THE INDUSTRIAL ARCHAEOLOGY OF SHROPSHIRE

Daniel's Mill, Eardington (SO 718917),
viewed through the viaduct of the Severn Valley Railway

The Industrial Archaeology of Shropshire

by

Barrie Trinder

Logaston Press

LOGASTON PRESS
Little Logaston Woonton Almeley
Herefordshire HR3 6QH
logastonpress.co.uk

First edition (ISBN 0 85033 989 8) published by Phillimore 1996
Second edition first published by Logaston Press 2016
Copyright © Barrie Trinder 2016
except for illustrations otherwise acknowledged

ISBN 978 1 910839 05 8

Typeset by Logaston Press
and printed and bound in Poland by
www.lfbookservices.co.uk

Contents

Other books written or edited by Barrie Trinder

A Victorian MP and his Constituents: the correspondence of H.W. Tancred 1841-1859 (1969).

Drink and Sobriety in an early Victorian Country Town (with Sir Brian Harrison, 1969).

The Pergamon General Historical Atlas (with A.C. Cave, 1970).

The Industrial Revolution in Shropshire (1973, 1981, 2000, 2016).

The Darbys of Coalbrookdale (1974, 1978, 1981, 1992).

The Most Extraordinary District in the World: Ironbridge and Coalbrookdale (1977, 1988, 2005).

The Iron Bridge: Symbol of the Industrial Revolution (with Sir Neil Cossons, 1979, 2002).

Yeomen & Colliers in Telford: the probate inventories of Dawley, Lilleshall, Wellington & Wrockwardine (with Jeff Cox, 1980).

Victorian Banbury (1982, 2005).

The Making of the Industrial Landscape (1982, 1986, 1997).

A History of Shropshire (1983, 1998).

Victorian Shrewsbury (1984).

Industrial Heritage of Britain (1988).

The Blackwell Encyclopedia of Industrial Archaeology (1992).

The English Heritage Book of Industrial England (with Michael Stratton, 1997).

Miners & Mariners of the Severn Gorge: the probate inventories of Benthall, Broseley, Little Wenlock & Madeley (with Nancy Cox, 2000).

Twentieth Century Industrial Archaeology (with Michael Stratton, 2000).

The Market Town Lodging House in Victorian England (2001).

Thomas Telford's Holyhead Road: the A5 in North Wales (with Jamie Quartermaine & Rick Turner, 2003).

Barges & Bargemen: A social history of the Upper Severn Navigation 1660-1900 (2005).

English Market Towns and their Suburbs in recent centuries (2005).

Beyond the Bridges: the Suburbs of Shrewsbury 1760-1960 (2006).

Britain's Industrial Revolution: the Making of a Manufacturing People (2013).

Victorian Banburyshire: Three Memoirs: Sarah Rusher, Thomas Ward Boss, Thomas Butler Gunn (2013).

ACKNOWLEDGEMENTS

The first edition of this book was written twenty years ago as I approached the end of three decades of teaching and fieldwork in Shropshire, and was shaped by conversations with countless students and colleagues to all of whom I renew my thanks, as I do to those who aided production of the first edition. My wife, Barbara, participated in numerous expeditions to sites considered here, and has constantly supported this new edition, and, as always, I am grateful for her patience and forbearance.

This edition appears on the occasion of the 44th annual conference of the Association of Industrial Archaeology held in Telford in September 2016, and I acknowledge with pleasure and gratitude the support of the AIA in making publication possible.

The pattern of the book is essentially that of the first edition, but there are many new illustrations and numerous changes have been made in detail, reflecting research during the last twenty years. Some tasks, particularly the recording of the Industrial Archaeology of the new town of Telford from the 1960s to the present, remain to be completed by others.

This new edition has been written in Buckinghamshire, and I wish to record my gratitude to those Shropshire scholars who have assisted in updating the text, to Dr Roger White of the University of Birmingham, to Neil Clarke, and particularly to John Powell, formerly librarian at Ironbridge.

I must also thank David de Haan for the efficiency with which he has represented the AIA in the negotiations leading to publication.

Thanks are due to the following for the use of images: the *Ironbridge Gorge Museum Trust* for: Industrial complexity p.4, Hadley Park Windmill p.20, Minsterley Cream label p.34, Groom catalogue page p.50, Broseley pit p.94, dome-shaped crossing-keeper's shelter p.105, tub boat p.106, Hay inclined plane when workable p.107, Granville Mines p.109, Lightmoor Brickfield p.111, Donnington Wood brickworks p.112, Coalport chinaworks p.115, Mountain Daisy p.117, Michaelangelo Rooker's image of the Iron Bridge p.117, Coalport Tar Tunnel p.119, Blists Hill coke heaps p.119, Priorslee furnaces p.123, Old Furnace, Coalbrookdale p.125, Hadley Castle works p.128, pumping engines p.130, Irish wolfhounds table p.131, William Williams view of the Iron Bridge p.132, Severn barges p.171, plateway at Horsehay p.212, Old Furnace, Coalbrookdale, p.214 and the G.R. Morton Ironworks p.214; *Shropshire Archives* for: Pipe Gate p.33, Billingsley Collier p.79, the yard at Ifton Colliery p.86, Calcutts' landscape p.95, Ditherington Flax Mill p.144 and the map of Hayton's Bent p.163; the collection of *Dr Paul Collins* for the Dean Goods locomotive p.205; *John Powell* for the tramcar p.129, Bridgnorth Town Mills p.153 and the Severn Valley Railway p.213; *The Science Museum, London* for the Trevithick engine p.53; the late *Russell Mulford* for the milk train p.34, Shrewsbury Station with roof p.203 and the engine sheds at Coleham p.204; and *Roger Edmondson* for Phillip Ballard's water colour p.103. Other illustrations are photographs by the author, or images from the author's collection.

Barrie Trinder
Olney, November 2015

Conventions

Measurements are given in metric, except for some approximate distances between places, quoted in miles, and some precise dimensions (e.g. railway gauges) originally measured in Imperial, for which metric equivalents are given. There appears no necessity in this study to give metric equivalents for Imperial tons, nor for shillings and pence.

The dates of birth and death of individuals mentioned in the text are given, where known, in the index of personal names.

National Grid references are given in the text for places whose locations are not obvious.

Abbreviations used

B&LJC	Birmingham & Liverpool Junction Canal
CBA	Council for British Archaeology
EcHR	Economic History Review
ESJ	Eddowes' Salopian Journal
GWR	Great Western Railway
HMSO	Her (or His) Majesty's Stationery Office
HRO	Herefordshire Record Office
IAR	Industrial Archaeology Review
IMS	Independent Milk Supplies
JRCHS	Journal of the Railway & Canal Historical Society
LJRO	Lichfield Joint Record Office
LMS	London, Midland & Scottish Railway
LNER	London & North Eastern Railway
LNWR	London & North Western Railway
MH	Midland History
NAAFI	Navy, Army & Air Force Institute
O&NR	Oswestry & Newtown Railway
PLUTO	Pipe Line under the Ocean
PMA	Post-Medieval Archaeology
PSNWR	Potteries, Shrewsbury & North Wales Railway
RAF	Royal Air Force
RASC	Royal Army Service Corps
RCAHMW	Royal Commission on the Ancient & Historical Monuments of Wales
RFC	Royal Flying Corps
SA	Shropshire Archives
SC	Shrewsbury Chronicle
SFWI	Shropshire Federation of Women's Institutes
SNL	Shropshire News Letter
SUR&CC	Shropshire Union Railway & Canal Company
TICCIH	The International Committee for the Conservation of the Industrial Heritage
TLH	The Local Historian
TSAS	Transactions of the Shropshire Archaeological Society (also Shropshire History & Archaeology)
UNESCO	United Nationals Educational, Scientific & Cultural Organisation
VCH	Victoria County History
WMH	West Midlands History
WMS	West Midlands Studies
WSMR	Wrexham, Shropshire & Marylebone Railway

1 INTRODUCTION

Shropshire was one of the birthplaces of Industrial Archaeology. Its monuments featured in Michael Rix's first article on the subject in 1955. A succession of publications on the county's industrial past began with John Randall's first writings in the late 1850s, and includes some notable scholarship of the 1920s and '30s. Shropshire hosted the first international conference on industrial heritage in 1973, which led to the formation of The International Committee for the Conservation of the Industrial Heritage (TICCIH). The Ironbridge Gorge was designated a UNESCO World Heritage Site in 1986, and its industrial monuments are much visited. Conservation of the Ellesmere Canal, the monuments of the Ironbridge Gorge and the Severn Valley Railway set standards which attracted international attention. One purpose of this book is to set those achievements in their context in a survey of industrial archaeology in the whole county.

Industrial archaeological scholarship was lively in Shropshire from the 1950s. A profusion of publications means that a topographically-based inventory of sites, which might be welcomed in less studied areas, is not an urgent necessity. Shropshire's principal industries – ironmaking, coalmining and ceramics in the Coalbrookdale Coalfield, lead-mining around the Stiperstones and flax-spinning in Shrewsbury – have been exhaustively analysed. The county's water mills, canals and railways are well-documented, and some of its products – Coalport and Caughley porcelain, Jackfield tiles and Sentinel steam wagons – are assiduously collected. One objective of this study is to integrate such specialised works with the less heroic elements in Shropshire's industrial history: to perceive the first iron-framed factory within a wider pattern of textile manufacturing, to see the Ironbridge Gorge not just as a 'cradle of the Industrial Revolution', but as one of several parts of the county with distinctive coalfield landscapes, to demonstrate the similarities between the manufacturing economies of the county's market towns.

The book aims to show what understanding has been gained from the disciplined archaeological study of Shropshire's industrial past, to bring together different kinds of research and to use them to create broader pictures of the roles of mining and manufacturing within different landscape contexts. By examining one county, some broader insights may emerge into the changing role of industry within British society during recent centuries. The book also tries to provide for the student of a particular watermill, foundry or copper mine, a context which enables the object of his or her study to be evaluated, showing whether it is an early or a late example, or an exceptionally large or merely modest enterprise of its kind. A further concern is with methodology. It can be argued that industrial archaeologists

*The Bleak Uplands: the White Grit engine house (SO 319979) in its landscape context.
There are several disused shafts in the disturbed ground to the left.
The Old Grit mines are just over the hill.*

*The fertile lowlands: a substantial malthouse at Diddlebury in the Corvedale,
one of Shropshire's most fertile regions.*

have paid insufficient attention to theoretical approaches to their discipline. This book is, consciously, an exercise in assessing the potential of one particular approach to the industrial past – the analysis of contrasting landscapes – through which it is hoped to explain how things were made and moved in the past.

Some justification is required for setting this kind of study in a county context. Shropshire is not a homogeneous region. It was the largest inland county, extending from the fringes of Wolverhampton to the Cheshire plain, from the outer edges of the Potteries to the uplands of Clun Forest. Geologists regard its landscapes as some of the most varied in Britain, with ten of the twelve characteristic rock types being found within its borders. Much of Shropshire is rural with few manufactures.

This variety can be a justification for analysing the industrial past in a county setting. This book considers the role of industry in contrasting settings – in the countryside, in market towns, in coalfields, in the uplands and along transport corridors. A county context ensures variety of subject matter, five coalfields, sixteen market towns, and a diverse range of countryside. These are arbitrary classifications. Some activities characteristic of market towns, such as tanning and malting, also took place in the countryside. Concentrations of water mills were as important in towns and in coalfields as in rural settings. In some parts of Shropshire coalmining was a small segment of an economy that was primarily agricultural. A landscape approach avoids some of the contradictions of an analysis based on technology, and avoids the necessity of having to decide whether a beam engine should be regarded as a prime mover or as part of a water supply system, or whether a bridge is a component of a transport route or a product of a foundry. The landscape approach dictates that some subjects are covered in different sections of the book – most ironworks that flourished before 1750 were located in the countryside, but those of the Industrial Revolution in the coalfields. Brickmaking was important in the countryside, on the fringes of market towns, and in the coalfields.

Some subjects are best approached from different angles. Non-ferrous metallic ores were extracted in several parts of Shropshire, but only in one did mining activities dominate the landscape. To examine the industry as a whole, including the processing stages, seems preferable. Textile manufacturing was primarily an urban activity, but the needs to analyse the origins of large-scale manufactures and to explain the persistence of domestic production make it preferable to take a holistic view of the industry.

Long-distance transport systems, the River Severn, turnpike roads, main line railways and some canals, pass through different landscapes and merit separate treatment. Some features of the Great Western Railway were identical whether in an urban setting at Shrewsbury, at Hollinswood in the heart of the Coalbrookdale Coalfield, or in the countryside at Hodnet. Short-distance transport systems, tub boat canals, mineral railways and brickworks tramways are treated in their appropriate landscape settings.

The Shropshire which is the subject of this study is the historic county, now governed by two unitary authorities, Telford and Wrekin in the east, which dates from 1998, and Shropshire Council which since 2009 has replaced five former non-metropolitan boroughs. The two authorities share some services – most importantly, in the context of this study, the Shropshire Archives – and together they comprise the current ceremonial county. The

Industrial complexity: an aerial view of the Upper Works, Coalbrookdale, probably in the 1920s. To the left (north) are the buildings covering the Old Furnace (SJ 667048), ranges of sheds, long demolished alongside the railway viaduct, the Long Warehouse (now the Ironbridge Gorge Museum Library) with north-lit sheds (now a museum store) to the east. In the centre is the Great Warehouse (now the Museum of Iron) with a bridge linking it to the offices on the other side of the road. In the shadow, to the right, is the Engineering Building of 1879. Carpenters' Row is left of centre, while the terrace next to the Wesleyan Chapel is Chapel Row.

A border county: Ludlow Castle with the complex industrial settlements on Titterstone Clee in the background.

area around Halesowen, an enclave of Shropshire that was incorporated into surrounding Worcestershire in 1844, is not included in this study. Enclaves of other counties within historic Shropshire, such as Farlow, which belonged to Herefordshire until 1844, and small portions of Shropshire that have passed into surrounding counties, such as Dowles, a suburb of Bewdley which became part of Worcestershire in 1895, are regarded pragmatically.

This survey does not have precise chronological limits. Its focus is on mining and manufacturing since 1660, but evidence from earlier periods is used where appropriate. No attempt has been made to evaluate the industrial buildings constructed in the new town of Telford since the 1960s, but it is acknowledged that they have undergone many changes and merit a study in their own right.

This study is based on a wide range of sources and recording methods, beginning with field observations, the phasing and recording of buildings and earthworks. Excavations too, formal or otherwise, have contributed to the archaeological record of industry in Shropshire. Much has been learned from images, whether from paintings and drawings by nationally acclaimed artists, or from scribbled sketches by tourists, crude woodcuts in newspaper advertisements, family snapshots or picture postcards. Inscriptions such as those on the tomb of the trowman Eustace Beard at St Bartholomew, Benthall and Sir Francis Chantrey's memorial to William Hazledine at St Chad, Shrewsbury have stimulated research. Perhaps the most powerful influence has been the experience of seeing manufacturing in progress, observing steel being rolled in the (by 1965) antiquated mill at Priorslee, barley being raked over at Ditherington, seams of coal being uncovered by mechanical excavators at Old Park and Little Wenlock, and steam locomotives being oiled before leaving Coleham sheds. Such activities, commonplace in the 1960s, are now part of Shropshire's distant history.

The book emphasises quantification, in the belief that analysis of one site or artefact makes sense only if there is some awareness of its typicality. There is a concern throughout to show how many manufacturing sites of particular kinds there were in Shropshire, and how they

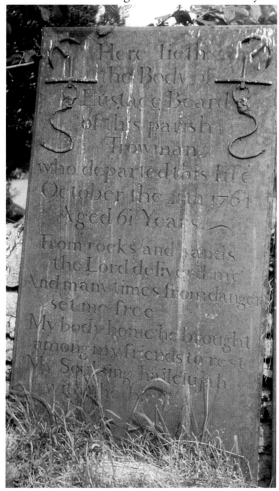

The power of inscriptions: the tomb of Eustace Beard at St Bartholomew, Benthall that stimulated research on the Severn Navigation.

related to others of the same types further afield. The study is also based on the premise that our understanding of the past can be increased by examining what is common and what is different in market towns as diverse as Shrewsbury and Bishop's Castle, or coalfield communities as unalike as St George's and Horsebridge.

A particular range of documentary sources has consciously been a foundation for this study. Fieldwork has been based on current 2½ inch (1:25,000) Pathfinder maps published by the Ordnance Survey. The two inch survey of 1827, the first edition 25 inch maps and those by Baugh and Greenwood have been analysed for all parts of the county supplemented by later editions and by the 1:500 map for Shrewsbury. Census enumerators' returns have been employed to locate and to quantify manufacturing and mining activities, and files of the county's newspapers have been exhaustively studied. Much use has been made of trade directories, of many hundreds of transcribed probate inventories, and of the database of the Port Books of Gloucester established in the 1980s at the University of Wolverhampton.

Like any historical study which attempts to provide a synthesis, this book depends on the work of others, and on numerous publications that are not primarily concerned with Industrial Archaeology. The full range of sources is recorded in the bibliography. A comprehensive index of places and liberal use of National Grid references make it possible to locate particular places in the text and on the ground.

Popular interest in Shropshire's industrial past increased enormously during the second half of the 20th century, and this was reflected in the establishment of the institutions now charged with the conservation of the county's heritage. This was due in part to the work of academics, but also to numerous scholars who are amateurs in the best sense – molinologists, the restorers of steam wagons, canal 'navvies', the explorers of abandoned mines, collectors of porcelain and tiles and enthusiasts for stage coaches. This study offers a context in which such enthusiasms can be placed. It is intended to do more than reveal to the many a range of sites known to a few, or elucidate the mysteries of processes understood only by the initiated. The justification for this survey must be that it uses archaeological evidence in a disciplined manner to enhance our understanding of the past. It aims to set up models, to pose questions, to accumulate and analyse data, and to reach conclusions about the artefacts, images, structures, sites and landscapes which form the subject matter of Industrial Archaeology. Its purposes is not merely to summarise, nor to ossify, nor to celebrate, but to stimulate; not to bring comfort and congratulations but to provoke; to consider not just questions of local history but the place of mining and manufacturing in man's past. If, by the mid-21st century, the hypotheses which follow are disputed and disproved, and the models discarded for something better, the book will have achieved its purpose.

2 RURAL INDUSTRIES

The idea of 'industry' in the countryside can seem paradoxical. The dominant economic activity in the Shropshire countryside has always been agriculture, yet water-power, space, minerals, the produce of farms and forests and the availability of labour have over many centuries sustained manufactures in the countryside, and rural entrepreneurs have shown remarkable ability in recent decades in adapting old sites to new uses.

Rural communities
Industrial as well as agricultural communities are shaped by patterns of landholding, and can equally be classed as 'open' (where there are many landowners and settlement is easy) or 'closed' (where there is usually one controlling landowner, and settlement is restricted) Ironically 'industry' could be most highly developed at either extreme. In an open community settlement was easy and incomers and successive generations could readily be accommodated. There was space for new enterprises, and there could be access to a range of skills. In an estate village there might be facilities to meet the needs of the thousands of acres dependent on a great house, a brick and tile works, a saw mill, a quarry which could be opened up when there was a demand for stone. A great house might utilise new technologies – there were gasworks at The Quinta, Apley Park and Eyton Hall and early electric lighting systems at Henley Hall, Yeaton Pevery and Acton Reynald.

Ruling class observers saw open communities as resorts of idleness rather than industry. Sir Richard Hill considered that those who lived on the waste of Prees Heath around 1800 could scarcely support themselves and that their children sank through idleness into vice and promiscuity. John Bishton in 1794 maintained that the miserable huts erected by the poor on open commons and the small plots that they enclosed around them encouraged a false sense of independence and that they could not sustain families.[1]

Nevertheless analysis of squatter communities shows that they stimulated rural manufactures. The remnants of such communities – crudely-built cottages, whose alignments are disrespectful of roads laid out as parts of enclosures – can be observed in all kinds of terrain: along the boggy margins of the Long Lane which leads from Wrockwardine to the Weald Moors, in the peaty depths of Whixall Moss, on parish boundaries at Vernolds Common, on sandy heathlands like Myddle Wood, and in the folds of hills at Cockshutford and Llanymynech.

Some squatter settlements were reservoirs of labour for industry. Cockshutford, on the edge of the extensive upland waste of Clee St Margaret, housed the colliers who worked in

A cottage on Hayton's Bent common in Stanton Lacy (SO 522807) (which has one of the largest gable end stacks in any squatter dwelling in Shropshire).

the coal mines on Brown Clee. Such communities could also provide skills. Cockshutford's residents in the 1840s and '50s included shoemakers, carpenters, a tea dealer, a weaver, a laundress, a carrier, blacksmiths, a schoolmaster, tailors and a dressmaker. Among the residents on Myddle Common in the 17th century were masons, carpenters, shoemakers, coopers, blacksmiths and weavers. Even in the mid 19th century, long after the common had been enclosed, the community included a butcher, stonemasons, a saddler, a rope-maker, a washerwoman, a woman carrier, a dressmaker, a wheelwright, a carpenter, a clock-maker and a weaver. Richard Gough recorded the encroachment of land in Newton Field by Morgan Clarke, a weaver, son of a squatter from Hadley who settled on Harmer Hill.[2] The fierce independence of those who lived on commons is revealed by such census entries

A cottage in a slang alongside the Shrewsbury-Ellesmere road at Burlton (SJ 466260), awaiting demolition in the mid-1980s. It was once occupied by a blacksmith.

as that for Evan Watkin of Stretton Heath in Westbury, whose occupation was described in 1861 as 'Cooper and holding 8 acres of land'. In that year cottagers at Cockshutford included Edward Howells, 'Stone Mason and Landowner of 2 acres 2 roods', 'William Edwards, Shoemaker and Landowner of 1 acre 2 roods', and Edward Woodhouse, 'Lime Maker and Landowner of 1 acre'. A cottage in an isolated part of Selattyn, occupied in 1871 by a miner holding seven acres of land, was called the 'Queen's Palace'.

On Vennington Common in Westbury, where a settlement of ten dwellings was established by 1677, and where cottage building reached a peak in the late 18th century, residents in 1851 included William Bradwick, a 54-year-old 'tinman', probably a repairer of domestic hardware, born in London, with four sons aged between 16 and 29 all following the same occupation. His wife, an Oxfordshire woman, was a basketmaker, as were her 78-year-old father and her daughter-in-law who shared the same cottage.

Clock cleaners were amongst the most skilled residents of open communities. There were two on Wattlesborough Heath in 1861, and in 1851 on the side of the Moelyd Hill in Trefonen lived Elex Hughes, a 49-year-old bachelor, of whom the census enumerator wrote:

> A country clock cleaner and maker who has spent a deal of his time in trying to complete perpetual motion, and I believe he is on the point of completing it.

Many cottages in open communities were built of turf or similar ephemeral materials, and can no longer be studied, although some sites would repay excavation. Most stone cottages have large gable chimney stacks and stand in irregularly-shaped enclosures bounded by banks topped with hedges of crab apple, hazel, damson, holly and laburnum.

Cornmills

Water-power was the most significant factor in rural manufacturing. Shropshire's principal river, the Severn, is a turbulent stream whose levels are variable, and it powered only five waterwheels. Most of the county's watermills were located on small streams; only a few on the lower reaches of the Tern, the Teme and the Worfe were of substantial size. The most intensive rural concentrations of mills were eight in a 3.75km stretch of the River Morda and five in 1.5km on the Morlas Brook. The most common application of water power was to the grinding of grain to make flour or animal feed. Flour-milling was ubiquitous in Shropshire; scarcely a settlement of consequence lay more than three miles from a mill.

Some 396 sites on which water power has been used since 1660 have been identified in Shropshire, of which 319 have been used for at least some time in grinding grain. Water remained the principal source of power for corn milling as long as grain was ground locally. No more than 30 windmills operated in Shropshire in the 18th and 19th centuries, and less than 20 cornmills in the county were totally dependent on steam power, of which only those at West Felton, Queen's Head, Whixall, Hadnall, Lower Hordley and Chinnel (Whitchurch) were in the countryside. Between 20 and 30 water cornmills employed supplementary steam power, including those at Cruckmeole, Eyton-on-the-Weald Moors, Wollerton and Hanwood. The ancient mill at Vennington, which had operated in conjunction with a windmill, acquired a third source of power, a steam engine, during the 1880s. A steam engine was installed before 1829 at the Hem Mill, Shifnal. After its removal and

1885	178
1891	169
1900	148
1905	131
1909	104
1913	98
1922	73
1926	71
1934	49
1937	47

Table 2.1
Numbers of
Watermills in
Shropshire.
Source: sundry
directories.

The imposing water corn mill at Penyllan (SJ 278281) on the River Morda in Oswestry parish. Steam power was never employed at the mill and the chimney, erected in the mid-19th century, was never put to use.

the abandonment of water-power *c.*1930, an oil engine and then an electric motor provided power for grinding. The mill retains its extensive pool.

The researches of molinologists and of the Victoria County History suggest that many watermills ceased working during the 18th century. In the area south of Shrewsbury, Leebotwood cornmill passed out of use before 1796, Cressage Mill was destroyed by fire in 1774 and never rebuilt, Pitchford Mill was demolished before 1795, and the last records of the mills at Langley and Stapleton are respectively in 1694 and 1678.[3]

About 200 cornmills were working in Shropshire in the mid 19th century, after which the decline of rural milling was rapid.

Henry Deacon's mill at Walcott is the only rural mill known to have adopted roller milling technology in the late 19th century. Only four mills – at Maesbury Hall, Market Drayton, Donnington Wood and Mytton – were still grinding flour in 1935. The remainder were sustained by modest local demands for cattle feed.

Many water cornmill buildings are still recognisable and more than 40 waterwheels remain *in situ*. Most surviving mill machinery was made by local foundries or millwrights of the 19th century. In the south there are examples of the work of Turtons of Kidderminster at Wrickton and Ditton. The iron wheel at Cleobury North Mill was made by John Hazledine at Bridgnorth, while the oak gearing at Broadstone Mill probably follows the plan of William Hazledine, who installed new machinery at a cost of £350 in 1794 in a manner commended by Thomas Telford in his treatise *On Mills*.[4]

Daniels Mill, Eardington (SO 718917) is one of the least conventional water corn-mills in Shropshire. Its source of water is a stream less than a mile long flowing from the Potseething Spring to the Severn. There was a mill on the site in the 15th century, but the present structure dates from a rebuilding in 1854-55. The 11.7m (38ft) wheel, with cast-iron hub and wrought-iron buckets, is on the same axle as an external pit wheel,

Daniel's Mill, Eardington (SO 718917) showing the wheel with its cast-iron hub and wrought-iron buckets.

which through a wallower drives a horizontal shaft powering three sets of French burr stones. Full-time operation of the mill was no longer viable by the 1890s, although it was worked part-time until 1957. It has been lovingly restored by its present owners.[5]

The mill at Bouldon (SO 547850), a three-storey, three-bay building of the late 18th century in grey sandstone, had a more conventional layout. It ceased work in 1934 and in the 1960s was a perfect time capsule. Its external cast-iron pitch-back waterwheel, 4.3m x 1m (14ft x 3ft 3in), drove the machinery through an internal cast-iron pit wheel, turning through a wallower a wooden upright shaft. A spur wheel worked two stone nuts, operating hopper-fed tuns, while a crown wheel on the first floor worked a sack hoist on the second. Conversion to residential use altered the character of the building and some machinery was removed.

The best-preserved watermill on a substantial river, driven by the Teme at Ashford Carbonel

The interior of Bouldon Mill (SO 547850) in the Corvedale, photographed in June 1965, showing the cast-iron pit wheel enmeshing with the wallower on the wooden upright shaft.

11

The horseshoe weir and restored undershot wheel at Ashford Carbonel Mill (SO 511711) on the River Teme.

(SO 511711), produced cattle feed until 1953. Water is diverted by a horseshoe weir to an undershot wheel, *c.*4.3m in diameter, which has a cast-iron rim and centre, with wooden paddles and spokes. The milling machinery in the stone building follows a conventional layout, with a cast-iron pit wheel, and wooden gearing, much of it having been renewed in recent decades in pear, apple, ash and hornbeam. A turbine drove sawmilling machinery, water pumps and an electric generator from which current was conveyed to Ashford Court by a cable hung on wooden poles.

Wrickton Mill (SO 642858) in Stottesdon parish on the Cleobury Brook is a stone building of the early 19th century, probably an extended version of an earlier brick building. The external overshot waterwheel, 2.85m x 1.77m (9ft 3in x 5ft 9in) retains its original iron rings, probably cast by Turtons of Kidderminster in the 1830s. An iron pit wheel meshes with a wallower on an iron upright shaft, from which a spur wheel drives two stone nuts. Most of the machinery appears to date from the 1830s, but equipment to operate a third pair of stones was added by Richard Wyer, a Cleobury Mortimer millwright, in 1863. Wrickton Mill worked until about 1950 and restoration began in 1979.[6]

Rindleford Mill (SJ 738955) on the River Worfe is a four-storey brick structure with a front elevation of four bays. It accommodated five pairs of French stones in the mid 19th century. The internal machinery has been removed but the undershot wheel, 4.6m (12ft 8in) in diameter and 2.2m (6ft) wide, remains in the outshot wheelhouse, together with a cast-iron pit wheel. An oil mill and a fulling mill once occupied the site where cattle feed was produced until 1950.[7]

Chadwell Mill (SJ 638208), on the Lynn Brook on the upper reaches of the River Meese, was one of the last Shropshire mills to be reconditioned for commercial use. It was substantially rebuilt in 1922 and ground cattle feed until 1950. The building, in Lilleshall Company brick, dates from 1881. An overshot wheel, 7m (19ft 3in) in diameter provides a conventional drive to two sets of stones through a pit wheel, a wallower and a crown wheel, all in cast-iron. The wheel also powered an endless rope system working machinery in a barn 300m distant.[8]

Clun Mill (SO 304813), now a Youth Hostel, is the best example in Shropshire of a mill converted to turbine operation. The mill is large, approximately 15.4m x 9.2m (42ft 3in x 25ft 3in). A Whitelaw turbine made in Glasgow was installed *c.*1854 in a pit in the middle of the building, and drove three sets of French burr stones which remain in a dormitory. Maps from the 1840s show substantial fish ponds, now dry, on the upstream side of the mill.[9]

Iron and Glass

Ironmaking after cornmilling was the principal use for water power in Shropshire. The indirect process for making iron, the smelting of ore in a blast furnace to produce cast-iron in the form of 'pigs' (so called because they resembled piglets feeding from a sow), and the subsequent reduction of the pig iron to wrought-iron in a finery-and-chafery forge (see below), was introduced to the county in the mid 16th century when furnaces were constructed at the Hurst in Aldenham Park, Morville (SO 672960), at Manor Mill, Shifnal (SJ 742067), at Willey (SO 672980), at Kenley (SO 564985) and Cleobury Park (SO 711764). A blast furnace of this period was a masonry stack, supported on at least two sides by arches, one accommodating the tuyère pipe, through which air was conveyed from water-powered bellows to the interior, the other the forehearth, from which were tapped molten iron and molten slag, the waste product of the process. Most furnaces were built into banks, or were approached by earthen ramps to facilitate the charging of iron ore, limestone, used as a flux, and the fuel, at this time charcoal. Other components of a furnace complex might include barns for storing ore and charcoal, and reservoirs where water could be stored to enable the bellows to work through a campaign of up to eight months' duration. Slag would be piled up around a furnace and might be utilised locally as road metal. Furnaces needed to be within convenient distance of iron ore supplies, which came from seams in the coalfields. Charcoal was burned from cord wood, grown as a crop, and might be drawn from an extensive hinterland. The principal demand in the 18th century was for wrought-iron, strong in tension but weak in compression, which could be used for horseshoes, nails and tools. It was refined from pig iron in a finery-and-chafery forge, which usually consisted of two hearths. At the finery hearth the iron was melted with charcoal using an air blast provided by water-powered bellows, and further carbon was then removed in the chafery hearth, also blown by water power. The resultant iron was then pounded under a water-powered hammer to produce a 'bloom' which might be rolled and cut into strips in a slitting mill, producing rods that could be used by nailers and other craftsmen.

Of the Shropshire blast furnaces with 16th-century origins, only Willey and possibly Kenley were still working in 1660, but seven furnaces of 17th-century foundation were probably operating in that year, at Abdon, Bouldon, Coalbrookdale, Ifton Rhyn, Leighton, Tilsop and Wombridge. By the second decade of the 18th century, Abdon, Ifton Rhyn, Tilsop and Wombridge had ceased working, but new furnaces had been erected at Charlcotte (SO 637861) and Kemberton (SJ 744045). The use of coke as fuel, developed by Abraham Darby at Coalbrookdale from 1709, ultimately caused the demise of Shropshire's rural ironworks, but only from the 1750s, and some charcoal-fired furnaces in the countryside worked for most of the 18th century, Charlcotte probably continuing until the 1780s, although working intermittently from the 1750s, and Bouldon into the 1790s.

There are archaeological remains at most of the rural ironworks in Shropshire which worked after 1660. At Kenley and Kemberton only scatterings of slag remain in the surrounding fields and along the banks of watercourses. At Abdon (SO 567867) foundations of the furnace remain, with a weir and a pool, and traces of slag along the bottom

The 18th-century blast furnace at Charlcotte, Aston Botterell (SO 637861)

of a wooded dingle. There is a complex pattern of leats at Bouldon and much slag, many lumps containing unconsumed charcoal. Tilsop furnace (SO 516725) lay alongside the Corn Brook. The site is surrounded by slag, and an iron casting in the nearby church of St Peter, Coreley commemorates Elinor, wife of Edward Hussey 'of Tilsop furnace', who died in 1684.[10]

Charlcotte is the best-preserved of Shropshire's rural blast furnaces. The red sandstone stack, 6.2m x 6.2m (20ft x 20ft) is complete and is approached by an earthen ramp. The print of a hand appears in the iron lintel above the forehearth. Slag surrounds the structure but an early 21st-century survey located the course of the leat to the furnace waterwheel.[11]

The remains of the blast furnace at Leighton (SJ 610055) are less complete but the landscape evidence is more comprehensive. Only the tuyère arch of the furnace remains, having been incorporated in 1762 into a cornmill whose wheel and machinery remain. The mill was rebuilt as a public house, the *Kynnersley Arms*, in the mid 19th century. On the opposite side of the B4380 the outline of the lowest pool of the water-power system can be recognised, while Myfanwy Eaves and Sharon Hall suggested that a steam pumping engine, noted at Leighton in 1753 by Reinhold Angerstein and in 1754 by Charles Wood, occupied the site of the modern 'Mill House' west of the inn, where there are large quantities of slag and cinder. The record of Leighton furnace is completed by a pair of 17th-century cast-iron memorials on the floor of the nearby church of St Mary.[12]

A forge can mean the workplace of a smith making useful objects by hammering red-hot iron. It can also mean a place where pig iron was reduced to wrought-iron. Until the late 18th century such a forge was a small water-powered and charcoal-fuelled establishment in the countryside, usually containing two hearths, a finery and a chafery and a water-powered hammer for shaping the wrought-iron. From the 1770s the stamping-and-potting process and from the 1780s puddling were used in some rural as well as in coalfield furnaces.

Eleven finery-and-chafery forges worked in Shropshire in the first decade of the 18th century. As many as seven others may have been operating in 1660 but had ceased working by 1700. A further nine were established in the 18th century, and three slitting mills worked in this period.

There were concentrations of forges along the River Tern and its tributaries in north Shropshire, and on the River Rea in the south. Most were modest concerns, some producing less than 150 tons of iron a year. Forges could work throughout the year, so that output could have been as little as three tons of iron rods per week. In 1766 Richard Whitworth estimated that Sambrook Forge consumed no more than three tons of pig iron, two tons of coal and three tons of charcoal per week.

Only at Eardington, a works of the late 18th century, do significant structures remain of a forge in a rural setting. Every other site retains at most the traces of a water-power system and lumps of slag.

There is documentary evidence of the characteristic components of rural forges. Most employed relatively few workers, the 40 forgemen who signed a loyalty declaration at Upton Forge in 1793 must have been one of the largest workforces in the county. Workers' cottages formed part of the 17th-century forge at Hubbals Mill, and dwellings that remain at the present farm at Upton Forge could well have been some of the 12 on the site in 1794. There were six houses at Uffington slitting mill in 1794 and the same number at Moreton Corbet Forge. A terrace at the Upper Forge, Cleobury Mortimer, remained until the 1960s, nine tenements for workmen and a house for the superintendent having formed part of the complex in 1811. At Eardington forgemen were accommodated in terraces that still survive.[14]

Warehouses for raw material or for finished iron were found at most forges. Upton Forge had one, and there were three at Uffington slitting mill in 1794. The Lower Forge, Cleobury Mortimer, had a charcoal barn and a coke house in 1811. All forges had smiths' shops for re-working tools.[15]

The most innovative of the Shropshire forges was Tern Works in Attingham Park, established in 1710 by a Bristol partnership for whom the first Abraham Darby was agent.[16] It was described as 'the first Joint Work of this kind in England', indicating that it fabricated both iron and brass. Components included a finery-and-chafery forge, a steel furnace, rolling mills for brass and for hoop iron, a slitting mill and a wire mill. Brass-working ceased after the death of Francis Pinnel, the expert on brass rolling, and the range of work

The causeway that follows the dam in which were sited the waterwheels of Tern Works, Attingham. (SJ 552098)

Name	Parish	Grid reference	First known date	Last known date
Bromley's Forge	Montford	SJ 439167	pre 1623	c.1660
Caynton/Kaynton	Edgmond	SJ 694230	pre 1694	c.1820
Cleobury Mortimer Lower Forge	Cleobury Mortimer	SO 688747	1571	c.1810
Cleobury Mortimer Upper Forge	Cleobury Mortimer	SO 787757	pre 1598	c.1810
Dorrington	Dorrington	SJ 487020	1606	c.1680
Eardington Lower Forge	Quatford	SJ 733895	1777-78	1889
Eardington Upper Forge	Quatford	SO 725897	1782-89	1889
Fernhill	Whittington	SJ 318333	1627	c.1660
Grindle	Ryton	SJ 753034	pre 1609	1670
Hampton Loade	Quatt	SO 748864	1796	1866
Hardwick/Rotherham	Stottesdon	SO 660818	pre 1757	c.1794
Harley	Harley	SO 588001	pre 1607	1664
Hubbals Mill	Morville	SO 691915	c.1631	c.1674
Lizard	Tong	SJ 784082	1564	c.1800
Longnor	Longnor	SJ 486014	1605	1800
Maesbury	Oswestry	SJ 304259	1627	c.1660
Moreton Corbet	Moreton Corbet	SJ 574228	1601	c.1794
Norton-in-Hales	Norton-in-Hales	SJ 704379	pre 1685	c.1794
Pendlestone/Bridgnorth	Worfield	SO 724944	1670	1795
Pitchford/Eaton Mascott	Pitchford	SJ 534054	1715	c.1800
Prescott	Stottesdon	SO 668820	c.1708	c.1794
Ryton Slitting Mill	Ryton	SJ 759028	1683	1714
Sambrook	Cheswardine	SJ 714248	pre 1690	c.1830
Sheinton	Sheinton	SJ 607041	pre 1637	1790
Sutton	Sutton	SJ 497608	c.1720	c.1790
Tern	Atcham	SJ 552098	1710	1757
Tibberton Slitting Mill	Edgmond	SJ 681203	pre 1653	1804
Uffington Slitting Mill	Uffington	SJ 527138	c.1790	pre 1828
Upton	Upton Magna	SJ 560112	1653	c.1830
Wytheford	Shawbury	SJ 569188	pre 1642	c.1796

Table 2.2 Rural Forges in Shropshire (Sources: various[13])

contracted. In 1717 output at Tern, some 300 tons a year, was the highest at any Shropshire forge, but by the 1750s production was no more than 150 tons a year. The works passed in 1725 to William and Richard Wood, and in 1733 to Joshua Gee, who claimed that closure, demanded by the landowner's agent, would 'put a stop to one of the biggest works in the county [and] turn fourscore people a starving'. The forge closed in 1756 to be replaced by cornmills which themselves were demolished in 1787-89. A causeway across the river 100m east of the mansion at Attingham is a relic of the dam which accommo-dated the many waterwheels of Tern Forge. Apart from a thin scatter of slag it is all that remains of the works.

The outstanding feature of the complex at Eardington is a canal that conveys water between the Upper and Lower forges, which was also used for transport between the two works. A deed of 1782 refers to a 'subterra-neous navigable cut' some 750 yards long. The canal was explored in the 1960s and is approximately 3m wide and 2m high, sufficient to allow a small boat to be legged through, although there are remains of a winch

Cottages built for workers at Eardington Forge (SO 743895).

at the upper end. The Upper Forge pool is silted but its curved stone weir remains, and the outline of the forge building, 21.5m x 12m, can be traced. At the Lower Forge is a 33m-high chimney built into a fissure in the sandstone, together with flue chambers, and the tail races from the water-power system. The upper forge was built in 1777-78 and the lower forge in the mid 1780s. The Eardington works used charcoal to make wrought-iron until its closure in 1889.[17]

The charcoal iron trade involved the carriage of iron over long distances. Pig iron was delivered at Wytheford in the 1680s, for example, from Willey and from the Forest of Dean. Iron in transit was stored at warehouses, the sites of three of which have been identi-fied, at Montford Bridge (SJ 432152) and Pimley (SJ 520142) on the River Severn, and at Roundthorn (SO 554788) east of Ludlow, but nothing remains on any of these sites.[18]

Several glassworks flourished in rural Shropshire before the patent of 1615 that prohib-ited the use of wood as fuel in glassmaking. The workers at the celebrated early 17th-century glasshouse in the Bishop's Wood on the county's eastern border, which was excavated in the 1930s, regarded themselves as parishioners of Cheswardine, where 15 events relating to glassworkers were recorded in the registers between 1600 and 1613, although the works itself (SJ 759313) was in Staffordshire. In 1967 fragments of crucibles and drinking glasses of the early 17th century were uncovered in a field called Glasshouse Bank at Ruyton-XI-Towns, but neither this works nor one that may have operated at Market Drayton is likely to have been working in 1660, and glassmaking in Shropshire, as elsewhere, was thereafter a coalfield industry.[19]

The Varied Uses of Water Power

Paper was made in Shropshire for three centuries. The mill at Cound, working in 1616, is the first of which there is any record. As many as five mills may have been working in 1660, and several more by 1700. The Gloucester Port Books indicate the despatch of considerable quantities of paper from the Severn ports of Shrewsbury, Broseley and Bridgnorth in the first decade of the 18th century. Around 15 mills were operating between 1750 and 1800, a total that increased slightly in the next three decades. As paper manufacturers elsewhere adopted Fourdrinier and other machines, production in Shropshire declined. Only six mills were working in 1851, and only that at Tibberton survived into the 20th century.[20]

Most Shropshire paper mill sites were used at other times for different manufactures. Except perhaps at Ludford, no significant buildings survive, most sites retaining only the overgrown remains of their water-power systems, or buildings relating to subsequent uses.

Paper was made from rags pulped by water-powered machinery. A 'vatman' would dip into the pulp a wire sieve called a mould, shake off surplus liquid, and turn out what remained on to a felt. Felts and paper were stacked by the 'coucher', and put beneath a screw press. The resulting sheets were then dried. Pure water was essential, and an advertisement for the Ludford mill in 1816 distinguished between the constant supply of water for power afforded by the River Teme and the never-failing spring that provided process water.[21] The probate inventory of Richard Fosbrook of Alveley, taken in 1730, lists best rags worth £5, second quality rags worth four guineas and cordage (old ropes) to the value of £12. William Fosbrook of Claverley,[22] whose possessions were listed in 1731, had 18cwt of rags worth £11 14s 0d. 'Ragg-men' were among those who worked at the Bolas mill in the 1660s. Richard Fosbrook had moulds worth £1 2s 6d, and felts worth 15s, while there were eight pairs of moulds and five posts of felts at Weston Rhyn in 1788, and double crown and foolscap lay boards at Longnor in 1825.[23] Most Shropshire mills produced brown wrapping paper, trade in which was said to be lucrative when a mill at Neen Sollars was offered for sale in 1831. Writing paper was made at Hopton Wafers, glazed boards at Longnor, paper for book-printing at Ludford, blue sugar paper at Ludford and Tibberton, and filter and blotting paper at Lloyds Mill, Neen Savage. At the Claverley Mill in 1731 were several grades of cap paper, one of which was used for printing, and two grades of pot paper. Paper made at the mill had been delivered to customers in Stafford, Worcester, Birmingham and Dublin.

The last paper-making establishment to work in Shropshire was the two-vat mill constructed in 1804 on the site of the former slitting mill on the River Meese at Tibberton by William Palmer, Thomas Brindley and George Brindley.[24] The main building, square in plan, spanned the leat. The complex was enlarged by Martin Billing, a Birmingham printer, who took it over in about 1860. The machinery was then worked by a steam engine supplied from a boiler house with a 47.5m chimney, constructed in 1874. The mill had 11 employees in 1861 and 21 in 1891, the largest workforce recorded at any Shropshire mill.

At Hopton Wafers three single-vat mills, one of which was working in 1736, were situated along a short section of the Hopton Brook. In 1798 the ironmaster Thomas Botfield bought the Hopton estate, and with his brother operated the three until 1824. Others worked them until 1840 after which they were vainly offered for sale. They had been demolished by 1858 and only traces of the water-power systems provide evidence of their existence.[25]

Name	Parish	Grid reference	Earliest date	Latest date
Alveley	Alveley	SO 765856	c.1705	1817
Besford	Lee Brockhurst	SJ 553258	pre 1640	pre 1750
Bouldon	Holgate	SO 547850	c.1790	c.1845
Charlcotte	Aston Bottrell	SO 637861	c.1725	c.1825
Chesterton	Worfield	SJ 792973	c.1690	c.1750
Claverley/Hopstone	Claverley	SJ 789945	c.1725	c.1805
Cound	Cound	SJ 553050	1616	1841
Ellerton	Cheswardine	SJ 714260	c.1730	1789
Great Bolas	Bolas	SJ 648208	c.1660	c.1760
Grindle	Ryton	SJ 753034	c.1650	c.1715

Hopton Wafers
    Upper Mill
    Middle Mill
    Lower Mill
	Hopton Wafers	
		SO 638769
		SO 639766
		SO 638762
			
			c.1730
			c.1730
			c.1730
				
				1826
				1840
				1840

Kemberton	Kemberton	SJ 744044	c.1790	c.1840
Longnor	Longnor	SJ 685013	c.1802	c.1825
Ludford	Ludford	SO 519743	c.1715	c.1870

Market Drayton
    Old Mill
    Walk Mill
    Tyrley Mill
	Market Drayton	
		SJ 656331
		SJ 671334
		SJ 679337
			
			c.1750
			c.1750
			c.1830
				
				c.1846
				c.1846
				c.1846

Morda	Oswestry	SJ 289281	c.1710	c.1875

Neen Savage
    Walford's Mill
    Lloyd's/Cleobury Mill
	Neen Savage	
		SO 675767
		SO 677763
			
			c.1827
			c.1827
				
				c.1885
				c.1885

Neen Sollars
    Langley Mill
    Sturt's/Bradley Mill
	Neen Sollars	
		SO 653730
		SO 654712
			
			c.1660
			pre 1830
				
				c.1880
				c.1850

Shifnal	Shifnal	SJ 741203	c.1810	c.1840
Tibberton	Edgmond	SJ 681203	1804	1912

Weston Rhyn
    Old Mill
    Wern Mill
	St Martin's	
		SJ 273344
		SJ 275345
			
			c.1745
			c.1745
				
				c.1875
				c.1875

Table 2.3 Papermills in Shropshire.
Sources: L.C. Lloyd, 'Paper-making in Shrophire', TSAS, vol 44 (1937-38)
and other sources.

NOTE: Mills of which there is only place-name or hearsay evidence,
uncorroborated from other sources, are omitted.

At least four water-powered oil mills worked in Shropshire. At Caynton (SJ 692214) a mill on the River Meese was operating in 1766 and continued until the bankruptcy of its owner, William Briscoe, in the late 1820s.[26] Rindleford Mill (SJ 738955) on the Worfe was adapted for crushing linseed by the mid 18th century and continued as an oil mill until c.1820.[27] The 23.5m diameter waterwheel at Swinney Mill, Coalport (SJ 706017) was utilised for oil manufacture, probably for colourings for the chinaworks.[28] The contents of an oil mill at Sandford (SJ 581341) are listed in the inventory of Thomas Sandford, taken in 1726.[29] The mill was processing both linseed and rape, and had a stock of 427 gallons and 1 pint of linseed oil, valued at £53 7s 6d, that is 2s 6d per gallon. Debts for oil supplied to customers amounted to £100. The largest item of movable equipment was a lead cistern. Oil was strained, leaving linseed dust, and linseed cakes for animal feed were made from the seed husks. Oil was delivered to customers in staved casks. The mill building at Sandford, a rectangular structure 16m x 6m in soft red brick, was used to grind grain in the 19th century. It bears the date 1728 which perhaps marks its conversion from an oil to a cornmill.

Water power has served other functions in rural Shropshire. Several fulling mills were working after 1660, and other stages of textile manufacture have used water power at Coleham (Shrewsbury), Knighton and Ludlow. Leather dressers used water power at Allscott, Hungerford, Widnal and Pontesford. Six mills were adapted to crush barytes, and water was used to power sawmills at Bromfield, Ashford Carbonel, Moreton Corbet and elsewhere. The Lower Mill at Cleobury Mortimer crushed cider apples. In the late 19th century small waterwheels were installed at Badger Hall, Stableford Hall, Faintree and elsewhere to pump water to mansions and farm houses, while the mills at Woolstaston and Ashford Carbonel are among those that have been used to generate electricity.

The remaining tower of the windmill at Hadley Park (SJ 657115)

Wind Power

Shropshire has never enjoyed the abundance of wind power generated in the Fylde or Lincolnshire. Only illustrative evidence remains of post mills, such as that on the racecourse at Bicton portrayed by W. Pearson in 1808. There is conclusive evidence for some 30 tower mills that have worked since 1660.[30] Most of the 16 surviving towers are of modest dimensions, when complete were of no more than three storeys, and were built for grinding grain in the late 18th or early 19th centuries. Lyth Hill Mill was used to prepare hemp for

Name	Parish	Grid reference	Earliest known date	Last known date
Asterley	Pontesbury	SJ 372075	1809	c.1890
Chetwynd/Sambrook	Chetwynd	SJ 695235	1845	-
Cluddley	Wrockwardine	SJ 630104	pre 1752	c.1890
Coton Wood	Wem	SJ 542351	1813	c.1900
Ditton Priors	Ditton Priors	SO 593877	c.1845	c.1880
Hadley Park	Hadley (Wellington)	SJ 657115	c.1787	c.1835
Hadnall	Hadnall	SJ 523210	1787	c.1800
Hawkstone	Weston-under-Redcastle	SJ 566297	pre 1808	-
Lyth Hill	Condover	SJ 469067	c.1835	c.1890
Madeley Court	Madeley	SJ 695053	pre 1827	c.1840
Much Wenlock	Much Wenlock	SJ 624008	pre 1750	c.1890
Rodington	Rodington	SJ 590144	pre 1830	c.1890
Rowton	Alberbury	SJ 365129	1774	c.1800
Shackerley	Albrighton	SJ 802039	1768	c.1895
Upton	Shifnal	SJ 756067	pre 1797	c.1890
Vennington	Westbury	SJ 337096	pre 1800	c.1912

Table 2.4 Windmills in Shropshire of which the towers remain
Source: W.A. Seaby & A.C. Smith, Windmills in Shropshire, Hereford and Worcester:
a contemporary survey, Stevenage: Stevenage Museum, 1984.

rope-making, while those at Chetwynd, Hadley Park and Uffington pumped water in addition to grinding grain. The mills at Asterley, Coton Wood, Vennington and Shackerley have been adapted as dwellings, while those at Hadnall, Much Wenlock and Hadley Park have the appearance of follies. The remainder are derelict or serve as stores. The largest tower mills in Shropshire were in towns. Most rural windmills closed between 1880 and 1900 although the towers remain of some that ceased work much earlier.

Building Materials

Building stone was quarried for local use in most parts of Shropshire. In Ditton Priors and in several squatter communities the dhustone, the dolerite from the summits of the Clee Hills, was employed in cottages although its porosity attracts dampness. Tolerably good local stones were employed in several distinct regions. The brecchia outcrop provided materials for buildings on the Loton Park and Rowton estates from the late 18th century, the last of them, Wattlesborough School, erected in 1904. The Chatwall Sandstone, characteristically banded in purple, brown and green, was widely used around Church Stretton. Rubble limestone is unsurprisingly found in the walls of older buildings around Much Wenlock and Ludlow.

Ann Scard observed that many quarries were exploited intermittently, whenever there was a need for quality building materials, such as when a school or bridge was being constructed or a mansion or church extended.[32] On the Sweeney Estate carboniferous sand-stone was employed in the walls of Sweeney Hall, but inferior sandstones from lower beds in the same quarries were used in farm buildings. Quarries in the Silurian limestone in Moor Park were opened up for the construction of Richard Norman Shaw's church of All Saints, Richard Castle (SJ 494707) in 1891-92, and a quarry called Rock Hollow was the source of stone for Benjamin Ferrey's church of St Luke, Sambrook (SJ 714245) in 1846. Former quarries of this type, accessible because they are protected for their ecological value, include Quarry Wood, Hinstock (SJ 685272) where the Bunter Sandstone was exploited until the 1880s, Tasker Quarry, Linley (SO 326956) where the Stapeley Volcanic rock was extracted, and Hope Mill Quarry (SJ 355021) in the Silurian limestone.

Some quarries provided stone for distant buildings of consequence and were worked over long periods. The sandstone workings at Alveley and Highley remain impressive. Severn barges enabled quarry masters to sell to customers as far away as Gloucester. Grinshill stone commanded wider markets. It was used in Shrewsbury's two 18th-century bridges, the Salopian Infirmary and in Georgian terraces in the county town, as well as in buildings in Birmingham, Liverpool and Aberystwyth. By the late 19th century powered machines, including two steam cranes, were used in the quarries, and stone was despatched from a siding at Yorton station. Several former quarries are accessible from Corbet Wood (SJ 526237), and a series of stone setts remains that was put down in 1839-40 to enable wagons to carry away stone for John Carline's rebuilding of All Saints, Grinshill (SJ 520234).[33] The sandstone at Nesscliffe was regularly worked in the 19th century but probably not for distant markets.

Quarries are also exploited for roadstone. The extraction of road metals on Pontesbury Hill (SJ 390046) began at about the time of its enclosure in 1848. At first only one or two men were involved, but the number increased to about a dozen in the 1880s, when Quarry Terrace was built to accommodate some of their number. Callow Hill Quarry (SJ 385050) was opened in 1926 and leased in 1931 to Salop County Council, who bought it in 1956, after hauling some of its produce along the Snailbeach District Railway with a farm tractor.[34]

The typical form of a brickworks drying shed, at Bourton, Much Wenlock (SO 601957).

22

Roadstone has also been extracted from Wenlock Edge, around Llanymynech Hill and on Sharpstones Hill. Quarries in the dolerite on the summits of the Clee Hills are considered in chapter 4.

Stones for abrasive purposes were produced in quarries in Highley and Alveley. Most, given the soft nature of the sandstones, must have been for grinding, but in 1821 a quarrymen was killed when trying to move what was described as a millstone from workings in Alveley. At the entrance to one quarry (SO 754825) about 1km downstream from Highley station, there remain five large circular grinding stones, the largest 1.75m in diameter.[35]

Sand is another quarry product. In the early 20th century moulding sand for foundries was extracted from quarries alongside the Wellington-Wolverhampton railway at Ruckley (SJ 773060). At Queen's Head (SJ 341267) on the Ellesmere Canal the face remains of a quarry from which, in the early 20th century, sand was conveyed to canal boats by a railway that passed under the road in a tunnel.[36]

Bricks were made in almost every part of Shropshire in the 18th and 19th centuries. The Coalbrookdale Coalfield supplied regional if not national markets, but until the 1890s most parts of Shropshire appear to have been self-sufficient in common bricks although those for prestigious buildings were purchased elsewhere.[37]

When bricks were required in rural areas in the 18th century it was common practice to dig local clay, mould it with a minimum of preparation, and fire the bricks in a clamp, or temporary kiln, for which coal would be brought from the nearest colliery. When the parish vestry at Prees decided in 1773 to build a workhouse, one Thomas Roberts agreed to build a kiln to fire 40,000 bricks. When the architect John Hiram Haycock contracted to build Apley Castle, Wellington, in 1791, it was agreed that the bricks would be made on the estate. Temporary clamps and shallow clay pits leave few traces on undisturbed ground.

In the 19th century, with improved roads and the ready availability of pug mills and other equipment, rural brickworks proliferated. By the 1880s there were about 50 in rural Shropshire, most with permanent kilns, and some with substantial buildings housing clay preparation and moulding machinery. Many made roofing tiles and field drainage pipes, and a few produced terracotta, glazed pipes and earthenware.

Evidence remains in the landscape of most of the brickworks of this period and some sites have continued in industrial use. The Chinnel brickworks outside Whitchurch became a creamery, while one of the two at Kinnerley was adapted as the locomotive depot of the Shropshire & Montgomeryshire Railway. The Osbaston works became the Brookside Kennels. Many brickmaking sites remain as rough ground, dotted with pools and partially covered with trees. Structures remain in some places. A brickworks at Bourton (SO 606956), operated in the 1880s and '90s by a local farmer, and probably closed c.1904, was surveyed in 1991. Its principal building was a single-storey rectangular drying shed, a little over 25m long and about 7m wide, with the bricks spaced to give perforated walls. The Scotch downdraught kiln, approximately 10m x 13m, had 16 fire holes. The clay pits could still be identified, and a small square pit appeared to have been the site of the pug mill.[38]

The brickworks at Long Wood was established by the 1830s, and in 1881 provided employment for five men and two boys. It closed before 1928. The drying shed has been demolished, but a downdraught kiln, approximately 9.5m x 5.5m, remains, probably in the form in which it was rebuilt in 1894, the date on the works chimney.

Site	Grid reference	Parish	Indications on map
Adeney	SJ 710185	Edgmond	Brick & tile works, kiln
Astley Abbots	SO 713957	Astley Abbots	Pool
Aston Eyre	SO 640941	Aston Eyre	Square kiln
Barkers Green	SJ 527282	Wem	Brick & tile works
The Bold	SO 642848	Aston Botterell	Kiln, pools
Bourton (i)	SO 602957	Much Wenlock	-
Bourton (ii)	SO 606956	Much Wenlock	Brick & pipe works, kiln
Brownhills	SJ 685361	Norton-in-Hales	Rectangular building, square kiln
Cantlop	SJ 508054	Berrington	Pools
Cherrington	SJ 668195	Edgmond	Brickfield
Cheswardine Park Farm	SJ 714313	Cheswardine	-
Chinnel	SJ 553432	Whitchurch	Kiln
Dernhill	SO 716794	Kinlet	Rectangular building, pool
Dorrington	SJ 727407	Woore	3 kilns, rectangular building
Dowles	SO 782761	Dowles	3 long rectangular kilns
Eaton	SO 378889	Lydbury North	Brickfield
Echoes Hill	SO 737994	Stockton	Brick & pipe works
Ensdon	SJ 405178	Montford	Brick & tile works, 2 round kilns, H-plan building
Frodesley	SJ 512017	Frodesley	-
Hadnall	SJ 525196	Myddle	Kiln
Hargrove	SO 497911	Rushbury	-
Hesterworth	SO 393828	Hopesay	Kiln
Highfields	SJ 509256	Wem	Rectangular building
Hughley	SJ 571975	Hughley	Brick & tile works
Kinnerley	SJ 336198	Kinnerley	Pool
Kinnerley	SJ 346200	Kinnerley	-
Lack Sarn	SO 267940	Churchstoke (Shrops)	Pool
Lane Green	SO 786864	Alveley	Pool
Lightwood	SO 808937	Claverley	Kilns
Long Lane	SJ 635155	Wrockwardine	Brick & pipe works
Long Wood	SJ 591067	Eaton Constantine	Kiln
Lower Fenemere	SJ 447215	Myddle	Rectangular building
Marshbrook	SO 638907	Church Stretton	Rectangular building, 2 round kilns, tramway
Marton	SJ 443241	Myddle	Round kiln

Millenheath	SJ 587356	Ightfield	Brickfield
Ollerton	SJ 652243	Stoke-on-Tern	Kiln
Oldwood	SJ 455203	Baschurch	Round kiln, rectangular kiln
Osbaston	SJ 595203	High Ercall	Kilns
Oswestry Waterworks	SJ 273304	Oswestry	Kilns
Painsmore	SO 778766	Dowles	Kilns
Prees Heath	SJ 551376	Prees	Clay pits
Ratlinghope	SO 404967	Ratlinghope	Kiln
Ruyton	SJ 386221	Ruyton-XI-Towns	Kiln, rectangular building
Tasley	SO 694947	Tasley	Square kiln
Ticklerton	SO 491917	Easton-under-Heywood	-
Westbury	SJ 346110	Westbury	Brick & tile works, tramway
Weston Common	SJ 426263	Baschurch	Brick & tile works, 2 round kilns
Wheathill	SO 602823	Wheathill	Brick & tile works
Wistanstow	SO 431857	Wistanstow	Brick & tile works
Yorton	SJ 505236	Broughton	-

Table 2.5 Rural Brickworks in Shropshire.
Source: Ordnance Survey First Edition 25 inch maps of the early 1880s

Concrete products were manufactured as an adjunct to limestone workings on Wenlock Edge in the second half of the 20th century, but the most significant rural concrete works was established at Ditton Priors (SO 612886) *c.*1915 by Hamish Cross of the Abdon Clee Stone Quarry Co. The houses around the hydro-electric power station at Dolgarrog in north Wales, erected in 1927 after earlier buildings were destroyed by a flood, were built from components made at Ditton Priors, as were estates in Neasden (London) and Wolverhampton, and some houses in Ditton Priors itself (SO 612893).[39]

Lime and Limestone

Wherever there was limestone in Shropshire it was quarried or mined. Some was used for building, and some quarries provided fluxing stone for ironmaking, but most was burned in kilns to produce lime (i.e. Calcium Oxide, CaO) for builders or farmers. Limestone is more easily transported than quicklime, and many kilns were located at the nodes of local transport systems, where they could readily be supplied with limestone and coal, and from which lime could conveniently be conveyed to customers.

The Silurian limestone extends in a south-westerly direction from Lincoln Hill, Coalbrookdale and Benthall Edge, along Wenlock Edge and south of Craven Arms to the Aymestrey limestones of Herefordshire. The archaeology of the quarries has been system-atically surveyed by Williams and by Holmes.[40] Documentary and field research revealed the existence of some 183 kilns between Lincoln Hill and Easthope, of which there are substantial remains of at least 80. The peak of quarrying activity was in the 19th century when stone was taken by rail to the blast furnaces of the Coalbrookdale Coalfield and South Staffordshire after the railway west of Much Wenlock opened in 1867. The despatch of fluxing stone to the Black Country continued until the 1930s. Lime burning in the area ceased in 1965, after which the quarries' principal product was aggregates.

North of Much Wenlock the Farley and Bradley quarries (SJ 637024-639024) were worked in the early 18th century, and for much of the 19th century were operated by ironworking companies. In the early 20th century Boulton & Co. employed up to 60 men there, using tramways to feed their kilns, and despatching lime from railway sidings. Photographic evidence suggests that there were three bottle-shaped kilns and a Hoffman kiln. The quarry became an RAF fuel depot in 1939 and there are no significant remains of limeworking structures.

The New Works, or Wenlock Edge and Smokey Hole quarries (SJ 609002-611003), were leased in 1801 by Thomas Telford and partners who had interests in the colliery at Lower Long Wood and in Cressage Bridge which linked the two undertakings. An inclined plane linked the quarries with three limes kilns alongside the Red House on the Shrewsbury-Wenlock road. Coal from Lower Long Wood was carried to the kilns by wagons that took a return freight of limestone to be burned in kilns at the colliery. Remnants of kilns remain in Smokey Hole quarry (SJ 611003), Trowes and Stokes Barn quarries (SJ 614999), Meakins quarry (SJ 610996) and Ballstone quarry (SJ 613997).[41]

The Stretton Westwood Quarry (SO 595984) occupies land allocated for stone production by the Enclosure Commission in 1808. From the 1860s it was worked by George Lloyd who constructed standard gauge railway sidings and a network of 3ft gauge tramways. Quarrying continued until 1954 after which the site was used for other industrial purposes. Two conventional kilns built against the quarry face remain.

The Lilleshall Quarry (SO 575968), one of the largest on Wenlock Edge, takes its name from the Lilleshall Company who, from 1862, extracted limestone for their blast furnaces as well as producing lime in kilns. Tramways linked quarry faces with kilns and with sidings on a mineral railway which joined the Great Western near Presthope station. Production reached 1,000 tons a week in 1900 but activities were subsequently run down and the rails were lifted in 1917. The mineral railway can still be traced but modern workings have destroyed ten kilns and all evidence of the tramways.

Elsewhere on the Edge several kilns and a tramway embankment remain at the Old Knowle quarry at Presthope (SO 585977), four kilns stand alongside the former GWR line at the Plough quarry (SO 583974) and a small kiln remains in the Edge Wood nature reserve (SO 479876).

At the southern end of Wenlock Edge there were two lime enterprises along the road from Craven Arms to Pedlars Rest, the Dinchope Works, where there were kilns at the roadside (SO 454828) and others within the workings stretching north into Halford Wood (SO 452836), and the Shawbank Lime Works (SO 463832). There were further kilns at Whettleton Bank (SO 445805) near the Shrewsbury-Ludlow road. The substantial View Edge Lime Works (SO 426807) in Aldon township was active by the 1770s, but must always have been difficult of access.

The beds of limestone around the Clee Hills also sustained lime-burning enterprises and until the late 18th century supplied some fluxing stone for blast furnaces. The Ditton Lime

Works (SO 601877) served a local market inaccessible to other suppliers. Two surviving kilns at the Studley Lime Works (SO 603745) must be amongst the smallest and crudest remaining in Shropshire. The workings at Oreton (SO 650805) in Stottesdon parish were on a larger scale and six individuals had businesses there in the 1870s. On the southern border of the county there were limestone mines at The Knowle, where 14 kilns produced 7,000 bushels of lime per week in 1814, Gorstley Rough (SO 593747) and the Novers (SO 596736) where an adit remains with a bank of four kilns. Cast-iron plate rails have been found on the site. Working ceased in 1912 having been on a small scale for some years previously.[42]

The Alberbury Breccia ridge was a source of lime before 1660. Small quarries line the north-eastern edge of Loton Deer Park (SJ 360140) and the road from Rowton to Cardington. There were 28 kilns on the Loton Park estate in 1834, and some 5,000 tons of rock were burned annually between 1828 and 1842.[43]

Llanymynech Hill was described by Thomas Pennant in 1773 as 'the magazine of limestone for a vast tract of country'. Output increased with the development of turnpike roads, but remained seasonal, carriage in the 1790s being possible only between March and October. Aikin in 1797 recorded that limestone was sent as far into Wales as Llanidloes, that it was sold at the kilns for 7d a bushel, and that a wagon-load was reckoned to be 36 bushels.[44] Lime was still being burned around the hill in the 1930s. In the mid 19th century limestone was despatched by canal to ironworks in the Coalbrookdale Coalfield and the Black Country. Evidence of the cutting of deeper levels in the top quarry on the hill suggests that owners remained optimistic about its prospects around 1900. Quarry workers at Llanymynech were universally called 'rockmen'. Their number declined from 45 to 33 between 1861 and 1871, with a further reduction to 21 ten years later. In the neighbouring hamlet of Pant the number fell from 43 to 11 during the 1870s.

Four tramway systems brought stone from the quarries on the hill to the main road, the canal and the railway at its foot. One was working as early as 1809, and in 1820 a man was killed at the 'Old Rail Road'. This was probably the line leading to the Ellesmere Canal along what remains a distinctive narrow plot in which stands Rock Cottage (SJ 266214). This line had fallen out of use by 1838. To the east is a system which in its final form linked the topmost quarries on the hill by means of three inclined planes, one through a tunnel, with wharfs on the canal. Foundations remain of the winding houses of all three inclines, on the slopes of which wooden sleepers and stones bearing the marks of winding ropes can still be seen.

To the north, a tramway in operation by 1838 ran on the level past Pant Methodist Church, across the turnpike road, and descended by an inclined plane to kilns alongside the Ellesmere Canal (SJ 275217). The winding drum at the head of the plane (SJ 273218) was restored by local enterprise in the 1970s, but the slope of the incline was subsequently destroyed by the construction of a house. The most northerly tramway, constructed between 1838 and 1882, ran from a wharf near Pant station (SJ 276223), through its own arch in the bridge carrying a lane over the canal, along what is now a footpath, past a pair of limekilns west of the Oswestry-Welshpool road (SJ 277236) and ascended to the Llynclys portion of the hill by a long inclined plane at the top of which remains a stable, probably for the horses that moved wagons to and from the quarries.

The winding drum at the head of one of the inclined planes on which wagons of limestone were lowered on their way from the quarries on Llanymynech Hill to wharfs on the Ellesmere Canal (SJ 273218).

The two southerly tramways ran into the canal basin at Llanymynech which had been constructed by 1838. Much of the stone was loaded into narrow boats to be shipped away, but considerable quantities were burned to make lime. Two large conventional lime kilns remain, one with a lining which appears to have been almost new when production was abandoned. Protruding rolled steel joists suggest that the kilns in their present form are of 20th-century date. The most prominent feature of the site is a Hoffman kiln, built after 1900, perhaps as an attempt to develop the market for lime as that for fluxing stone declined.

North of Llanymynech Hill is a further range of limestone quarries, partly in Llanyblodwell and partly in the township of Treflach in Oswestry, and incorporating workings at Porthywaen, Whitehaven and Nant Mawr. These also reached a peak of production in the mid 19th century. In 1841 there were 27 'rockmen' in Oswestry parish, but the total rose to 98 by 1861, and reached a peak of 118 ten years later before declining to 66 in 1881. The quarries were served by the Porthywaen branch of the Cambrian Railways opened in 1861, by the Nant Mawr extension of the Potteries, Shrewsbury & North Wales Railway opened in 1866, and by the Tanat Valley Light Railway which utilised part of the track of the PS&NWR and opened in 1904. The quarries became one of the principal sources of ballast for the Great Western Railway, and many ballast wagons bore the legend 'Return empty to Llynclys'. Dolgoch quarry (SJ 276244) is accessible as a nature reserve.

The scale of working in this area is revealed by a sale notice of 1841 for a set of kilns at Porthywaen. Three were 7.6m (25ft) deep and held 14 wagon-loads of lime each, three were 4.9m (16ft) deep and held six wagon-loads of lime each. Stone came from a breast of rock 165m (180yds) wide. Equipment included 105.2m (115 yds) of railway plates and sleepers, railway stone carriages, eight iron crowbars, six stone hammers, five pick mattocks, four iron and eight wooden wheelbarrows, eight lime shovels and an iron-bound lime measure.[45]

A scatter of small quarries serving local markets and each employing no more than two or three workers extended north towards the River Ceiriog. There was a limestone quarry

Lime kilns on the line of Offa's Dyke and on the Welsh border at Craignant (SJ 252349).

west of Trefonen Hall (SJ 245263) and further quarries with kilns south of Wernddu (SJ 233261). The landscape around Craig-llwyn (SJ 237276) is scarred with remnants of quarries, and there were further workings with kilns at Cynynion (SJ 2433030).

At Llawnt (SJ 249309) on the turnpike road from Oswestry to Llansilin, quarries line the eastern bank of the infant River Morda. In the late 19th century there were two banks of kilns. Further quarries lie along the turnpike from Oswestry to Glyn Ceiriog at Craignant (SJ 252349) near the Victorian tower marking the course of Offa's Dyke. Some kilns remain alongside the lane north of the main road.

The celebrated lime kilns of Bron-y-garth stand on Shropshire's north-west frontier, south of the River Ceiriog, across which a bridge gave access to the Chirk-Glyn Ceiriog turnpike road. It also carried a siding from the Glyn Valley Tramway to the kilns. Customers to the east were supplied along the road from Wem turnpiked in 1771. A quarry remains in the angle between the road and Offa's Dyke, and a bank of four kilns stands behind a retaining wall more than 10m high, from the mortar joints of which sprout hazel saplings, hart's tongue ferns and wild strawberries.

Malting and Tanning

In the 18th and early 19th centuries much of the barley used for brewing beer in Shropshire was malted in small malthouses that formed parts of farmsteads or inns. The maltings at Barrow Farm, Barrow was probably converted from a barn when the adjacent malt kiln was built around 1830. The *Hare and Hounds* at Cruckton (SJ 432107) is one of many inns that had malthouses.[46] Some rural malthouses were of the same order of size as their urban equivalents. At Diddlebury (SO 518851) is a three-storey malthouse in neatly coursed sandstone with a clay tile roof, L-shaped in plan, with five bays on the main elevation and

The bow-ended malt-house at Minsterley (SJ 372050)

taking-in doors on each floor. At Minsterley (SJ 372050) is a bow-ended, three-storey malthouse of eight bays, in rubble stone, with a lucam on the top storey, and the remains of a taking-in door on the first floor. Malting became an essentially urban trade in the 19th century.

The processing of leather similarly progressed towards the towns. In the 18th century there were tanners at Myddle, Worthen, Wollerton (Hodnet), Pontesford, Whittington, Hungerford Mill in Munslow, Gadlis in Ellesmere and Cheney Longville, of which only the last three appear to have been working in 1851. There are substantial remains of the tannery buildings at Hungerford Mill (SO 537790).

Woodworking

Wood is one of the principal natural resources of the Shropshire countryside. Until the late 18th century the most important product of the county's woodlands was charcoal for smelting iron ore and refining iron, much of which was carried long distances to furnaces and forges. Trevor Rowley showed that the costs of charcoal at Bouldon furnace increased from £1 16s 0d in 1736 to £2 16s 0d in 1775, and that the owners of Charlcotte furnace after 1750 obtained supplies from 16km away, as far as Nash, Acton Scott and Spoonhill Wood. An early 19th-century writer, acknowledging the diminished consumption of charcoal resulting from the use of coke in blast furnaces, noted that there were still many thousand acres of coppice woodland in the county, valued at seven shillings an acre.[48] In some areas a modest level of charcoal production continued through the 19th century – there was a wood collier (i.e. charcoal burner) in Leighton, for example, until the 1890s, and coppices continued to be sources of pit props.

The largest extent of woodland in Shropshire is the Wyre Forest in the parishes of Kinlet and Dowles on the Worcestershire border. Seven woodcutters lived in Kinlet in 1871. Disciplined study of the forest revealed changing patterns of past management reflected in the distribution of species, in different patterns of coppice, and in the effects on ground flora of charcoal burning.[49]

Shropshire oak was used in shipbuilding both within the county and at ports on the lower Severn. Sale notices for timber trees in the early 19th century usually detail the means of access from the point of sale to the Severn. Sawmills powered by water and steam proliferated in the 19th century, especially on the great estates. The buildings of the mill at Uppington (SJ 602097) built for the Dukes of Cleveland remain little altered. The reciprocating saw from the Bromfield mill, made by John Pickles & Son of Hebden Bridge *c.*1890, together with the Fielding & Platt oil engine of *c.*1914 which once powered it, is preserved at Blists Hill. Overhead cranes were installed at some rural railway stations to aid the loading of timber, including those at Bromfield, Marshbrook, Ludlow and Woofferton on the Shrewsbury & Hereford line. Trackside sawmills remained long after they ceased to use the railway at Bucknell (SO 355736), Elson (SJ 313360) and Woofferton (SO 514680).

Shropshire's woodlands were also a source of bark for use in tanning. An early 20th-century photograph of the Bucknell sawmill shows huge piles of bark awaiting despatch by rail. Coppice products included crate heads, crate rods and stales for shovels and hammers, all of which were offered for sale at Cressage in 1868.[50] Alders were sought by itinerant cloggers. The 1861 census revealed the presence of five cloggers from Lancashire at the *Raven Inn*, Ludlow. William Dudley of Welshampton made his living as a clogwood dealer in the 1870s, and the practice continued at Wistanstow in the 1920s when alder wood was taken away by lorry. Basket-making was a significant manufacture at Montford and Welshampton. Besoms were made from twigs, usually by itinerant besom makers who stayed in market town lodging houses, but two resident tradesmen in Button Oak were thus occupied in the late 1870s. J.C. Edge of Craven Arms, John Upton of Church Aston and Richard Kay of Prees all made bendware, while during the 1870s a 'Steam Chair Manufactory' at Whittington was manned by skilled workers from High Wycombe.

Artificial Manure

There were artificial manure (i.e. superphosphate) works in the late 19th century at Allscott, Maesbury, Rednal, Ruckley, the Calcutts and Quatford. The best evidence of the technology employed comes from the Calcutts in the Ironbridge Gorge. In 1871 the premises comprised a mill room, oil room, acid rooms and rectifying room, with power provided by a 7hp steam engine, together with two warehouses, 18.5m x 5.2m and 12.3m x 4.6m, and a dwelling house. Equipment included a bone mill, wrought-iron cisterns, glass retorts, Woulfe's Jars and about a hundred carboys, together with stocks of acetic acid, sodium acetate, sulphur, hydrochloric acid, palm nuts and cotton seed.[51]

The largest of the manure works was established in 1858 by John Austin alongside the railway at Allscott (SJ 614126). Austin, born at Longdon-on-Tern, was a farmer who began making manure on a small scale in Wellington in 1854, and was working 1,170 acres and employing 24 men in 1871. His chief chemist was Edward Smith, a Liverpudlian, who, like Austin, lived in Allscott village. The works operated until 1958 and was subsequently used as a fertiliser depot.[52]

Technical expertise from Merseyside also supported superphosphate works in north Shropshire. A factory at Maesbury on the site of the former lead smelter was established by Edward Richards, a Welshman who had lived in Liverpool where his sons, David, an analytical chemist, and Robert, who also worked in the business, were born in 1853 and 1858. The building remains alongside the Ellesmere Canal behind the *Navigation Inn*, a

The former artificial manure (superphosphate) works on the banks of the Ellesmere Canal behind the Navigation Inn at Maesbury (SJ 315250), established in the 1860s by Edward Richards on the site of a former lead smelter.

two-storey structure, rectangular in plan and sparsely fenestrated, with a round chimney. A larger chimney, 46m high and 7.6m in diameter, was demolished in 1892 after the company moved to a former warehouse at Rednal Canal Wharf (SJ 350280) where manufacturing continued until the 1950s.[53]

Nothing remains of the bone works at the Calcutts, and Bonehill Bridge over the Wolverhampton-Shrewsbury railway (SJ 770064) is almost the only evidence on the ground of what seems to have been the first artificial manure works in Shropshire, established at Ruckley by William Bradburn before 1851. A few mounds remain on the site of the water-powered mill at Dudmaston (SO 737896), which was operated by George Fisher between *c.*1860 and 1880.[54]

The Food Industries

Cheese was produced on a large scale in Shropshire for national markets before 1700. The county formed the southern part of what agrarian historians have defined as the Cheshire Cheese Region. Cheese-making was particularly important at Adderley, a closed parish of large farms. Richard Furber who died in 1660 had a dairy herd of 134 beasts and cheese worth £168, probably about eight tons, stored in his house. William Tankard, who died in 1695, had 80cwt of cheese, valued at £80.[55] Cheese from Shropshire was carried down the Severn through Gloucester. During 1713 the *Prosperity* of Shrewsbury carried 230 tons in the course of 17 downstream voyages, and in 1722 the *Thomas & Mary* of Broseley made 11 journeys, carrying in all 140 tons of cheese.[56]

The scale of the cheese trade in the early 19th century is indicated by the county's cheese markets, particularly the three in Shrewsbury, but cheese making remained a farmhouse activity until the 1870s. The first cheese factory in England was opened at Longford, Derbyshire, in 1870, utilising American technology.[57] The first in Shropshire came a little later. By 1879 Thomas Pugh Johnson had a 'milk and cheese factory' at Tern Hill (SJ 635321), probably opened in 1878, the date on the adjacent cottages.[58] The factory subsequently passed into other hands and was still used for dairying in the 1930s, although it has since been adapted for other purposes. Dairy factories multiplied in Shropshire from

The first cheese factory in Shropshire opened by Thomas Pugh Johnson at Tern Hill (SJ 635321) c.1878.

the 1880s until the 1930s, both in adapted premises and in purpose-built creameries. Most balanced the production of cheese and butter with the supply of liquid milk for distribution to households. In more recent times global companies have dominated dairying in Shropshire, and chilled products, cottage cheese, yoghurt and fromage frais have been made on a large scale.

Thomas William Horner was making butter and dealing in cheese by the early 1890s at the Chinnel, Whitchurch (SJ 552430) on a site that had previously been a brickyard. The creamery alongside the North Staffordshire Railway at Pipe Gate, Woore (SJ 737408) was established before 1909 by Henry Edwards & Son of Market Drayton and continued after the Second World War. The buildings were subsequently occupied by a rubber manufacturer. The most prominent is a three-storey polychrome brick tower, with a north elevation of four bays and an east elevation of five bays, which is flanked by pairs of high, single-storey brick sheds in the same combination of red and buff bricks.

The creamery at Minsterley (SJ 375051) originated in 1909 when the barytes mill south of the village was adapted by Wathes Bros of Birmingham as a collecting depot for liquid milk. After the First World War the company purchased a military forage depot, which itself had been adapted from a sawmill, and established a model creamery. Products in the 1930s

A picture postcard of the 1930s showing the creamery alongside the North Staffordshire Railway at Pipe Gate (SJ 737408). The line of the road has since been altered leaving the cottages on the right on a service road.

included cheese, butter, fresh and tinned cream and evaporated milk. A herd of 300 pigs consumed by-products. Pork and bacon were processed in an adjacent factory which continues to operate as a meat cannery under different ownership. The buildings at the creamery have been constantly adapted to new uses and few structures remain from before the Second World War, although the cottages on the opposite side of the A488 bear the initials of the original owners of the sawmill.[59]

A label of the 1930s for tinned cream produced at Minsterley

A farmers' co-operative established the creamery at Ruyton-XI-Towns (SJ 391223) during the First World War. Until its closure in 1992 it was celebrated for its cheese, made in varied buildings including brick sheds that probably dated from the time of its foundation. There were some modern structures such as the evaporator tower that produced whey powder. The factory had subsidiary plants at Whittington (SJ 323310), which was closed in 1990 and demolished in 1992, and a three-storey structure, clad in corrugated iron at Baschurch (SJ 423216) which ceased to be used as a dairy in the late 1940s and was then adapted to pack frozen peas.[60]

The creamery by the former station at Dorrington (SJ 480032) on the Shrewsbury & Hereford Railway was opened by a farmers' consortium in 1921 and supplied milk to London. A new dairy company, Independent Milk Supplies (IMS), was established in the

Right: The Marylebone milk train in 1954, approaching Shrewsbury from Dorrington. The five glass-lined 3,000 gallon tankers are hauled by locomotive No.6976 Graythwaite Hall *from Banbury shed which shared the working with Coleham depot at Shrewsbury. The inscription on the left is on a bogie brake van preserved by the Severn Valley Railway.*

capital in 1928 in competition with the two dominant firms, United Dairies and Express Dairies, and in 1934 built a depot at Rossmore Road alongside Marylebone station. The following year IMS took over and rebuilt the creamery at Dorrington, and in June 1936 bought ten six-wheel tank wagons (Nos 2567-76) built by the GWR at Swindon. The Dorrington-Marylebone (sometimes called the Dorrington-Banbury) milk train began to run soon afterwards. The tanks were worked to Banbury during the afternoon then attached to a train to Woodford and added to the 20.50 for Marylebone, where they arrived at 23.11. The empty tanks for Dorrington left Marylebone at 14.09 and were returned to Shropshire by the same route. After the nationalisation of the railways the milk train travelled direct from Banbury to Marylebone through Bicester and High Wycombe. The Dorrington milk train was still running in 1965, but ceased soon afterwards when the creamery closed. The Severn Valley Railway has a bogie brake van inscribed 'Banbury and Dorrington Milk Train'.[61]

Apart from the meat-packing plant next to Minsterley creamery, Shropshire's principal cannery in the inter-war period was at Walford, Baschurch (SJ 442203), established in 1933 by Col C.R. Morris-Eyton, initially to can locally-grown peas. After harvesting, the peas were taken to a viner which extracted them from their pods. They were blanched and graded at the factory before being placed in cans and put into an exhauster. They were marketed as *Golden Mere* and *Silver Mere* peas. Strawberries, raspberries, gooseberries, plums, bilberries and damsons were canned in the late summer. At its peak the factory employed about 300 girls, mostly on a seasonal basis. It closed soon after the outbreak of the Second World War.[62]

A new industry arrived in Shropshire in 1927 with the construction by the Shropshire Beet Sugar Co. Ltd of the factory at Allscott (actually in Walcot, SJ 605125). It employed German technology and the menus at the dinner celebrating its completion on 10 November 1927 were bilingual. The factory was one of the first building projects in the county to employ concrete construction on a large scale. For 80 years its clouds of steam and distinctive aromas were features of autumns and early winters in east Shropshire but the factory closed in 2007 and the site awaits re-development.[63]

The essence of rural manufactures
Varied manufacturing enterprises flourish in the Shropshire countryside in the 21st century, most of them in places whose industrial use is historically determined – the sites of watermills, railway stations and brickworks. The most significant influence on industrial location has been the availability of space on military bases constructed during the two world wars. The sales that followed the Armistice of 1918 indicate the scale of the changes that the First World War brought to the countryside. Nearly 1,200 wooden buildings were sold between February 1920 and April 1922 from the training camp established in 1915 at Prees Heath, more than 2,000 beds from Park Hall, Oswestry, and 933m (1020 yds) of 2ft (6m) gauge railway track at a forestry depot at Acton Burnell.[64]

PMC (Shrewsbury) Ltd was one of the first companies to be involved in the redevelopment of the military bases of the Second World War from the time that it acquired part of Condover airfield (SO 503037) in 1964.[65] A hangar, some personnel buildings and a tower used for training bomb aimers were taken over and initially used largely by metal-working concerns. In the early 1970s the company converted to industrial uses the NAAFI, the dining block, the sergeants' mess and numerous personnel buildings of the Rosehill base (SJ 660301) which had accommodated servicemen from the flying field at Tern Hill. In 1969 PMC bought the ex-RASC base at Leaton (SJ 473186) where there had been a military butchery and a bakery. Corrugated iron huts and precast concrete buildings were adapted for industrial uses, principally motor car body workshops and plating concerns.

There are two industrial estates on the Second World War airfield at Rednal. On Site A (SJ 370286) a timber company and a piling concern occupy wartime buildings that are now surrounded by conifers. On Site B (SJ 368277) scarcely-altered accommodation blocks provide space for a road haulage depot and firms making paint and upholstery, while a farmer makes use of a multi-storey concrete structure.

The Royal Navy base at Ditton Priors was constructed for the storage of ammunition and the industrial units are 'magazines', substantial buildings protected by earthen banks extending 2km south-east of the entrance. (SO 613893). Present-day uses include engineering workshops, motor body shops and a fireworks factory. Some buildings on the huge army base at Nesscliffe that was served by the Shropshire & Montgomeryshire Railway have been similarly adapted.

The word 'industry' conjures up stereotyped images of multi-storeyed mills, smoking chimneys and blazing furnaces, making it difficult to link the term with activities in the Corvedale or on Whixall Moss. The landscape of rural Shropshire nevertheless reflects a long history of manufactures, centred round the availability of water power, raw materials, labour or simply space. Timber, milk and stone are still transported along Shropshire's rural roads and the enterprises that flourish in former military camps or in the yards of closed railway stations continue a tradition which has its origins in the squatter settlements of the 17th and 18th centuries, of making the most economic use of available space and labour.

Buildings from the former Royal Navy depot at Ditton Priors (SO 613893) now adapted for industrial use.

3   MARKET TOWN INDUSTRIES

George Eliot described her fictional St Ogg's as 'one of those old, old towns which impress one as a continuation and outgrowth of nature, a town which carries the trades of its long growth and history like a millennial tree'.[1] Towns in the 18th and 19th centuries were places for trade, for accessing the services of professional men, and for religious, cultural and recreational activities. Most had distinctive 'manufactures', producing goods, on however small a scale, for national markets. Towns were also locations for particular kinds of industry, some of which demanded specialised buildings. A market town was as much a cluster of millers, maltsters, tanners and brickmakers, and later of iron founders and brewers, as it was a concentration of bankers, attorneys, grocers, linen drapers and dissenting ministers.[2]

The Shropshire Towns

Sixteen communities in Shropshire can reasonably be regarded as market towns between 1660 and 1960. Shrewsbury, by far the largest with a population in 1801 of nearly 15,000, remained at that date amongst the 30 largest towns in England, slightly smaller than Leicester, Exeter and Coventry, rather larger than Derby, Oxford, Preston and Reading, a regional capital whose influence extended to the Welsh coast. Shrewsbury grew rapidly in the late 18th century, but actually lost population in the 1830s, and in the course of the 19th century the number of its inhabitants only doubled, a much slower rate of growth than that of the nation as a whole. Wellington, the market town for the Coalbrookdale Coalfield and for the agricultural parishes to the north, came next in order of size. Bridgnorth, one of the principal ports on the River Severn, and Ludlow, which had prospered on the business brought by the Council in the Marches and Wales, had pretensions as resorts as well as market towns. Oswestry, market centre for the Welsh uplands to the west, prospered in the early 19th century and from the 1860s became a railway town, a miniature Ashford or Swindon. The five market towns of north Shropshire – Whitchurch, Market Drayton, Newport, Ellesmere and Wem – all owed some of their 19th-century prosperity to canals. Wem was the smallest Shropshire town to have all the characteristic market town industries. The remaining six, all with populations below 2,000 in 1841, were little more than local retailing centres, although all had maltsters and millers and most had tanners.

Distribution and Exchange

Towns were places of distribution and exchange for which purposes some had buildings that were already venerable in 1660, among them Walter Hancock's Market Hall of 1596 in Shrewsbury – used for buying cloth by the Drapers' Company, as a corn market and as the focus of the Saturday pannier market – or Much Wenlock's Guildhall of 1577. William Baker's Butter Cross of 1743-44 at Ludlow was the most distinguished market building constructed in the county in the 18th century. Market buildings proliferated in the reign of Victoria. In Shrewsbury three establishments competed for the wholesale trade in butter and cheese: Henry Newton's Circus near the Welsh Bridge, completed in 1822, a Doric market hall by Edward Haycock on Pride Hill, built in 1819 and extended in 1844, and the Butter Market in Howard Street, designed by the Birmingham architects Fallows & Hart, and opened at the terminus of the Shrewsbury Canal in 1836.[3] In Oswestry the Powis Market and the Cross Market both opened in 1849. The Butter Market in Market Drayton, a shelter for sellers of dairy produce, supported by Tuscan columns, dates from 1826.

After 1850 the tendency was towards larger multi-purpose market buildings, which were usually given a measure of civic recognition even if built by private companies. One of the first, and certainly the least successful, was the New Market Hall in Bridgnorth,

Market towns in Shropshire

The Butter Market in Howard Street, Shrewsbury, whose foundation stone was laid in 1835 soon after the adjacent canal wharf was linked with the national waterways network. It was designed by the Birmingham architects Fallows & Hart.

	Population in 1841	No. of houses in 1841
Shrewsbury	18,285	4,092
Wellington	6.084	1,300
Bridgnorth	5,770	1,204
Ludlow	5,064	1,086
Oswestry	4,566	987
Whitchurch	3,403	668
Market Drayton	3,161	713
Newport	2,497	553
Ellesmere	2,326	446
Wem	1,932	874
Shifnal	1,872	412
Much Wenlock	1,627	504
Bishop's Castle	1,510	373
Cleobury Mortimer	1,122	211
Clun	913	191
Church Stretton	860	183

Table 3.1 Shropshire Market Towns in 1841, in order of size by population.
Source: 1841 census.
NOTE: *For towns which were parts of large parishes, such as Wellington, Clun or Shifnal, the figures given refer only to the township(s) which comprised the urban areas.*

built in 1855, an exercise in red, white and blue Italianate by John Smallman of Quatford, which failed, after much legal contention, to draw in the town's market traders, who even now remain in the open air in the High Street on Saturday mornings.[4] Shrewsbury's general market, designed by Robert Griffith and completed in 1869, accommodated the corn exchange, the wholesale market for dairy produce and retail markets for fish, meat, fruit and vegetables.[5] Ludlow's combination of town hall and market hall was completed in 1887. In Much Wenlock the Corn Exchange was opened in 1852 and the Market Hall in 1878, both designed by Samuel Pountney Smith.

Facilities for trading in cattle were improved in most Shropshire towns. The pattern was set in Shrewsbury where the ambitious project, completed in 1851, to drain and drive a road across riverside land upstream from the Welsh Bridge included the construction of the Smithfield on a site which it was to occupy for more than a century.[6] At Ellesmere cattle selling moved to a

Ludlow's open air market in the 1950s outside the market hall (now demolished) opened in 1887.

Smithfield alongside the railway station soon after its opening. Two markets on the fringe of the town centre, one close to the station, were opened in Ludlow.

Warehouses for wool and grain were natural appendages of markets. Most surviving buildings are of relatively late date, such as the wool warehouse by the Welsh Bridge in Shrewsbury, now solicitors' offices, a three-storey brick structure of 1888 with a Mansard roof, designed by A.B. Deakin for the merchant Isaac Eakin.[7] The Corn House, a four-storey polychrome brick warehouse on the corner of Wyle Cop and St Julian Friars, was built about 1880 for the grain merchant T.E. Matthews.

Shops are the essence of a market town. The late-medieval frontages in Butcher Row, Shrewsbury, were still hung with joints of meat in the 19th century. In Ludlow small shop fronts of the late 18th and early 19th centuries remain at Nos.9/11 Bell Lane (SO 511743). Typical retailing properties of the mid 19th century, with spacious accommodation for shopkeepers' families on the upper floors, remain in most towns. Higgins's Leeds Warehouse in the Square, Shrewsbury, portrayed in an advertisement of 1847, is an archetypal building of this type. Birchalls, agricultural implement dealers, installed an outstanding shop front at No.40 High Street, Whitchurch (SJ 541415) in 1904, a nine-bay, three-storey, arcaded cast-iron façade supplied by McFarlanes of Glasgow, with semi-circular headed arches, and tracery springing from cylindrical columns. On the top floor it follows the Decorated style with trefoils.[8] Early chain stores secured only a modest presence in Shropshire but some premises can readily be recognised. A mosaic doorstep and a panel in decorative tiles at No.15 King Street, Ludlow (SO 512745) show that a Maypole Dairy once occupied this ancient timber-framed building, and in Pride Hill, Shrewsbury, the Boots store (SJ 492125) of 1907 and 1920 is in the characteristic style of the company's architect, A.N.

An advertisement from the Shrewsbury Chronicle for 1845 for Higgins's Leeds Warehouse, a woollen draper's shop in The Square, Shrewsbury. This is an archetypal Victorian shop front, with two doors, one for the house, one for the shop, reception rooms with high ceilings on the first floor, family bedrooms above and servants' bedrooms on the top storey.

IN CONSEQUENCE OF THE IMMENSE INCREASE OF BUSINESS,

H. HIGGINS

H AS made a great addition to the STOCK at the above Establishment, and begs to inform the Nobility, Clergy, and Public of SHROPSHIRE, that it now consists of EVERY DESCRIPTION OF GOODS SUITABLE FOR THE SUMMER SEASON, and which he will sell at such prices as cannot fail to meet the approbation of a discerning public.

WEST OF ENGLAND AND YORKSHIRE BROAD AND NARROW CLOTHS, in every shade of colour ; plain and fancy CASAMERES, DOESKINS, TWEEDS, SUMMER CLOTHS, &c.

The WAISTCOATING department is beautifully assorted, viz. Plain and Fancy SILK VELVETS, ditto PLUSHES, ditto FRENCH SATINS, MOSELLAS, VALENTIAS, CASHMERES, &c. &c.

Gentlemen's Silk Handkerchiefs, Satin Stocks, Scarfs, &c.

TAILORS' TRIMMINGS, in every variety, at the wholesale prices.

All Goods are marked in plain figures.

Bromley. Most co-operative stores were located in existing buildings. The one-time department store in Castle Street, Shrewsbury, a three-storey, seven-bay building with three gables and a corner turret, combining star-panelled cosmetic timber-framing with precisely-laid Ruabon bricks and stone dressing, opened in 1923, is the outstanding exception.

Until the late 19th century most consumer goods, footwear, furniture, clothing and some kinds of metalware, were made in the towns where they were purchased. The larger the town the more specialised its trades. Every town had shoemakers, tailors, blacksmiths and cabinet makers. Ludlow could boast makers of guns, trunks and straw hats. Shrewsbury had a sword cutler in the 1690s, and in 1851 numbered amongst its tradesmen five clog and patten makers, a cork cutter, three soda water manufacturers and a stained glass maker. The premises in which such traders worked were rarely distinctive, and most master craftsmen employed no more than two or three workers. Thomas Bowen, upholsterer in the Bullring, Ludlow, in 1871 employed six men and two apprentices, but there is nothing to distinguish his premises. A notable record of a craft workshop is a picture taken *c.*1870 of the Old Cooperage in Whitchurch, where in a timber-framed building whose oldest parts date from the 16th century a cooper displays barrels and dolly pegs on an open counter.[9] Customers in market towns often chose to deal with traders who shared their political and religious opinions, and some craftsmen sought markets elsewhere which were free from such pressures. The outstanding example in Shropshire is the Whitchurch clockmaker J.B. Joyce, who, as a result of his successes with church clocks, moved in 1904 from a conventional shop at No.40 High Street to a factory on Station Road (SJ 546414). The company supplied clocks for buildings all over the world, including the Refuge Assurance Building in Manchester, the government buildings in Sydney, the Dilkusha Palace in Kabul, the Shanghai Custom House and the Chamberlain Tower of the University of Birmingham. Above all Joyce provided 1,500 clocks for stations on the London & North Western Railway. The firm was taken over in the 1960s by a company from Derby. Heritage items from the factory were sold in 2012. The gingerbread bakers of Market Drayton pursued a similar if more modest course. Billingtons, established in 1817, and Chesters, founded in 1850, exported gingerbread to Australia, India, China and America.

The factory of the clockmaker J.B. Joyce in Station Road, Whitchurch (SJ 546414), built in 1904.

Town Mills

Every market town had access to water power. The citizens of Shrewsbury utilised the seven mills along the 4km course of the Rea Brook between Meole Brace and its confluence with the Severn. Ludlovians enjoyed the services of a mill on the River Corve and six on the Teme.

The power of water: the River Teme in full flood sweeps over the mill weirs downstream from Ludford Bridge (SO 513742).

The infant River Tern powered seven mills as it passed through Market Drayton. The ancient link between urban status and water power is demonstrated by the inclusion in the parish of Wellington of the detached hamlet of Walcot, with its powerful mill on the Tern, some 6km distant from the parish church, and by the Town Mills of Bridgnorth, situated at Pendlestone in Worfield parish, given to the corporation by Henry III in 1227. Urban mills, like those in the countryside, were used for purposes other than grinding grain. An iron forge flourished in the 18th century at Sutton, Shrewsbury, while there were paper mills at Market Drayton and Cleobury Mortimer. The power of the Ludlow mills was used by a foundry, by makers of woollen cloth and paper, and by throwers of silk. Pendlestone Mill had five pairs of stones in 1817, and, in addition to the cornmill, its waters powered an iron forge between 1760 and the 1790s, and wool-spinning machinery in the mid-19th century.

The citizens of Shrewsbury, Wellington, Bishop's Castle, Wem, Ellesmere, Much Wenlock and Newport also used wind power for grinding grain. In 1796 the Marsh Trustees at Newport built an outstanding windmill, a five-storey structure designed by Joseph Jackson of Lane End, Staffordshire. It cost £2,000, was 16.76m high and 8.23m in diameter at the base. Its 16.76m long oak stocks drove two pairs of stones, one 1.52m the other 1.73m in diameter. The mill was sold in 1802 for less than half the cost of erection, but was still standing in 1846 when it was claimed to be the largest and best windmill in the county. All traces have now disappeared.[10]

The earliest surviving steam mill building in Shropshire is the four-storey, five-bay structure of 1826 at the canal terminus at Whitchurch (SJ 541414). The Castle Mills at

The steam mill in Shifnal (SJ 747078).

The mill on the River Roden at Wem (SJ 512285), where power was also obtained by 1800 from a windmill, from a steam engine by 1819, and subsequently from a gas engine and then from electric motors.

Notepaper from the flour mill of W. Rogers & Son, at Market Drayton (SJ 633344) constructed in the 1890s.

Shrewsbury (SJ 496132), on the west bank of the canal north of New Park Road, formed the largest steam milling complex in the county. They were adapted from canal carriers' warehouses by Richard and William Blakeway about 1852. In the 1850s two beam engines, of 40hp and 30hp drove 14 pairs of French burr stones.[11] The steam mill alongside the Wesley Brook in Shifnal (SJ 747078) was built in about 1870 and its engine powered its stones for about 30 years until it was adapted as a brewery. It subsequently served as a provision warehouse, military stables and a garden centre, and the stub of its chimney remains. The ancient watermill on the River Roden at Wem (SJ 512285), supplemented by 1800 by a windmill on the mill dam, was enlarged in 1819 when the miller, John Boughey, installed a steam engine, and in the 1890s when a gas engine was added.[12] The remaining mill buildings have been adapted as apartments.

The introduction of roller-milling which transformed the milling trade from the early 1880s made relatively little impact in Shropshire. In Ludlow, the substantial buildings of the Ludford Papermill (SO 518742) were adapted to accommodate roller-milling equipment in the early 1880s. A purpose-built, three-storey, steam-powered roller mill was constructed at Station Road, Market Drayton (SJ 673344) by W. Rogers & Sons shortly before 1900. Cast-iron columns support massive timber beams, and some traces remain of line shafting. It was used for milling cattle feed until the early 1990s.

Malting

Malting was the most characteristic of market town industries. Probate inventories suggest that in the early 18th century many people both in town and country were involved in malting, but that few relied upon it for their livings. One of those few was William Podmore of Newport, who died in 1744 with 500 strikes of malt worth £60 in his malthouse.[13] By the 1850s there were about 250 malting businesses in Shropshire, about 60 per cent of them in the market towns.

After 1850 the number of malting enterprises contracted and the trade became essentially urban. There were 139 maltsters in the county in 1879, 90 in 1885, 81 in 1900, 68 in 1906, 39 in 1913, and only 13 by 1934. In some towns malting disappeared early. The malthouses in Watergate, reckoned to be the economic mainstay of Ellesmere, ceased to be profitable in the 1860s and all have subsequently been demolished.[14]

There were 11 malting businesses in Much Wenlock in 1808, but only four by 1851. Three buildings remain, one, active before 1800 and now adapted as apartments, on the Bourton Road (SO 620996), one in the High Street (SO 621997), now a café, and the third at the rear of the *Talbot Hotel* (SO 623997), a three-storey, three-bay structure, with a west elevation of brick and an east elevation in local limestone, which is now the residential wing of the hotel. In Wem a characteristic maltings building, with low ceilings and the recognisable remnants of a kiln, stands in Noble Street (SJ 511289), but the maltings near the station that formed part of the town's brewery have been demolished. Two maltings complexes remain in Low Town, Bridgnorth. One, next to the Crown Meadow football ground (SO 719932), consists of two parallel two-storey, 11-bay malthouses with iron-barred windows. They abut against a three-storey building at the east end of the plot, while the kiln remains at the west end. The other complex at No.48 Mill Street (SO 720931) consists of two three-storey buildings, one of

Shrewsbury	29
Bridgnorth	20
Oswestry	17
Ludlow	12
Wellington	12
Ellesmere	10
Shifnal	10
Newport	9
Whitchurch	8
Wem	7
Market Drayton	6
Much Wenlock	4
Bishop's Castle	2
Church Stretton	2
Cleobury Mortimer	2
Clun	2
Total	152

Table 3.2 Malsters in Shropshire market towns in 1851.
Source: S. Bagshaw, History, Gazetteer and Directory of Shropshire *(1851).*

The malthouse at the rear of the Talbot, Much Wenlock (SO 623997), now the residential wing of the hotel.

six and one of 12 bays, with a kiln at the eastern end extending from a three-storey, three-bay house of 1700.

The largest malthouse in Ludlow, behind Nos.23-24 Corve Street (SO 511749) was built about 1800 and was valued with adjacent residential property at £2,000 in 1827. After use as a brewery and a laundry it was demolished to make way for a garage. Ludlow's best preserved maltings, at No.139a Corve Street (SO 512749), is rather smaller. Fronting Corve Street is a three-storey, four-bay Georgian house, behind which are a cottage and an eight-bay, three-storey building, originally sparsely fenestrated, which appears to have been intended for malting, although part was adapted as cottages. Beyond this building is a six-bay, three-storey malthouse at the end of which is a pyramid-topped kiln which retains its tiled floor.

Malthouse buildings are often associated with adaptive re-use, a celebrated example being the Snape Maltings in Suffolk, converted *to* a concert hall complex at the instigation of Benjamin Britten. In Oswestry a maltings was adapted in the 1850s *from* the towns's theatre, which had opened in 1819 in Willow Street, next to the *White Lion Inn* (SJ 288297).[15] The main building, of red brick, stands on a stone plinth, and has a stone cornice below the pediment on the three-storey, three-bay Willow Street elevation. The north elevation is of five bays with taking-in doors on all three floors in the bays nearest the street. Bars on the windows were intended to deter the entry of birds. The south wall is of rubble stone and the west elevation of ashlar. The building has been restored and adapted as a wood-working shop. Malting was still reckoned one of Oswestry's principal trades in the 1870s.

Malting was especially important in Shrewsbury and several maltings buildings can still be identified in the town centre. One stands within a tangled pattern of old buildings behind No.53 Mardol (SJ 490126), a four-storey brick structure, retaining a lucam and windows indicating characteristically low ceiling heights. Construction of maltings of relatively modest size continued into the 1880s. At the junction of Roushill and Phoenix Place (SJ 491127) is a two-storey 18.2m x 11m malthouse designed for Edward Mullard by the architect A.B. Deakin in 1888. It was built in Ruabon-type brick with blue brick string courses, and a taking-in door in the wide central bay of the nine-bay Roushill elevation.[16]

The largest malting complex before the 1880s was The Glen, Frankwell (SJ 489127), which was operated by John Hughes

The maltings complex adapted from the town theatre in Willow Street, Oswestry (SJ 288297). It now houses a woodworking shop. The building to the left was the White Lion Inn.

Barley laid out on the fourth floor of the Ditherington Maltings, Shrewsbury.

between 1836 and 1855. It comprises a three-storey, twelve-bay double malthouse, in red brick, with a wetting floor 24m x 11m, capable of wetting 160 bushels every four days, with two adjacent kilns, another three-storey, eight-bay malthouse alongside, with a 22m x 5m floor, capable of wetting 80 bushels every four days, with a kiln, together with a large house and three cottages.[17] As in other malthouses, the windows were barred. The capacity of the Glen was 240 bushels, yet a malthouse in Park Street, Wellington, that still survives was offered for sale in 1847 with a capacity of only 130 bushels, and was described as 'gigantic'.

From the 1860s the Shropshire malting trade was dominated by the company established by William Jones in 1869. A native of Llanbrynmair, Jones migrated to Ohio in 1857 with the intention of settling in a Welsh-speaking colony, but returned to Britain during the American Civil War. He established his company in 1869 when his first malt-house was probably the red brick building at No.17a Hills Lane which measures *c.*17m x 6m. He acquired other malthouses in Shrewsbury, including The Glen, and businesses at Oswestry, Gobowen, Whittington, Ackleton and Pontesford. He built a newly-designed maltings, which was also the company headquarters, in Bynner Street (SJ 497128) in 1888. It has been re-used as offices since the early 1990s. In March 1897 Jones acquired the former flax mill at Ditherington (SJ 498137) which was adapted as a maltings with a pyramid-topped kiln at the north end of the main building. Subsequently Jones acquired the Castle Foregate cornmills (SJ 496132). There was already a malthouse at the west end, but Jones adapted the whole site for malting. Much of the complex has been demolished to make way for housing but two small two-storey malthouses remain, which probably pre-date Jones's purchase of the site.[18]

Brewing

Shropshire was more celebrated for malting than for brewing. The county was largely self-sufficient in beer until the late 19th century, although Guinness and some beers bottled in Burton were advertised from the 1830s. Most beer was brewed in public houses or private homes until, as in other counties, commercial breweries with chains of tied houses were established in most market towns between 1780 and 1850. Few Shropshire breweries despatched beer beyond the hinterlands of their tied houses. The Wem Brewery (SJ 513290) was the last in the county to brew on an industrial scale. Since it closed in 1987 its buildings have been adapted as industrial units.

The most important survival in Shropshire is the brewery attached to the *Three Tuns*, Bishop's Castle (SO 324889). It is more than a brewhouse attached to an inn, but rather a small-scale Victorian tower brewery of the type that flourished in many towns.

A brewery stood on the site of The Gateway in Chester Street, Shrewsbury (SJ 492131) for at least 150 years. It was established probably in 1792, the date on a windlass, by

The tower brewery at the Three Tuns, Bishop's Castle (SO 324889).

Thomas Hawley of Caus Castle. Its first brewhouse was topped by a lead reservoir and housed a 120-bushel mash tun and two large coppers. There were six oak vats, the largest with a capacity of 260 barrels, and the output was calculated at 5,000 barrels per year. By 1868 power was provided by a steam engine and a well of spring water was regarded as one of the assets of the site. For a time the building was used for manufacturing oilcake but the machinery was sent to Japan, and in 1880 it was bought at auction by Thomas Southam who rebuilt it in 1889, the date recorded on an inscribed stone in the Gateway car park, and again in 1903. Southam's main building, an eight-bay, three-storey structure with bold string courses, presented a forbidding elevation to the river.[19]

The Circus Brewery (SJ 488126) by the Welsh Bridge was established by Henry Newton in 1822 as part of a complex which included a dairy market and a venue for public performances. Its components in the 1890s, when it was worked by Richards & Hearn, were the original

47

'circus' building, a high, two-storey rectangular structure, with six bays of blind arcading on its west elevation, a tall narrow brewhouse on its south side, and a new steam engine that had replaced the 10hp engine working there in the 1860s. Richards & Hearn later amalgamated with the Wem Brewery. Brewing ceased in 1912 and the site was cleared in the 1920s.[20]

The most complete surviving brewery complex in the county is in Coleham, Shrewsbury (SJ 492119). It was established in 1806-07, purchased in 1830 by William Hazledine for use as a timber depot, and sold in 1846 to Thomas and Thomas William Trouncer, whose family brewed there until 1955. In 1828 the

Trouncer's Brewery, Longden Road, Shrewsbury, which continued brewing until the 1950s.

brewery supposedly produced 120 barrels per day. It had eight vats holding 17,000 barrels, and a nearly new 6hp steam engine. The site was taken over in 1959 by a greengrocery wholesaler. The four-storey brewhouse stands alongside a three-storey engine house and a tall, square-section chimney, the adjacent boiler house having been demolished. The two-storey cooling house consists of three arcaded bays, and formerly housed the condensing vessel on the first floor with a racking room and cellars beneath. The vat house, a single-storey structure of eight arcaded bays, was partially demolished to provide space for a modern building.[21] A four-storey malt store remains, but the malthouse has been replaced by apartments called *Pengrove*.

The Crown Brewery, Market Drayton (SJ 673345) is the most imposing of Shropshire's surviving brewery buildings. It comprises a steel-framed, six-storey, three-bay brick tower, flanked to the south by a two-storey, four-bay block, through which a wagon arch gives access to a yard. It was constructed in 1899 to the design of T. Tindal of Longton (Staffs.). Power was provided by a 35hp steam engine.[22]

The Leather Trades

A tannery in 1800 was one of the age-old symbols of a market town. Around 20 were working in Shropshire in the 1850s, but numbers steadily declined. There were four in Market Drayton in 1837, but only one in 1849, and by 1905 there were only seven tanning concerns in the whole county. Only five, in Ludlow, Shrewsbury, Oswestry, Bridgnorth and Wem, remained in 1913, and only two, in Shrewsbury and Oswestry, by 1926. The last, Cock's Tannery in Shrewsbury, closed in the early 1960s.[23]

The drying sheds of the tannery at the south end of Church Street, Bishop's Castle (SO 324884) photographed in the mid-1980s.

Terrace Buildings, Nos. 131-33 Longden Coleham, Shrewsbury (SJ 495122), once the drying house of a tannery.

Most tanneries remained in the same locations over long periods, as in Corve Street in Ludlow, below the church at Market Drayton and by the English and Welsh bridges in Shrewsbury. Characteristic components are detailed in the sale in 1891 of the tannery in Much Wenlock (SJ 623003), which was subsequently converted into a brewery. It included a 'lofty barn', 6m x 18m, capable of holding 100 tons of bark, a bark mill room, a scoring room and shed, a large three-storey building, 8.8m x 8.8m with drying rooms and storage facilities, a building 27.5m x 6m accommodating another drying room and an office, beneath which were 31 pits, an inner yard with 22 large and 20 small pits, and an outer yard with 11 pits.[24]

The only significant monument of the trade in Shrewsbury is Nos.131-33 Longden Coleham (SJ 495121), a three-storey, eight-bay structure called Terrace Buildings used as a brush factory from the 1890s. Charles Hulbert recalled that it was built in the early 19th century as part of a tannery. Its piered construction and the shallow depth suggest that it was the drying house.[25]

The tannery at the south end of Church Street in Bishop's Castle (SO 624884), established at least as early as 1750, retained a large drying shed with wooden louvred sides until c.1990. It was occupied until 1831 by William Beddoes who was succeeded by John Norton, who combined tanning with farming, malting and running a butcher's business.[26]

Curriers, who prepared tanned leather for shoemakers, glovers and saddlers, occupied less distinctive premises, but at Much Wenlock the top floor of St Milburga Row in Barrow Street (SO 623998) retains hooks, rails and hoists which are relics of its use as a currier's workshop. The making of leather gloves in Ludlow enjoyed a boom during the Napoleonic

Wars, when it was recalled, perhaps none too accurately, that a thousand people had once been employed.[27] Certainly it declined after 1815, had disappeared by 1840, and has left no significant monuments.

Woodworkers

All the Shropshire market towns had sawmills which cut locally-grown and imported timber, and manufactured a variety of products for the building trade. The timber yard in the appropriately-named Wood Street (SJ 494135) in Shrewsbury was opened in the 1890s by Treasures the builders as a complement to their brickworks at Buttington.[28] An account in 1897 of the business of Henry Farmer of Wyle Cop, who produced mouldings and joinery, referred to 'the phenomenal activity of the building trade in and near Shrewsbury'. Woodworkers also served traders and made household goods. There were 17 makers of baskets and sieves in the county in 1879, almost all in the towns. A business in Oswestry in 1827 worked lime and sycamore for curriers' and shoemakers' cutting boards. Isherwoods of Wem, who occupied an extensive site alongside the railway (SJ 516289) until the 1980s, were noted in the 1930s for their butchers' blocks. Henry Addison who established the Waterloo Works in Wellington (SJ 642117) in 1881, manufactured seating and interior woodwork, including the reredos panels at St Lawrence, Little Wenlock.

The widest range of products was made by Grooms of Wellington. Richard Groom began basketmaking in New Street about 1841, then developed a timber business, subsequently expanding into sawmilling and the making of turned and bendware. In the late 19th century his range included washing dollies, wooden bowls in sycamore or willow, butter boards and butter workers in sycamore, butchers' skewers in maple, bakers' peels in ash, oval tubs in oak, children's hoops, toy spades and timbers for heavy engineering. Many products were stamped 'R.G.S. & Co.' By 1882 the company occupied the Shropshire Works, the former railway engineering works south of the railway and west of Bridge Street (SJ 647116), which had extensive sidings.[29]

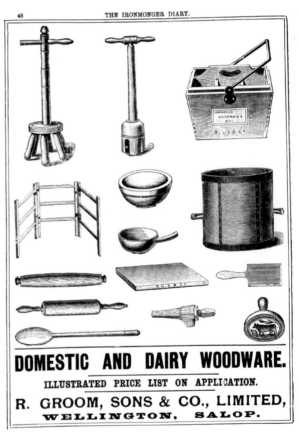

A page from an early 20th-century catalogue published by Richard Groom & Sons of Wellington tannery.

The carriage works behind the Six Bells, Bishop's Castle (SO 323884).

Coachbuilders

The opening of railways stimulated short-distance road transport all over Britain and increased the demand for carriages of many kinds. Coach-building flourished in provincial England in the second half of the 19th century.[30] There were coach-builders in eight Shropshire towns in the 1850s, and a new workshop was built at Bishop's Castle as late as 1904-05. The most venerable works, the County Carriage Works in Dogpole, Shrewsbury (SJ 493124), was opened in 1819 by Thomas Mountford, who, like other coachbuilders, combined the construction of vehicles with a hiring business. He was proud in 1864 that his omnibuses were built by a craftsmen who had once worked for Silk & Co. in London. Mountfords had 18 employees in 1888, but in 1894 the firm was taken over by Charles Hughes and by 1914 it was part of the Shrewsbury Motor Garage, whose principal premises were on Coton Hill. The building in Dogpole was subsequently adapted as offices.[31]

The carriage works in St Julian Friars, Shrewsbury (SJ 494123) was established by David Davies in the 1830s. In 1854 he offered a range of small carriages, dog carts at £21, Whitechapels at £14 and £18, and Phaetons between £20 and £40. He went bankrupt in 1892 after a spell in which his business had been restricted to repair work. The premises later became part of a motor car showroom, now replaced by apartments.[32]

The Tan Bank coachworks in Wellington (SJ 651113), examined before demolition in the 1960s, had a broad staircase with flaps fixed to the banister which were lowered to enable carriages to be pushed up to or lowered from workshops on the first floor. The building was used as a coachworks in the 1850s and was subsequently the Excelsior Carriage Works of Clift & Son.[33]

The carriage works behind the *Six Bells*, No.1 Church Street, Bishop's Castle (SO 323884) was built by the inn's landlord, Charles Jones, in 1904-05, and closed when he died in 1922, by which time the premises were also used as a motor garage. The principal range of buildings, measuring 26.6m x 5.6m, is built into a bank at the western end, while the eastern end projects over the yard on cast-iron columns. There is a blacksmith's shop on the ground floor. The building was probably constructed cheaply. The walls are a mixture of rubble limestone and brick, while the timbers are of irregular size, and were probably re-used.[34]

Foundries: the first generation

A foundry in the 1850s was as much a sign of a town's vitality as a market hall, a railway station or a Member of Parliament. Shropshire's most celebrated foundries were, of course, in the Coalbrookdale Coalfield, but the spread to every market town of consequence in England of the basic techniques of mechanical engineering, the ability to make castings and forgings, to machine them to fine tolerances, and to assemble components into machines, was amongst the most significant developments of the Industrial Revolution. Most such enterprises developed from the businesses of millwrights, ironmongers or blacksmiths.[35]

In the 18th century, machines were assembled by their users, usually with the assistance of a consultant who might prepare drawings and supervise erection. The best-known example of such practice is the system by which Boulton & Watt provided steam engines for their customers. During the 1790s a new pattern of engineering works emerged, which undertook the complete manufacture of machines or structures. The best-documented examples are the Soho Foundry in Smethwick, opened by Boulton & Watt in 1796, and Matthew Murray's Round Foundry in Leeds established the previous year. Foundries in the Coalbrookdale Coalfield began to produce complete steam engines at much the same time. Two market town foundries opened in Shrewsbury and Bridgnorth in the 1790s and were pioneers of the species.[36]

The four brothers Hazledine – John, William, Robert and Thomas – born, sons of a millwright, between 1760 and 1771, grew up in the Shropshire iron trade. By 1795 John, Robert and Thomas had established a foundry in Mill Street, Bridgnorth (SO 179932). They began by making millwright's castings, but by 1804 the foundry was associated with Richard Trevithick, pioneer of high pressure steam engines. John Hazledine died in 1810, when his principal partner was Joel Shuttleworth, but between July 1811 and February 1812 the engineer John Urpeth Rastrick became managing partner, and the company was known as Hazledine, Rastrick & Co. Rastrick withdrew from the business around 1816. The foundry ceased work in the early 1820s, but had resumed by 1827 when a recently-cast cannon burst when it was fired, killing a bystander. By 1838 the business was the subject of a suit in Chancery, and the land and machinery were sold. William Pope, who worked as a smith under the Hazledines, subsequently operated a foundry that was only of local significance. None of the buildings of Hazledine's foundry remains, although a plaque commemorates its existence. In 1834 the components of the works included the iron foundry building, a steam engine, air furnaces, stoves, carpenters' and smiths' shops, turning and boring mills, fitting-up rooms, two offices and three dwelling houses. J.U. Rastrick recalled that the pig iron

A Trevithick engine built by John Hazledine's foundry, Bridgnorth. Nothing is known of its working life but it was rescued from a scrapyard at Hereford and presented to the Science Museum in the 1880s by the locomotive engineer Francis William Webb.

melted at Bridgnorth came from the Coalbrookdale, Lightmoor and Old Park companies.[37]

The products of the Bridgnorth foundry confirm that it was a pioneering works of its kind. The foundry made many Trevithick engines. Some were used locally, at a tannery and a cornmill in Bridgnorth, at the ironworks at Billingsley, and at a farm at Stableford in Worfield parish. The company was among the first manufacturers of threshing machines, seven of which were offered for sale in 1812. Machinery ordered by Richard Trevithick was exported to South America, one consignment in 1814 being valued at £16,152. The company cast the iron bridge at Stourport (SO 808710), which replaced Thomas Farnolls Pritchard's bridge destroyed in the great flood of 1795, and the five-arch bridge completed in 1808 linking Gloucestershire with Monmouthshire across the River Wye at Chepstow (ST 536944). A steam engine numbered 14 was rescued from scrapping in Hereford in the 1880s by Francis William Webb, chief mechanical engineer of the LNWR, and is now in the Science Museum, London. The waterwheel at Cleobury North Mill (SO 626872) and possibly some grave slabs in St Mary's churchyard, Bridgnorth (SO 716928) are the only other products of the foundry that survive.[38]

William, the second of the four Hazledine brothers, established a foundry in Shrewsbury at about the

The remaining street frontage of William Hazledine's foundry in Longden Coleham,
Shrewsbury (SJ 493120).

time that his brothers began their works at Bridgnorth. It was the first of many enterprises, but even when he was the owner of blast furnaces, coal mines, limestone quarries and much of Shrewsbury, Hazledine was known to leading engineers as *the great ironfounder*. He is commemorated by a bust by Sir Francis Chantrey in St Chad's church, Shrewsbury.[39]

William Hazledine was apprenticed in 1778 to his uncle, a millwright, and by 1789 was working as a millwright from premises on Wyle Cop, Shrewsbury. He subsequently established a foundry in Colehall off Claremont Street, and about 1793 moved to Longden Coleham (SJ 493120). When he died in 1840 the foundry had a street frontage of 93m, the exact distance from the eastern end of the *Crown Inn* to the western end of Terrace Buildings, and occupied a space of 4,350 sq m between Longden Coleham and the Severn. At the centre of the works was a clock tower being the date 1805. A steam engine provided power for lathes, cranes and other machinery, and in the early 19th century the labour force totalled over 400 workers. The works declined after Hazledine's death in 1840 when it was managed by William Stuttle, once his clerk, and some buildings had been abandoned by 1856. Operations ceased during the 1870s but in 1878 the foundry was taken over by Lowcock & Barr, and by Arthur Lowcock alone the following year. The main components were then a foundry building 30m x 15m, a fitting shop 21m x 12m, a turning shop, a smiths' shop, an engine house and a showroom 30m x 16m next to the river. Lowcock used only about two-thirds of the premises; the remainder, east of the approach to Greyfriars Bridge which opened in 1882, was adapted to other uses and remained in the ownership of the Hazledine family. Lowcock's business continued until the mid 1920s after which most of the buildings were replaced by shops and houses. The only remaining building, now Nos.116-17 Longden Coleham, is a three-storey, 10-bay structure in soft red brick. A photograph taken when the premises were complete suggests that two buildings on the riverside with ventilators in their roofs housed the cupolas.[40]

Hazledine was a pioneer in producing castings for millwrights and supplied ironwork for many of Thomas Telford's bridges and canal installations, but he had three foundries and it is not possible to credit particular structures to Coleham, except for the Cleveland Bridge at Bath completed in 1827, the roof of a bonded warehouse in Dublin cast for Sir John Rennie in 1821, and gates for the docks at Newport (Mon.) made in 1840, each pair of which weighed 120 tons. He probably cast the iron plates for the Chirk Aqueduct at Coleham and sent them by road to Weston Lullingfields wharf and thence by canal. Several iron chimney pots on houses in Coleham that once belonged to the Hazledine family were probably cast at the foundry. In the late 19th century the foundry was famous for the Lowcock economiser, a device developed in 1882-83 which used waste heat from boilers to pre-heat feed water. In 1888 an economiser weighing 400 tons was supplied to the Merrimack Mill Co. at Lowell (Massachusetts), a celebrated textile concern in the United States.[41]

Victorian Foundries

There were several other engineering works in Shrewsbury in the early 19th century. By 1841 a blacksmith's shop on the road to Welshpool owned by John Rowlands had become the Bicton Heath Foundry, making malt mills, threshing machines and even steam engines. It closed after Rowlands' sons Thomas and Henry Rowlands dissolved their partnership in 1872. The Eagle Foundry owned by Cyrus Gittins and a Mr Cartwright was established in 1808 and stood at the bottom of the Seventy Steps (SJ 491127). In 1832 its workers carried a model steam engine in Shrewsbury's procession celebrating the passing of the Reform Act. Its equipment in 1847 included a 10hp steam engine and a cupola furnace. An inscription on a gate in Prees churchyard (SJ 556335) is perhaps its only memorial. Nearby, south-west of the cattle market, stood the Smithfield Foundry, which in 1879 had a 10hp horizontal engine and three 3hp vertical engines. No traces remain of either foundry, both of which made agricultural implements.[42]

The Phoenix Foundry near the canal wharf in Castle Foregate was worked in the 1830s by William Picken. It was one of several foundries in the vicinity, from one of which, the Salopian Ironworks, Lowcock & Barr moved in 1878 to Coleham. The best-known concern in the area was Thomas Corbett's Perseverance Ironworks.[43]

Thomas Corbett was a self-made and self-congratulating entrepreneur. His deferential obituarist recalled that:

> It was Mr Corbett's privilege to have conversed with half a dozen crowned heads and to have received from them warm congratulations on the services he had rendered to civilisation by his innovations.

He travelled as far as Australia and South Africa selling his machines. The son of Samuel Corbett, a Wellington ironmonger, Corbett acted from 1863 as Shropshire agent for reaping machines made by Bernhard Samuelson in Banbury, selling 377 within five years. In 1867 he began to manufacture his Eclipse Winnower in a workshop in Chester Street and soon employed nearly 40 men. In 1868-69 he purchased a yard in Castle Foregate (SJ 495133) from Henry Treasure the builder, which was the nucleus of a factory which by 1900 had a street frontage of 76m, occupied 1.6ha, and employed up to 150 men.

The buildings were designed by Corbett's kinsman, A.B. Deakin, and were crowned by a 20m-high clock tower which incorporated a water tank. Components in 1876 included a 26m x 8m erecting shop, a 24m x 9m smiths' shop with 10 hearths, an 18m x 6m packing room, a 15m x 7m machine and implement store equipped with a crane, and a 16m x 12m moulding shop with two cupolas. Machine tools were powered by a 10hp steam engine, and the sawmill complex by a 12hp engine by Marshalls of Gainsborough.

The Perseverance Ironworks suffered a fire in 1905 and was subsequently rebuilt, although the clock tower was never fully restored. Thomas Corbett died in 1917 after which his executors maintained the business for more than a decade, but in 1929 it was closed and the premises were adapted for oil blending. The façade on Castle Foregate reflects five phases in the growth of Corbett's enterprise. The oldest and most altered portion is a four-bay, two-storey structure with an arched entrance, now blocked, bearing the date 1871 and the still readable inscription 'Speed the Plough'. On the western side are two two-storey buildings flanking the four-storey clock tower, each in red brick with blue and yellow brick dressings, each of 10 bays, in pairs divided by pilasters, and with a blocked wagon arch in each central bay. The northerly building is dated 1873, while the clock tower and the southerly building are inscribed 1876. North of the 1871 building is a later two-storey structure in red brick with blue brick dressings, of five wide bays divided by pilasters with elliptical arcading above the first-floor windows. The ground-floor windows are divided by miniature cast-iron columns inscribed 'Corbett'. On the west side of Castle Foregate is a two-storey, ten-bay building in red brick with blue brick dressings bearing the date 1884. Corbett's products are preserved in several agricultural museums. One 'Eclipse' winnower is displayed in Welshpool, and another adorns a shopping mall near the RMS *Queen Mary* at Long Beach, California.[44]

Thomas Corbett's name cast on the ironwork of a window in one of the buildings of the Perseverance Ironworks.

Three foundries were making agricultural implements in Market Drayton from the mid 19th century. The Eagle (sometimes the Raven) Foundry in Cheshire Street (SJ 674343) was established in 1849 by the ironmongers William and John Rodenhurst. The buildings have been demolished but the name is preserved in the shopping centre Rodenhurst Court. The Britannia Foundry in Stafford Street (SJ 677343), one of many to bear that name, was operated from 1841 by A.W. Gower. Several small buildings remain and some old cast-iron columns have been incorporated into a

A cellar cover in Ludlow cast at the foundry of Chaplin Hodges.

modern structure. Only advertisements for elevators provide evidence of the foundry worked by John Bruckshaw in Tinker's Lane (SJ 676342) in the 1860s and 1870s.[45]

In Ludlow the Castle Foundry was established in 1822 in the Castle Mill (SO 507754) by Chaplin Hodges (1790-1877), a Leominster-born millwright. Its products include several decorative coal cellar covers that remain in the town's main streets. Hodges was employing 20 people in 1851 but subsequently his workforce diminished. The foundry had eight employees in 1861 and eleven in 1871 by which time it was managed by one of his sons. The foundry's patterns were sold in 1892 to William Roberts, a Coalbrookdale-born ironfounder whose Phoenix Foundry from 1855 occupied the premises of Ludlow's first gasworks in Upper Galdeford (SO 514750) and specialised in casting jaws for stone-breaking machines.[46]

In Ellesmere W. Clay operated the Bridgwater Foundry on the canal wharf (SJ 397345) in the 1850s. After 1920 its site was occupied by a creamery whose buildings have now been demolished. Robert Thursfield Smith established a foundry in Dodington, Whitchurch (SJ 542411) before 1856, with the intention of supplying 'anything his neighbours might want'. After his death in 1907 it took the name of W.H. Smith & Co. by which it is best known. The frontage building remains, a two-storey, three-bay structure later occupied by

The weir at Castle Mill, Ludlow (SO 507754) which provided power for the foundry established by Chaplin Hodges in 1822.

a garage. Smith moved to a site near the station (SJ 549415) where the company continued until the 1970s. The firm's specialisms included cheese presses, meeting local demands, but it was best known for Dutch barns.[47]

One of the leading British suppliers of valves evolved from the ironmonger's business of William Underhill of Newport. In 1869 he erected a foundry near the town's gasworks (SJ 748190) which produced some steam engines in the 1870s. In 1906 the foundry was taken over by the Audley Engineering Co. who manufactured valves bearing the inscription AUDCO, which subsequently became the name of the company. It continued to operate in Newport until the 1980s.[48]

Railway Engineering

The first railway engineering works in the county was the Shropshire Works, which occupied a 3.2ha site west of Wellington station (SJ 647116). It was established by John Dickson, the railway contractor, in 1852. Its products ranged from keys for fixing rails to chairs, to passenger carriages for the Great Western Railway. The business was wound up in 1856 and the site was taken over by Richard Groom, the woodworker.[49]

The construction of the locomotive and carriage works at Oswestry (SJ 296300) was authorised by the Oswestry & Newtown Railway (O&NR) in 1864. It was in operation by May 1866, by which time the O&NR was part of the Cambrian Railways. The main components were an erecting shop, a carriage-building shop, a foundry, a tender shop, a boiler shop, a locomotive machine shop, a carriage machine shop, a brass foundry, a smith, a wagon shop and a paint shop. All were accommodated within a 247m x 64m factory designed by John Robinson of Manchester. The main front is the north elevation that looks across the tracks that once led to Whittington. In the centre of the elevation is a three-storey block with two bays of arcading on the ground floor and a cupola above. It is flanked on each side by five-bay structures with semi-circular arcading and circular lights in the gables. A seven-bay building at the north end is the only non-symmetrical element.[50]

After the establishment of the works, Oswestry's population increased from 5,414 in 1861 to 7,306 in 1871. Nevertheless the works gave direct employment to only 137 people in 1893. Its main concern was the construction of passenger carriages and freight wagons and the maintenance of the locomotives of the Cambrian Railways, most of which came from outside contractors, although two express locomotives, the 4-4-0s Nos.11 and 19 were built at Oswestry. The works was retained by the Great Western Railway (GWR) after the grouping of 1923 and by British Railways after nationalisation, and steam locomotives were overhauled there until it closed in 1966. It has subsequently been tenemented. No locomotives of the Cambrian Railways survive, but several carriages made at Oswestry are held by heritage railways.

The Shrewsbury & Hereford Railway established engineering shops at Coleham, Shrewsbury which operated between 1852 and 1863, and were adapted as carriage shops by the GWR. The stock, sold in 1863, included a 25hp steam engine and a traversing crane.[51] The redundancy of skilled workers that followed the closure was perceived as an opportunity by Richard France, promoter of the Potteries, Shrewsbury & North Wales Railway (PSNWR), who, in 1863, acquired property in Abbey Foregate on which he destroyed several distinguished medieval buildings. In 1866 the PSNWR opened its Abbey Station on part of the property, but from 1864 France developed the remainder alongside the Shrewsbury & Hereford Railway where he intended to establish a depot for unloading coal and lime, and an engineering works providing structural iron, locomotives, wagons and construction equipment for railway contractors. The *Shrewsbury Chronicle* hoped that the works would make Shrewsbury 'as it was in the days of Mr (William) Hazledine, a great rival of the Coalbrookdale and Lilleshall companies'. France found his project obstructed by the established railway companies, and by a rival firm supplying coal to the county town, and neither business flourished. The workshops – fitted with two cupolas, heating furnaces, smiths' hearths, two powerful cranes, lathes, shaping-, shearing-, drilling-, punching-, planning-, boring-, slotting- and plate-bending-machines, a sawmill, weighing machines and four steam engines – lay disused. The plant was put up for sale in 1869 but it was not until 1876 that the works was purchased and brought into production by the Birmingham-based Midland Railway Carriage & Wagon Co.[52] During 1880 it produced vehicles for railways in New Zealand, South Australia and India, coaches for the London, Brighton & South Coast Railway, sleeping cars for use in Italy by the Compagnie Internationale des Wagons-Lits, tramcars for Southwark and Deptford, and very large numbers of wagons for the East Indian Railways. About 300 men were employed at the factory in 1881, and more than 500 people enjoyed the annual works outing to Blackpool in 1890. The works closed when the company enlarged its plant at Saltley, Birmingham, in 1912. Eleven sidings ran into the main building of the works. Fanning out from a turntable at the southern end, two lines ran to an engine shed in the north-eastern corner of the premises and another to five short sidings between the Abbey Pool and the Shrewsbury & Hereford viaduct. The only connection to the national rail network in 1882 was by a siding from the PSNWR, but after its closure a link was established with the Hereford line near the Coleham locomotive depot. The site was used as a prisoner-of-war camp during the First World War, and the construction of a supermarket and a new road in the 1990s removed the last traces of the works.

Twentieth-Century Engineering

The Sentinel Waggon Works originated in Shropshire *c.*1900 when Daniel Simpson experimented with a steam-powered road vehicle at his uncle's engineering works at Horsehay. Development was taken over in 1903 by Alley & MacLellen and transferred to their works at Polmadie, Glasgow. By 1914 the company lacked space for expansion and George Woodvine, an apprentice from Horsehay who had progressed to works manager, was instructed to seek a location for a new factory. He chose a 20ha plot on the Whitchurch Road, Shrewsbury (SJ 505146), where construction began in March 1915. A new company, the Sentinel Waggonworks Co. Ltd, was formed in 1917 and from 1919 a model estate, Sentinel Gardens, was built on the opposite side of the Whitchurch Road.[53]

By 1920 the Sentinel works employed 500 men and produced up to 32 vehicles a week. The principal product in the 1920s was the Super Sentinel steam wagon. A new model, the DG or double-geared wagon, was produced in 1927, and new shaft-driven vehicles, the S6 and S8, appeared in 1933. Variants included tipper wagons for quarries, tar sprayers, logging tractors and the first British ready-mixed concrete vehicle supplied in 1930 to the British Steel Piling Co. As competition from oil-engined vehicles increased the company made

*A celebratory gathering of Sentinel vehicles
at a County of Salop Steam Engine Society rally at Onslow Park.*

losses, and it was liquidated in 1935 but a new concern, Sentinel (1936) Ltd, was formed the following year. During the Second World War products included turret lathes and Bren gun carriers, and kitchen and bathroom units for prefabricated houses were made between 1946 and 1949. The last steam wagons, a hundred for a coal-mining project in Argentina, were delivered in 1949-50. The principal products of the 1950s were 140 buses, and more than 1,200 oil-engined lorries. In 1956 the company was taken over by Rolls Royce who,

A bus built at the Sentinel Works in the 1950s.

three years later, launched a range of diesel hydraulic shunting locomotives, some 292 of which were built by 1971, along with a range of oil engines. After problems with the RB211 jet engine led to the collapse of Rolls Royce Ltd in 1971, the Shrewsbury works became part of Rolls Royce Motors and was sold in 1985 to Perkins plc, who built a new factory for building and maintaining diesel engines west of the railway. Other companies use parts of the original factory and office block but much of the site is occupied by a supermarket.

The Sentinel Works was celebrated for its locomotives and steam railcars, coachwork for which was supplied by outside contractors. The first Sentinel locomotive was completed in 1923, and more than 600 had been built by 1958. Traction equipment was supplied for 292 railcars, more than two-thirds of which were completed before 1930. The principal customer in Britain was the London & North Eastern Railway (LNER) which acquired 81 railcars and 58 steam shunting locomotives. More than 20 Sentinel locomotives are preserved together with more than 130 Sentinel steam wagons, nine motor coaches and more than 30 diesel lorries. Documentary records are held by the Sentinel Trust.

Muller & Co, makers of watch screws, established a factory at Cleobury Mortimer (SO 670756) during the Second World War. Joseph Muller and Jacob Schweizer of Soleure, Switzerland, opened a branch in London in 1932. Such was its importance in the manufacture of armaments that it was moved to a location unlikely to be affected by bombing. The crooked tower of the church of St Mary at Cleobury Mortimer, similar to that at Soleure, was a factor in the choice of site. The firm employed 350 people by 1945 and 500 in the 1950s. The growing sophistication of machinery necessitated two generations of new buildings in the 1950s and the 1980s. The houses in Curdale Close were built by the company for their employees, together with a canteen and a sports field.[54]

Electrical Engineering

One Shropshire company was for a spell in the forefront of electrical engineering. It sprang from the ironmongery trade, from the shop of Messrs Alltree at No.43 Castle Street, Shrewsbury, in which James Aran Lea became a partner on 1 January 1867, when the business was already involved in hiring out lighting for balls and bazaars. Between 1880 and 1886 the company acquired premises at No.8 Castle Street (SJ 493130), where Lea's son, Francis James Lea began to manufacture electrical equipment. He came to public notice when he installed a 16,000 candle power electric beacon on Titterstone Clee to mark Queen Victoria's Golden Jubilee in 1887. By 1893 he was working independently of the ironmonger's shop, supplying bells, lightning conductors and telecommunications equipment, but his speciality was the manufacture of high quality light fittings in wrought-iron, brass and copper. Fittings were installed locally at Yeaton Pevery, Acton Reynald and the *Victoria Hotel*, Wolverhampton, but the most notable contracts he fulfilled were at the royal residence at Sandringham in 1903, at McGill University, Montreal, and, in 1894, at Cragside, Northumberland, the mansion built by Richard Norman Shaw for Lord Armstrong where the National Trust still proudly displays Lea's lamps and electroliers. After the Sandringham contract the company subsided to become a local electrical contracting concern. The Chester Street workshop, demolished in the 1960s, was a three-storey, three-bay structure, with a broad bow window at first floor level, and two scalloped gables topped by pediments and spheres, above which was a sign in cut-out lettering.[55]

Building Materials

Landscape evidence from Shropshire towns accords well with the hypothesis that until late in the 19th century materials for most urban dwellings were obtained locally. Rubble limestone was used in the majority of houses in Much Wenlock and there are stone cottages that appear to be of 18th-century date in Shrewsbury, Ludlow and Bridgnorth, but brick was the predominant building material in the county. Only in Bridgnorth, where most 19th-century buildings were in the characteristic buff-coloured bricks manufactured in the

Primrose Terrace, St Michael's Street, Shrewsbury, built in phases by Thomas Williams, brickmaker, and his family between 1886 and 1907. Behind the terrace lay one of Shrewsbury's principal brickfields.

Ironbridge Gorge, does there appear to have been significant use of bricks that were not made locally. Brickyards in the countryside and in the coalfields are considered in chapters 2 and 4. The urban or suburban brickyard was a distinctive species. Substantial structures other than kilns were rare until after 1850, and the nature of many bricks in earlier buildings suggests that clay preparation was minimal. Most yards operated seasonally and employed no more than three or four brickmakers.[56]

In Shrewsbury an irregularly-shaped recreation ground alongside the former canal is evidence of the brickfields of Castle Foregate. Examples of their products can be seen in the adjacent Primrose Terrace (SJ 496134), built in eight stages between 1886 and 1907 by the brickmakers Thomas and William Thomas Williams. For most of the 19th century bricks seem to have been made in open clamps, but in the 1880s a substantial clay preparation plant fed by two short tramways was built behind Primrose Terrace, together with a trio of round kilns. Production in Castle Foregate had ceased by the 1920s.[57]

The Shrewsbury suburb of Kingsland was built on leasehold plots made available from the early 1880s by the borough corporation as part of a process that included the closure of Old Shrewsbury Show from 1878, the re-location of Shrewsbury School, which opened on its new site in 1882, and the construction of the Kingsland toll bridge, completed in the same year. Common bricks were delivered to the plots on Kingsland along a tramway constructed by the builders Treasure & Son, and authorised in 1879.[58] It began at a brick-field near Copthorne Road (SJ 477126), whose site, formerly rough ground, was covered with houses in 1993. The tramway continued along the line of Porthill Drive, which is still an unusually narrow thoroughfare, and passed along the east side of Porthill Road, and the north side of the lane that was widened into the Shrewsbury by-pass in the 1930s, before cutting across the fields towards the school and the sites of the new houses. Many of Kingsland's houses were roofed with tiles made by J. Pearson Smith, builder of Nos.13/15

Kennedy Road. Facing bricks came from further afield. In the White House, built in 1881, the Shrewsbury architect A.H. Taylor combined white-faced bricks, which were certainly not of local origin, with stone dressings and red brick string courses. Lloyd Oswell, architect of Nos.13/15 Kennedy Road, used bricks supplied by the Lilleshall Company, while the home of the tanner James Cock, later the Junior High School, was constructed with bricks and terracotta provided by J.C. Edwards of Ruabon.[59]

A similar change from locally-produced bricks to those obtained from a distance is revealed in the humbler suburb of Greenfields. Eighty lots off the Ellesmere Road, potentially 'one of the most attractive suburbs in the town', were offered for sale in 1880, but found few buyers. Nevertheless the streets were laid out by May 1881, and the first houses, No.25 Falstaff Street (SJ 493138) and Nos.34/35 Hotspur Street were completed by the end of the year. No.30 Hotspur Street was built in 1882 but most of the plots were not developed until late in the decade. At least six houses date from 1888, seventeen from 1889, four from 1890, twelve from 1891 and eight from 1892. Most of the later buildings are fronted with hard, shiny red bricks, which might have come from Ruabon or the Lilleshall Company, but the earliest houses of 1881-82 are of the soft, buff-coloured brick, typical of many Shrewsbury dwellings up to that time. Many of the houses in Greenfields were constructed by Thomas Pace, a self-made builder, Liberal and Congregationalist, who migrated to Shrewsbury and worked as foreman for Henry Treasure before setting up his own company in 1888. His political opinions may be reflected in the names of Hawarden Cottage and Gladstone Terrace, although Cecil Cottages and Primrose Cottages indicate that some builders may have held contrary views. In 1925 Pace reflected that there were seven or eight brickyards when he began work in Shrewsbury in the 1880s but all had since closed.[60]

There were brickyards in all Shrewsbury's suburbs in the 19th century. The availability of brick clay was one of the supposed merits of nine building plots along Wenlock Road and Sutton Road (SJ 506116) advertised in 1831, while 'an almost inexhaustible bed of superior clay' was available on a building site opposite Trinity Church in Belle Vue (SJ 496119) offered for sale in 1865.[61] Near The Column the present-day Preston Street was called Brickyard Lane, and an irregularly-shaped enclosure, Brickyard Field, which appears to have been a working brickyard in the 1840s, bordered its northern side. Seven enclosures south-east of Belvidere Road, known as Brick Kiln Fields in the 1840s, were occupied by Portland Nurseries before being covered with houses in the 1960s.

The change from local to regional sources for bricks was marked by the opening in 1896 of the brickyard at Buttington, (Monts., SJ 263097), constructed by Treasure & Son with the specific purposes of supplying Shrewsbury with 'a good, hard-burnt, sound, red common pressed brick'.[62]

Most other Shropshire towns drew their building materials from local brickyards which flourished until about 1900. In Ludlow the quarry face of the clay pit used by brickyards north of the town and immediately east of the railway, remains a feature of the landscape, and vitrified bricks, used for stopping the entrances of kilns, have been re-used in garden walls along New Road (SO 513753). In Market Drayton there were clay pits in the 1880s just north of the railway (SJ 667345) and at Cleobury Mortimer two brickworks in the 1880s lined the road to Ludlow (SO 667757; SO 669757).

Houses in Lime Street, Shrewsbury (SJ 493118),
constructed just before the First World War with concrete blocks.

About a hundred suburban houses in Shrewsbury were built with concrete blocks in the years before the First World War. The principal concentration is in Copthorne (SJ 498127) where there are 37, including dated examples of 1909 and 1911 on Copthorne Road. Others are in Longden Road, Armoury Gardens, Ditherington and Cherry Orchard. Four houses in Copthorne Drive, eleven in Porthill Drive and six in Oakley Street are of brick with concrete block dressings, as if utilising concrete blocks remaining on the site when building resumed after the First World War. Most of the blocks are of 'Cyclops' concrete stone, supplied by G. & W. Edwards from their works next to the *Quarry Inn* by the Welsh Bridge (SJ 487126).[63]

Market Town Housing

Shropshire's market towns provide evidence of various patterns of housing and of several kinds of housing agency. In most towns by 1800, burgage plots, the inheritance of medieval planning, were lined with cottages, often of an insanitary nature. Picken's Court in Castle Foregate (later Britannia Place), Shrewsbury (SJ 494131) was lined by 27 dwellings, two workshops and a block of 16 privies. Only the entrance arch remains. Similar entrances to courts remain in Longden Coleham and in Frankwell where a visitor in 1912 described:

> many tortuous passages, shiny with the grease of generations, that lead to the holes where men and women live and little children are dragged up … The courts and alleys lead nowhere, their entrances are difficult to find; their inhabitants are uninviting, the odours an abomination.[64]

In Shrewsbury most of the cottages which lined such plots have long since gone, but some remain, in a more sanitary condition, in Ludlow, Bishop's Castle and Bridgnorth.

Shropshire towns began to expand beyond their medieval limits only in the closing years of the 18th century. The first buildings to colonise the fields were often small mansions, such as The Mount in Shrewsbury, built by Dr Robert Darwin in 1797.[65] Next came terraces which might be four-storey dwellings for the middle class, such as Holywell Terrace (SJ 501125) in Shrewsbury, built about 1830 by the bricklayer Thomas Groves, or the two ranges of artisans' cottages now numbered Nos.26-48 and 50-76 Copthorne Road (SJ 483128), built by the Whitehouse family at about the same date.[66] Charlotte Row in Ellesmere (SJ 398350) is of the same period, a terrace of 20 catslide outshot cottages, built in four phases and characterised by exceptionally thick roofing slates.

In Shrewsbury houses for different social classes were built on the corner of Belle Vue Road and Trinity Street by the architect Daniel Climie. On the main road he erected the *Masonic Arms* public house (SJ 496117), and Honiton Terrace, consisting of three identical four-storey dwellings in blue and yellow brick, and a larger double-fronted house with a schoolroom attached where he himself lived. Round the corner in Trinity Street was a row of 15 simple two-storey cottages in red brick. Climie used a similar system of colour-coding on the railway between Shrewsbury and Crewe, where he built the first-class stations at Wem, Whitchurch and Nantwich in blue brick, and the lesser stations in red brick. On the opposite corner of Trinity Street is a development of the early 1860s, comprising a corner shop with living accommodation, next to which are four dwelling houses, adjoining 12 smaller cottages which together form the north side of Besford Square (SJ 495116). The terrace had been built by the spring of 1866 when the ten houses on the opposite side of the Square, which differ in detail, were standing half-completed.[67] The first houses built in Oswestry as the town's growth was stimulated by the railway works, of which Llwyn Place (SJ 293298) is an example, were terraces of similar dimensions.

Archaeological analysis of the speculator-built housing of the last quarter of the 19th century reveals something of the slumps and booms of the period, and of the scale of individual developments. Building activity in Shrewsbury seems to have reached a peak in 1882 when Edward Burley, an incomer from Birmingham, constructed many houses in Tankerville Street and Cleveland Street in the polychrome style popular elsewhere in the town at the time.[68]

The best reflection of the rhythms and fashions of late 19th-century building is found in Oswestry, particularly in the area around York Street (SJ 288299-SJ 290302) and Albert Road (SJ 289301-SJ 292299), where it is possible to sense how many dwellings a builder might complete during a summer season, and the waxing and waning of fashions such as polychrome brickwork. In Gittins Street (SJ 294301), Walnut Cottage (No.3) was built in 1881 by R. Jones, and Stanley Villas (Nos.7/9/11) by S. Price. In Albert Road there are houses of 1880, 1884, 1885, 1886, 1889 and 1895. The houses in the area show that soft, locally produced bricks were gradually supplanted during the 1880s by hard Ruabon-type bricks, and pressed ornamental bricks were increasingly used in the later buildings.

The Shrewsbury Freehold Land Society was formed after the originator of such schemes, James Taylor of Birmingham, lectured in the town in October 1851. Within 15 months subscriptions for 278 shares had been received, and plots on the garden ground behind the prison (SJ 496130) had been laid out pending distribution. Albert Street, Victoria Street, the south side of Severn Street, Benyon Street and part of North Street had been built up by Society members by 1861. In 1866 another phase was developed across the Dorsetts Barn estate, incorporating the remainder of North Street, Queen Street, Burton Street and Severn Bank.[69]

The Society was less successful in Monkmoor where it acquired the five-acre property on which John Beck, a banker, had built the dwelling now called Orchard House (SJ 503130) in 1819. By 1855 plots were laid out along a new thoroughfare then called Union Street (now Bradford Street), with several along Underdale Road. All the plots in the latter (Nos.26-46) were occupied by houses in 1875 when only five dwellings had been erected in Union Street.[70] In 1860 the Society laid out the Oakley Cottage estate (SJ 493113) in Belle Vue, consisting of Oak Street, the east end of Oakley Street and Drawwell Street, originally Cemetery Road.[71]

Castlefields and Drawwell Street illustrate well the characteristic pattern of Freehold Land Society developments. Houses are built singly or in short terraces that rarely extend to more than four dwellings, with differences in building materials, roof lines and fenestration. It seems that in Shrewsbury, as elsewhere, the Freehold Land Society provided a vehicle for the small-scale speculator, gradually acquiring a portfolio of residential property as an investment, rather than a means by which significant numbers of working-class people could become property-holders. Societies in other Shropshire towns were insignificant. A Bridgnorth society built a pair of cottages in Oldbury, while the Ludlow society in 1853 gave the name Constitution Hill to a property on Sheet Road, but probably never developed it.[72]

The suburbs of Shrewsbury include two company villages. The Sentinel Waggonworks Co. began construction of Sentinel Gardens, opposite their factory, in 1919. The houses, modelled on Garden City principles, were of a high standard, some arranged in cul-de-sacs, resembling those at New Earswick, York. A district heating system was installed but corrosion in the pipes led to its abandonment in the late 1920s, although its water tower remains in Albert Road (SJ 5071480).[73]

An ambitious 'new town' was planned at Harlescott in the 1920s, promoted by Atcham Rural District Council on land outside the borough of Shrewsbury. The only part of the plan to be realised was the re-location of the factory of the Chatwood Security Co. from Bolton (Lancs.) to Little Harlescott Lane on part of an estate which was purchased by the parent company, Hall Engineering. On the opposite side of the lane

The water tower of the Sentinel Gardens factory village, Albert Road, Shrewsbury (SJ 507148).

Houses in Harlescott Crescent, Shrewsbury (SJ 505160), built for the Chatwood Security Co. to the design of William Green in 1926.

the company built Harlescott Crescent, a 'garden village' of 44 dwellings (SJ 505160), gabled semi-detached pairs, with brickwork and woodwork of exceptional quality, grouped around a tennis court. The architect was William Green of Birmingham, who designed a similar estate for Hall Engineering at Burton Manor, Stafford. For three decades Harlescott Crescent stood isolated in the fields alongside the factory, but it was engulfed in a tide of suburban expansion from the late 1950s. The estate has been designated a Conservation Area.[74]

The construction by local authorities of 'homes fit for heroes' began soon after the conclusion of the First World War. Shrewsbury Borough Council in 1919 intended to range its houses on Longden Green (SJ 489114) around an institute on a village green, but such refinements were abandoned and by the end of the decade councillors were regretting the poor quality of the cheap houses they had constructed in Sultan Road. After the Second World War most local authorities built various forms of prefabricated housing. A few much-altered examples of single-storey 'prefabs' remain in the Clee View area of

Single-storey 'prefabs' constructed after the Second World War in the Clee View area of Ludlow (SO 518751).

'Airey houses', to the design of the Leeds builder Sir Edwin Airey,
built in the late 1940s in the Clee View area of Ludlow (SO 519752).

Ludlow (SO 520750) together with some two-storey concrete 'Airey houses', and there are examples of BISF (British Iron & Steel Federation) houses in Crowmere Road (SJ 505126) and Crowmeole (SJ 470122) in Shrewsbury.[75]

The outstanding private developer of the mid 20th century was Fletcher Homes Ltd, a Blackpool company, who in 1934 acquired the former Royal Flying Corps (RFC) road transport depot alongside Whitchurch Road, Harlescott (SJ 506152). Some of the depot's concrete buildings were rented to commercial tenants, but most were replaced by housing, typical semi-detached pairs of the 1930s, with characteristic steel-framed windows. Some were sold in 1935 for as little as £430. Some of the RFC buildings in Harlescott remain in commercial use. The former married quarters of the RFC base were purchased by Shrewsbury Borough Council early in 1934, and the 38 two-storey rendered houses, with dormers breaking into the clay tile roofs and with ground-floor bow windows, remain on Whitchurch Road, and in Harlescott Close, Haughmond Avenue and Roselyn.[76]

On the other side of the River Severn in Monkmoor (SJ 514136) a First World War flying field was converted to industrial and residential use. The base closed before the end of 1918 but was re-occupied by a non-flying maintenance unit in the Second World War. Two Belfast-truss hangars remain in commercial use, and some barrack blocks and offices of the First World War have been adapted as private residences.[77]

Several Shropshire towns had 'rough suburbs' resembling Mixen Lane in Hardy's Casterbridge:

... the hiding place of those who were in distress and in debt and trouble of every kind. Farm labourers and other peasants who combined a little poaching with their farming, and a little brawling and bibbing with their poaching. The land and its surround thicket of thatched cottages stretched out like a spit into the moist and misty lowland ...[78]

Such characteristics were found in Shrewsbury in the courts on the burgage plots of the town's medieval suburbs and on the Old Heath at Ditherington. The Bank in Much Wenlock, a collection of crudely-built limestone cottages on the road to Church Stretton (SO 618996), housed 396 residents in 1851, most of them farm labourers and lime burners. Bernard's Hill (SO 723927), one of whose thoroughfares was ironically called 'The Mall', was a similar extra-mural suburb on the edge of Bridgnorth. Market Drayton's western suburb, Little Drayton Common (SJ 663336), was made up of small, ill-ventilated cottages of miserable appearance. By 1837 there were 27 encroachments on the common which was enclosed in 1852, after which the settlement grew rapidly. By 1861 some 37 new houses had been erected, most of them occupied by migrants from nearby parishes. It had a small Baptist chapel, but lacked the traditional beerhouse.[79] Ludlow's Rock Lane (SO 521749) was an archetypal rough suburb with an alehouse, the *Mousetrap*, a minuscule Baptist chapel and a changing population of agricultural labourers, brickmakers, knife grinders and washerwomen. A visitor in the 1870s commented on 'the squalid appearance of the poor cottagers'.[80]

A 'rough suburb', The Bank, on the edge of Much Wenlock.

Public Utilities
The relatively early provision of public utilities distinguishes most towns from the countryside. The most venerable of Shropshire's public water supply systems was installed in Shrewsbury in the late 16th century, a line of lead pipes from springs at Mousecroft Lane

(SJ 472112) to a cistern on Pride Hill. A second system, installed in the county town in the early 18th century, incorporated a waterwheel in one of the arches of the English Bridge of the adjustable pattern designed by John Hadley for London Bridge. It worked pumps which lifted water to a cistern near the top of Pride Hill. The latter was replaced in 1827-32 by a steam-powered waterworks in Chester Street (SJ 493131). Many Salopians nevertheless drew their water from contaminated wells or directly from the Severn for decades afterwards, and the quality of the town's drinking water was a source of scandal until a new waterworks was built in 1934 at Shelton (SJ 464133).[81]

Bridgnorth too had a Hadley-style waterwheel alongside the bridge, pumping water to a tank on Castle Wharf. Wellington by the late 17th century had a conduit system leading water along the Town Brook to a point of public supply on Tan Bank. A water company, established in 1851, built the Ercall Pool reservoir soon afterwards. In the early 19th century the corporation in Ludlow was responsible for pumps which raised water from the River Teme to a reservoir at the top of the Butter Market, from which pipes led to various parts of the town. Whitchurch gained its public supply from the waterworks at Fenns Bank in 1882. Wem's supply, pumped from Preston Brockhurst, was completed two years later. By 1900 most towns had healthy supplies. Some 19th-century reservoirs and small pumping installations remain and there is a modest interpretative display at Conduit Head, source of Shrewsbury's 16th-century supply, from which some water is still extracted.

The process of draining towns took a similar course. Lord Brownlow was instrumental in draining Ellesmere in 1869 after the formation of a Local Board of Health a decade earlier. Wellington's sewage flowed into the Bratton Brook until 1898 when a disposal works was built at Dothill. In Shrewsbury ancient sewers decanted their contents into the Severn at 'mudholes' near the two bridges. They remained in use until 1901 when a pumping station in Longden Coleham (SJ 496122) began to pump sewage to a treatment works at Monkmoor (SJ 520137). The station's two Woolf compound beam engines by W.R. Renshaw & Co. of Stoke-on-Trent, which were replaced by electric pumps in 1970, are cared for by the County of Salop Steam Engine Society.[82]

The first gas lighting installations in Shropshire were at the flax mills at Ditherington and Castlefields, drawings for which were prepared in 1811.[83] Gas lighting was demonstrated at the theatre in Oswestry in 1819, and the county's first public supply, in Shrewsbury, began in 1820. Gasworks were built soon afterwards at Wellington and Oswestry, and by the 1880s every town except Clun was supplied. There were also gasworks outside the market towns, in the Coalbrookdale Coalfield and in the large villages of Albrighton and Craven Arms, while the works for the Worcestershire towns of Tenbury Wells and Bewdley were actually in Shropshire.

Some of the small companies amalgamated, the industry was nationalised in 1949, and during the 1960s coal gas production was abandoned to be replaced by natural gas. There are few significant monuments of the gas industry, although several former gasworks sites retain equipment used in the distribution network. A muted expression of the industry's importance is provided by the truncated remains of the Shrewsbury Gas Light Company's office in Castle Foregate (SJ 495133), a flamboyant building of 1884 in polychrome brick and terracotta, now reduced from three to two storeys.

The benefits of electricity supply were demonstrated in Shrewsbury through the 1880s by F.J. Lea, who was supposedly closely concerned with the establishment of the town's power station in Roushill (SJ 492127) in 1893. It was initially steam-powered but diesel engines were used up to the time of closure in 1956.[84] A power station opened in Oswestry, also in 1893, and subsequently supplies were made available in Church Stretton in 1904, Ludlow in 1906 and Bishop's Castle in 1914. It was not until the early 1930s that electric power was brought to other towns. The North Wales Power Co. began to supply Whitchurch in 1931, and the completion of the Ironbridge 'A' Power Station in 1932 enabled the West Midlands Joint Electricity Authority to bring electric power to Newport, Shifnal, Wellington and Much Wenlock.[85]

The sites of several of Shropshire's power stations are occupied by sub-stations, including those at Roushill in Shrewsbury, and Corporation Street in Bishop's Castle (SO 322888). Fragments of buildings remain at Station Road in Bishop's Castle (SO 324886), Crossways, Church Stretton (SO 458935), Portcullis Lane, Ludlow (SO 513749) and Coney Green, Oswestry (SJ 292296).[86]

Less is recorded of the development of telecommunications. The first telephone installation appears to have been the network established in Shrewsbury by the Western & South Wales Telephone Company in August 1887, with a switchboard in Dogpole Court (SJ 673124) and subsequently in the *Clarendon Hotel*. From 1912 when the General Post Office took over telephone services the exchange was part of the post office in St Mary's Street, where it remained until the exchange on Town Walls was commissioned in the late 1950s. Early exchanges in other towns were in shops or private houses such as that at No.11, The Wharfage, Ironbridge (SJ 670035) where the National Telephone Company opened for business in 1905, and remained until the late 1940s.[87]

Conclusions

Shropshire's 16 market towns shared certain characteristic manufactures, the range and importance of which depended on the size of the town – the larger the town the greater the number of maltings and the more likely it was to have a tannery and a foundry. The larger towns – Shrewsbury, Wellington, Bridgnorth, Ludlow, Oswestry, Market Drayton and Whitchurch – were concerned with textiles, but none was primarily a manufacturing town. Many Salopians in the late 19th century expressed regret at the loss of manufacturing capacity. Twentieth-century industry in Shrewsbury flourished largely on land that became available for manufacturing during the First World War, and on that envisaged as the site of a visionary new town in the 1920s. In Ludlow a government factory was built towards the end of the First World War on the Bromfield Road. It had a rail connection to the line from Shrewsbury and was officially opened in June 1918. It was intended to distil benzole and naptha from wood and was known as the 'Wood Spirit Factory'. It was offered for sale by the Disposals & Liquidation Commission in 1923, with about 30,250 sq ft of space available in a range of brick buildings. The factory was bought by a local entrepreneur, Charles Edwards, who exported the equipment to India and disposed of the timber. The buildings were let for various purposes, the repair of railway wagons, storing fruit, making toys and, after the Second World War for the manufacture of lanterns and small stoves, and for

*One of the two hangars from the First World War flying field
at Monkmoor (SJ 512136) Shrewsbury that was subsequently put to industrial use.*

die-casting. The chimney and a tower have been demolished and at least one building has burned down, but others are still used by the motor trade.[88] On the other side of Ludlow the Board of Trade allocated the site of a 'buffer depot' on Temeside, established during the war for the stockpiling of food for use in emergencies, to McConnels, the agricultural engineering company established at Martley (Worcs.) in 1935. Some of the first products were saw benches made from the wheels of decommissioned Spitfires, but the firm became well-known for its tractor-mounted hedge cutters, and now manufactures remote control machines.[89] Construction of the prototype logistics base for the United States forces in Britain began on the north side of Wem on 14 December 1942, and was completed on 30 June of the following year. Many ranks of huts with corrugated asbestos and corrugated iron ends accommodated food, clothing and munitions. Alongside was a camp for 1,250 men, and 11 miles of railway sidings were linked to the line from Shrewsbury to Crewe. Since the war ended the remaining huts have been put to varied industrial uses, part of the depot is occupied by a caravan site and the remainder has been restored to agriculture.[90] Military bases of the Second World War have also provided space for industrial developments at Oswestry and Bridgnorth.

The traditional market town manufactures have disappeared. Shropshire's last tannery, by the Welsh Bridge in Shrewsbury, closed in the 1960s. Wem brewery, the last industrial-scale brewing enterprise in the county, Wem Mill, the last to grind grain on a traditional urban water-power site, and Albrew Maltsters in Shrewsbury, all ceased to operate during the 1980s. Coach-making was absorbed in the motor trade. The Atlas Foundry (SJ 488127) in Shrewsbury was probably the last market town foundry in the county to produce castings, in the 1970s. Nevertheless the historic identities of Shropshire towns have been shaped in part by their manufactures. Over many centuries each was a concentration of cornmilling, malting, brewing and tanning. Each had a range of craft occupations, all provided most of their own building materials, most by 1850 had foundries, and most developed public utilities. When reminiscing about his schooldays at Wem around 1850, General Sir Charles Warren recalled not only 'the sound of lowing cattle and squealing pigs and the rumble of carts and vans along the streets' but also 'the smell of tanyards and breweries'. Manufactures were part of the essence of market towns.

4 COALFIELD LANDSCAPES

Coalfield landscapes, even when they have long ceased to be productive, are unmistakable. Clay mounts topped with gangly birches, fringes of prickly grass at the bases of clay-faced cliffs, soot-grubby red brick terraces, underfoot layers of shale, clinker, crushed bricks or blast furnace slag, apparently purposeless tracks across ill-drained squelchy fields enclosed with fences of wrought-iron rattle chain, are the signs of economic patterns which differ radically from those of market towns or the agricultural countryside.

The five Shropshire coalfields are small by comparison with those of Northumberland and Durham, South Wales, Nottinghamshire and south Yorkshire, with less than a dozen mines worked in the 20th century. This study uses archaeological evidence to draw out the economic and social significance of each, in the belief that coalfields comprise distinct types of community, and that our understanding of them is increased by a comparative approach.

Shropshire's Coalfields

The Shrewsbury Coalfield

The Shrewsbury coalfield extends 20km west from the banks of the Severn at Uffington and Eaton Constantine to the slopes of the Breiddens and the Welsh border at Bragginton, and 15km south from the county town to Leebotwood.[1] The widely dispersed mines in the Upper Coal Measures were small, shallow and isolated, with the most productive pits around Hanwood, Exfords Green, Pontesbury and Westbury. The deepest workings extended from the 128m shaft of Hanwood Colliery.

The discovery of coal near Shrewsbury in the 16th century was greeted with enthusiasm, but it is doubtful whether local supplies ever satisfied the needs of the county town. In Shrewsbury in the 1840s coal from

73

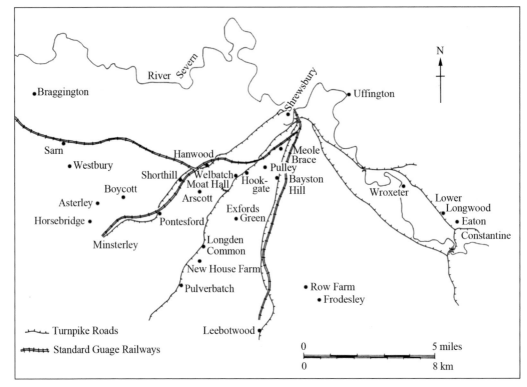

The Shrewsbury Coalfield

nearby pits ranged in price from 10s to 15s a ton, while that from the Coalbrookdale Coalfield cost between 12s and 17s, but large quantities of the latter were consumed nevertheless.[2] The peak of activity in the Shrewsbury Coalfield was reached in the 1850s and 1860s when more than 300 miners were employed, the majority living at Hanwood, Longden Common, Asterley and on Pontesbury Hill. Most miners and colliery proprietors were locally born although Thomas Proctor, who worked the Arscott pits in the 1870s, was from Whaley Bridge, Derbyshire, and several mining engineers from Lancashire worked at Hanwood in the 1880s and '90s.

The economic significance of a coalfield can be determined by its markets, and the best archaeological indications of markets are the remains of transport systems. Few pits in the Shrewsbury Coalfield were linked with regional and still fewer with national networks. Most coal was consumed in the vicinity of pitheads or was distributed by road over short distances. In the 1840s coal from the mines at Uffington (SJ 533126), which Murchison called 'the little patch of coal measures occupying the low ground between Haughmond Hill and the Severn', was taken along the Shrewsbury Canal to the *Golden Ball* basin (SJ 499138) near the Ditherington Flax Mills.[3] In 1812 Richard Boothby built a railway from the colliery north of Moat Hall (SJ 450090) to a landsale wharf (i.e. where it was sold to local customers who collected it by road) at Annscroft on the Shrewsbury-Longden road. The line was extended in 1886 and continued in use until the colliery closed in 1934. In its last years wagons were pulled by a horse called *Curley*. This was the only early railway in the area except for short tramways at Bragginton and Pontesford. In 1800 and in 1831 customers were urged to collect coal by road from the pits at Welbatch alongside the Longden turnpike. In 1868 coal from Asterley was sold at a wharf in Minsterley to which it could only have been delivered by road.[4]

The only pits with standard gauge railway sidings were at Shorthill and Hanwood alongside the branch line to Minsterley, and pits near Moat Hall (SJ 444081) served by the only standard gauge mineral railway in the coalfield which extended 2km south-east from a junction west of Hanwood (SJ 434093).

Almost all the coal mined in the Shrewsbury Coalfield was for landsale, for lime-burning, or for brickmaking. The only ceramics works which catered for distant markets was the Sarn Terracotta Works (later the Sarn Brick & Tile Works) near Westbury Station (SJ 347110), established in the 1860s by Thomas Kough, and later worked by Edward and Thomas Greenwood. It probably employed most of the 18 brickmakers living in Westbury parish in 1871.[5] Bricks marked 'Sarn' were used in many late 19th-century middle-class houses in Shrewsbury. Clay was delivered until the 1960s by a 2ft (0.6m) gauge railway laid in 1886 from pits 400m north. The only other significant use for coal in the area was in smelting lead ore, for which the Nag's Head Colliery at Pontesford and the Boycott mine near Malehurst were the chief suppliers.[6]

The late 18th-century coalmine pumping engine house at Pontesford (SJ 410065)

Some steam engines were used in the coalfield, the first of them a Boulton & Watt pumping engine erected at Westbury Colliery (SJ 366087) in 1781. An 18hp engine was offered for sale at a colliery at Meole Brace in 1843, and a 12hp machine at Homley Pit, Hookagate, in 1857. Fourteen colliery steam engine drivers were living in Pontesbury in 1861. A surviving pumping engine house at Pontesford (SJ 410065) was probably constructed by Samuel or William Heighway before 1800. The first documentary reference to it dates from 1817. It was out of use by 1828 and by 1842 was adapted as a dwelling, a purpose it still serves. The pump shaft lies about 2m from the bob wall. Insufficient evidence remains to determine whether the building housed a Newcomen or a Boulton & Watt engine.[7]

A mine had been sunk near Row Farm, Frodesley (SJ 505019) by the 1740s. In the 1830s it produced only 200 tons p.a. of coal, and only two miners were living in the parish in 1841. Extraction ceased soon afterwards but traces of the shafts remain. Coal was mined in Pulverbatch as early as 1717. In the 19th century the centre of operations was New House Farm (SJ 436036), home of George Fenn, who combined farming 250 acres (112 ha) with mining. He employed ten miners in 1851, and 28, including the driver of an engine, in 1871, when his colliery manager lived near the pits at Castle Place (SJ 446039). The mines at Lower Long Wood (SJ 588062), between Wroxeter and Eaton Constantine, were sunk in the late 1790s and were worked until the 1840s in conjunction with a limeworks at Harley and a nearby brickworks.[8] There were workings at Bragginton (SJ 3311350) in Alberbury parish in the 18th century, but in about 1830 an investment was made in the colliery which included the building of a tramway with both wrought-iron and cast-iron rails. Llanymynech limestone was burned there, and the proprietors offered to deliver the resultant lime to customers in Shrewsbury by Severn barge. Murchison observed that the thinness of the seams and extensive faulting, coupled with the remoteness of the mine from markets, led to its closure before 1840, although some activity continued in the 1850s.[9]

The most southerly workings in the Shrewsbury Coalfield, on the borders of Leebotwood and Longnor, were established in 1784 and continued until the 1870s, extending over 2.8ha in 1796, 7.7ha in 1807, and 16.6ha in 1832-33, when annual output was 3,664 tons. The main colliery lay close to the turnpike road (SO 482999) where waste tips remain. A steam engine was working at the mine by 1815. Most of the coal was used in lime kilns built before 1810 and at two brickworks, one near the Shrewsbury & Hereford Railway (SO 475997), the other east of the colliery (SO 482000). Coal was still being produced in 1874.[10]

South-west of Shrewsbury there is little evidence of mining activity at Meole Brace and Pulley Common other than some old cottages amongst the suburban sprawl of Bayston Hill. On the turnpike road to Longden, the settlements of Hookagate and Annscroft retain traces of their origins as communities of squatter miners. Around 20 miners lived at Hookagate throughout the second half of the 19th century. North of the Longden

A restored and extended cottage at Hookagate (SJ 465092), a community of squatter coalminers in the 19th century.

turnpike waste tips mark the sites of the Moat Hall (SJ 450802), Arscott (SJ 436081) and Asterley (SJ 375075) collieries. Along the Minsterley turnpike the pithead buildings of the Hanwood (SJ 436093) and Shorthill (SJ 430092) mines have been adapted for residential purposes. The Hanwood shaft was sunk in the 1870s. In 1921 as many as 248 miners were employed, although only 50 were working there when the mine closed in 1942.[11]

The best surviving mining landscape in the coalfield is between Westbury, Minsterley and Pontesbury. The Westbury Colliery (SJ 366087) had four shafts in the 1820s and closed in 1862, after which the Old Engine and the weighing machine (SJ 361087) were adapted as dwellings. Fifty-five coal miners were living in Westbury parish in 1861, but only one remained 30 years later. There were six coal pits in the mid-19th century around Asterley in Pontesbury parish (SJ 374071), celebrated as the birthplace in 1827 of Richard Weaver, the Victorian evangelist known as the 'converted collier'. Waste tips remain at the Windmill Pit (SJ 373075) and the Farley Mine (SJ 382076), and mounts extend along the road east of the lancet-windowed mission church of 1869, which is now a dwelling. North of the road a ruin remains on the site of the Big Engine (SJ 375075) adjacent to which was a brickworks. Many of the miners' houses in Asterley have been replaced or altered, but the ex-Primitive Methodist chapel still stands. Horsebridge (SJ 368061), 1km south of Asterley, typifies the mining settlements of the coalfield, consisting of about a dozen small brick cottages in short terraces, all with long garden plots.[12]

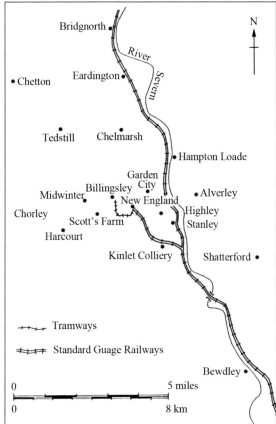

The Wyre Forest Coalfield

The Wyre Forest Coalfield

The luxuriantly wooded valleys through which the Borle Brook and the Mor Brook flow to the River Severn form one of the most idyllic landscapes in England, but beneath the surface lies the metre-thick Brooch seam in the Upper Coal Measures, and the countryside retains many traces of past mining activities.[13] The Wyre Forest Coalfield occupies much of the west bank of the Severn between Eardington, downstream from Bridgnorth, and Bewdley. Most of the coalfield lies within Shropshire although there were productive workings around Mamble in Worcestershire. The coalfield experienced two principal periods of activity, one during the Napoleonic Wars, the other in the last quarter of the 19th century and the first years of the 20th century, when the Brooch seam was worked for markets made accessible by the Severn Valley Railway.

Spoil tips provide evidence of small-scale mining. A 220m-deep colliery with a steam winding engine was working near Eardington Mill (SO 715903) by 1847, but only three colliers and an 'engine tender' were living in the 'enclosure about the coal pits' in 1851. West of Chelmarsh (SO 720872) are the remains of a colliery that employed about a dozen miners in the 1850s, and around 20 in the 1880s and 1890s. It provided fuel for William Partridge, a Broseley man, who owned a nearby brickworks. Mining on a modest scale took place for most of the 19th century around Chorley and Harcourt in Stottesdon parish, and the coal from the pits at Lower Harcourt (SO 693827) was prized in the 1830s for its low sulphur content. In 1881 nine miners and an engine driver worked in the area, and in 1891 some 17 miners lived in scattered cottages between Chorley, Harcourt, Midwinter (SO 702841) and Scots Farm (SO 707835). Mining at Harcourt ceased in 1924, but some workings at Chorley continued until 1933. Tips of coal waste are encountered from time to time during ploughing. Waste tips around old shafts at Tedstill (SO 693884) in Chetton parish indicate the sites of coal and iron ore mines offered for sale in 1827. Only ten miners lived in the parish in 1851, by which time a steam engine was employed at the pit and one Thomas Evans operated an adjacent brick and tile works.

Stanley Colliery (SO 749828) in Highley on the west bank of the Severn was developed in the opening years of the 19th century. A 20hp pumping engine was installed together with two 7hp engines which wound coal up a 100-yard shaft. Some 900 yards of plateway conveyed coal to the Severn where it was loaded into the partners' two 60-ton barges, *Sarah Mytton* and *Bridget*. Coal was supplied to the forges at Hampton Loade, to lime kilns at Shatterford and to a brickworks near Stourport. The colliery closed in the 1820s but was revived by Bigger & Co. of Newcastle-under-Lyme in 1878.[14] Highley was certainly not a mining community in 1851, when only four miners lived in the parish. There were two in 1861 and just one ten years later.

The other substantial venture of the Industrial Revolution period in the Wyre Forest was at Billingsley, based on a 1,000-acre (405ha) estate leased from William Pulteney. The parish clerk noted in his register in 1796 that a pit was being sunk by miners 'from the North of England', chief amongst whom was George Johnson of Byker (Northumberland), who was buried at Billingsley four years later. Two blast furnaces were constructed by his successor, George Stokes, the first completed by 1800. They were blown by a 52-inch steam engine which cost more than £4,000, and had a cast-iron beam, still a novelty at that date. Adjacent to the furnace were coke hearths and calcining kilns. The mine was drained by a 38-inch pumping engine, and minerals were wound up the shafts by two Trevithick steam engines and several horse gins. Coal was carried 4km to the River Severn along a plateway, with cast-iron rails and a mixture of cast-iron and wooden sleepers. It descended into the valley of the Borle Brook by an inclined plane at the head of which (SO 716842) was a 2hp steam engine. The track bed beyond the foot of the incline is about 2m wide. About 50 wagons were used on the line. The ironworks was taken over after Johnson's death by partners who went bankrupt in 1812. It was offered for sale between 1814 and 1817, but no buyer was found and the buildings were demolished.[15]

The colliery at Billingsley (SO 715844) was revived in the 1870s after William Birchley discovered the Brooch seam beneath sulphur-rich deposits. A man was killed during the sinking of a new 200-yard shaft in 1876. By 1881 a steam engine was employed, driven by

An early 20th-century photograph of the colliery at Billingsley (SO 715844).

Isaacher Jones, then aged 27, who lived next door to the *Cape of Good Hope* public house. Much of the coal was used by Thomas Davies, a brickmaker with eight employees who lived at Brickhill House. Coal was also carted about 800m to a wharf on the mineral railway built in 1881 which later served Kinlet Colliery, along which it was conveyed about 5km to the Severn Valley Railway. In 1908 the colliery was acquired by the Powell Duffryn company from South Wales, but it closed in 1921 with the loss of 200 jobs. The site is marked by waste tips and by several red brick colliery buildings.[16]

The shafts of Kinlet Colliery (SO 738818) were sunk from 1892 and the substantial engine house of 1896 remains in ruins. It stood close to a brickworks whose clay pit (SO 373819) is now a pool, and was linked with the Severn Valley Railway (SO 752815) by a mineral line along the south bank of the Borle Brook. The mine closed in the early 1930s.

The Highley Mining Co. located the Brooch seam in 1879 and began producing coal soon afterwards. The company had links with the North Staffordshire Coalfield, both William Viggars, the contractor and engineer, and Jabez Lawton, the company secretary being natives of Silverdale. By contrast, most of the 71 miners living in the parish in 1891 were from Shropshire, either from other parishes in the Wyre Forest, or from the Coalbrookdale or Clee Hill coalfields. Coal was despatched from the colliery (SO 745830) by a rope-worked inclined plane to a siding off the Severn Valley Railway south of Highley Station (SO 748830), but some was used at a nearby brickworks (SO 742829). The workings extended beneath the Severn and in the 1930s the company sank a 345m shaft on the east bank at Alveley (SO 752842). Its concrete headstock began winding in 1935 and it became the main production shaft for the mine, although the shafts at Highley were retained for ventilation and access. The new facilities were linked with the Severn Valley Railway by a cable-worked inclined plane crossing the Severn on a concrete bridge, and subsequently by an aerial ropeway. In the 1950s the mine employed 1,250 men and produced up to 30,000 tons of coal a year. It closed in 1969.[17]

Clee View (SO 783843), the longest terrace in Highley, comprising 35 two-storey, tunnel-back dwellings, probably constructed in the 1890s.

Nos. 1/3 Woodhill Road, Highley (SO 733844), part of the Garden Village built in the second decade of the 20th century.

The plaque on No. 1 Woodhill Road identifying it as part of Block 1 of the Garden Village.

The sites of the Alveley and Highley pits are now part of the Severn Valley Country Park. At Highley (SO 745830) only an administrative building remains at what is now the entrance to the country park. The bridge (SO 753839) which carried coal over the river has been replaced by a footbridge leading to the Alveley site, where there is a visitor centre (SO 753839) giving panoramic views across the valley. The bridge is on the route of the Mercian Way, the National Cycle Network Route 45. The remainder of the mine complex, including a weighbridge house and pithead baths (SO 753842), is in commercial use.

Highley is an archetypal mining village, reminiscent of settlements in South Wales, Yorkshire or Co. Durham. Its character is determined as much by the history of the parish as by its coal deposits. From medieval times Highley was an 'open' parish, with many landowners, where settlement was easy. In 1841 its 1,527 acres (618 ha) were shared by 30 owners. As new pits were sunk in the late 19th century their owners sought to accommodate their workers in Highley rather than in closed parishes such as Billingsley or Kinlet. Highley's population grew from 293 in 1871 to 1,985 in 1921, while in the same period that of Kinlet rose from 432 to 501 and that of Billingsley from 119 to 148. Highley is characterised by long brick terraces. Silverdale Terrace (previously Providence Terrace), a row of 25 dwellings (SO 741835), was built during the 1880s and recalls

Highley's links with north Staffordshire. The longest terrace, Clee View (SO 783843), consists of 35 two-storey tunnel-back houses in soft red brick, and appears to have been built in the 1890s. In Church Street are six pairs of villas with terracotta ornamentation, mostly built in 1911-12, which were probably intended for supervisory staff at the mine. The Co-operative Store, built in 1905 and extended in 1912, retains its beehive emblem, and is remembered for its support of the miners during strikes, and for organising chara-banc outings, sporting events and children's parties. The Methodist chapel of 1913, a fiery red brick building with a Decorated Gothic window at its ecclesiastical west end, is simi-larly remembered as a centre of social life. The choir sang in the village on summer Sunday evenings, while the local brass band and representatives from other Midlands collieries attended the annual miners' service, when the names of pitmen who had died during the previous year were recited with respect.[18]

The most interesting housing is at the north end of Highley, more than a mile from the colliery, in a triangular area including Oak Street, Ash Street and Beech Street (SO 733847). Construction began before the First World War, and it appears that it was intended for miners from Billingsley. Nearly a hundred dwellings in what was called 'Garden City' style were inexplicably standing empty in 1919. They were built in 'blocks' whose numbers, on blue enamel plaques, remain on No.13 Oak Street (Block 25), No.13 Ash Street (Block 19) and No.1 Woodhill Road (Block 1). The houses are constructed of bright red Ruabon-type bricks, with some rough cast and some cosmetic timber framing. There are floral devices in some gables, and the original doors have stained glass panels. The inclusion of bathrooms in houses in the countryside was considered a luxury in 1919.[19]

The Oswestry Coalfield

The mines in the extensive parishes of Oswestry and St Martin's form the southern part of the North Wales Coalfield, whose productive seams were in the Middle Coal Measures.[20] There were mines in most parts of St Martin's, except on the limestone slopes along its western border. In Oswestry most pits were in the upper reaches of the Morda Valley around Coed-y-go and Trefonen. Some miners lived in neighbouring Selattyn and by 1891 about 40 were resident in Whittington. Mining was established by the late 18th century and was stimulated by the new markets made accessible by the Ellesmere Canal during the Napoleonic Wars.

The mines in the south of the coalfield lay in the townships of Trefonen, Sweeney and Trefarclawdd, within an area less than 4km from north to south, and extending less than 4km west from the Oswestry-Welshpool turnpike. At least 200 colliers were working in the area in the 1790s. The Croxon family, bankers of Oswestry, were operating ten or more pits soon after 1800. The outlet to the Ellesmere Canal was a tramway from the Gronwen pits (SJ 277264) to Redwith. In 1863 a standard gauge rail connection was constructed to join the Porthywaen branch of the Cambrian Railways, on which a 0-4-0 saddle tank locomo-tive, *Tiny*, conveyed about 20 wagons a day until the colliery ceased operation in 1881. The northern part of the route is now a footpath west of Sweeney Mountain.[21]

There were 140 miners in Oswestry parish in 1841, doubtless fewer than during the boom years of the Napoleonic Wars. The number declined to 113 in 1851, and to 99 in 1861, but rose to 127 in 1871, probably as a result of increased use of coal in ceramics

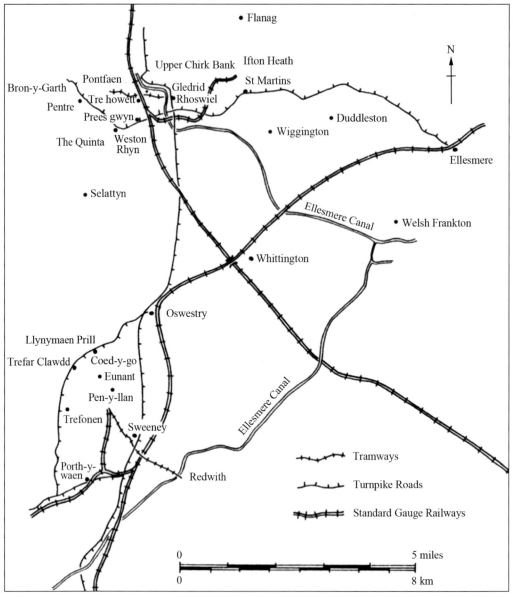

The Oswestry and St Martin's Coalfield

works. The number of brickmakers in the area rose from nine in 1861 to 34 in 1871. Subsequently both brickmaking and mining declined. Only seven brickmakers lived in the area in 1881, while the number of miners fell to 39 in that year and remained at that level in 1891. Coalmining had ceased in Trefonen by 1900, and large-scale brickmaking by 1905.

The monuments of this part of the coalfield are unspectacular. West of Morda village the coal wharf of the Drill Colliery (SO 286277) became a road transport depot, bordered by waste tips. Adjacent to it are six pairs of two-storey tunnel-back houses. Along the road to

The waste tip is all that remains of the Penyllan Colliery (SJ 278282, which was worked in the mid 19th century.

Trefonen the sites of two more pits are indicated by waste tips (SJ 282277; SJ 279278) as is that of the Pen-y-llan Colliery (SJ 278282) on the north bank of the Morda. The British Colliery opened by the Croxons in the 1830s, leased in 1860 by the railway contractor Thomas Savin and closed three years later, was at Coed-y-go (SJ 276277). The terrace called Eunant (SJ 272276), double-fronted, two-storey cottages in rubble sandstone, bears the date 1859 and formerly incorporated the British Colliery's company shop. To the west is a terrace of six two-storey cottages (SJ 271275) dating from 1860.[22]

The turnpike road from Oswestry to Trefonen south of Llwyn-y-Maen (SJ 272283) was lined with coal workings in the early 19th century, most of them closing in the 1830s.

Eunant, a terrace adjacent to the site of the British Colliery at Coed-y-go (SJ 272276). The terrace was built in 1859 and accommodated the company store, a butcher's shop and a beerhouse. The cross-wing dates from 1875.

Some tips of waste coal remain near Pottery Cottages (SJ 262274), which were adapted from the drying sheds of the associated ceramics works.[23] Trefonen, where mine workings were scattered around Offa's Dyke, is a squatter settlement where in 1881 two groups of cottages bore the ironically grandiose names of Piccadilly Row and Babylon. East of the turnpike road a waste tip has been adapted as a children's playground (SJ 262270) and what appears to be a former weighbridge house became a hairdressing salon (SJ 261269). From 1870 Trefonen Colliery was worked by the railway promoter Richard France, in association with limestone quarries at Nant Mawr. France re-ordered the workings, closing the Old Trefonen Pit and in 1880 opening the New Trefonen Mine, which had two shafts, 44m and 50m deep accessing a 6ft seam of coal, and a 4ft bed of fireclay. It was forecast that the mine would produce 24,000 tons of coal a year. Surface installations included a 15hp winding engine, workers' cabins, a blacksmith's shop and a weighing machine. The colliery continued to work after France's bankruptcy in 1881, and the census of 1891 recorded 25 miners at Trefonen, but it closed later that year.

Lime-burning and ceramics manufactures were the only industries consuming coal in the Oswestry portion of the coalfield. In 1851 at a works opposite the rectory in Trefonen, John Howell was making tiles and firebricks. There was a steam engine at the works by 1871 but it had closed by 1891. In that year the principal works in the area was a brick-yard at Sweeney, managed by Philip Kent from Silverdale (Staffs.), who employed eight men. Characteristic bricks, which can be seen in 19th-century houses in the coalfield and in Oswestry, were of a yellowish hue. The neo-Romanesque ornamentation of the west front of Thomas Penson's church of St Agatha, Llanymynech (SJ 268308) may have come from Trefonen, as may the yellow firebricks used in the astonishing Gothic façade of the Congregational Chapel in New Street, Welshpool.[24]

Mining flourished in the St Martin's portion of the coalfield during the Napoleonic Wars, particularly around Chirk Bank. Activity declined thereafter and the number of miners in the parish fell from 128 in 1841 to 97 in 1851, but with the stimulus of the Shrewsbury & Chester Railway, numbers subsequently increased, to 215 in 1861, 261 in 1871, 299 in 1881 and 405 in 1891. The scale of investment is indicated by the numbers of

Upper Chirk Bank – the footpath following the line of the Glyn Valley Tramway, constructed in 1873, cuts through the early 19th-century waste tip of Upper Chirk Bank Colliery (SJ 292368).

colliery enginemen – four in 1851, 10 in 1861 and 16 in 1871. Initially the focus of growth was at Rhoswiel, where the turnpike road to Bron-y-garth crosses the canal and the railway.

A cosmopolitan mining community developed in the area. The principal investor in Ifton Colliery was Thomas Barnes, the Lancashire cotton manufacturer, railway director and Congregationalist, who built the Gothic-style mansion, The Quinta, in 1858.[25] Colliery managers in 1871 included men from Tynemouth (Northumberland), Kearsley (Lancashire) and Easington (Co. Durham). Most miners were born in north Shropshire or adjoining parts of Wales. In the 1860s terraces at The Lodge, principally occupied by miners, were named after Prince Albert, Giuseppe Garibaldi and Abraham Lincoln. By 1881 there was a *British Workman*, a temperance public house, at Pentre.

The landscape around Weston Rhyn illustrates two centuries of mining history. The outstanding building in the village is the Sunday School on the High Street, designed by T. Raffles Davidson for Thomas Barnes, a red brick and red terracotta building with a drum tower. Originally it served also as a day school and a communal meeting place. The Quinta Chapel, a Congregationalist place of worship built for Barnes in 1858, stands close to the mansion. In the early 19th century the principal mines were at Chirk Bank between the Holyhead Road and the Ellesmere Canal. At Upper Chirk Bank, the Glyn Valley Tramway, opened in 1873, cuts through pit mounts of the early 19th-century, providing a perfect example of archaeological phasing (SJ 292367). Two terraces are evidence of different periods of mining. Quinta Terrace (SJ 291366), a row of six two-storey cottages in soft yellow brick, appears to date from the third quarter of the 19th century, and, on the opposite side of the road, a terrace of six very small houses, now largely rendered, is of much earlier date. Pit mounts east of the main line railway (SJ 291363) mark the site of other early 19th-century workings. Further north are traces of Trehowell Colliery (SJ 290365), which was active in the 1880s. Only stunted mounds survive of the extensive surface buildings and adjacent brickworks of the Quinta Colliery (SJ 286367), which closed in 1880. East of the canal a range of coke ovens at Gledrid (SJ 297365) had been replaced by the 1880s by a brickworks, from which a short tramway led to the canal bank opposite the Glyn Valley Tramway's Gledrid Wharf. The brickyard was derelict in 1900 and was subsequently replaced by a sawmill.

East of the Shrewsbury & Chester Railway John McKiernin's brickyard, working in the 1840s, was displaced by Preesgwyn Colliery (SJ 293363) whose components in the 1880s included a headstock above a 152m shaft, a tall chimney, a powder magazine, a smithy, screens and railway sidings. The colliery had closed by 1900 but its site became the terminus of the 3.2km mineral railway from St Martin's (or Ifton Heath) Colliery authorised in December 1915.[26] Miners were taken from Weston Rhyn to St Martin's along the mineral line in three ex-GWR six-wheel carriages. Garden City style cottages in Weston Rhyn were commended by the Council for the Preservation of Rural England in the late 1920s, and Salop County Council built a new school there in the early 1930s.

Mining in the eastern townships of St Martin's was on a small scale in the mid 19th century. In 1851 the Flanag pit (SJ 323397) was being worked by a spinster, Magalene (*sic*) Evans, who employed 12 men and five boys. Most of the coal was used in the manufacture at Duddleston of bricks, tiles and black and brown earthenware. Ten years later it was worked by Evan Davies, a local preacher as well as a miner, who employed 13 men and four boys. The Wigginton Colliery in 1857 was worked by four partners, all of them illiterate.[27] From *c*.1880 the area round the parish church became the chief focus of mining. The number of miners in Wigginton and Ifton grew from 101 in 1881 to 181 in 1891. A new shaft was sunk by W.T. Craig & Son in 1912 at Ifton Heath, where production began

The yard at Ifton Colliery, St Martin's (SJ 323363), not long before its closure in 1968

The pithead baths at Ifton Colliery, St Martin's (SJ 323363)

in 1921. Two years later it was linked underground with the earlier Brynkinalt pit, and the two were developed jointly into the largest mine ever worked in Shropshire, which employed 1,357 men by 1928. It was closed in 1968.

The new pit stimulated growth in St Martin's village, although many miners lived at Weston Rhyn which became a dormitory satellite. A mass of small fields around the pit suggest that the northern part of the village had squatter origins, and the irregular pattern of the older housing in the area appears to predate the modern roads. St Martin's was a 20th-century village, and had none of the long terraces typical of Victorian mining settlements. The village takes its character from houses like those at Garden Village (SJ 321367), a T-plan cul-de-sac of semi-detached pairs in Ruabon brick on the ground floors, with rough-cast first floors, low-pitched slate roofs and integrated porches. A Methodist church in Tudor Revival style has rough-cast walls rising from a stone plinth. The Miners' Welfare, with its Baroque lozenge windows, remains at the centre of the village. Part of the site of the pit is used by road transport contractors, while the Cubist pithead baths building has been adapted as industrial units.

The Clee Hill Coalfield

The mines on the Clee Hills, between Bridgnorth and Ludlow, the highest points in Shropshire, form a coalfield unusual for its situation, its longevity, and for the variety of its manufactures. Almost all of it lies above the 1,000ft contour, and workings are recorded from the 13th century until the 1930s. Numerous bell pits remain on the slopes of the hills. The coal seams on Brown Clee, Titterstone Clee and around the village of Clee Hill lie below and around the dolerite or dhustone, which was penetrated by shafts into the coal

A bell pit was a shallow shaft up to about 10m in depth. Miners excavated coal from all sides creating a bell-shaped cavity which, once the mine was abandoned, left a saucer-shaped depression on the surface. This example is from Catherton Common on Clee Hill (SO 630782).

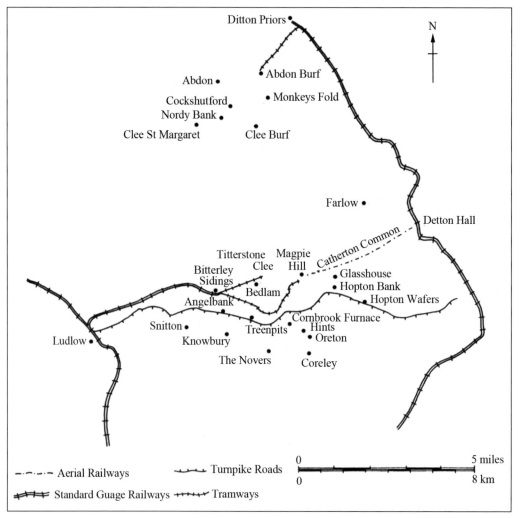

The Clee Hill Coalfield

measures from the late 18th century. Since the 1860s the landscape has been re-shaped by quarrying of the dhustone itself.[28]

Brown Clee has two principal summits, Clee Burf and Abdon Burf, the height of the latter of which was reduced from 1,806ft to less than 1,800ft by 20th-century quarrying. Until the 18th century most of the summit was common pasture for surrounding parishes and parts remain unenclosed. A third, lower summit, Nordy Bank, shelters the squatter community of Cockshutford north of the hill.

The most prominent industrial monuments on Brown Clee are those of dhustone quarrying. From 1908 until 1936 a 2.4km long inclined plane lifted railway wagons 244m from Ditton Priors station yard (SO 610882) to the summit of the hill (SO 596866). The foundations of the winding drum remain, together with traces of the railway sidings where wagons were shunted by four standard gauge steam locomotives and two 2ft gauge petrol locomotives. Smith & Beddoes provide a detailed description of the railway system.[29]

Around the rim of the flooded quarry on the summit are ruins of crushing machinery, and a tarmac plant of concrete construction, built in the 1930s, remains at Cockshutford (SO 580850).

The mines on Brown Clee were more important as a source of iron ore than for the coal extracted from their thin seams. Ironstone was mined in the mid 17th and early 18th centuries, and in the 1830s Sir Roderick Murchison observed heaps of high quality ore lying on the hill.[30] The route by which ore was conveyed by packhorse down the track from Monkeys' Fold through Cockshutford and Clee St Margaret to the blast furnace at Bouldon can still be followed. Bell pits on Abdon Burf south of the inclined plane, below the 1,600ft contour (SO 597871) form an early industrial landscape of outstanding interest.

Some mines on the summit of Abdon Burf were 64m deep but all traces of them were destroyed by quarrying. The sites of some 19th-century shafts are evident on Clee Burf (SO 592844). Murchison noted in 1830 that they were between 12m and 73m deep. All were wound by windlasses, and funnels of canvas fixed to wooden frames were erected at pitheads to reduce the turbulence in ventilating systems caused by high winds on the exposed summit.[31] Twenty-two miners lived around Brown Clee in 1851, nine in the hill-side area of Ditton Priors in 1851, and 13 in Cockshutford and adjacent parts of Abdon. The total fell to ten in 1861, three in 1871 and to two in 1881. Ten years later one man and a 14-year-old boy were extracting coal in the area. The lack of turnpike roads around Brown Clee restricted the market for coal, but some was used in kilns between Cockshutford and Ditton Priors to burn the sandy limestone which underlies the Coal Measures.

Coal workings around Clee Hill village, south of Titterstone Clee, extended 7km east from Angel Bank and Knowbury to Hopton Brook and the edge of Catherton Common. The area includes parts of the parishes of Caynham, Bitterley, Coreley and Hopton Wafers. The early history of mining on the hill was analysed by Keith Goodman, who showed that large-scale extraction had begun by the 1660s.[32] Much of the area remains unenclosed. Many cottages on the common were built by squatters, and between 1745 and 1778 the number of cottages on the wastes of Snitton in Caynham parish increased from 49 to 68. The Knight family of Downton were mining ore for the blast furnaces at Charlcotte and Bringewood (Herefordshire, SO 453750) in the early 18th century. Ore was transported by packhorses but the construction of the turnpike road from Ludlow to Cleobury Mortimer opened up new markets for coal, and the passage of Mr Botfield's cumbersome coal wagons down Angel Bank was regarded as a characteristic feature of the area in the early 19th century. Output from the principal group of mines, those of the Earls of Craven, was estimated to be about 9,000 tons in the 1780s. By 1830 coal was being carried to Radnorshire and other parts of mid-Wales.[33]

Coal-using manufactures were established on Clee Hill in the 17th century. The lime kilns at Oreton and the Novers consumed small coal until the early 20th century. Bricks were being made at Hints (SO 611252) in the 1660s, and tobacco pipes from white clay deposits near Hopton Bank (SO 620768) in the 1670s.[34] The name of the settlement at Glass House (SO 626773) suggests that glass may have been made on the hill. There were several potteries, and by the 1690s *Clee Hill ware*, distinguishable from *Boslom ware* (i.e. Burslem) from north Staffordshire, was on sale in Ludlow.[35] Wares and sherds have yet to be identified and analysed but pottery manufacture certainly continued into the 19th century.

One potbank in the 1820s was on Angel Bank (SO 582758). Eight potters were working on the hill in 1851, but only one lived there in 1881, and he was out of employment.

The Industrial Revolution brought changes on the Clee Hills in the late 18th century with the introduction of new technologies in mining, and the establishment of ironworks. The principal agents of change were the Botfield family, ironmasters of Dawley, who from the 1780s worked the pits in Coreley township that belonged to the Earls of Craven. Mines on a high plateau from which streams flowed through ravines were drained relatively easily, but a navigable level serving the mines in Snitton township was proposed in 1778 and steam winding engines were introduced from the 1790s[36] Two substantial ironworks were built in the area during the Industrial Revolution. Each was sometimes called the Clee Hill Furnace, but they are better distinguished as the Cornbrook and Knowbury works.

The Cornbrook Furnace (SO 604754) was constructed in 1783-84 by Thomas Botfield, who considered at length whether it should be fired with coke or charcoal, and whether its bellows should be worked by steam or water power.[37] When the furnace was blown in it appears that it was fired with coke, and that its bellows were powered by the Corn Brook. In 1786 the furnace produced 822 tons of pig iron, but its output in 1796 was only 482 tons. It was out of blast in 1804, and produced only 292 tons in 1805. In the 1780s the pig iron was probably refined into wrought-iron at Botfield's Cleobury Dale Forge. By 1810 the furnace appears to have been blown out and it is doubtful whether it was ever commercially successful.

The shaft of the Cornbrook Furnace is no longer visible, but it may remain under the trees that now cover the site. The high level charging area can readily be recognised, and there are traces of a leat from the bubbling Corn Brook, which was later utilised to generate electricity. A waste tip remains, of hard, brittle, blue-black, glass-like slag intermingled with strata of a hardened, whitish material, rather like a coarse cement.

The ironworks at Knowbury (SO 580752) lasted rather longer, yet remained unrecorded in national listings. The blast furnace was built c.1804 by James George who worked the ancient charcoal-fired furnace and forge at Bringewood (Herefordshire). Knowbury produced 303 tons of iron in 1805. In 1825 it was reported to be out of blast, but it resumed operation, and a forge with puddling furnaces was built alongside. In 1845 and again in 1851 the furnace and forge, capable of producing 40 tons of wrought-iron a week, were offered for sale. The furnace was blown by a 34hp steam engine, whilst an engine with a 28-inch cylinder operated the rolling mill, and a smaller high pressure engine worked the forge hammer. Eighteen coke ovens stood alongside the furnace. Plateways and railways with wrought-iron rails provided transport within the site. The works was again offered for sale in 1853, together with associated coal mines and brickyards, the whole enterprise employing 13 steam engines.[38] Iron-making ceased but the manufacture of bricks and tiles continued into the 20th century. A residence, probably adapted from an engine house, remains on the site alongside a slag tip. John George Lewis, the last operator of the ironworks, sailed to New Zealand, arriving on the ship *Stately* on 22 February 1854. He developed coalmining in his adopted country, and died in Otago at the age of 88 in 1887 at the house which he named Knowbury Villa.[39]

The three principal coalmining enterprises on Clee Hill in the early 19th century were the Cleehill Colliery in Hopton Wafers worked by the Botfields, the Treen Pits in Bitterley, north of Clee Hill village, and the collieries alongside the Corn Brook in Coreley worked by J. & W. Pearson. Peter Hewitt showed that the Botfield mines achieved a peak annual output of 20,983 tons in 1845. Output remained just below 10,000 tons during the 1860s. Much of the coal mined in the 1850s was used for brick- and tile-making. There were only two brickmakers on the hill in 1841, but 40 in 1861, eight of them migrants from Broseley. Ten years later the trade had declined and only eight men were making bricks in the area.[40]

There were 193 coal miners on Titterstone Clee in 1841, 273 in 1851, 186 in 1861, and 194 in 1871, but only 99 ten years later. Catherton Colliery ceased work in 1889 and its site was destroyed by quarrying. Watsill mine closed in 1912 and Cutley in 1922, while the last workings in Knowbury were abandoned in 1908. The Barn Pit had 27 employees when it closed in 1927. A short-lived mine with a wooden headstock above a 73m shaft was opened at Coreley in 1935.[41]

From the 1860s the quarrying of dhustone became the principal industry of the Clee Hills. The economy of quarrying depended critically on railways. When the Ludlow & Clee Hill Railway was projected it was acknowledged that the market for Clee Hill coal in Ludlow had been destroyed by the delivery of coal from elsewhere by the Shrewsbury & Hereford Railway. It was anticipated that the railway to Clee Hill would stimulate iron-making and ceramics manufactures.[42] Iron-making proved to be beyond revival and brick-making enjoyed only a brief spell of prosperity, but quarrying flourished. The Clee Hill Dhu Stone Co. under the direction of William Clark began quarrying in 1863. Most stone was shaped into setts (small cube-shaped blocks used for paving city streets in the late 19th century) in sheds around the quarries. By 1881, 194 quarrymen were living on the hill, 75 of whom were sett makers. More than half were migrants from other counties, chiefly from the Mountsorrel district of Leicestershire. By 1893 the annual output of stone from the Clee Hill quarries totalled 90,000 tons.[43]

The Ludlow & Clee Hill Railway extended 8km from its junction with the Shrewsbury & Hereford Railway north of Ludlow station to Bitterley Sidings (SO 574768), at the foot of a 2km long self-acting inclined plane which raised wagons to sidings on the south

The sidings at the top of the incline from Middleton Sidings on the Ludlow & Clee Hill Railway (SO 590768)

side of the Dhustone quarries which were served by a system of 3ft gauge tramways. The railway was operated jointly by the GWR and the LNWR (later the LMSR), the usual practice being for Great Western locomotives to work between Ludlow and Bitterley, and for the North Western to keep a shunting engine in the sidings at the top of the incline. A concrete-framed shed was built to shelter it in the 20th century. At the end of the sidings (SO 599761) was a warehouse where goods from shops in Clee Hill village were received, and from where a standard gauge mineral line opened early in 1867 crossed the bleak, boulder-strewn common, past the boundary marker (probably of medieval date) known as the Stooping Stone (SO 604771) to Catherton Colliery (SO 611774).[44]

In 1881 another company, formed by William Field and John Mackay, opened quarries on land they leased on Titterstone Clee. They laid down a 3ft gauge railway system that extended down a long inclined plane, opened in May 1881, to Bitterley Sidings, where stone was transferred to standard gauge wagons.[45]

In 1909 Thomas Roberts, who had an engineering works in Ludlow, commenced large-scale quarrying on Magpie Hill (SO 313774) east of Titterstone Clee. Stone was conveyed to Detton Ford station (SO 663795), on the Cleobury Mortimer & Ditton Priors Light Railway, by a 5.6km-long aerial ropeway installed by J.M. Henderson of Aberdeen.[46] The development of quarrying brought new patterns of housing to the Clee Hills, such as the terrace at Bedlam (SO 582773) below the Titterstone quarries.

Field & Mackay began to manufacture tarmac on Titterstone Clee in 1911, and the quarries increasingly provided materials for roads designed for motor traffic. Quarrying reached a peak of prosperity in the Edwardian period. The population of the area reached 3,587 in 1901, then fell to 3,290 in 1911, and to 3,033 in 1921, before falling sharply to 1,856 ten years later. The demand for setts, the most labour-intensive quarry product, declined, although production continued until the 1950s. The Magpie Hill quarries closed and the Detton Hall ropeway stopped working by 1928.[47] The narrow gauge incline to Titterstone Clee survived the Second World War but ceased operation soon afterwards. The standard gauge incline to Clee Hill was closed in 1960 and the railway from Ludlow to Bitterley Sidings in 1962.

The Clee Hills remain one of the most interesting industrial landscapes in Britain. On Catherton Common is an area of bell pits where the nature of 18th-century and earlier mining can readily be sensed. The sites of two blast furnaces are evidence of the ambitions of the entrepreneurs of the Industrial Revolution. The cottages, crudely built in dhustone, and extended into terraces to accommodate succeeding generations, their plots delineated by low ramparts topped by hedges of holly, damson, crab apple and hazel, show the importance of squatter settlement, a key element in the industrialisation of other regions where the physical evidence has been destroyed by urban growth.

The Coalbrookdale Coalfield

The Coalbrookdale Coalfield is celebrated as the scene of innovations in iron-making in the 18th century, as a region whose growth after 1750 characterised the 'Industrial Revolution', and, above all, as the location of the Iron Bridge. In the 1970s and '80s the museum which takes its name from the bridge set internationally acknowledged standards for the conservation and interpretation of industrial monuments, which were recognised when the

Ironbridge Gorge was designated a UNESCO World Heritage Site in 1986. Nevertheless it is enlightening to examine the region in the context of other Shropshire coalfields.

The Coalbrookdale Coalfield is compact in area but rich in mineral deposits. It extends no more than 16km north to south from Lilleshall to Linley, and is nowhere more than 6km from east to west. Twenty-one seams of coal in the Lower and Middle Coal Measures bear specific names, indicating that they have been worked at some time in the past. Several seams of iron ore, of fire clay and brick clay have also been worked. Carboniferous limestone occurs at Lilleshall and around Little Wenlock, while the Silurian or Wenlock limestone forms Lincoln Hill, the east side of Coalbrookdale, and Benthall Edge. Brine, natural bitumen and sands that can be used for moulding in foundries are also found in the coalfield. The Ironbridge Gorge, where the River Severn passes through the Silurian Limestone and the Carboniferous Measures, was cut by the overflow of a glacial lake, and the river proved the principal outlet for the area's mineral wealth.[48] The natural resources of the Coalbrookdale Coalfield were infinitely greater than those of others in Shropshire, and the means of transporting them more convenient.

The economy of the coalfield expanded in the late 16th century and through the 17th century. Malcolm Wanklyn showed that the population of Broseley grew from less than 150 in 1570 to around 2,000 in 1700, while that of Benthall rose from less than 80 to more than 500. This prosperity was based on the export of coal, on the application of new technology to mining, and, increasingly, on coal-based manufactures.[49] In the 18th century the industrial uses of coal increased further, and in particular it came to be used in iron-making. In the 1750s nine blast furnaces were built in the coalfield, transforming its economy, which was dominated for more than a century by large concerns which leased mines from landowners, extracted coal, iron ore, clay and limestone, smelted iron in blast furnaces, refined pig iron in forges, made iron castings, put together machines in assembly shops, and sold coal, limestone, lime, bricks, pig iron, wrought-iron and iron products. The population of the coalfield increased from around 20,000 in 1760 to 34,000 in 1801, and exceeded 50,000 by 1851. The closing years of the 18th century and the first of the 19th century were a time of intellectual ferment, sometimes called the 'Shropshire Enlightenment'. Its industrial manifestations included a steam locomotive constructed at Coalbrookdale, and the contemplation given by William Reynolds and his colleagues to the establishment of an integrated chemical works at Coalport, and the building of an oil engine. This zeal for innovation subsided after Reynolds died in 1803. The iron industry suffered severely during the recession that followed the Napoleonic Wars. It recovered in the 1820s when new ironworks were constructed along the eastern edge of the coalfield, but never regained the intellectual energy that it displayed a generation earlier.

The region subsequently lost its zeal for innovation but in some areas remained in the vanguard of industrial progress. The Coalbrookdale Company was one of the principal manufacturers of decorative castings, some of which imitated those made in Germany, Belgium and Sweden. The New Yard of the Lilleshall Company, built in the 1850s, was one of Britain's leading engineering works. The decorative tile factories built in Jackfield by Maw & Co. and Craven Dunnill & Co. were matched in size by only one other works in Britain. From the 1870s the ironworks began to close, the integrated companies were broken up and the economy of the coalfield went into decline, while its population fell as people sought employment elsewhere. Some companies, notably GKN at Hadley, prospered in the 20th century, and low labour costs and the availability of cheap housing, combined with the removal of the Woolwich Arsenal to Donnington in the late 1930s, created a veneer of economic well-being after the Second World War. Nevertheless traditional industries – mining, ceramics, ironworking, railways – continued to decline, and the underlying situation in the 1960s was not essentially different from that of three decades earlier when Ramsay Macdonald described the Wrekin area as 'a summary of the nation's problems'.

From the mid 1960s the coalfield was transformed by the creation of the new town of Telford, which brought to the region new

Coal seams revealed during open-cast mining at Little Wenlock, 1968.

The classic image of early mining in the Severn Gorge: George Robertson's engraving of a pit at Broseley published in 1788.

manufactures and transformed its housing and landscape. Traditional industries continued to decline. The last blast furnace ceased operation in 1959, the last coal mine 20 years later, large-scale tile-making ceased about 1970, and just one brickworks remains. Many monuments of the industrial past were conserved, particularly in the Ironbridge Gorge, but much archaeological evidence was lost. Some houses were recorded, if inadequately, and those parts of the canal system which disappeared were reasonably well documented and photographed. The opportunity presented by open-cast workings for coal and clay to learn more about early mining technology was largely lost. Some old workings with their pit props, and slack-filled gobs were photographed, and some tools, rails and pipes were retrieved, but the authorities resisted most demands for coherent programmes of recording.

The Coalbrookdale Coalfield: Settlements

The growth of mining and manufactures was not due just to natural resources and entrepreneurial will-power. It depended crucially on the availability of labour and of settlements where workers could live. Some parts of the coalfield were areas of open settlement, either common land on which newcomers could erect squatter cottages, or land of low agricultural value where owners readily permitted the construction or extension of dwellings. The Ironbridge Gorge is the prime area of such settlement but it also occurred in Broseley Wood, in parts of Little Dawley, at Ketley Bank, at Wrockwardine Wood and in smaller pockets. Such patterns of settlement began before 1600, but the earliest buildings of which there is archaeological evidence, whether surviving structures or photographs, date from the late 17th century, and it is clear that they were constructed by specialist builders.[50] Evidence from wills shows that many small houses were extended into terraces to accommodate succeeding generations of families.

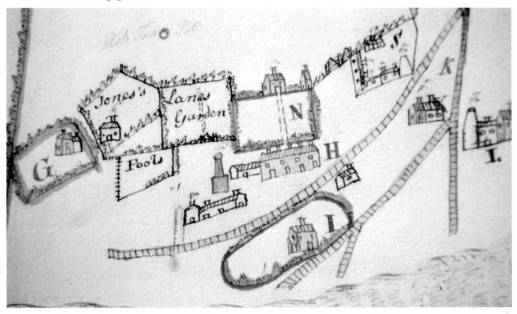

The landscape of squatter settlement in the Severn Gorge: an 18th-century map of the Calcutts from the Broseley Estate Book.

*The landscape of squatter settlement in the northern part of the Coalfield:
a postcard of Wrockwardine Wood, c.1910.*

The building of more formal terraced housing accompanied the growth of industrial enterprises in the mid-18th century. Tea Kettle Row (SJ 66604), the first terrace in Coalbrookdale, was built in three phases between 1735 and 1742 as a private speculation by Richard Ford, manager of the ironworks. Each dwelling had two rooms and a pantry.[51] When the Coalbrookdale partners set up the ironworks at Horsehay in the 1750s, a terrace of 27 four-room cottages, the Old Row (SJ 673072) was built in three stages and into the 19th century accommodated the more skilled workers. The company built a row of 28 back-to-back houses alongside their projected works at New Dale (SJ 674095) *c.*1760. Several rows of interlocking cottages with L-plans were built in Coalbrookdale in the 1780s and 1790s, of which Carpenters' Row (SJ 668046) and Engine Row (SJ 669048) remain. At Horsehay the New Row (SJ 672073), built in the 1830s alongside the furnace pool, with ceramic devices over the doors and drip moulds above the windows, was intended for

*The terrace of back-to-back cottages at Newdale (SJ 675095)
built by the Coalbrookdale Company c.1760.*

The terrace of interlocking L-plan cottages at Dark Lane (SJ 703087)
built by the Old Park Company c.1830.

'the principal workmen', while the plainer Sandy Bank Row (SJ 679066) and Frame Lane Row (SJ 677068), both now demolished, were designed for brickmakers. The Old Park Company built more than 50 houses near their ironworks in the 1790s. Some, in Forge Row (SJ 673093), were spacious and were doubtless designed to attract skilled workers at a time of labour shortage. All were demolished in the 1970s, as were the less eligible dwellings built by the company in the 1820s, the interlocking cottages at Dark Lane (SJ 703087) and the back-to-back row which formed part of the village at Hinkshay (SJ 696074). Terraces were also built by the Lightmoor Company, by the Madeley Wood Company at Blists Hill (SJ 696036), by William Reynolds at Coalport, and by James Foster, who in the 1840s established the village at The Aqueduct (SJ 694058) to accommodate workers moving from Wombridge to the Madeley Court ironworks. In the north of the coalfield the long terraces

Some of the cottages that comprised Hinkshay Row SJ 696075), built by the Old Park Company
in the 1830s to accommodate workers at the Hinkshay Furnaces and the Stirchley Ironworks.

97

A row of barrack houses *that accommodated limestone workers at Lilleshall (SJ 727154), now demolished.*

A cottage in the classic industrial settlement at Holywell Lane, Little Dawley (SJ 677058) showing the brewhouse that was a feature both of squatter and company housing.

Granville Buildings, St George's (SJ 706111), built c.1860 to accommodate workers at the Lilleshall Company's New Yard engineering works.

of single-storey cottages, known as *barrack houses*, appear to have been built in the 18th century, not by entrepreneurs, nor by landlords, but by speculators. Some isolated examples remain, together with a short terrace at Lilleshall (SJ 732164), but only maps now provide evidence of the long rows at Donnington Barracks and Waxhill Barracks.[52]

While the ironworking companies provided terraced housing, the tradition of squatter building continued. In 1772 there were six cottages in Holywell Lane (SJ 677058) in Little Dawley, but 20 more had been constructed by 1825, untidily crammed together on what had been garden plots, with the bedrooms of some dwellings extending over the ground floor rooms of others. The cottage from nearby Burroughs Bank (SJ 675056) which was removed to the museum at Blists Hill in 1978 was not built until the 1840s. It is a crude structure in Coal Measure sandstone with a roof of uncut timbers. It accommodated a family of nine in 1861. Building of squatter cottages at Ketley Bank was probably curtailed when James Loch became agent on the Marquess of Stafford's estate in 1812, and had probably ceased throughout the coalfield by 1850.[53]

St George's, which grew up in the 1850s and 1860s to accommodate workers at the Lilleshall Company's Priorslee Furnaces and New Yard engineering works, was formally named at a public meeting on 19 December 1859, and was the most urban part of the coalfield. While its communal facilities were provided by the Lilleshall Company or the Dukes of Sutherland, its terraced housing appears to have been constructed by speculators.[54]

The coalfield failed to develop a single commercial, administrative and cultural centre. Only at Ironbridge were shops and public buildings consciously designed to be part of an urban landscape. The settlement at the north end of the bridge was developed in the last 20 years of the 18th century, probably by the bridge proprietors acting in other capacities. Most of the buildings which overlook The Square have a distinct urban quality, but the

The commercial centre at the north end of the Iron Bridge (SJ 672033)
was one of the few consciously urban landscapes in the Coalfield.

shops on its fringes are domestic in scale. Further buildings of some distinction were built in the early 1860s when the Severn Valley Railway was opened. The *Station Inn* on the south bank of the river, the police station and St Luke's School were all constructed with the blue bricks which were produced for a short time by the Coalbrookdale Company.[55]

Archaeological study of other retailing centres – Dawley, Madeley and Oakengates – shows that almost all the shops, public houses and even the branch banks were built in the mid 19th century and were domestic in scale, probably replacing the first generations of buildings on the sites concerned. Few are more than three bays wide or more than two storeys in height. Most look like converted houses even if they were built as shops. Competition between centres, between Broseley, Ironbridge and Madeley in the south, and between Wellington, Oakengates, St George's and Dawley in the north, prevented the emergence of any one of them as the acknowledged urban centre of the region.[56]

The Coalbrookdale Coalfield: Markets and Transport

One difference between the Coalbrookdale Coalfield and others is expressed in two archaic expressions, *landsale* of coal, which occurred in all the Shropshire mining regions, and *Severn sale*, the despatch of coal along the river, which was significant only in the Ironbridge Gorge. There was some landsale in the Coalbrookdale Coalfield – a railway in the 1740s took coal from the Horse Pasture workings in Wombridge to a wharf on Watling Street, somewhere on the site of the main street of Oakengates (SJ 697109); coal from Little Wenlock was conveyed to a wharf at the Old Hall (SJ 656110), also on Watling Street; and the Donnington Wood Canal, dug in the 1760s, terminated at a landsale wharf on the Newport-Wolverhampton road at Pave Lane (SJ 760115). Nevertheless, it was the trade in coal on the Severn which was the basis of the area's prosperity from the late 16th century until after 1850. In the 1660s it was claimed that the coal trade supported 2,500 families, and that as much as 100,000 tons of coal per year were sent down the Severn from the Gorge. By 1800 around 50,000 tons were being despatched from Coalport alone, a total which reached a peak of nearly 80,000 tons in 1830. Navigation on the Severn was unpredictable, but the river remained the chief outlet until the third quarter of the 19th century, not just for coal but for all the varied products of the coalfield.

The role of the Severn was emphasised by the early railway systems which terminated at wharfs on its banks.[57] The first to be recorded ran from Birch Leasows, near Broseley parish church (SJ 678014) to a riverside wharf near the Calcutts (SJ 686030) and was the subject of a dispute in the court of Star Chamber in 1608.[58] When, in 1634, John Weld wrote a memorandum on the prospects for his Willey estate, he mentioned railways in a way that shows that they were an accepted and unremarkable part of the local landscape. At least five lines ran to the Severn by 1700. Most early railways had few cuttings, embankments or bridges of note, and they have left few traces, even in ploughed soil. A flanged wheel, found at Caughley early in the 20th century and now in the custody of the Ironbridge Gorge Museum, is one of the few surviving artefacts of early Shropshire railways. Shaped from a single block of elm, it is 25cm in diameter over the flange, and 20cm over the tread, the latter being 9.5cm wide. Some wooden railway track was uncovered near the Bedlam Furnaces in 1986. Rails and sleepers were of oak, the gauge was 1.14m

The wooden railway wheel found at Caughley in the 19th century, now held at Ironbridge.

(3ft 9in), and furnace slag had been used as ballast.[59]

Iron wheels for railway vehicles were cast at Coalbrookdale in 1729, probably for a line built by Richard Hartshorne from Little Wenlock to the riverside wharf at Strethill (SJ 658041). From the 1750s a system of wooden rails known as 'double way' was devised, and was observed in 1767 by the young Joseph Banks. In that year iron rails, 6ft long, 3¼in wide and 1¼in thick (1.85m x 8.26cm x 3.18cm) were used by Richard Reynolds to replace the top layers of wood. Rails of this kind found at Blists Hill in the 1990s are displayed in the Museum of Iron, and after their discovery similar rails were recognised, incorporated within the waterwheel pit and the Snapper Furnace at Coalbrookdale.[60] In the late 1780s, at the instigation of the Sheffield coal viewer John Curr, L-section iron plate rails, known in Shropshire as *jinny* or *jenny rails* were introduced, necessitating the replacement of flanged wheels by smooth-rimmed wheels on railway vehicles. The new system had many advantages, and wooden rails and iron edge rails appear to have been replaced quickly.[61]

Plate rails in wrought-iron or cast-iron are frequently found in the coalfield. Sleepers were mostly of cast-iron but some wrought-iron examples have been collected, together with some stone blocks, and documentary sources show that wooden sleepers were used on some lines. Archaeological investigations have demonstrated a contrast between those plateways which were laid simply, for such purposes as carrying waste to tips, and others which were constructed with great care, with sleepers at the joints and mid-points of rails, brick trotting paths between the rails, hammered clay over the sleepers at joints, and wooden longitudinal sleepers beneath the rails. Railways of at least six gauges were used in the area, and the Coalbrookdale Co. had some dual-gauge plateways, of which a siding remains *in situ* at Rose Cottage, Coalbrookdale (SJ 668041). The characteristic early railway vehicle, with low sides, so that minerals had to be affixed by wrought-iron hoops, was unaffected by the introduction of plateway track. Some specialist vehicles were used. A box wagon with a sloping top is shown in an early 19th-century picture. A tank wagon appears in a photograph of the 1860s, and a similar vehicle, once used for carrying waste tar at Horsehay, is preserved at Blists Hill, together with chassis of conventional wagons from the Coalbrookdale and Madeley Wood companies. The Ironbridge Gorge Museum holds a collections of rails, sleepers and wagon wheels, with some stone blocks from the Yard Rails at Donnington Wood (SJ 706124). The longest plateway, extending 9km from Oakengates to Sutton Wharf (SJ 709015), was built in 1797, and closed, by agreement with the rival

A stone sleeper block from the Yard Rails, Donnington Wood (SJ 706124), now held at Ironbridge.

Wrought-iron, T-section Birkinshaw rails uncovered during building work in 1969, part of the railway system installed by James Foster when the Madeley Court furnaces were being built.

The archaeology of early railways

Plateway track carefully laid by the Madeley Wood Company at Blists Hill, excavated in 1968.

Dual gauge plateway track at Rose Cottage (SJ 668041) that formed a siding off the Coalbrookdale Company's 'main line' through the Dale.

Shropshire Canal Co., in 1814. Excavations on its course through Halesfield in the 1960s revealed that its trotting path was made from puddling furnace slag. The density of the mid-19th-century network of plateways in the coalfield is illustrated on Greenwood's map of 1827. Plateways acted as feeders to standard gauge railways, which crossed them on bridges which allowed them much narrower tracks than those for roads, examples of which survive at Lightmoor (SJ 677050) and Trench (SJ 683126). Plateways were used on a small scale into the 1960s.[62]

The most impressive civil engineering monument of an 18th-century railway in Shropshire is a two-arch masonry bridge over the Ketley Brook at Newdale (SJ 675095), probably of *c.*1760. The high-level latticework bridge across Lee Dingle (SJ 694035), built in the 1880s, is evidence of the continuing use of plateways through the 19th century. Several early railways descended the slopes of the Ironbridge Gorge on inclined planes, the first of them before 1750. The best traces of such inclines are at Bagley's Wind (SJ 693036)

The imagery of early railways

Little Dawley's Bath Spout (SJ 675063), a spring whose curative properties were highly rated, still ran out of the ground on a plate rail in the 1960s, as it did when this post-card was published half-a-century earlier.

One of the railway inclined planes that descended the sides of the Ironbridge Gorge. A water colour of the 1830s by the china painter Phillip Ballard.

The two-arch railway bridge at Newdale (SJ 676095), which probably dates from c.1760.

west of Blists Hill, on Benthall Edge, rising from the lime kilns alongside the Severn Valley Railway (SJ 666034), and the Old Wind above Coalbrookdale (SJ 670015), but there were others that are currently untraced. The outstanding innovation in railway mechanical engineering was the construction at Coalbrookdale by Richard Trevithick in 1802 of one of the first steam railway locomotives. There is no evidence that it was set to work, and the death of William Reynolds in 1803 may have brought the experiment to a halt. Parts that survived into the 1870s have been lost. A drawing survives in the Science Museum and was the basis of a working replica that now runs at Blists Hill. The discoveries about the original made during the reconstruction have yet to be published.[63]

Innovation in railway technology ceased with the building of Trevithick's locomotive, and the developments from which evolved the main line railway in 1830 took place in the north of England. Archaeological evidence has revealed just one intermediate phase in the Coalbrookdale Coalfield, the construction by James Foster of narrow gauge lines laid with Birkinshaw track, wrought-iron, T-section edge rails set in cast-iron sleepers, when he developed the Madeley Court collieries and ironworks in the 1840s. Samples are held by the Ironbridge Gorge Museum. In the 1830s Foster had supplied similar rails to the Liverpool & Manchester Railway.[64] In the 1920s and '30s several companies replaced or supplemented plateway systems with narrow gauge 'Jubilee' edge rails of the type used on the Western Front during the First World War.

The main line railways from Shrewsbury to Wellington and thence to Stafford and Wolverhampton opened in 1849. Lines which ultimately belonged to the Great Western extended from Wellington and from Madeley Junction near Shifnal to Lightmoor and Coalbrookdale, crossing the Severn by the Coalbrookdale Company's Albert Edward Bridge, opened in 1862, and joining the Severn Valley Railway at Buildwas Junction. The London & North Western Railway converted much of the Shropshire Canal, which it owned, into the branch line from Hadley Junction to Coalport.

Most of the principal ironworking companies built their own links to mainline railways. The most extensive system was that of the Lilleshall Company, built in 1851-55, which

A dome-shaped crossing-keeper's shelter recorded in 1986 on part of the Lilleshall Company's mineral railway system near Donnington (SJ 703136) which was closed by 1887.

joined the LNWR at Donnington (SJ 705141) and the Great Western at Hollinswood (SJ 706091). At its maximum extent during the First World War the system totalled 42 track km, with 200 wagons for use on the main lines and 250 whose use was confined to the company's own tracks, and was worked by five locomotives. The principal engine shed adjoined the New Yard works (SJ 704116). During a century of operation, 22 locomotives were used, six of them built by the company. Crossing keepers' shelters, dome-shaped and constructed with bricks, were an unusual feature of the line. An example recorded in 1986 was 2.85m high and 2.5m in diameter. The company staff marked the closure of the system in 1959 by a rail tour in open wagons headed by the locomotive *Constance*.[65]

No Lilleshall Company locomotives survive, but one of the six saddle tanks built by the Coalbrookdale Company when standard gauge tracks reached Coalbrookdale in 1862-63 is displayed by the Ironbridge Gorge Museum, and another adapted for Sentinel drive also survives. Other companies who used locomotives for shunting sidings were the brickworks of William Exley at Jackfield, connected to the Severn Valley Railway, where traffic ceased in 1956; the Hadley Castle Works of GKN Sankey, rail-served until 1972; C. and W. Walkers' factory at Donnington where three saddle tanks worked until 1952; and the Old Park Ironworks, which closed before the end of the 19th century.[66] In the 20th century connections were laid to the Ordnance Depot at Donnington where conventional traffic ceased in 1991. A freight terminal on land that had been part of the depot, 4km from Wellington station on the former line to Stafford, was opened in 2009, but has failed to attract the anticipated traffic. The Ironbridge Power Stations were served by rail from the time that the 'A' station opened in 1932 until the 'B' station closed in November 2015.

The construction of the first tub boat canal in the coalfield was foreseen in the agreement of 1764 which established the Lilleshall Company (not then so named), and within a few years a canal linked the mines at Donnington Wood (SJ 705125) with a landsale wharf at Pave Lane (SJ 760165) and with limestone quarries at Lilleshall. A tunnel-and-shaft

The curious tunnel near the western terminus of the Wombridge Canal (SJ 609115) revealed by roadworks in the late 1960s.

system, replaced in 1796 by an inclined plane, achieved a change of level of 13m at the junction of the Lilleshall and Pave Lane lines at Hugh's Bridge (SJ 740151), and seven locks took boats 10.6m down to the level of the canal at the Lilleshall quarries where the line terminated in three distinct branches. In 1798 the canal was principally worked by rectangular boats measuring 20ft x 6ft 4in (6m x 1.9m), 70 carrying eight and 20 carrying five tons, but 19 boats were of approximately twice that size. In 1787 the ironmaster William Reynolds built the 2.8km Wombridge Canal from a junction with the south end of the Donnington Wood Canal to mines near Wombridge Church. Its only engineering feature of note was a seemingly inexplicable tunnel near the church (SJ 691115) which was visible for a time during roadworks in the 1960s. In the same year Reynolds built a canal servicing his ironworks at Ketley, which was approached by an inclined plane (SJ 679108), a pair of railway tracks on which boats were conveyed 22m in cradles to and from a level serving the works. A short tunnel nearby (SJ 683110) is blocked but probably intact.[67]

In 1788 an Act of Parliament was obtained for the Shropshire Canal by which the iron-masters of the coalfield hoped to convey their produce to the Severn. It began at a junction with the Donnington Wood Canal and ran though Oakengates, where it was joined by the Ketley Canal to Southall Bank (SJ 694065), from where one branch, probably opened in 1793, led to the eastern end of the Ironbridge Gorge, to the settlement which was to gain the name 'Coalport'. The other line, operating by 1791, followed a circuitous course which was intended to terminate by the Severn, but ended at Brierly Hill (SJ 670051) above Coalbrookdale, whence a tunnel-and-shaft system conveyed cargoes to plateway wagons which took them to the riverside. Three inclined planes were built, at Wrockwardine Wood (SJ 702123), Windmill Farm (SJ 693064) and The Hay (SJ 695028). They followed a design by Henry Williams and John Loudon, which utilised docks at the summit instead

The wrought-iron tub boat, typical of those used on the canals of the Coalbrookdale Coalfield, restored by the Ironbridge Gorge Museum in 1973.

One of the few photographs of the Hay Inclined Plane (SJ 695028) taken while it was still workable if not working.

The Hay Inclined Plane (SJ 695028) in 2002 about 35 years after its initial clearance.

of the locks employed on Reynolds' Ketley Canal. A steam engine provided water from reservoirs at Hinkshay (SJ 695070). A stone aqueduct crossing the turnpike road on the borders of Dawley and Madeley (SJ 694058) gave the name 'Aqueduct' to the adjoining settlement. The canal company paid substantial dividends, but by the 1840s its fabric had been severely damaged by subsidence. As part of the Shropshire Union Railways & Canal Co. it was acquired by the London & North Western Railway, and closed, apart from the section between Tweedale (SJ 701050) and Coalport. Much of the canal bed was used for the railway from Hadley Junction to Coalport opened in 1861. The Hay Inclined Plane worked for the last time *c*.1890, after which only the 1.5km stretch of canal between Tweedale and Blists Hill remained in use.[68]

Many surviving features of the tub boat system were recorded by industrial archaeologists in the 1960s, notably by the late W.H. Williams and by Roger Tonkinson, who provided a definitive record of the inclined planes.[69] Relatively little now remains. The section of canal through the museum at Blists Hill is still in water, as is a curving stretch by-passed by the railway which is now in the Hinkshay Nature Study Area (SJ 695071). Several stretches near Lilleshall can be followed on footpaths. The Trench incline on the Shrewsbury Canal (SJ 688121) was destroyed by a new main road. The foot of the Wrockwardine Wood incline was obliterated when bungalows were built in the 1960s, and the section immediately above by a new road in the 1980s, but the remainder survives as a track. All traces of Windmill Farm were destroyed when the Brookside estate was built.

The slope of the Ketley incline disappeared under a housing estate in the 1970s. Hugh's Bridge (SJ 740150) remains in rural seclusion, the lines of both the upper and lower canals surviving, together with the embanked slope of the incline and the portal of the tunnel-and-shaft system which preceded it. The Hay Incline, part of the museum at Blists Hill, is much visited, although excavation still has more to reveal of its history. The basin at the Brierly Hill interchange above Coalbrookdale remains, together with the cutting of the plateway incline that replaced the tunnel-and-shaft system after 1794.[70]

The movable effects of the Shropshire Canal were sold in 1861 and included the engines from the Wrockwardine Wood and Windmill Farm inclines, of 20 and 22hp, the beam pumping engine from Hinkshay, three oak incline carriages with cast-iron wheels, the building materials that once comprised a ticket office, and 26 iron and 20 wooden tub boats.[71] It is evident that many tub boats were made of wrought-iron and fortunate that one which served as a water tank on a farm near Newport has been preserved at Blists Hill since 1973. An unsuccessful attempt was made to preserve a wooden boat from Tweedale, but the remains of another are in the bed of the canal near the Lubstree Wharf (SJ 686163).

The Coalbrookdale Coalfield: Coal-mining

The Coalbrookdale Coalfield was the birthplace of the longwall method of mining coal, by which the whole of a seam is removed and the roof of the resulting space (known as the 'gob' or 'goof') is sustained by pit props. Malcolm Wanklyn showed that in the mid 17th century there were drift mines up to 1,000 yards long in Madeley Wood where the method was possibly pioneered.[72] The earliest archaeological evidence of mining is not of such large-scale operations but of humble bell pits, which are difficult to date. Landscapes of bell pits remain at the Deer Leap (SJ 668015) in Broseley, and in the woods near Caughley (SJ 695001).[73] Many of the mines in the Severn Gorge were adits (horizontal drifts driven into the sides of hills), which are illustrated on 17th-century maps. One, from which the Crawstone iron ore was extracted, remains in Ironbridge (SJ 670035) in good condition.[74] Roadways give access to the face from which the ore was extracted by longwall methods. The last adits in the Gorge, clay workings on the south bank of the river near the Iron Bridge (SJ 670032), were worked until 1953, and remained recognisable as mines in the 1960s, but slumping has reduced them to mere depressions amongst the trees.

The first steam engine to drain a mine in the coalfield was probably set to work in Madeley in 1719. Within a few years the Coalbrookdale Company was casting iron cylinders for such engines and installed several more in the following decades. At the Lloyds (SJ 688031) is a pumping shaft in which the pump rod of the last engine remains, alongside the foundations of the last engine house. It is possible that this is the site of one of the earliest engines in the coalfield, erected during the 1720s. There were probably between 20 and 30 pumping engines in local mines by 1800. The first colliery winding engine in the coalfield was probably installed at Wombridge in 1787 and such engines quickly became dominant features of the landscape. An aged miner born in 1779 recalled the time when 'there was not a single steam engine in the district to draw up the coals'. There were probably more than a hundred steam winding engines in operation by 1800, suggesting a substantial increase in coal production in the previous decade. Many more were built in the 19th century.[75] The foundations of some engines have been revealed during building

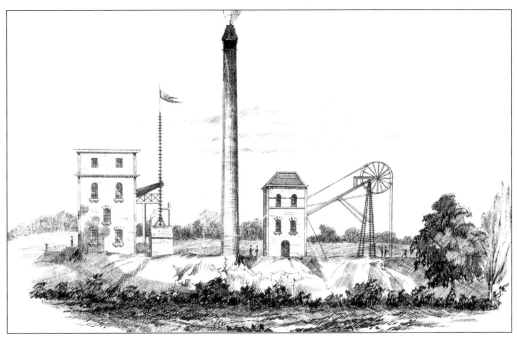

A drawing from a geological section of the Granville Mines (SJ 725120) made in 1864 by T. Doody. The engine house on the left accommodates a Cornish pumping engine, while that on the right contained a vertical winding engine.

developments but few survive to be examined. At Blists Hill (SJ 694034) are the foundations of a Heslop engine built in the 1790s and, with amazement, observed working by a visitor from New York in 1912.[76] The nearby horizontal winding engine was removed from the Milburgh Tileries, Jackfield (SJ 684026) and occupies the site of a somewhat larger engine. The winding engine house at Muxton Bridge Colliery (SJ 722133), which dates from *c.*1884 and accommodated two horizontal engines which worked until 1912, remains in Granville Country Park alongside fragments of an earlier beam engine house. The only headstocks remaining *in situ* are those of Granville Colliery (SJ 721114), the last deep mine in Shropshire, which worked until 1979. The surface area of the colliery has been adapted as the headquarters of a naturist club. Some surface buildings remain of the Madeley Wood mine within the Halesfield industrial estate (SJ 713055). Components of collieries discovered during archaeological investigations include a horse gin found in 1987 near Granville Colliery (SJ 711117) of which an oak rope roll nearly 2m in diameter remained, and a powder house, built by the Madeley Wood Company in the 19th century, which measured approximately 10m x 10m, had a brick-vaulted roof, and was built into a hillside.[77]

The Coalbrookdale Coalfield: Manufactures

Lime-burning was perhaps the oldest coal-dependent manufacture in the coalfield. The Silurian limestone on Benthall Edge was quarried as early as the 13th century. Kate Clark used a Harris Matrix to show that the first stage of subsequent large-scale extraction was concerned with the beds of stone best suited for use as flux in blast furnaces, and documentary

Lime kilns on the Wharfage at Ironbridge (SJ 668034)

evidence shows that limestone from Benthall Edge was used at Coalbrookdale in the early 18th century. The lower quality beds were quarried later for lime-burning. There is little evidence of lime-burning during the first stage of exploitation, but the tramway that was part of the later phase, running south away from the Severn, delivered stone to as many as 20 kilns. Another railway, constructed before 1801, descended by an inclined plane (SJ 666034) to the side of the river where a bank of kilns remains.[78]

The limestone workings on Lincoln Hill, Coalbrookdale, were more extensive. Many visitors in the late 18th century went to the Rotunda (SJ 668038), constructed by Richard Reynolds at the south end of the ridge, and looked down on a chasm, 400m long and 48m wide in 1758, on whose floor were ranks of kilns, and from which adits penetrated the cliff faces. The tithe map of 1847 marks 32 kilns in the area. The hill has been distorted by collapses and the tipping of waste, and the shafts that gave access to the underground workings have been grouted. Exploration in the 1970s when the mine was accessible revealed pillars up to 10m high and 7m square supporting a working area approximately 100m x 48m. Two lime kilns are preserved on the Wharfage, Ironbridge (SJ 668036) close to what appears to be a third, a substantial structure cylindrical in plan, which may have been painted by J.M.W. Turner and Paul Sandby Munn.[79]

By 1800 ironmasters were looking further afield for limestone. On the fringes of the Ironbridge Gorge supplies were obtained from the southern end of Wenlock Edge by tramways running from Gleedon Hill to a wharf on the River Severn by Buildwas Bridge (SJ 632041) and from Tickwood to the Stoneport (SJ 660038) further downstream.[80] Archaeological evidence shows that large scale lime-burning took place in the Ironbridge Gorge until the mid 19th century. The kilns were not well located for the distribution by road of agricultural lime, nor was the pace of building sufficient to account for the local use of all that was produced. A substantial river-borne trade in lime ended in 1854 when Hiram Hill of Benthall, one of the principal producers, sold his set of barges.[81] Small-scale workings continued on Benthall Edge and Lincoln Hill into the 20th century.

The mines and quarries of the carboniferous limestone outcrop at Lilleshall and Church Aston were chronicled by Adams and Hazeley.[82] Archaeological evidence for early working is provided by squatter cottages, one of which dates from 1681 or earlier. Large-scale extraction began with the construction in the 1760s of the Donnington Wood Canal, whose three branches extended into the quarries. Stone from some beds was burned to make hydraulic cement. Underground workings reached a depth of 75m, and stone was taken from beds up to 20m thick. By the 1840s stone suitable for fluxing in blast furnaces was running out in Lilleshall although some remained on the Church Aston side of the parish boundary. The underground workings flooded in 1860 and the principal site (SJ 735165) is now a lake, surrounded by vegetation and bounded on one side by a steep cliff of pink limestone. In the early 1880s more than 7,000 tons a year were being produced by more than 30 men. Traces of tramways, the canal system and shafts remain, together with several substantial kilns. The longer terraces of 'barrack' houses which accommodated miners and quarrymen hves been demolished, although a short row survives under cosmetic timber-framing (SJ 733165).

There were also workings in the Carboniferous limestone on the fringes of the Wrekin at Steeraway (SJ 694095) and The Hatch (SJ 645084). The former included underground workings. An early railway linked them with the Watling Street turnpike at the Old Hall (SJ 656110) by the 1730s, and carried limestone in the opposite direction to the furnaces at Horsehay in the 1750s. A steam winding engine was employed in the early 19th century in mines 36m deep. By the 1870s the two sites were in the same ownership and employed up to 20 men, but operations ceased in 1918.[83]

The manufacture of bricks in the Ironbridge Gorge appears to have commenced in the 17th century. The bricks used in the octagonal tower of 1618 at Willey Hall were

The Coalbrookdale Company's extensive brickfield at Lightmoor (SJ 676053) in the 1920s. A steam engine to the left is almost concealed by waste tips. Materials are being moved on a narrow gauge 'Jubilee' track railway system, probably military surplus.

The Lilleshall Company's Donnington Wood brickworks (SJ 712114) with its Hoffman kiln, one of a series of photographs taken for the Company in the 1930s.

almost certainly made in the area. Nevertheless the earliest surviving working-class houses in the Gorge are of Coal Measure sandstone, and some which do not survive were probably of more ephemeral materials. It was only in the 18th century that the one-and-a-half storey cottage with brick walls and a clay tile roof became commonplace. A cottage on Hodge Bower dated 1714 and Tea Kettle Row in Coalbrookdale (SJ 666047) built between 1735 and 1742 show that brick became the accustomed building material.[84] From the mid 18th century the Coalbrookdale Company began to exploit the deposits of clay between Lightmoor and Coalbrookdale, where brickmaking continued well into the 20th century, and many remains are now shrouded by trees. Brickmaking was part of the activities of most of the principal ironmaking companies from the late 18th century.

Roofing tiles were made at Jackfield from the mid 19th century in substantial manufacturing units some of which can still be recognised. By the 1840s there were up to half a dozen works in the riverside parts of Broseley, with sheds for clay preparation, moulding and drying, with round kilns and rectangular drying stoves on the downhill side of each complex. From the 1870s there was increasing mechanisation. The Milburgh Tileries (SJ 683025) at Jackfield, built by Thomas Prestage in the 1870s, continued in production until the 1940s, but was scarcely altered until the late 1960s when the steam engines and much of the production machinery were salvaged by the Ironbridge Gorge Museum. The brick and tile works at Blists Hill (SJ 695034) is well-preserved, and exemplified the semi-plastic process for making roof tiles introduced in the 1890s. Alfrey & Clark suggested that the huge dumps of waster tiles on the riverside in Jackfield are evidence of problems in production, the consequence either of attempts to use inferior clays or insufficient drying times. The tile manufacturers formed a trade association in the 1880s, after which their products were stamped with makers' names and with inscriptions indicating the type of tile, such as *Iron Broseley* and *Sovereign Broseley*. Some roofing tiles were fired in the same kilns as the characteristic buff-coloured bricks of the Ironbridge Gorge, and chevron-shaped 'kiss-marks' on the sides of bricks, indicating that tiles were laid on them during firing, can be seen in many buildings.[85]

Larger brickworks developed in the late 19th century in the northern part of the coal-field where the Blockleys works still flourishes (SJ 682120). The most spectacular was the Donnington Wood works of the Lilleshall Company (SJ 712114) of 1875, which had a 13-compartment, circular Hoffman kiln.[86]

An early 18th-century chamber pot, slip-washed, trailed and marbled, with a flat-topped rim, reassembled from sherds found at Jackfield in 1982.

The making of pottery was well-established in the Ironbridge Gorge in the early 18th century. Investigation of waste tips in the 1980s revealed evidence of the manufacture of plates, dishes, storage jars, chamber pots, mugs, teapots, coffee pots, posset pots, strainers and ointment pots. They were generally similar to contemporary wares in north Staffordshire, although decoration tended to be less ornate. Some white salt-glazed stoneware was found, as well as red-bodied earthenwares, slip wares and the black-glazed wares on red or buff bodies that are known to collectors as *Jackfield wares*. Systematic study of walls made up of waste materials revealed saggars with holes in their sides, which were used for making salt-glazed pottery. Similar wares were discovered in the early 1970s on a site at Little Wenlock (SJ 664069) that was occupied by a pottery in the mid 18th century.[87]

Alfrey & Clark used cartographic and archaeological evidence to show how the earthenware potworks evolved from a cottage with a kiln on the end into a semi-courtyard 'factory', exemplified in the 1720s by Morris Thursfield's works at Jackfield and in the 1770s at Benthall (SJ 668022). While earthenware manufacture continued in the Ironbridge Gorge in the 19th century, its scale remained modest, and Thursfield's pottery was displaced by the Craven Dunnill decorative tile factory. William Allen produced the well-regarded Salopian art pottery at Benthall between 1882 and the First World War.[88]

The name 'Broseley' was synonymous with clay tobacco pipes in the 17th century. Of all industrial archaeological artefacts, the tobacco pipe, usually stamped with its maker's name, and usually datable by its shape, is perhaps the most useful. The Broseley industry was studied in depth by David Higgins. The site of Henry Bradley's works at No.11 Lodge Lane, Benthall, dating from the late 17th century, was investigated in 1986. Remains

Tobacco pipes in a saggar in a works at Broseley in the 1930s

of a muffle kiln were found, together with about 100 mould types and different marks, suggesting that this was a sizeable workshop employing several journeymen. Richard Shaw's workshop of the early 19th century at Benthall Villa Farm, seems to have been a modest family-scale business.[89]

Only 12 men and six women were engaged in making tobacco pipes in Broseley and Benthall in 1841, but the industry subsequently boomed. The number of workers rose to 36 in 1851 and peaked at 91 in 1861. There were 74 in 1871 and 49 in 1881. The increase in the scale of production in the 1850s is reflected in the premises used and the numbers employed by the principal manufacturers, the Southorn family. In 1861 both William and Edwin Southorn employed 28, while seven people worked for Joseph Southorn. In 1871 Edwin Southorn had 40 employees, and in 1881 William Southorn had 70. William Southorn, born at Cardington in the early 1790s, probably established a pipemaking business in Broseley in 1823, which by 1838 was located off Legge's Hill (SJ 671023), and remained there until the 1930s. William's son Edwin set up an independent concern, taking over *c.*1850 the building alongside the *New Inn* at Benthall (SJ 670027) which had been the pipeworks of Noah Roden. He was credited with making some of the best English pipes of the period. After 1876 the works passed into other hands and probably fell out of use in the 1890s. An older building in King Street, Broseley (SJ 671022) was adapted for pipe-making in 1881 by R. Smitheman & Co., who employed five men and two boys. The Southorn family bought it in 1923 although they did not use it until the 1930s. Pipes were made there until 1960, using a kiln that remains a distinctive feature of the Broseley townscape. The factory is conserved and managed by the Ironbridge Gorge Museum.[90]

A late 19th-century photograph of the chinaworks at Coalport (SJ 696024)

The establishment of the china works at Caughley (SJ 697705) marked a revolution in the ceramics industries of the coalfield, both in technology, since the manufacture of porcelain was still new to Britain, and in the organisation of production. This was the first 'ceramics factory' in Shropshire, and was comparable to contemporary potbanks in north Staffordshire. The buildings were arranged in a square, and a clock was prominent on the front elevation. China clay and ball clay, imported from the west of England, were delivered by an early railway from a wharf on the Severn. Coal and refractory clay for saggars were obtained locally. The factory closed in 1814 and its buildings have disappeared, although excavations revealed sherds which considerably enlarged our knowledge of its products.[91]

The china works at Coalport (SJ 696024) was part of an ambitious plan by William Reynolds to create a new town alongside the interchange between the Shropshire Canal and the River Severn at the eastern end of the Ironbridge Gorge. The first part, the works of John Rose on the north side of the canal, was in operation by 1795, and the oldest surviving building, a three-storey brick structure of five bays, was built in that year. Essentially it is a building designed to accommodate workers sitting at rows of benches. The adjacent premises, occupied by Anstice, Horton & Rose, were incorporated into John Rose's factory in 1814, when the Caughley works was also absorbed and closed. The Coalport works remained one of the largest producers of pottery in England for much of the 19th century, employing at times up to 400 people, but there were few changes to the modes of production until Charles Bruff undertook major alterations from 1902. The works closed in 1926, when production was transferred to Stoke-on-Trent and the buildings were adapted for other industrial uses. Part was opened as a museum in 1976 and the site is now managed by the Ironbridge Gorge Museum Trust. Two bottle ovens remain, with part of a third, and in some of the buildings it remains possible to sense the workshop scale of operations. Excavations have added to our understanding of what was produced at Coalport, showing, for example, that mocha, marbled and cream wares were made during the factory's early years.[92]

The Coalport china works was dwarfed after 1870 by the construction of even larger ceramics factories on the opposite bank of the Severn. George and Arthur Maw, from Worcester, leased the former Benthall Ironworks in 1852, and began to manufacture encaustic tiles of the kind then in demand for the decoration and restoration of Gothic churches. In 1867 Henry Powell Dunnill, a Yorkshireman, moved to Broseley and took over the former Hargreaves & Craven roofing tile works. He formed a new company in 1870, and in 1871, when he was employing 89 people, Dunnill sought tenders for the construction of the Jackfield Encaustic Tile Works, opened with a 'warehouse warming' on 25 February 1874. The factory was designed by Charles Lynham, architect of many potbanks in north Staffordshire. Lynham was also commissioned by Maw & Co. to build a factory at Jackfield, which opened in 1883 and was reckoned the largest tileworks in the world in 1900. Both factories were designed for logical sequences of production, from clay reception and preparation to decoration, packing and selling. Both companies produced diverse ranges of tiles in the late 19th and early 20th centuries. Their products decorate state parliament houses in Canada and railway stations in India. The Craven Dunnill works closed in the 1940s, and after use as a foundry, is now part of the Ironbridge Gorge Museum. Most of the original buildings remain. The kilns have been demolished, but evidence of the foundations, together with those of the Ash Tree Pottery, which previously stood on the site, has been uncovered. The Maws factory closed in 1969 and is now a craft centre. Collections of samples and moulds are held by the Ironbridge Gorge Museum. Installations of tiles by Maw & Co. and Craven Dunnill are recorded in the Tile Location Index maintained by the Tiles & Architectural Ceramics Society.[93]

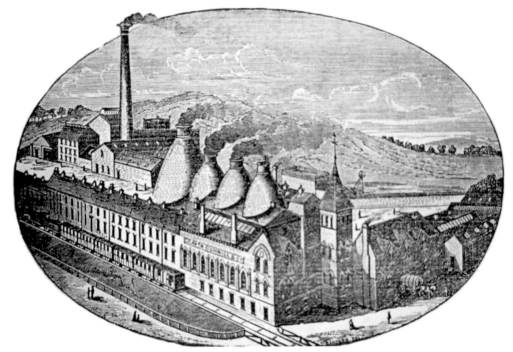

The tile factory of Messrs Craven Dunnill at Jackfield (SJ 686029)

The interior of the Mountain Daisy public house, Sunderland, with tiles by Craven Dunnill of Jackfield.

The first Abraham Darby and his partners smelted copper ores and made brass in Coalbrookdale in the first two decades of the 18th century, but brassmaking probably ceased in 1714, when the equipment was sent to Bristol. It is doubtful whether copper smelting continued after Darby's death in 1717, and there are no visible remains of either operation.[94] Nevertheless, the smelting of non-ferrous metals in the Ironbridge Gorge continued for most of the 18th century. By 1731 Thomas Barker had built a smelter in Benthall (SJ 671034) for lead ores mined by the London Lead Company at Llangynog (Monts.), which from 1739 was used for smelting ores from The Bog in Shropshire. The smelter was used at least until 1786, and appears in early views of the Iron Bridge, a single-storey structure with a clerestory ventilator in the roof and an iron-banded chimney. A second smelter in Benthall, close to the subsequent site of the Iron Bridge (SJ 673033), had been adapted as a malthouse by 1765. Fragments of the building remain in section on the river bank. A third lead smelter, known only from documentary records, stood on the

The lead smelter on the bank of the River Severn at Benthall (SJ 670033), recorded c.1780 in Michaelangelo Rooker's image of the Iron Bridge, by which time it was at least 60 years old.

boundary of the Coalbrookdale Company's property at Dale End (SJ 668036) and was working in the 1750s and 1770s. A fourth, whose name was preserved by the name of the terrace 'Smelthouse Row', stood on the river bank near Coalport (SJ 691028), and was worked by William Reynolds and his successors for a short time in the first decade of the 19th century. A piece of zinc blende (sphalerite) was found on the site in 1981. Nothing remains above ground of the lead smelters in the Gorge, one of which was described in 1746 as 'vastly poisonous, and destructive of everything near it'.[95]

Glassmaking was of modest importance in the Coalbrookdale Coalfield. A manufactory of both window panes and bottles, set up at Snedshill between 1673 and 1676, was working 20 years later, but there are no subsequent references to it and its precise site is unknown. There was also a short-lived glassworks at Broseley in the early 18th century. The erection of a glassworks at Wrockwardine Wood (SJ 698126) was proposed by William Reynolds in 1791, and it continued under different ownership until c.1841. Plans and an engraving show that there were two English glass cones. The works used crucibles made from local refractory clays, and for a time furnace slag was a raw material, along with sand from Little Dawley. The principal products were green bottles, but some jugs and 'friggers' (ornamental pieces) are held by the Ironbridge Gorge Museum and the Victoria & Albert Museum. Fragments of wasters and crucibles are occasionally found in the gardens of the dwellings which occupy the glassworks site.[96] William Reynolds also had an interest in an alkali works in the parish of Wombridge where for a short period after 1799 John Biddle used the process developed in France by Malherbes and Athenais to make sodium carbonate for use in glass manufacture.[97]

The only well-documented workings for salt in the coalfield were at Preston-on-the-Weald Moors (SJ 672148). Two adjacent works, one owned by the Charltons of Apley Castle, the other by the Newport family, pumped up brine which was boiled in iron pans, using coal from Oakengates, with the evaporation process accelerated by the addition of blood delivered in barrels from butchers' shops. The works were derelict in 1799 and probably never worked afterwards. Traditions that salt was produced from the 'Tar Tunnel' and other sources in the Ironbridge Gorge have yet to be confirmed by documentary or archaeological evidence.[98]

The manufacture of tar and other hydrocarbons had a long history in the coalfield. In 1696 Martin Eele set up cauldrons at Jackfield (SJ 686030) for extracting tar, pitch and oil from coal. An oily layer, which could have related to this period, was observed during deep non-archaeological excavations on the site in the 1980s. In 1786 William Reynolds drove a tunnel intended to accommodate a canal into the hillside on the north bank of the Severn (SJ 693025) near the settlement subsequently called Coalport. His miners struck a spring of natural bitumen which was collected and sold in barrels, initially producing as much as 55 gallons a week, although output had declined to no more than two or three barrels a year when production ceased in 1843. The tunnel was extended until it was more than 1,000m long, and served as a ventilation outlet and drainage level for mines in Madeley. From 1796 it was the route of a plateway which brought out coal from the mines. The tunnel was 'lost' for some years, but was explored in the 1960s by the Shropshire Caving & Mining Club, and a section was subsequently cleared of debris and opened to the public as part of the Ironbridge Gorge Museum.[99]

The Tar Tunnel at Coalport (SJ 693025) which produced bitumen for more than 50 years.

British Oil was being made in 1767 from bituminous rocks alongside the early railway between Coalbrookdale and Horsehay, and there was a range of 'coal tar buildings' at the Madeley Wood iron-works when it was purchased by Abraham Darby III in 1776. Two groups of kilns for making coke and utilising the by-products were built in the 1780s by Archibald Cochrane, 9th Earl Dundonald, who took out a patent for the process in 1781. A bank of 20 kilns, with adjacent plant for refining by-products was built alongside the Calcutts ironworks (685029) and a similar range at the Benthall furnaces (SJ 671030). The latter ceased working before 1799, but the Calcutts kilns were still in use when the ironworks was sold in the early 1830s. Coke was also made in kilns built by William Reynolds at Ketley and Madeley Wood in the 1790s, and by John Wilkinson at Willey. Nevertheless in the 1840s iron-works were using coke made by traditional open heap methods, which continued to be used at Blists Hill until 1912. The Lilleshall

While coke ovens were pioneered in the Coalbrookdale Coalfield by Lord Dundonald and others, much of the coke produced for blast furnaces in the late 19th century was still made in open heaps, as shown in this photograph of Blists Hill.

Company set up coke ovens at Lodge Bank (SJ 717121), which continued for 20 years after the blowing-out of the adjacent Lodge Furnaces, and at the Priorslee ironworks, where there were more than 40 beehive ovens by 1870. In 1912 the only integrated coke and by-product plant in Shropshire was built at Priorslee and continued until 1928.[100]

One of the most significant uses of steam power during the Industrial Revolution was in milling grain. At the very birth of the rotative steam engine, William Reynolds sought the advice of James Watt on the construction of an engine to power two sets of millstones. There were steam-powered cornmills, probably dating from the 1780s, near Reynolds' works at Ketley and Madeley, and more were built in the 19th century. The most significant survivor is the mill at Wrockwardine Wood (SJ 697126), a four-storey brick building alongside the canal, dating from 1818 when it had three sets of stones. The mill was the last customer whose boats used the canal inclined plane at Trench, and it continued to grind animal feed until the 1970s.[101]

The principal new use for coal in the 20th century was in generating electricity. There was no public supply of electricity in the coalfield until 1930, but in 1925 the West Midlands Joint Electricity Authority, a consortium of municipal and private undertakings, decided that Ironbridge (SJ 653042) was an ideal site for a large power station. Construction began in 1929, most of the plant and building materials arriving by rail. The generating plant began to work on 13 October 1932. The chief engineer was E.F. Hetherington and Ivor Daughtry acted as consultant architect. Initially just one 50MW generating set was used, but a second was installed in 1935-36, and two more in 1938-39. Wellington had received its first electricity supply via Bridgnorth in 1930, taking in current at a sub-station in Watling Street, topped with a pylon (SJ 663110), and with the opening of the Ironbridge station supplies were made available throughout the coalfield. A new station, 'Ironbridge B', was constructed on an adjacent site (SJ 658039) in the 1960s but ceased generating in November 2015. The 'A' station of 1929-32 was demolished in 1983 although the steel truss bridge over the Severn which provided road access remains in place. Coal from Halesfield Colliery was regularly carried to the 'A' station, and, until it ceased production in 1979, coal from Granville went to the 'B' station.[102]

The Coalbrookdale Coalfield: Iron & Engineering

The Coalbrookdale Coalfield was of most importance for its role in the manufacture of iron. In the late 17th century it was a source of iron ore, which was smelted at water-powered, charcoal-fuelled blast furnaces on the periphery of the coal measures, at Coalbrookdale, Kemberton, Leighton, Willey and Wombridge.

The mining of iron ore profoundly influenced the landscape. The Ballstone, Blackstone and Pennystone ores occur in nodules in strata of clay or shale. The whole of a stratum was mined by longwall methods, deposited on the surface and allowed to weather before gangs of women and girls collected the nodules in baskets and carried them to the 'ranks' where the ore was loaded into plateway wagons and taken to the furnaces. This was one of the principal forms of employment for women in the coalfield. The gangs seem to have been self-directing, once contracts were agreed with the iron companies. Each summer many young ore pickers migrated to London to work in market gardens. Middle-class objections to the employment of women as ore pickers seem to have been motivated as much by the self-reliance which it engendered as by the arduous nature of the tasks involved.[103] Tips of clay and shale, in which small, rejected nodules of iron ore can still be found, remain in many parts of the coalfield, most notably in Telford Town Park and the Granville Country Park.

Alfrey & Clark showed the significance of early investment in water power in Coalbrookdale, and how the concept of recycling water was introduced by Abraham Darby II, using horse pumps in 1734 and a steam engine by 1744. The system was extended with the installation of the *Resolution* engine in 1781, after which water from the Boring Mill Pool that had powered several wheels, flowed along a tunnel 800m long to be pumped 37m up a shaft from which it was released into the Upper Furnace Pool.[104]

Our understanding of the beginnings of the use of mineral fuel in the smelting of iron ore has been transformed in recent decades by the documentary researches of Peter King and Nancy Cox. It has become evident that iron-making in the late 17th century should not be seen as an isolated industry, but rather as part of a metals industry. The first Abraham Darby, who used coke to smelt iron ore at Coalbrookdale from 1709, owned a manuscript copy of Dud Dudley's *De Metallum Martis*, the printed version of which appeared in 1665. Capital for one of Dud Dudley's experiments, a furnace for smelting iron ore blown by a horse mill, which worked for some years until 1676, came from Sir Clement Clerke of Laund Abbey, Leicestershire. With his son Talbot Clerke, Sir Clement became involved with litigation relating to the use of reverberatory furnaces for smelting lead and copper ores. Sir Clement also had interests in 'The Company for Making Iron with Pit coal', which built a short-lived blast furnace at Cleator, Cumberland in 1694. The company had contacts with Shadrack Fox, who worked the blast furnace at Coalbrookdale from 1696, and it seems likely that he used coal or coke in smelting iron ore there. Certainly his brother Thomas Fox, who managed the furnace at nearby Wombridge, stocked coal there in 1701. The furnace at Coalbrookdale was damaged by an explosion, probably in 1706, after which Shadrack Fox left England for Russia.[105]

Abraham Darby I was born in 1678 into a Quaker family at the Wren's Nest in the Black Country, near the location of Dud Dudley's experiments. He was apprenticed to a maker of malt mills in Birmingham, moved to Bristol in 1698, and married Mary Sergeant the following year. From 1702 he was a partner with other Quakers in a brass works at Baptist Mills, where he doubtless gained some experience of the use of coal in smelting metallic ores. A year or so later he began to employ 'Dutchmen', probably from the brassworking area near Aachen on the borders of Germany, the Netherlands and Belgium, to work brass by 'battery', that is, beating it cold between water-powered hammers. In 1703 he set up an iron foundry in Cheese Lane, Bristol, and in 1707 took out a patent for casting bellied pots in sand rather than loam. He purchased pig iron from blast furnaces at Blakeney, Redbrook and Guns Mill in the Forest of Dean, and melted it in an 'air furnace', a reverberatory furnace of a kind with which he was familiar from his involvement in working brass.

Darby's presence in Shropshire was first recorded on 24 July 1706 when he witnessed the deed of purchase for the burial ground adjacent to the Friends' Meeting House at Broseley. About that time he and other Bristol Quakers established a brass works in Coalbrookdale that would have necessitated their withdrawal from the Baptist Mills partnership. Calamine, the zinc oxide used in making brass, was carried by barge from Bristol. Darby also set up a furnace in Coalbrookdale for melting copper, the other raw material used in brass-making, and on 29 April 1710 signed deeds granting him and his partners the rights to mine copper ore at Harmer Hill north of Shrewsbury. In June 1710 he became a partner in Tern Works, in the present-day Attingham Park, where it was intended to refine pig iron into wrought-iron, to roll brass plates and hoop iron, to make wire and to slit iron into nailers' rods. The brassworks at Coalbrookdale appears to have ceased operation in 1714, when its moveable equipment was carried down the Severn to Bristol, but the copper furnace may have worked until Darby's death in 1717, and the 'Copper House' and 'Copper Warehouse' survived to have their contents listed in an inventory of the Coalbrookdale works made in July 1718.

In 1708 Darby leased the blast furnace in Coalbrookdale and began to rebuild it that October. It was in blast by January 1709 and the regular workmen received their first wages on 17 January. One of them, Richard Dorrell (or Darrall), was paid for 'charking coals', showing that from the first it was fired with coke. Darby encountered difficulties with the furnaces over the next five years and carried out experiments with other fuels – charcoal, coke made in Bristol and coal (perhaps anthracite) from Neath, as well as a mixture of coke, brays (charcoal) and peat. The experiments were over by 1715, by which time it appears that the process was successful. Shipments of iron castings increased substantially from 1713 and in 1714 Darby was sufficiently confident in his process to build another blast furnace.[106]

Abraham Darby's use of coke in the smelting process at Coalbrookdale in 1709 stimulated the growth of iron-making in the coalfield, although it was not until the 1750s, in the time of the second Abraham Darby, that any degree of 'take-off' was achieved. The reasons for the delay are not wholly evident, although the iron that the first Darby produced was better suited to founding than for forging into wrought-iron, which restricted its sales. Moreover, there was probably no clear cost advantage in operating a furnace with coke rather than with charcoal. A change in the operation of the furnace, of which the details are uncertain, seems to have been achieved in about 1753, after which coke-blast iron found a ready market with forgemasters.[107] The second Abraham Darby built a furnace at Horsehay which came into blast in May 1755 and supplied the principal forges in the Midlands. In the next 45 years more than 30 blast furnaces were built in the coalfield, which in 1805 produced 50,000 tons of pig iron, a fifth of the national output. The proportion could have been much higher in the 1780s.

Coal and coke displaced charcoal in the forging of wrought-iron with the adoption of the 'stamping and potting' process patented by John Wright and Richard Jesson in 1773, and widely used in Shropshire, together with the puddling process, patented by Henry Cort in 1784, which gradually displaced 'stamping and potting' after 1800. Some Shropshire ironmasters adopted 'buzzing', the re-working of scrap wrought-iron which gave forgemen experience of reverberatory furnaces. A buzzing furnace was one of the first structures installed in a new forge at Old Park built by Thomas Botfield in 1789-90. The development by James Watt of the rotative steam engine freed ironworks from dependence on water power and by 1800 steam engines were operating bellows, hammers and rolling mills.

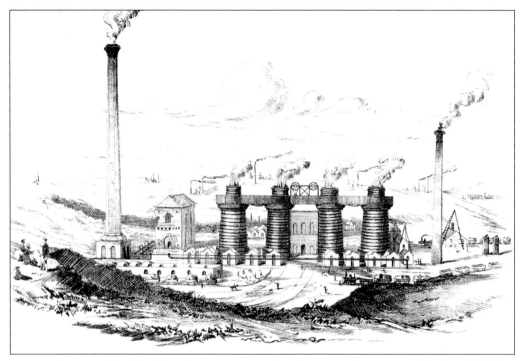

An early view of the four blast furnaces at Priorslee (SJ 702099) constructed by the Lilleshall Company in 1851. The engine house on the left accommodated the beam blowing engines David *and* Sampson, *now at Blists Hill.*

Some ironworks in the coalfield closed after the Napoleonic Wars as difficulties in finding markets were compounded by the exhaustion of mines. The industry recovered nevertheless. Twelve new blast furnaces were constructed between 1800 and 1851, while some older works remained in use. Production continued to rise, reaching a peak of nearly 200,000 tons in 1869, four times as much as in 1805, but by then only two per cent of national output. Subsequent decline was rapid. Most blast furnaces in the coalfield ceased to operate before 1900. The plant of the Stirchley Ironworks with a 100hp steam engine, three mill furnaces, a forge train, a guide mill and two steam hammers was sold in 1904 for £3,600.[108] The Blists Hill furnaces worked until 1912, and those of the Lilleshall Company at Priorslee until 1959. Only at Priorslee was a steel plant established alongside blast furnaces, and that only worked between 1882 and 1922.

Iron ore was smelted with coke at 32 sites in the Coalbrookdale Coalfield (see Table overleaf). There are substantial remains of blast furnaces at seven of them, and landscape evidence at others.

Much of the upper part of the water-power system at Coalbrookdale remains, including the Upper Furnace Pool and the New Pool further upstream. The furnace complexes constructed between 1755 and 1780 all used recycling systems copying that at Coalbrookdale. The pool at Horsehay, which, as hostile observers predicted, proved difficult to make watertight in 1754, is now all that remains of the ironworks. The pool system constructed by John Wilkinson for the New Willey furnace in the 1750s can still be traced, but a road of the early 19th century, built after the furnace was blown out, cuts through the bottom pool. The site of the Old Willey furnace can readily be recognised, on a hillside, supported by stone retaining walls and surrounded by slag. There are substantial remains of the dams of the Benthall ironworks. A different system was employed at Madeley Wood,

Name	Ancient parish	Grid reference	Approx. period of operation
Barnett's Leasow	Broseley	SJ 679032	1797-1830
Benthall	Benthall	SJ 672030	1778-1821
Blists Hill	Madeley	SJ 694033	1832-1912
Broseley	Broseley	SJ 682013	1806-1830
Calcutts	Broseley	SJ 686030	1767-1828
Coalbrookdale Lower	Madeley	SJ 667045	1714-1818
Coalbrookdale Upper	Madeley	SJ 667048	1638-1818
Coneybury	Broseley	SJ 683017	1786-1830
Dark Lane	Dawley	SJ 703086	1832-1875
Dawley Castle	Dawley	SJ 688061	1810-1883
Donnington Wood	Lilleshall	SJ 704125	1785-1859
Hinkshay	Dawley	SJ 693072	1825-1875
Hollinswood	Dawley	SJ 697108	1786-1793
Horsehay	Dawley	SJ 673071	1755-1862
Ketley	Wellington	SJ 670108	1758-1876
Langley Field	Dawley	SJ 600972	1824-1870
Lawley	Wellington	SJ 666094	1822-1866
Lightmoor	Dawley	SJ 682053	1758-1883
Lodge	Lilleshall	SJ 721123	1825-1888
Madeley Court	Madeley	SJ 698052	1845-1902
Madeley Wood (Bedlam)	Madeley	SJ 678033	1756-1840
Newdale	Wellington	SJ 672097	1759?
New Hadley	Wellington	SJ 682115	1804-1825
Old Park	Dawley	SJ 694094	1790-1873
Priorslee	Shifnal	SJ 702099	1851-1959
Queenswood	Wombridge	SJ 696108	1804-1815
Snedshill	Shifnal	SJ 701115	1779-1830
Stirchley	Stirchley	SJ 699074	1825-1885
Willey (New)	Willey	SJ 673006	1757-1804
Willey (Old)	Willey	SO 672978	1594-1774
Wombridge	Wombridge	SJ 691115	1818-1843
Wrockwardine Wood	Wrockwardine	SJ 702115	1801-1825

Table 4.1 Coke-blast furnaces in the Coalbrookdale Coalfield

where water was lifted from the Severn by a steam engine whose bob wall remains. It flowed into a substantial stone reservoir, still *in situ*, and from it through a deep wheel pit.

In 1780 John Wilkinson blew in a new furnace at Snedshill. Nothing has remained on the site for many decades but the furnace was important as the first to be built to be blown directly by a steam engine. Subsequent ironworks did not require water-powered blowing systems, and the development of the rotative engine in the 1780s obviated the need for waterwheels to work hammers and rolling mills. The best remaining blowing engine houses, one of 1841 and one of the early 1870s, are at Blists Hill, near the only remaining steam blowing engines in Britain, the pair of beam engines *David* and *Sampson*, constructed by Murdoch, Aitken & Co. of Glasgow for the Lilleshall Company's Priorslee furnaces in 1851, and a vertical engine once used in the same company's steel plant.

The Old Furnace at Coalbrookdale still has much to reveal to archaeologists. The furnace ceased operation *c*.1818, and in its present form probably dates from re-building after an explosion in 1801. The inscriptions on its lower beams were interpreted by a German expert on the rebus to mean 'Brooke, Basil & Ethelfleda: 1638: Ethelfleda and Basil Brooke'. Michael Vanns has argued convincingly that older pictures of the beam suggest that the date was 1658, and that the interpretation of it to read 1638 dates from the restoration of the furnace in 1959. In either case it is difficult to match the date with the documentary evidence that there was probably no blast furnace at Coalbrookdale before the outbreak of the Civil War in 1642, and that the Brooke family did not occupy the site in 1658. It was shown in 1981 that in its final years the furnace was blown from three sides, and there is plentiful evidence of a large-scale re-building before the furnace took its final form, probably when the beams inscribed 'Abraham Darby 1777' were inserted, perhaps as a means of increasing output when the components of the Iron Bridge were being cast.

The forehearth of the Old Furnace, Coalbrookdale (SJ 667048) with its intriguing inscriptions, photographed in the 19th century.

At Madeley Wood the stacks remain of two of the three furnaces that worked on the site. Several attempts have been made to interpret the remains, but a fuller understanding must await further uncovering. The two furnaces at Hinkshay were torn apart by explosives, but substantial parts remain within a nature study area. The bases of the Stirchley furnaces stand in the Telford Town Park, alongside the high chimney, built, to no avail, by the Wellington Coal & Iron Company in 1872. The bases of three furnaces at the Lodge, left after the works was demolished in 1905, were restored as part of the Granville Country Park. The massive retaining wall, in ashlar sandstone, and the adjoining canal make this an impressive site. The bases of the blast furnaces at Old Park and Dark Lane were briefly revealed during site clearance in the 1970s.

In 1873 there were 11 forges in the coalfield producing wrought-iron, with a total of 232 puddling furnaces. Nothing remains of any of them other than some fragments of

The bob wall of the engine house at the Bedlam or Madeley Wood furnaces (SJ 677034).

Remains of the Hinkshay blast furnaces (SJ 699078), built by the Old Park Company c.1930, now in a nature reserve.

the foundations of the Stirchley Ironworks (SJ 700075) observed in the mid 1980s. There were 26 puddling furnaces at the Stirchley works and 43 in the forge at Old Park, where there were eight steam engines, a steam hammer, and rolling mills for plate, sheet and hoop iron, and for ships' plates. Fortunately the process of forging wrought-iron by puddling, with structures and machines brought in from elsewhere or newly built as replicas has been illustrated at the G.R. Morton Ironworks at Blists Hill. The manufacture of 'rattle' chain from tough charcoal wrought-iron bars, used originally for winding in mines, was developed at Coalport from the 1790s at works owned by William Horton and Benjamin Edge, and subsequently by Gilbert Gilpin at The Aqueduct.[109]

Two important forges of earlier date have been studied in detail. The Upper Forge at Coalbrookdale (SJ 669041) occupies a site that was used for working iron for at least two centuries, and for other industrial purposes after it ceased to produce wrought-iron in 1843. The surviving main building was probably built soon after 1753, but was altered to accommodate new processes and Boulton & Watt rotative engines. It is an unequalled record of the adaptation of an existing ironworks building to new technology, but it is doubtful whether it will ever be possible to identify remains of structures in use when the Cranage brothers experimented there in the 1760s with the use of coal and coke in refining wrought-iron.[110]

The three forges linked by iron railways at Wrens Nest near the confluence of the Linley Brook with the River Severn were probably constructed before 1771 on the site of two ancient corn mills by George Matthews of the Calcutts furnaces. They passed into the possession of John Wright and Richard Jesson, pioneers of the 'stamping-and-potting' process for refining iron, who in 1779 installed a steam engine which initially recycled water, but later worked hammers directly. The stamping-and-potting process was used

The Upper Forge building, Coalbrookdale (SJ 669041)

127

but the works had a relatively short life, ceasing operation in about 1812. Traces of the water-power system remain, together with slag, vitrified bricks and some fragments of the refractory clay pots used in the process.[111] Two large double-gabled buildings of 1759-60 at Newdale, surveyed before demolition in 1985, provided rare evidence of 18th-century ironworks buildings, but their purpose is uncertain.[112]

It has long been known that Sir Basil Brooke worked a steel furnace in Coalbrookdale in the 17th century. Excavations near the Upper Forge in the opening years of the present century revealed the remains of a cementation furnace, similar to those that survive in the centre of Sheffield. It probably dated from the 1620s, and evidence from the Gloucester Port Book suggests that it was no longer used by the 1680s. The site was subsequently used as a malthouse and as domestic accommodation.[113]

Steam hammers were used in all mid 19th century forges. This restored example is in the G.R. Morton Ironworks at Blists Hill.

The Hadley Castle works (SJ 675124) of G.R. Milnes & Co. On the right is the Shrewsbury Canal with the Castle Lock, and the basin serving the works. In the centre of the works tramcars await despatch, while the Stafford-Wellington line of the LNWR is to the left. The works was taken over by Joseph Sankey in 1910.

Several companies making wire and wire rods were established in the northern part of the coalfield in the late 19th century. The Trench Ironworks (SJ 685124), which had 24 puddling furnaces and was established in the 1860s, and the Shropshire Ironworks (SJ 686122) were located alongside the canal basin at Trench and were in the same ownership from 1872. They closed in 1931. The works of the Haybridge Company, which carried on similar processes and dated from the late 1850s, occupied the fork between the railways from Wellington to Stafford and Wolverhampton. It closed in 1983.[114]

Shropshire's principal 20th-century engineering concern had similar origins, and was served by both the Shrewsbury Canal and the Wellington-Stafford railway. The Castle Iron Works at Hadley (SJ 675124) was established in 1871 to make bar iron and wire. The company went bankrupt in 1888, and between 1900 and 1904 the site was used by G.R. Milnes & Co. Ltd for the production of tramcars; it served the same purpose for different owners between 1905 and 1908. A tramcar constructed by Milnes for Lowestoft Corporation in 1904 is preserved by East Anglia Transport Museum, and there are vehicles from Birkenhead and the Hill of Howth Tramway in the museum at Crich. In 1910 the Castle Works was bought by Joseph Sankey & Co., who used it to make motor vehicle wheels and body parts. In the 1920s and '30s it was one of the few prosperous companies in the coalfield, making steel pressings of many kinds, and had about 1,500 employees in 1939, a total which rose to more than 6,000 by the 1960s. The company survived the

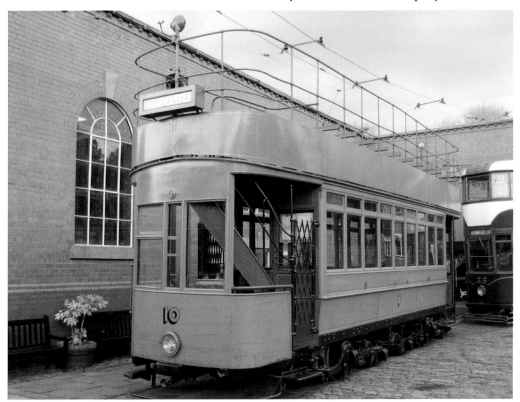

Tramcar No.10 from the Hill of Howth Tramway in Ireland, built by Milnes in 1902, and preserved at the Crich Tramway Museum, Derbyshire.

economic crisis of the early 1980s with a much reduced workforce. The archaeology of the site has yet to be investigated.

Another engineering concern alongside the Wellington-Stafford railway was that of C. & W. Walker of Donnington (SJ 710142), makers of gas purification plant and gas holders, established in 1859. By 1900 the firm had about 800 workers, and was supplying global markets. Operations ceased in the 1980s and the site was cleared without being surveyed. Some of its products survived in the 1990s, such as the No.3 gasholder at the former Banbury Gasworks which bore the inscription 'C. & W. Walker, Donnington, Shropshire, 1933', but most gasholders in England have been demolished in the past two decades as new methods have been used to store natural gas.[115]

Six of the blast furnace complexes in the coalfield in 1800 were significantly involved in engineering, making steam engines and bridges, and in some cases great varieties of smaller castings. No buildings of the period survive but there are substantial remains of two late 19th-century engineering works.

The Lilleshall Company dated from 1764 when Granville Leveson Gower, 2nd Earl Gower, formed a partnership with John and Thomas Gilbert for exploiting the mineral wealth of his Shropshire estates. It became a significant iron-making concern under the direction of John Bishton after the partnership was renewed and was named the Lilleshall Company in 1802. In 1861, with the construction of the New Yard (sometimes called the Phoenix Foundry) at St George's, it became a leading engineering concern. Within the next decade it supplied eight pairs of blowing engines for blast furnaces, and numerous steam hammers and saddle tank locomotives. The works extended over 4.4ha. In the 1870s there were more than 70 machine tools in the machine shop, two steam hammers in the forge, and cranes in the foundry capable of lifting the heaviest castings then in demand. Steam engines were supplied for the waterworks in Shanghai, and a large gas engine was

Pumping engines for a waterworks in Shanghai under construction at the New Yard works in 1927.

despatched to a railway in Japan. Further substantial orders were gained in the 1920s, but the works suffered a crisis of management and closed in 1931. The company re-opened the premises in 1937, leasing portions to other firms. The buildings remain in a multiplicity of uses, and await evaluation. The principal surviving product of the New Yard, the beam engines constructed in 1895-1900 to pump sewage from the borough of West Ham in London into the capital's Northern Outfall Sewer, have been saved from destruction, but remain inaccessible. A late product, an inverted vertical triple expansion pumping engine supplied to the Bristol Waterworks Company in 1923, is conserved at the Chelvey Pumping Station.[116]

The Coalbrookdale Company has a long history in engineering. It supplied parts for Newcomen steam engines in the 1720s and made complete steam engines in the 1790s. Its engineering shops were located in the upper part of the site near the Old Furnace and were water-powered until 1872. The present erecting shop, approx. 77m x 12m, was constructed in 1878-79. Steam engines powered line-shafting driving machine tools, there was an overhead crane and standard gauge railway sidings extended through the building. It is ironic that this great building was completed long after the company's best-known products had been despatched to customers. The shop is now part of the headquarters of the Ironbridge Gorge Museum.[117]

Like the Lilleshall Company, the Coalbrookdale Company enjoyed global markets. Whaling pots of indeterminate date bearing the inscription 'Coalbrookdale' have been found on several shores of the Pacific Ocean. In 1838 the company began to make art castings, and their display in the Crystal Palace in 1851 attracted much attention. The ceremonial gates which featured in it stand near the Albert Hall. Subsequently displays were mounted at most of the international exhibitions of the second half of the 19th century. The most distant artefact is probably the statue of the colonial administrator John Robert Godley, cast at

John Bell's statue of Andromeda, cast at Coalbrookdale and displayed at the Great Exhibition of 1851, now in the grounds of Queen Victoria's home at Osborne on the Isle of Wight.

An ornamental table in cast-iron featuring Irish wolfhounds, one of the most extravagant art castings made at Coalbrookdale.

Coalbrookdale in 1865, which stands, restored after the earthquake of 2011, outside the cathedral in Christchurch, New Zealand.[118]

Nevertheless, it is not a work of art but a useful object which is Coalbrookdale's best-known product. The Iron Bridge, built in 1777-81, was universally acknowledged at the time as the first in the world, and drew the world's attention to what was happening in the coalfield. It was proposed in 1773 by the Shrewsbury architect Thomas Farnolls Pritchard in a letter to the ironmaster John Wilkinson. Pritchard had carried out commissions for Wilkinson as well as for the Harries family of Benthall and, probably, for Abraham Darby III at Hay Farm. In February 1774 proposals for an iron bridge across the Severn near Coalbrookdale were formally announced. The first subscribers' meeting took place in 1775, when Abraham Darby III agreed to take responsibility for the construction. An Act of Parliament was obtained the following year, and after some disagreements among the share-holders, work began on a small scale late in 1777. The iron ribs were placed in position during the summer of 1779, perhaps before the completion of the stone abutments. The bridge was opened to traffic on New Year's Day 1781. In the following decades it attracted many visitors and was depicted in numerous paintings and engravings. It symbolised the scale and significance of the developments in mining and manufacturing that took place in the area. It is also a measure of the difference between the Coalbrookdale Coalfield and other coalfields in Shropshire.[119]

The landscape of the Coalbrookdale Coalfield was transformed in the second half of the 20th century by the creation of the new town of Telford. In the 1960s the landscape of the

One of the commissioned views of the Iron Bridge made by William Williams
shortly before it opened.

The inscription on the Iron Bridge revealing where the castings (or some of them) were made.

coalfield reflected many aspects of its industrial past. The skyline was punctuated by several headstocks of small abandoned mines worked earlier in the century. Adits, mostly the remnants of recent workings for clay and by now obliterated by slumping strata, still penetrated the slopes of the Ironbridge Gorge. A walk across any range of pit heaps could reveal plate rails or lengths of rattle chain. Terraces at Dark Lane, Hinkshay, Sandy Bank Row and Coalport, remained as reminders of past periods of expansion. In many areas they would have been demolished or modernised, but they remained homes for some families. The new town made possible the conservation of most of the coalfield's principal industrial monuments, although much information about mining, ironmaking and early railways was lost in earth-moving that might have

An adit in Benthall Edge Woods (SJ 669033) from which clay was extracted for the nearby White Brickworks, when it was still recognisable in 1965.

133

been recorded by a concerted archaeo-logical programme. It is to the credit of those who reshaped the landscape that it is possible to admire the Iron Bridge and the Hay Inclined Plane, and also that there are areas such as the Town Park, the Granville Country Park and Benthall Edge Woods where it is possible to sense less spectacular aspects of the area's past.

Conclusions

The most evident contrast between the Shropshire coalfields is in their markets. All the coalfields supplied landsale coal for local customers, for brickworks and for lime kilns. The pits of the Shrewsbury Coalfield had only one other significant type of custom, the lead smelters at Pontesford and Malehurst. The only other use for coal in the Oswestry coalfield was in making coke, but substantial quantities of coal

An abandoned steel headstock from a coal mine at Heath Hill, Dawley (SJ 680082), 1965.

were carried by rail to distant markets. Coal from the Wyre Forest was used in iron-making for a short time, and was later taken to distant customers along the Severn Valley Railway. Coal from the Clee Hills was used for iron-making, pottery manufacture and the making of clay pipes, and for a time was taken by road into Wales, but long-distance trade was destroyed by the standard gauge railway.

The Coalbrookdale Coalfield presents many contrasts. For three centuries coal was supplied along the Severn to customers 90km distant in Gloucestershire. From the 1720s the Coalbrookdale ironworks provided parts for steam engines being erected throughout England. By the end of the 19th century tiles made in the Ironbridge Gorge were being installed in prestigious buildings throughout the British Empire. For a time between 1780 and 1803 the entrepreneurs of the coalfield displayed a remarkable degree of intellectual prowess, contemplating ideas like the oil engine and the integrated alkali works that did not come to fruition for many decades, and attracting the attention of leading figures of the time.

Even so, the Shropshire coalfields had much in common. All were affected by the major changes of the Industrial Revolution. All except Clee Hill were making use of steam pumping and winding engines by 1800. All employed plateways. All, except the Oswestry Coalfield, became involved with iron-making. All were stimulated by turnpike roads. All were affected by canals, although the Clee Hill and Shrewsbury coalfields were affected adversely.

The standard gauge railway affected the coalfields in different ways. While the Coalbrookdale Coalfield gained from the easier despatch of secondary products, it may have lost ground in the market for coal. The Oswestry and Wyre Forest coalfields obviously benefitted from their railway links, but the Shrewsbury and more particularly the Clee Hill coalfield demonstrably lost markets when railways opened. The pits that remained open in the second half of the 20th century in the Coalbrookdale Coalfield were modernised, with steel headstocks, compressed air and electrical systems, and pithead baths, as were the large single pits developed in the 1920s in the Oswestry Coalfield and in the 1930s in the Wyre Forest. The mines in the Shrewsbury Coalfield and on the Clee Hills were never updated in this fashion.

There are similarities in the patterns of settlement in the five coalfields. Squatting did much to shape the Ironbridge Gorge, Ketley Bank and Wrockwardine Wood in the Coalbrookdale Coalfield, it dominates the landscape of Clee Hill and can be observed at Trefonen and in parts of St Martin's in the Oswestry Coalfield, at Hookagate and Annscroft near Shrewsbury, and on Chelmarsh Common in the Wyre Forest. Terraced housing built by entrepreneurs for their workpeople is evident in all five coalfields, and the example of Highley shows how an industrial landscape can be shaped by patterns of land ownership which date from the middle ages. The most characteristic miners' housing of the 20th century dates from the first quarter of the century and consists of semi-detached pairs and short terraces in the 'Garden City' style, visible at St Martin's and at Highley, but except for the 12 dwellings forming Castle Houses at Hadley, it is absent from the Coalbrookdale Coalfield.

Few structures survive which relate directly to coalmining, although there are rather more constructed for secondary, coal-using industries. Some engine houses are well-known and are cared for. There are probably rather more weighbridge offices, which tend to survive when other colliery buildings are demolished. The county retains two pithead baths.

Waste tips remain in all five coalfields. They have slowly been colonised by grass, by birch, and then by oak trees. In the same way mining landscapes have changed slowly as the evidence of mining activity has been supplanted, by agriculture and forestry in the Wyre Forest, by the housing estates and factories of the new town of Telford in the Coalbrookdale Coalfield. The scattered cottages on Clee Hill would never have been built were it not for the coal beneath the dhustone. There would not be a new town in the Coalbrookdale Coalfield if the area had not undergone an industrial revolution in the 18th century. Highley, Weston Rhyn and St Martin's are unmistakably mining villages, whatever the current occupations of their inhabitants.

Mining anywhere on earth is a passing phase in human history. Minerals are exhausted or their exploitation ceases to be profitable. Many centuries of non-ferrous mining have ended in recent decades at Falun in Sweden, the Erzebirge in Saxony and the Harz Mountains in central Germany. The effective cessation of coal mining in Northumberland and Co. Durham, in South Wales and in Belgium would only recently have been regarded as beyond credulity. Yet even when mining has ceased, it shapes the present and the future of both landscapes and communities.

Just as a pit heap may merge into the landscape, and, with a covering of trees and shrubs, come to look like any other small hill, so a mining community may come to look like a commuting settlement, whether in the rural isolation of Asterley or the planned landscape of Telford. Just as a closer examination of the pit heap will show that its vegetation is determined by past mining activity, so closer examination of a community, of its building materials, its house types, its shops and places of worship, will reveal its origins. The miners' trains stop running. There are no more Sunday School anniversaries at Primitive Methodist chapels. The Co-operative Store no longer pays a dividend. Brass bands do not march through the streets and the miners' lodge banners have been laid up. No one now reads the *Colliery Guardian* and the mutual improvement class no longer meets. Nevertheless, the railway embankment, the chapel, the Co-op mini-supermarket, the banners and miner's lamps in museums, together with the waste tips, remain as evidence of the reasons why communities grew up, and the task of the industrial archaeologist is to subject that evidence to continuing analysis.

5   THE TEXTILE INDUSTRIES

Changes in the ways in which the production of fabrics was organised were at the heart of the Industrial Revolution. Shropshire has never been one of the principal textile-manufacturing counties, yet one of the most formal early modern textile manufactures focussed on Shrewsbury, the county was substantially influenced by the growth of textile factories around 1800, and small-scale production of fabrics for local markets continued into the 20th century.

Vernacular production

The most widespread textile activity in Shropshire in the 18th century was a form of 'vernacular' or subsistence manufacturing. In most parts of the county flax and hemp were grown on small plots, often adjacent to farmsteads and called 'hemp butts'. Arthur Young in 1776 noted that almost every Shropshire farmer grew about two acres of hemp, and every cottager devoted to the crop all he could spare from potatoes and beans.[1] The first stage in processing flax was retting, soaking the stalks which decomposed the gum that bound the fibres together. In Shropshire it appears that this was usually done in containers rather than pools, although there are field names that suggest the existence of retting ponds in Ellesmere, West Felton and Eyton-on-the-Weald-Moors. It was then scutched, heckled and spun by the families who grew it, and the resulting yarn was woven by 'custom weavers', defined in 1840 as 'domestic artisans … employed to weave the yarn spun in private houses'.[2]

In the northern part of the Coalbrookdale Coalfield some 156 of 846 probate inventories made between 1660 and 1750, 18.4% of the total, refer to hemp or flax, and the same proportion list spinning wheels. By contrast, ownership of looms was confined to 23 specialist weavers.[3] A similar pattern occurs elsewhere in the county. In the 1660s 'Shropshire Canvas' was being shipped down the Severn through Gloucester, but the manufacture of hempen or flaxen fabrics for national markets seems to have ceased by 1700. Edward Harries in 1795 insisted that Shropshire spinners did not spin 'for manufactures', and Nightingale in 1813 noted that hemp and flax, like cabbages, were grown in small quantities.[4]

Custom weaving continued in Shropshire after the middle of the 19th century. Thomas Rogers of Pontesbury was making his living as a weaver in 1851, when he was aged 68, while in Minsterley William Hughes was still weaving at the age of 86, employed a journeyman, and served as parish clerk. In the same year Charles Manley was weaving at Myddle Wood when he was 70. Two weavers, Richard Rogers and Nathan Davies, lived in adjacent households at Ifton Rhyn in 1841. The latter was still working 20 years later at the age of 84.

Samuel Hall's loom shop at Cockshutford (SO 580850)

Other aged custom weavers included John Edwards of Craignant, Selattyn, working at the age of 85 in 1851, and Joseph Windsor of Rhosygadfa, Whittington, a hand loom weaver in 1861 when he was 76. The best-documented custom weaver, and reputedly the last in Shropshire to make linen cloth, was John Jeffreys of Llanymynech, born in 1825, the last of several generations of weavers. He was apprenticed at Welshpool before succeeding to his father's trade. He operated two looms in a shed adjacent to his cottage, and produced table-cloths, towels, sheeting and striped linsey-woolsey cloth until the end of the 19th century, in the latter years using yarn from Yorkshire.[5]

The best archaeological evidence of custom weaving is the workshop at Cockshutford (SO 580850), the squatter settlement in Clee St Margaret parish, occupied in 1861 by Samuel Hall, a 73-year-old woollen weaver who had used the premises for at least 20 years. It is located in the grounds of a stone cottage, occupied in the mid 19th century by a blacksmith, but the tithe map identifies it as Hall's loom shop. Hall's cottage, replaced by a 20th-century building, stood on the adjacent plot. The workshop, of rubble sandstone intermixed with dhustone and brick, is 3.94m long x 3.52m wide, with a height to the eaves of 2.5m.

Some custom weavers made woollen as well as linen cloth, and there is plentiful evidence in Shropshire of 'vernacular' production of woollen fabrics in small factories. Several rural fulling mills remained active for most of the 18th century. Strafford's Mill at Wrickton (SO 646853), for example, was still working in 1783. On the slopes of the Long Mynd, the Upper Mill at Smethcott remained in use, at least as a dyehouse, until after 1800, while the fulling mill at Woolstaston worked until sometime between 1757 and 1777. A fulling mill at Allscot (SJ 613133), built in 1689, remained in operation in 1745. Field name evidence suggests that more fulling mills operated before the 17th century.[6]

The tradition of local production for local markets continued through the 19th century. The preparation and spinning phases, as well as fulling, were mechanised, but cloth continued to be woven on hand looms. In 1814 a woollen factory at Upper Mill, Wentnor

(SO 381940) was offered for sale, newly built, with its fulling stock and tenters, and the prospect of 'plenty of good country work'.[7] Broad Street Mill in Ludlow (SO 512742) had included a fulling mill since the 16th century. In the mid 19th century the mill was a small woollen manufactory, with five hand looms, making flannel, blankets and cloth for horse collars, all sold locally. It operated until the 1870s.[8]

Nineteenth-century woollen cloth production at Morda followed the same tradition. In 1841 Edward Evans, woollen manufacturer, was employing about half a dozen weavers. His mill at Weston (SJ 297275), which in 1817 had two pairs of fulling stocks and detached buildings used for spinning and weaving, appears to have been destroyed by fire and rebuilt as a cornmill. Morda (Lower) Mill (SJ 289281) used for cotton manufacture in the early 19th century and subsequently for paper-making, was taken over in the 1880s by D. Rogers & Co., who made blankets, tweeds and flannels until the 1930s. A farmer who grew up at Hengoed recalled in 1994 that in 1922 his mother took fleeces to Morda Mill to be made into blankets.[9]

At Church Stretton, Carding Mill Valley takes its name from Brooks Mill (SO 445945), which in the 19th century worked on the same scale as Morda and served similar markets. In 1841 it employed ten males and two females, including two wool pickers and a sorter, two yarn slubbers and a carding engine feeder, two spinners and two flannel weavers. Ten years later the labour force had grown to 19, of whom nine were from Newtown, centre of the Welsh flannel industry, and one from Ossett, Yorkshire. There were only seven employees in 1861 and six in 1871. By 1891 the works was operated by two members of the Williams family who had owned it since the 1850s, other members gaining employment in their adjacent aerated water works and in the operation of the refreshment rooms and tea gardens in the valley. Richard Williams was advertising tweeds and blankets in the 1890s, and offering to provide cloth to farmers in part-exchange for wool.[10] The Silurian Mill on the Shropshire bank of the River Teme at Knighton (SO 287725) was converted from a cornmill in 1860. It was disused in 1880, but still workable when offered for sale in 1906, when its equipment included a 4.2m diameter waterwheel, a steam engine with a 12 inch (0.3m) cylinder, self-acting mules and 22 plain flannel looms.[11]

The only place in Shropshire producing woollen fabrics for national markets in 1660 was Bridgnorth, where probate records show that large-scale manufacture of the woollen cloth called frieze continued into the second decade of the 18th century. Entrepreneurs appear to have undertaken the preparation and finishing of cloth on their own premises, but to have entrusted spinning and weaving to outworkers. George Southall, a clothier who died in 1667, owned equipment for preparing, spinning and finishing cloth, as well as 'on(e) piece at the weaver's'. Samuel Higgins in 1681 had stocks of cloth and wool, together with cards for carding, boards and shears for finishing, and dyestuffs. George Bickerton in 1718 had possessions worth £870, including quantities of wool, yarn and cloth. Twenty pieces of cloth worth £20 were with weavers, and 375lbs of wool had been put out for spinning. The scale of the Bridgnorth trade is best indicated by the inventory of Moses Law, made in 1712. He had wool of various kinds worth £93, yarn for 48 pieces of cloth worth £104, 141 pieces of completed frieze worth £423, kerseys, plains, druggetts and other cloth worth £110, tools for carding, eight looms and dying equipment. The whole of his possessions were valued at £1,864. Law lived in Underhill Street, north of the bridge (SO

717931). After George Bickerton died there is no further evidence of large-scale woollen cloth manufacturing in Bridgnorth, and there appears to be no continuity between frieze manufacture and the carpet weaving introduced to the town in the late 18th century.[12]

The Shrewsbury Drapers

Shropshire was involved in one of the most important textile trades of the early modern period – the production of woollen fabrics, 'cottons' or 'webs', in north and mid Wales, for export through Blackwell Hall, London, to the poorest parts of Europe, and to the Americas, where it clothed black slaves. The *de facto* ability to manage the trade in such fabrics was acquired by 1623-24 by the Shrewsbury Drapers' Company, based in their 16th-century hall by St Mary's Church, and they controlled it until the 1790s.[13]

Membership of the Drapers' Company slowly declined in the late 17th and early 18th centuries. There were 61 Drapers resident in the town in 1660, 52 in 1680, 41 in 1700 and 32 in 1740. Seventy-six apprentices were indentured between 1700 and 1750, 51 in the next half-century and only 29 in the 50 years after 1780. Thomas Pennant noted in the 1770s that Shrewsbury profited from the woollen cloth manufactures of Montgomeryshire, about 700,000 yards a year passing through the town's market. Owen and Blakeway in 1826 recalled how, each Thursday, Welshmen in blue cloth coats and striped linsey waistcoats sold cloth to the Drapers in The Square, the end of the market being marked by the ascent of members of the Company in order of seniority into the market hall. The formal market ended about 1795, the year after the spectacular bankruptcy of Joshua Blakeway, a leading Draper, and in 1803 the Company gave up the lease of the upper room of the market hall. The ancient and somewhat archaic market ceased to be viable as the Welsh concentrated on the production of flannel, involving the mechanisation of preparation and spinning and consequently the concentration of production, while new wholesale markets were established in Welshpool, Newtown and Llanidloes.[14]

Welsh cloth was finished by shearmen in Shrewsbury, who were traditionally perceived to be poor, and exploited by the Drapers. In the late 17th century the prosperity of finishers and dyers in Wellington suggests that some work may have been contracted out to that town. The scale of the finishing trade gradually diminished: probate records survive for 29 cloth workers and shearmen who died in Shrewsbury between 1660 and 1679, but for only seven between 1730 and 1749.[15] The frankpledge list in 1709 includes 47 cloth workers, but there are only 21 on that for 1731. Nevertheless the trade continued, and 14 cloth dressers and nine shearmen claimed votes in the Shrewsbury election of 1796.

Shrewsbury merchants continued to participate in the Welsh cloth trade after the loss of the market. As late as 1865 a property sale included a warehouse in Frankwell that had for many years been used to store wool and flannel. An insight into the operation of such warehouses is provided by the sale notice of 1794 for Joshua Blakeway's warehouse on St Chad's Hill, where 12,000 yards of cloth were stored, together with 40 quires of packing paper and 400 ells of hurden packing cloths.[16]

Shrewsbury's diminishing role in the Welsh cloth trade had two significant effects on the county's textile industry. First, it stimulated an element of imitation as flannel manufactories, based on Welsh practice, were established in and around the county town. It also stimulated some entrepreneurs to seek other outlets for their capital.

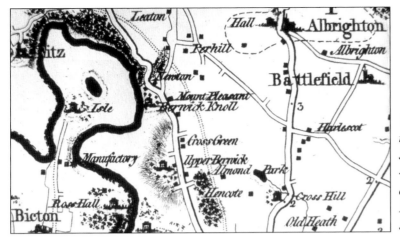

The flannel mill in the bend of the River Severn at The Isle (SJ 457159), the location of which is depicted on Robert Baugh's Map of Shropshire in 1808.

Welsh-style Flannel

Arthur Aikin remarked in 1797 that flannel was being made in Shropshire. The 'greatest undertaking' he considered to be the mill erected by Cook & Mason at the Isle (SJ 457159) on the Severn upstream from Shrewsbury, where a tunnel across the neck of the isthmus conveyed water to a wheel which powered spinning and fulling machinery. The mill operated until the 1820s, when the plant included two carding engines, nine jennies, 20 looms and two sets of fulling stocks. The site would repay archaeological investigation.[17]

In Shrewsbury itself flannel manufacture took place in Barker Street, traditionally the area where shearmen lived. In 1800 Thomas Child, flannel manufacturer, was using a chestnut mare to power carding machinery in premises where he also had looms. By 1813 Rowley's Mansion (SJ 489125) was in use as a woollen factory. The principal manufacturer, the demise of whose business was remembered with regret in the 1890s, was a Mr Rowbottom whose stock, when he sold up in 1830, included carding machines, jennies and frames for spinning and looms. The machinery was powered by a single horse.[18]

The distinguished early 17th-century buildings Rowley's House and Rowley's Mansion (SJ 489125) were used as a textile factory in the early 19th century.

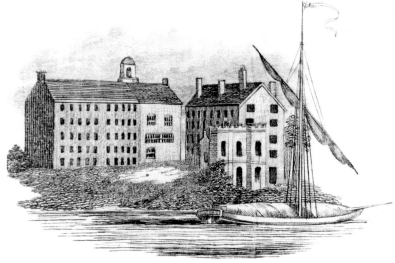

The textile mill in Coleham, Shrewsbury (SJ 496172) constructed for Powis & Hodges in 1790 and leased by Charles Hulbert from 1803. To the right is Hulbert's 'Castle', the home which he built for himself.

A more ambitious enterprise was the integrated woollen factory built by Powis & Hodges in 1790 in Coleham, Shrewsbury (SJ 496122) at the confluence of the Severn and the Rea Brook. With two five-storey ranges, one 33.9m x 12m, the other 31.3m x 12m, and a four-storey block, 13.8m x 12m, it was amongst the largest woollen mills built by that time anywhere in Britain. Power was derived from a small steam engine and a 4.57m diameter waterwheel, and equipment included billies for carding, jennies for spinning, looms and fulling stocks. The enterprise soon went bankrupt and for about a decade the mill stood empty, and was used for a time to accommodate prisoners captured during the Napoleonic Wars.[19]

Cotton Manufacture

In 1803, during the period of commercial optimism that followed the Treaty of Amiens, the Coleham factory was leased by Charles Hulbert, a Mancunian who intended to weave yarn spun at Turner's Mill, Llangollen, producing calicoes to be printed at the works of Roberts & Warren at Morda.[20] He encountered difficulties, losing skilled workers to factories in Stockport and Manchester which offered higher wages. In 1811 Luddite threats prevented him from operating power looms. The hope of a legacy which would have increased his capital proved unavailing and by 1814 he turned towards retailing. The property was gradually tenemented as dwellings and workshops and was sold in 1825. Homes in the former mill came to be regarded as some of Shrewsbury's worst slums. A militia drill hall was built in place of the four-storey building in 1881 and the military acquired the whole site shortly before the Second World War after the remaining dwellings had been condemned and demolished. The Territorial Army remained in possession until 1995-96 when the property was sold to the Barnabas Church. A photograph taken *c.*1900 during the construction of the adjacent pumping stations shows the longer of the five-storey buildings alongside the road, and part of the other five-storey block at right angles to it. Having sold the property, Hulbert made his living as an auctioneer, publisher and antiquarian writer.[21]

There was a concentration of textile manufactures on the River Morda, south of Oswestry. Hulbert's associates, Henry Warren of Bury (Lancs.) and John Roberts of Oswestry leased two of the mills on the Morda Brook, Morda (Lower) Mill (SJ 289281) and Upper Weston Mill (SJ 297275). A printworks was operating in 1804, when it was valued at over £24,000. The partnership was dissolved in 1806 but production continued under the direction of Henry Warren until 1818. Upper Weston Mill was later used for grinding grain and has been demolished. Morda (Lower) Mill, after being used for paper-making in the mid 19th century, reverted to textile use as Rogers' woollen factory from the 1880s until the 1930s. The site remains in industrial use but the only old buildings are some low, stone structures which may have been drying sheds for the papermill.[22]

There were two other cottonmills in Shropshire. Little is known of that in Broseley, except that in 1792 it was worked by Messrs Jennings, Latham and Jennings, who stored fabrics in an adjacent warehouse. The mill might be the three-storey west range of the preserved Broseley Pipe Works (SJ 671022), which measures 11m x 5m, and is probably of late 18th-century date, but this can only be surmise.[23] A mill on the River Rea in Stottesdon parish (SO 662804) was built c.1794 at a cost of £4,000, had a 4.26m diameter, 3.65m wide waterwheel, and machines for carding and spinning. All that is known about it comes from attempts to sell it between 1804 and 1827. It appears to have been demolished by 1840, but the leats remain. Slag deposits suggest that it occupied the site of Prescot Forge which closed in the early 1790s.[24]

Mighty Flax Mills

Shropshire's most important role in the Industrial Revolution in textiles was in the linen sector. Capital originated in the traditional trade in Welsh woollens. In the 1790s the brothers Thomas and Benjamin Benyon stored flannel in warehouses in Shrewsbury and Dolgellau. Both lived in Quarry Place, suggesting that they were amongst Shrewsbury's wealthiest citizens. By 1792 they were acquainted with John Marshall, the pioneer of mechanisation in the Yorkshire linen industry. The following year the brothers invested £9,000 in Marshall's mill in Water Lane, Leeds. A second mill was completed in Leeds in 1795, but it was damaged in a fire on 13 February 1796, recommencing production in July of that year. By May 1796 Marshall and the Benyons had decided to build a mill in Shrewsbury, and the following month admitted Charles Bage to their partnership. On 26 September 1796 they purchased land at Ditherington (SJ 497136) on the north side of Shrewsbury, and within a year had constructed a remarkable iron-framed spinning mill.[25]

Charles Bage, designer of the mill, was the son of the novelist-mechanic Robert Bage, and had made his living in Shrewsbury since 1776 as a wine merchant and surveyor. He had a profound understanding of the structural properties of iron, shown by his comments in 1801 on Thomas Telford's design for a bridge of a single iron arch to replace London Bridge. He corresponded with William Strutt of Belper, who first used iron columns in textile mills, and knew William Reynolds, who made available the results of tests on the structural properties of iron made during the design of the aqueduct at Longdon-on-Tern.[26]

The mill began production in 1797 and was soon profitable. In 1804 Marshall bought out his partners and for the next 82 years the complex was operated by the Leeds company which claimed to be Europe's largest flax-spinning concern. Until c.1830 some cloth was

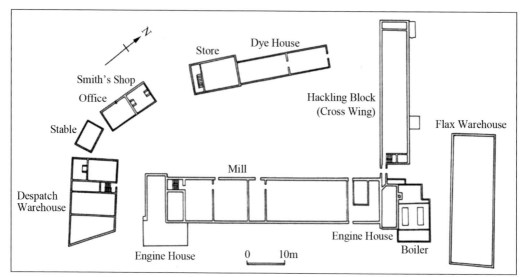

*Plan of the Ditherington Flax mill, re-drawn from an original of 1811
in the Boulton & Watt Collection, Birmingham Libraries.*

*The east elevation of Ditherington Flax Mill (SJ 499139) c.1900
after alteration by William Jones & Co., maltsters. The lean-to alongside the canal
and the pyramidal malt kiln had just been completed, and it is clear that the windows
had recently been bricked-in.*

The first floor of the Ditherington Flax mill showing three lines of cruciform columns, the cross beams abutting to the right of the central columns and the wrought-iron tie rods holding together the brick arches.

woven on hand looms, and from 1820 on power looms, but increasingly the mill special-ised in making thread. John Marshall's grandsons wound up the company in 1885 and the Ditherington Mill ceased operation the following year. It then stood empty for more than a decade, although attempts were made to re-open it. The business was not, as has been suggested, transferred to the United States, although some skilled workers probably migrated to Jersey City, NJ.[27]

The *Shrewsbury Chronicle* in 1797 hailed the Ditherington Mill as a fireproof building.[28] Its importance was acknowledged for a few years afterwards, but it was subsequently neglected by historians of architecture and it was not until the 1940s that it was 're-discov-ered' by Turpin Bannister of the University of Illinois and by Professor A.W. Skempton, who demonstrated that it was the first wholly iron-framed building. The main building remains, with most of its subsidiary structures, two of which are iron-framed. They have provided stimulating evidence about the development of the factory and about the evolu-tion of textile mills in general.

The spinning mill is 53.94m long and 12.04m wide, and consists of four floors with an additional attic storey. On each floor are three lines of cruciform cast-iron columns supporting cross beams from which spring shallow brick arches, the nine northerly bays being 3.04m in span, the six to the south 3.2m, which form the floors above. The cross-beams have triangular bottoms and slightly tapered webs and would have been cast upside down on the foundry floor. The vertical holes cast in the beams probably accommodated bolts fixing brackets for the power transmission system. The cross-beams are fixed to 7.62cm thick flat end plates mounted in the side walls of the mill, fixed in place by single iron pins driven into timber pads built into the core of the wall. These features have been discovered during investigation of the mill prior to its re-use. The pads show that the mill was not built entirely of fireproof materials, and some wood was also used in the staircases and possibly as battens for affixing slates. Wrought-iron tie rods 2.54cm square run through the mill to the east of each line of pillars.

Just south of the mid-point of the mill is a bay 3.66m wide which originally contained a cross-wall rising through the first three floors. The existence of this bay supports the theory that the main mill was built in two closely successive stages, first the six bays at the south end with two short bays accommodating the prime mover, and immediately afterwards the 10 full bays at the north end whose machinery was powered from an adjacent engine house. On the attic floor a central line of columns supports sloping beams from which spring arches of shorter radius. This structure, used in no other known mill, would have excluded from the factory any fire in the roof above. No original doors or windows remain in the mill, but they were certainly of iron. Recent discoveries of features hitherto obscured by the concrete floors installed for malting show carefully contrived architectural detailing at the bases of the columns, and suggest that the beams were cast with minor variations to match the planned layout of machinery.[29]

A 20hp Boulton & Watt engine was installed at the south end of the mill in 1797. It was replaced in 1811 by a 60hp engine, probably by Fenton, Murray & Wood of Leeds, which was succeeded in 1874-75 by a 30hp Corliss engine by Hicks & Son of Bolton. Subsequently, perhaps when the mill was adapted as a maltings, a further storey was added to the south engine house providing additional storage space. At the north end of the mill a 40 or 45hp engine was installed by mid-1800. It was replaced by a 56hp engine in 1819-20, probably in a newly-built engine house, and by another Corliss engine in 1875.[30]

Access to the mill was by means of the staircase at the south end alongside the original steam engine. Since the mill used less than 600 tons of flax a year in the 1820s, less than 12 tons a week, materials could have been carried between floors, and no evidence survives of hoists or taking-in doors. Nor are there significant traces of early sanitation, heating or lighting systems, although the complex was lit by gas from 1811.

The mill is built of 'great bricks' made in the vicinity, measuring 10 x 11 x 24cm (approx.), a size which seems to have been used in all the buildings on the site built before 1810. The principal subsidiary buildings are the cross-wing or hackling block and the flax warehouse, both of which are iron-framed. The cross-wing, completed by 1803, originally had a timber frame but was destroyed by fire on 24 October 1811. It was rebuilt with an iron frame, its length shortened from 41.68m to 36.6m, and its width increased from 6.27m to 10m with the northern wall on a new alignment. The iron frame consists of two lines of pillars carrying nine sets of beam-supporting brick arches similar to those in the main mill. The cruciform columns have moulded star-shaped capitals, now encrusted with paint. The cross-wing has a pitched roof carried on cast-iron queen-post trusses.

The flax warehouse was probably built c.1810, the first significant building in the complex to be constructed with 'standard' (7.5 x 9 x 21cm) bricks. It is a four-storey structure of nine bays, 26.8m long and 11.9m wide. Eight cast-iron cross-beams are carried on two rows of cruciform columns, and the roof is brick-vaulted. The warehouse was minimally fenestrated. One small iron-framed window, apparently from the primary phase of construction, remains in the south wall.

The work of researchers elsewhere in Britain makes it possible to see the Ditherington Mill in its wider context.[31] Iron-framing was adopted in Shropshire as elsewhere because it was perceived as being fireproof, and the Ditherington mill was the beginning of a sequence of iron-framed textile factories that continued until steel began to be incorporated into the frames of buildings from the 1880s. It has also been shown that iron-framing was particularly associated in its early years with linen manufacturing. By 1816 iron-framed structures formed the principal buildings used for spinning in nine flax-manufacturing complexes, appreciably more than in the much larger cotton and woollen sectors.

In the early years of operation at Ditherington most of the processes involved with the preparation and spinning of flax were probably carried out in the main mill. Subsequently some tasks were moved to new buildings, while machinery throughout the factory was constantly renewed. Bundles of flax were produced seasonally and, once delivered to mills, were stored in warehouses which did not need windows. Flax was then heckled in a building separate from the main mill, the process dividing the short fibres, the *tow*, from the long fibres, *line*. At Ditherington the line was probably conveyed to the fourth floor of the main mill where preparation continued on drawing and roving frames, the resultant sliver proceeding to the third floor for spinning. The tow was prepared on heavier machines on the third floor. Both line and tow sliver descended to the second floor for spinning. Twisting and further line spinning took place on the first floor, while turners' workshops occupied at least half of the ground floor. A new process, wet spinning, was introduced *c.*1830. By the 1850s thread was being manufactured, finished and dyed at Ditherington from yarns spun at Leeds. An engineering shop was established on the ground floor of the main mill, where by the 1860s the turners' shop was making reels from Swedish timber, and a printing department produced labels for the many varieties of thread then being manufactured. Selling thread on reels rather than in packs, and providing distinctive labels, gave Marshall's products a strong brand image.[32]

Most of the other buildings which formed the mill complex still stand. Near the south entrance one wall remains of a small warehouse for finished products that was subsequently used as a packing shop. It was completed by 1801 and constructed from the same 'great bricks' as the main mill. It was demolished in the 1970s. The adjacent blacksmiths' shop and stable date from before 1805. The next building on the west side of the courtyard is the stove block, substantially altered in 1841-43. The presence of some 'great bricks' suggests that it originally dates from before 1805, and it was probably this building for which Bage was preparing drawings in October 1802. The first dyehouse was built before 1804, but the present building was constructed in the 1850s with fine quality brickwork and a roof with composite trusses of cast-iron and wrought-iron members. There were two gasworks, one built in 1811 and later converted to a carpenters' shop, the other of 1842, but nothing remains of either. The iron-framed roof of a small stable block was removed to the Ironbridge Gorge Museum in the 1970s.

The first accommodation for parish apprentices and 'the clerks' (or the clerk's) house were constructed before June 1800 by John Simpson. The former was the terrace, now Nos.56-59 St Michael's Street (SJ 496137), named Ann's Hill after Simpson's daughter,

The Apprentice House of the Ditherington flax mill in St Michael's Street, outside the perimeter of the mill, built for the proprietors by John Simpson before June 1800, and later named Ann's Hill after Simpson's daughter.

while the latter was the adjacent No.55 St Michael's Street. Both are constructed from the 'great bricks' used in the mill. The apprentice house at the north end of the mill complex was built in 1812 at a cost of £3,329.[33]

Ditherington Mill bordered the Shrewsbury Canal north of the Factory Bridge which carried the turnpike road to Market Drayton north of the waterway. Some of the land between the road and the canal was used for the construction of eight blocks of houses, each consisting of four dwellings and measuring 11.04m x 7.38m. The landowner John Mytton agreed with the partners early in 1797 that he would construct four blocks and rent them to the millowners for £80 p.a.[34] The other four blocks were doubtless built soon afterwards. Dwellings of this type, called 'cluster' or 'quaduplex' houses, were built by the Strutts at Belper and by the Evans family at the textile village of Darley Abbey near Derby, both places with which Bage was familiar. The design was subsequently used in the celebrated *cité ouvrière* at Mulhouse, in Spain and in the Ruhrgebiet. At Ditherington only these 32 dwellings were constructed by the mill owners. Two terraces at the south end of the complex, one of up to seven dwellings called Davies's Buildings, the other numbered 1-12 St Michael's Street, were built by others, although William Jones & Co., the malsters who later occupied the mill buildings, owned both between 1926 and 1936.

The Ditherington Mill was one of the principal employers in Shrewsbury for nearly a century. In 1813 some 433 people were employed there, a total that had risen to 475 by 1819. An estimate that there were 800 employees in the 1840s is probably an exaggeration. After a period of diminishing activity, the total was no more than 300 when closure was announced in 1885. Census evidence suggests that the workforce was overwhelmingly made up of young people. In a sample of 377 flax workers in 1851, 207 or 55% were aged under 20, and 123 or 33% under 16. There were 65 females between 18 and 24 employed, compared with only 41 males, suggesting that many boys left for other work in their late teens while girls continued at the mill until they married. There were more men than women among the workers aged over 30.

In 1811-12 John Marshall established a bleachworks on the site of a cornmill on the Rea Brook at Hanwood (SJ 441093).[35] He opened a similar detached bleachworks at Wortley, serving his Leeds mills, in the following year. The main building at Hanwood was an iron-framed, four-storey structure, in which, by the 1880s, power was provided by a waterwheel and a compound horizontal steam engine. In 1851, 64 men and boys were employed. Six young skilled men in their 20s lived in a cottage within the complex, while other employees were accommodated in the 23 dwellings in Factory Row, the terrace on the eastern side of the lane which approached the works from the Shrewsbury-Minsterley road. The mill was adapted to grind barytes in the late 19th century and has since been demolished, as have the older, four-room cottages in Factory Row, but five cottages at the southern end, built in the mid 19th century, remain.

The Benyon brothers and Charles Bage, having terminated their partnership with John Marshall in 1804, established a parallel flax-spinning business by constructing new iron-framed mills both in Leeds and Shrewsbury. The latter was a five-storey structure in Castlefields (SJ 497131), 63.65m long and 10.83m wide, with a 20hp engine at the south end and a 75hp engine by Fenton, Murray & Wood of Leeds at the north end. A cross-wing west of the main block provided accommodation

A plan and the only known image of the Castlefields flaxmill built in 1804 and demolished in 1837. The plan has been re-drawn from an original of 1811 in the Boulton & Watt Collection, Birmingham Libraries.

in 1811 for reeling and warping, the counting house and the stoves. Detached buildings included a dyehouse, a bleach works, a wood-working shop, a smithy, a gasworks and a warehouse. Thomas Benyon died in 1833 and Benjamin Benyon in 1834. The mill was offered for sale as a working concern in October 1833 and again in 1835 and 1836, when Charles Hulbert observed a 'spirit of discord' among the Benyon family. It was eventually sold and most of the buildings were demolished by May 1837. The shock to the local economy was severe, and the closure was perceived as a reason for the fall in Shrewsbury's population during the 1830s.[36]

The main building of the Castlefields mill stood close to the line of the appropriately named Benyon Street, built in the 1850s. The only remaining part of the complex, known in 1811 as the 'new building', is the iron-framed 23.3 x 7.16m block which now forms Nos.5-8a Severn Street, which stood about 25m south-west of the cross-wing. A sale plan shows that this was a warehouse. The herringbone lintels above the windows of Nos.5-8a Severn Street are identical with those of the later cottages on either side of the block, suggesting that, like other flax warehouses, it was sparsely fenestrated, and that windows were inserted when it was adapted as housing. West of the warehouse, a building that probably served as an apprentice house was converted to Cadran Place, a block of ten back-to-back dwellings, and remained until it was replaced after the Second World War by flats. The warehouse became one of several linen-weaving workshops in Shrewsbury, first, in the 1830s, the property of one Sacheverell Harwood, then, after 1843, of Robert Minn, a Yorkshireman who had been book keeper to the Benyons. The inscription 'Minn & Co., Home Made Linen Warehouse' was legible on the wall of an adjacent cottage until the 1970s. Apart from Minn, seven weavers lived in the Castlefields area in 1851, and Hannah Minn, widow of Robert, still had a linen-weaving business at No.13 Severn Street in 1871.[37]

The south-west elevation of Nos.5-8a Severn Street (SJ 496131), once the flax warehouse of the Castlefields mill, and later linen weaving workshops.

Another weaving concern, Paddock & Davies, from *c.*1814 until 1818 worked in three rented rooms within Hulbert's cotton factory in Coleham. The Benyons also had a weaving workshop in Coleham, probably the 'noggin manufactory' noted by Charles Hulbert in 1802, and another in Barker Street.[38]

The most significant weaving factory in Shrewsbury was built by Charles Bage in Kingsland (SJ 489119) after he withdrew from his partnership with the Benyons in 1815-16. It was a single-storey structure, 27.43m long with a brick-vaulted roof, spanning 9.14m and 22cm thick. Bage employed up to 70 people working 30 hand looms and 24 power looms powered by a 4hp steam engine. Products included linen, huckaback (a rough linen fabric used for towels), and sailcloth. After Bage died in 1822 the business went bankrupt and his widow closed the factory on 26 October 1826. The main building subsequently became part of the Burr family's leadworks.[39]

The Shrewsbury linen industry reached its zenith about 1820 when the Ditherington and Castlefields spinning mills together employed nearly a thousand people and 70 weavers were working for Charles Bage, with others working for smaller concerns. The main buildings at Ditherington and Castlefield were the largest built for the flax industry before the late 1830s and larger than any individual building in Yorkshire, although the complexes in Leeds of John Marshall and the Benyons were more extensive than those in Shrewsbury. The power deployed within the Shrewsbury mills was similarly exceptional. The engines at Ditherington provided 116hp by 1820, while 95hp was available at Castlefields by 1811. By 1820 Marshall's mill in Leeds had 234hp available, and Benyons' mill 136hp, but no other Yorkshire mill approached the power output of those in Shrewsbury. The Ditherington and Castlefields mills were in the vanguard of flax-spinning technology and structural innovation, but Shrewsbury failed to develop a baggage train of smaller concerns like the 'old, irregular-looking houses seemly much disfigured with alterations and additions' which comprised the majority of the flaxmills in Leeds in 1821. It was perhaps for this reason that no buyer emerged to take over the Kingsland Mill in the 1820s or the Castlefields Mill in the 1830s. Linen weaving thereafter was no more than an urban version of the vernacular trade in the countryside, while Marshall's mill specialised in thread manufacture and employed fewer and fewer people. The Shrewsbury mills were an artificial transplant, made possible by the Benyons' capital and their love for their native town. Flax-spinning did not make significant use of local raw materials, nor did it draw on local textile traditions, and with the exception of Marshall's mill, which operated for 90 years, the industry failed to take sufficient root to survive beyond a single generation.

Silk: ripples from afar

Shropshire was also affected by the Industrial Revolution in silk manufacture in other parts of England. In the 1770s a water-powered silkmill was operated by William Jackson in Mill Street, Ludlow. It was offered for sale in 1777 and 1786 and subsequently converted to a wool warehouse which has been demolished.[40] In Whitchurch in the 1820s Messrs Whitfield & Sergeant constructed a two-storey brick silkmill, 44m long and 10.6m wide, alongside the canal. (SJ 535415) It provided working space for 200 people, and was so designed that three further storeys could have been added. Power was provided by a 10hp

151

steam engine by Galloway of Manchester for four 104-bobbin doubling frames, a hard silk engine with 100 swifts, and four 100-bobbin drawing frames. It was offered for sale in 1831, and by 1851 had been adapted as a warehouse by Thomas Burgess, cheese factor and corn merchant.[41]

Local Specialisms

Carpet manufacture was established in Bridgnorth by entrepreneurs from nearby Kidderminster in the 1790s and became the town's principal industry. The two largest factories, in Friars Street (SO 718933) and the Pale Meadow Mills in Spital Street (SO 721927), consisted largely of north-lit sheds of mid- or late 19th-century date, and were demolished in the 1980s. Other buildings, in Listley Street and St Mary Street, were used by carpetmakers in the early 19th century. Several wool-spinning enterprises in the town, as well as some rural mills, produced yarn for carpet manufacture. The three-storey mill at Burcote (SJ 746954) was built in 1799 by William and Joseph MacMichael specifically to provide yarn for Bridgnorth's carpet weavers. Power was provided by a 6m diameter waterwheel which worked a devil and three carding engines on the ground floor, and drawing frames and six spinning frames with 256 spindles on the floor above. The mill was offered for sale in 1815 and was subsequently adapted as a cornmill. A four-storey mill at

An aerial view of the north-lit sheds that comprised one of the carpet factories in Bridgnorth (SO 718933)

The woollen factory on the site of the Town Mills of Bridgnorth at the confluence of the River Worfe and the Severn (SO 725944).

Eardington (SO 708899), 18.28m long and 8.53m wide, was built in 1794 by William and George Hallen to spin flaxen and woollen yarn, for which there were, respectively, 96 and 104 spindles. It was sold in 1798 after the Hallens went bankrupt and the building was then used as a cornmill. The town mills at Pendlestone were reconstructed in 1844-45. The main two-storey building, in the Tudor Gothic style and crenellated, is iron-framed. Its upper floor is illuminated by cone-shaped lights set into the roof in the same style as those used by Ignatius Bonomi in Marshall's Mill at Leeds about five years earlier. Power was provided by a waterwheel at the northern end, later replaced by a turbine, supplemented by a steam engine at the opposite end. The mill is now adapted as apartments.[42]

Market Drayton in the 19th century supplied national markets with horsehair cloth. Cotton, which was usually mixed with horsehair yarn, was spun at the parish workhouse from the 1760s, and the workhouse governor appointed in 1783 was sometimes described as a 'cotton manufacturer'. In 1810 Samuel and Peter Davies began to build an iron-framed mill for the manufacture of thread. Iron castings were supplied by William Hazledine and machinery was delivered, but when the property was offered for sale in 1811 buyers were asked to remove the buildings.[43] The manufacture of horsehair cloth for use as sieves in malt houses and dairies, and in upholstery, had begun by the 1790s. The principal building became the Victoria Mill, rebuilt for horse cloth manufacture in 1855 by H. & W. Sandbrook. It was commonly remarked that the three manufacturers in the town in the mid-19th century together employed about 200 people, most of them females. In 1861 Joseph Haslam employed three men, six boys, 34 women and 20 girls. Four weavers in that year were unmarried women living in some of the worst accommodation in the town, some of their children working as hair weavers' servers. The industry declined before the end of the century. Haslam's business was sold in 1903 to H.W. Woodcock, who continued to make horsecloth until 1934. His factory in Shropshire Street (SJ 674340 can still be recognised.[44]

Shropshire's textile industry extends from the 'vernacular' mode of production for local markets, through the modest specialisms of Bridgnorth and Market Drayton and flannel factories and silkmills representing the distant ripples of large-scale growth in other counties, to the Shrewsbury flaxmills, in their time larger and more innovative than any in the world, save their owners' parallel works in Leeds. The county's textile history highlights two contrasting themes – the profound impact of the Industrial Revolution of the late 18th century and the dogged persistence of small-scale local manufactures through the 19th century into the 20th. Study of the industry also shows the contrast between our understanding of Ditherington Mill, which is increasing because the mill still stands and can be viewed in new contexts as research progresses, and our ignorance of those textile factories that have long been demolished.

6 UNTOLD TREASURES: THE LANDSCAPE OF UPLAND MINING

Shropshire was for a time one of Britain's principal sources of lead ore. At its peak in the early 1870s the ore field around the Stiperstones produced about 10% of national output. Lead ore was mined on a significant scale in the region for nearly two centuries and the monuments of the industry are amongst the most impressive in Britain. Other workings for non-ferrous ores are dispersed across the county. None is of national significance, but their surviving remains illuminate the perpetual optimism of mining speculators.

The Stiperstones Region: Minerals and Economy

The principal minerals which occur in veins in the Stiperstones regions are *galena* or lead sulphide (PbS), *sphalerite* – zinc sulphide or zinc blend (ZnS) – and *barytes* or barium sulphate (BaSO4). Small quantities of silver and fluorspar have also been extracted. The metallic ores are found in three principal setts, one around Snailbeach, another between The Bog and Tankerville mines, and a third along the valley of the Hope Brook, incorporating The Grit and The Gravels mines. Barytes deposits occur more widely and were exploited from Cothercot in the east to Wotherton and Bulthy in the west.[1]

A pig of lead preserved at Linley Hall bears the inscription of the Emperor Hadrian and is evidence of Roman mining activity in the Stiperstones region. Lead ore was being worked on a substantial scale by 1739 at the Bog mine (SO 356978), and taken to be smelted in the Severn Gorge.[2] In 1777 Jonathan Scott constructed there the first Boulton & Watt steam pumping engine in the orefield, its arrival symbolising increased mining activity. Jonathan Lawrence of the White Grit Co. leased mineral rights, worked a smelter at Malehurst and coal mines at Pontesford, built pumping engines at Roman Gravels (SO 334998) in 1783 and the Grit in 1793, and had interests in the Pennerley and Bog mines. His family prospered during the Napoleonic Wars but their wealth was destroyed by litigation in the 1820s.[3]

The most productive mine in the orefield was at Snailbeach, where modern exploitation began in 1761 when Thomas Powys leased the mineral rights. His workers quickly established that this was a rich mine. In 1782 it was leased by the Snailbeach Mining Company, which worked it for more than a century.[4]

Falling prices and the law suits faced by the Lawrence family led to a decline in the industry after 1815, but prosperity gradually returned. In 1845 some 3,551 tons of lead ore were mined in Shropshire, some 4.54% of national output. *Mineral Statistics* show that over the next 20 years production varied between 2,729 tons and 4,491 tons, following no particular pattern.[5]

Swelling confidence was indicated by the installation in 1839 by a reconstituted Bog Mine Co. of a 370hp steam pumping engine, with a 70-inch x 9ft (1.78m x 2.74m) cylinder named the *Queen Victoria* and built by the Coalbrookdale Company. Spectators from as far away as Shrewsbury and Bishop's Castle swarmed over the hill, cannon were fired, and visitors feasted on ale, bread and cheese, while being serenaded by harpists and fiddlers. The company's agent delighted in the building of a chapel and the reform in morals that it represented. Optimism was not sustained. The mine closed in 1844 and was re-opened in 1856 by a fraudulent company which went into liquidation three years later.[6]

In the mid-1860s the Shropshire mines attracted speculative capital from the City of London and elsewhere, and a tide of new investment raised production year by year from 1867.[7] Output of lead ore reached a peak of 7,932 tons in 1875, and did not fall below 7,000 tons for six years from 1871. There was a slight decline after 1877, but 6,495 tons in 1883 represented 12.7% of national output. Thereafter decline was rapid. Less than 2,000 tons were extracted in 1889 and output exceeded that figure in only three years during the 1890s. It fell below 1,000 tons in 1902, and only 132 tons were mined in 1911. Lead mining in Shropshire effectively ceased before the outbreak of the First World War. In the parishes of Westbury and Pontesbury 178 men were employed in lead mining and smelting in 1841, a total which increased to 304 in 1851, but fell back to 201 ten years later. There was a modest increase to 248 by 1871, a slight falling back to 191 by 1881, and a sharp fall to 61 during the following decade.

The silver content of Shropshire ores was rarely high enough to make refining profitable, but small quantities were produced in 1854 and 1861, and then annually from 1872 until 1883, the peak year of production, when 11,388 ounces were extracted, amounting to 3.31% of UK output. Zinc ore production was recorded in 1858 and annually from 1863 until 1913. Output was 210 tons in 1863, rising to peaks of 837 tons in 1875, 914 tons in 1882 and 880 tons in 1897. Production slumped to 37 tons in 1910, but 444 tons were extracted in 1913. The 759 tons mined in 1872 formed 4.09% of UK output. Some fluorspar production was recorded in 1874-75 and between 1877 and 1879.

Silver, zinc and fluorspar were marginal to the mining economy of south Shropshire, but barytes sustained the industry on a modest scale for more than three decades after lead mining ceased. Barytes production was first recorded in 1857 when 1,000 tons mined in Shropshire represented 7.99% of UK output. No production was recorded in 1859, 1863 and 1866, but annual output figures subsequently appeared regularly, reaching peaks of 4,870 tons in 1875, 4,939 in 1884, 7,170 in 1890, 8,771 in 1901, 9,597 in 1906 and 13,772 in 1913. Between 1890 and 1893 and between 1901 and 1906 more than a quarter of the national output of barytes came from Shropshire, and production continued until after the Second World War.

The Stiperstones Region: The Archaeology of Lead-mining

The archaeology of the region is dominated by the remains of Snailbeach Mine, one of the richest sources of lead in Europe, which produced 131,900 tons of lead ore between 1845 and 1913, with a maximum output of 3,852 tons in 1846. Modest quantities of zinc ore were produced between 1858 and 1912, with a maximum output of 378 tons in 1902. Some fluorspar was extracted in the 1870s, and some silver in the early 1880s. Barytes

One of the wooden head-stocks which remained at Snailbeach (SJ 375021) in the 1960s.

production was first recorded in 1860, but remained at a low level until after 1900, reaching a peak of 3,734 tons in 1913. Extraction continued until the 1950s. Numbers of workers at Snailbeach are recorded from 1877, when 356 men were employed, 176 underground and 180 on the surface. The number fell during the early 1880s, no more than 86 being employed in 1885, but revived to 150 in the following year and remained around that level until the end of the century. It fell to less than a hundred by 1910. The pumping engine was halted in 1911 and the sections of the mine below the drainage adit were allowed to flood.[8]

Conservation and evaluation of the surviving components of the Snailbeach Mine only began in the early 1990s, by which time much that remained in the 1960s had been destroyed or allowed to decay, including two headstocks, an engine house, a dressing plant with a rake of wrought-iron kibbles filled with ore, and a jig with a spiral classifier. Most

Kibbles filled with lead ore that remained at the Snailbeach mines in the 1960s.

surviving buildings date from the 1870s, when the Cornishman Henry Dennis re-organised the mine. The site of a dressing shed once occupied by eight jigging machines and four buddles has yet to be excavated. The reservoir from which the machines were supplied with water remains at the head of the valley. There is a winding engine house of 1872, a compressor house of 1881 and a blacksmiths' shop. On Lordshill, above the main concentration of buildings, stands a Cornish engine house of 1856. The white tips of spoil from the dressing processes, one of Shropshire's most prominent landmarks, were removed at great expense in 1994. English Heritage has contributed substantially since the early 1990s to the conservation of the site which is now managed on behalf of Shropshire Council by the Shropshire Mines Trust, which arranges guided tours, some of which include visits to shallow underground workings.

Snailbeach ore was smelted at Pontesford from the early 1780s until 1862-63, when a reverberatory smelter was constructed on the hillside about 800m north of the mine (SJ 373030). Fumes were conveyed through a flue which cuts across the site to a chimney high on Lordshill, which also served the boilers of the nearby Cornish engine. The chimney, used until the smelter ceased working in 1895, remains intact, and some stretches of the flue can be traced.[9]

Henry Dennis was largely responsible for the construction of the 2ft 4in (0.71m) gauge Snailbeach District Railways, authorised by Act of Parliament (36/37 Vic. c.207) in 1873. The line opened in 1877 and linked the standard gauge line at Pontesbury (SJ 393063) with Crows Nest (SJ 371018), where there were sidings for ore delivered by road from mines to the south. A reverse siding ran up to the shafts and dressing floors of the Snailbeach Mine, and a further branch served the smelter. Between 1878 and 1883 the railway carried on average 14,000 tons of minerals per year.[10]

The best-preserved remains of the Snailbeach District Railway are within the mine complex, where the locomotive depot has been restored, and some track remains. The depot was photographed in the 1920s with 4-6-0T locomotives built by the Baldwin corporation in the United States for military service in the First World War and used at Snailbeach from 1923.

The railway outlasted the mine. In 1905 a branch was opened serving the quarry of the Ceiriog Granite Co. on the north side of Eastridge Wood near Habberley. Carriage of roadstone increased the railway's revenue and in 1909 some 38,000 tons were transported. The branch was closed in 1922. In the following year the celebrated Colonel H.F. Stephens took over the railway and receipts from the carriage of barytes and of roadstone from a quarry on Callow Hill remained buoyant through the 1930s. Loads of stone were worked by steam locomotives until 1946 when Salop County Council, which leased the line the follow year, began to use a farm tractor. The track was abandoned in 1959 when the quarry was made accessible to lorries.[11]

The Roman Gravels Mine ranked second after Snailbeach in terms of size and output and its site remains an absorbingly interesting landscape. Output declined after the demise of the Lawrence family and in 1859 totalled only 61 tons. It rose to 1,550 tons by 1873, and exceeded 2,000 tons for the rest of the decade, peaking at 3,109 tons in 1883. By 1892 it had fallen to 993 tons and never again reached significant levels. In 1877 there were 252 employees, 156 of them working underground, but only four men were employed

The engine house of the Ladywell Mine (SO 328994) erected by Arthur Waters in 1875.

by 1894. East Roman Gravels employed 89 miners in 1881, suffered severely in the recession in the following years but subsequently recovered. The workforce numbered 111 in 1898, but had slumped to four by 1901. The workings were developed in the 1870s by Arthur Waters, a Cornish engineer who was also concerned with the Tankerville and Ladywell mines. Spoil tips line the A488 road, which was crossed by a three-level wooden bridge (SO 334998), photographed about 1890 with miners filling the top deck, probably queuing for their wages. An engine house for a 60-inch Cornish engine by Harveys of Hayle, erected in 1878, stands on the hillside, with some pump rods remaining in the shaft. Below it in the valley stands a pumping engine house constructed about 1865 and the ruins of engines which drove winding gear and compressors. Another Cornish engine house of *c.*1850 remains at the East Roman Gravels mine, together with the ruins of a winding engine house.[12]

Most surviving structures in the Stiperstones orefield reflect the period of investment with speculators' funds from the City of London in the third quarter of the 19th century, or of later workings for barytes. The most prominent features of the landscape are the 19 engines houses of which there are significant remains.

The Tankerville or Ovenpipe Mine (SO 355995) is characteristic of the speculative investments of the 1860s and '70s. It was worked on a small scale until it came under the management of Arthur Waters, who discovered a new vein of ore in 1862. A new shaft was sunk and an underground engine installed. For a time in the mid-1870s the mine was prosperous. Output in 1875 peaked at 1,700 tons of ore, but by 1877 costs were increasing as prices were falling. A new company was formed and the workforce increased to 171 in 1880, but mining ceased and was never resumed. Two pumping engine houses built by Waters remain, together with the ruins of a winding engine house. Some of the structures at Tankerville have been conserved and the site is now managed by the Shropshire Mines Trust.[13]

At the Bog (SO 356979) the monuments of lead-mining have mostly been destroyed except for a small powder magazine and a blind adit. Two reservoirs which supplied water for dressing ore remain. One of them, dating from 1872, is bisected by a tramway built by Sir James Ramsden to carry barytes in the early 20th century.[14]

Mine	Purpose	Date	Grid reference
Central Snailbeach	Pumping	1860s	SJ 347022
East Grit	Pumping	1870s	SO 326981
East Roman Gravels (or West Tankerville)	Pumping Winding (California)	1850s 1870s	SJ 336003 SJ 336002
Ladywell	Pumping & Winding	1875	SO 328994
Old Grit	Pumping	1783	SO 326981
Roman Gravels	Pumping Pumping Winding & Compressor	1878 1860s 1870s	)) SJ 334000)
Ritton Castle	Pumping	1853	SO 349980
Snailbeach	Pumping Compressor Pumping (Lordshill) Halvans	1872 1881 1857-58 1899	SJ 373021 SJ 373021 SJ 374020 SJ 373023
Tankerville. Watson's Shaft	Pumping	1876	SO 355995
Tankerville. Ovenpipe	Pumping & Winding	1870s	SO 355995
White Grit	Pumping	1860s	SO 319979
Wotherton	Pumping	1865	SJ 279004

Table 6.1 Steam engine houses in the Stiperstones lead-mining region

The pumping engine house at the White Grit Mine (SO 319979) dating from the 1860s.

The Boat Level, a 2.8km-adit which drains water from The Bog and other mines into the valley of the Minsterley Brook (SJ 358002), is an outstanding monument to local mining skills. Its excavation was directed by John Lawrence and it was probably completed in 1797, the year in which the Boulton & Watt engine draining the Bog Mine was sold. Explorers of the level in the 1960s surmised that it was too narrow to have been used for transport, but when the Bog Mine was sold in 1830, it was described as navigable and the sale included two wooden boats and an iron one.[15] It thus appears that the Boat Level was used for carrying ore although the vessels must have been small.

The outlets remain of two drainage levels in the Hope Valley, the Wood (or Hope) Level (SJ 339008), driven in the 1790s by John Lawrence, and the Leigh Tunnel (SJ 331034), the venture which brought his son to bankruptcy. Water from Snailbeach is drained into the Hope Brook along a 1.3km-adit driven in the late 1790s. For a time it carried a rod-drive system from a waterwheel on the brook which pumped water up the mine shaft to the adit level.

Archaeological evidence of the growing sophistication of ore-dressing techniques in the 19th century is not plentiful in the Stiperstones orefield, although the accumulations of fine waste materials at Snailbeach, Roman Gravels, Pennerley and elsewhere show that Shropshire mine owners were concerned to increase the quality of the concentrates they sent to smelters. The change is reflected in the occupations of people working at the mines. In 1851 four lead ore washers were living on Pontesbury Hill. Ten years later two lead ore washers and two lead buddlers resided in the area, and there were 13 ore washers in Westbury parish, some of them women.

The first lead smelter in the region was established at Malehurst (SJ 384060) in 1778 and acquired by John Lawrence in the 1790s, when he also built a smelter adjacent to the *Nag's Head* at Pontesford. Both were adjacent to mines in the Shrewsbury Coalfield. The Maleshurst smelter closed before 1831. The Snailbeach Company built a smelter at Pontesford (SJ 409061) in 1784, in which water power was employed to blow ore hearths. The smelter building measures 55m x 7.3m, and from it a 110m flue led to a pair of chimneys constructed in 1832, one 48m, the other 55m high. Smelting at Pontesford ceased in 1863, when the reverberatory smelter on the hillside below Snailbeach came into operation. Parts of the Pontesford building incorporated within an agricultural warehouse, together with vitrified bricks re-used in farmyard walls, are the only significant remains. Lawrence's smelter at Pontesford was worked by the White Grit Co. in the 1830s, and by George Burr of the lead works in Shrewsbury in the years before its closure c.1880. The Bog Mining Co. had a smelter in the 1840s alongside Pontesbury Colliery. In 1851 Thomas Bennett, lead and coal mine agent, who was responsible for one of the smelters, employed 40 men and 15 boys, while Robert Rogers, who managed the other smelter, employed 50 men and 20 boys. Lead was also smelted in the 18th and early 19th centuries in the Severn Gorge.[16]

Most lead miners lived in the ancient parishes of Pontesbury, Westbury (including Minsterley) and Worthen, whose boundary lay close to Snailbeach. In 1851, 50 lead mine workers were living on Pontesbury Hill, where John Lawrence had encouraged squatting in the early 19th century. Some lead miners lived in the coal-mining community of Horsebridge (SJ 368061) some 4km from the nearest lead mine. Squatter cottages on the margins of cultivation line the road southward from Snailbeach, which runs past the

Tankerville and Pennerley Mines towards The Bog, and a similar pattern of settlement can be observed in the Hope Valley around the Roman Gravels mine. Investment in the extraction of lead ore always carried risks, and companies were clearly reluctant to put their own capital into housing. In the depression of the 1880s many mining families were sustained by the modest holdings which surrounded their cottages.

Barytes Mining

While lead mining in Shropshire had effectively ceased by 1914, the extraction of barytes continued into the 1950s. Some came from the unflooded upper workings of the major mines such as Snailbeach and The Bog, which yielded, respectively, 3,734 and 2,904 tons in 1913, and the remainder from smaller mines which only produced barytes. Amongst these was the Wotherton No.2 Mine (SJ 279004) which operated between 1865 and 1911 and achieved a maximum output of 6,100 tons in 1901. The sandstone engine house has been adapted as a dwelling. Barytes was loaded on to trailers in a lay-by off the B4386, and was hauled away by traction engines. The Huglith Mine (SJ 405015) began operation in 1910, employed up to 65 miners, and produced up to 20,000 tons a year in the 1930s. More than a dozen other mines were worked for barytes in the late 19th and early 20th centuries, but only two, Bulthy (SJ 309133) and Gatten (SO 387992) produced more than a thousand tons in any one year.[17]

The marketing of barytes depended on mills where the mineral could be ground into a form in which it could be used in the manufacture of paint or cosmetics. At least five water-powered mills served the Stiperstones region. A barytes miller is mentioned in the census for Minsterley in 1871. The Cliffdale Barytes Co. operated at Waterwheel (SJ 365024) in the Hope Valley from 1863 until c.1926. Tayler, Gilbertson & Co. worked a mill on the brook south of Minsterley (SJ 374045) between 1893 and 1909, when it was converted to a milk depot. Barytes was crushed at Sutton Mill (SJ 504107) on the edge of Shrewsbury, and at Hanwood (SJ 441093) where the mill, established in the buildings of the flax bleachworks after its closure in 1886, worked until 1922, and was supplied with barytes from Wotherton. The mill at Malehurst (SJ 384060) opened in 1922 and worked until c.1948. Barytes from Huglith Mine was conveyed to Malehurst by an aerial ropeway 5.6km long, built in 1911, while a similar 8.8km ropeway took the produce of The Bog mine to Minsterley.[18]

The engine house of the barytes mine at Wotherton (SJ 297004) which operated from the 1860s until shortly before the First World War.

162

There was also a barytes mill at Maesbury (SJ 304259), set up before 1861 by Edward Peate, which supplied materials to paint makers. Crushed barytes was taken to Oswestry to be sent by rail to Liverpool. Just one paint grinder, William Williams aged 60, born in Cropredy, Oxfordshire, was living in Maesbury in 1861, but subsequently the mill employed three or four people. It closed soon after 1900. A pair of mid-Victorian dwellings, 'Paint Mill Cottages', marks its site.

Copper Mining

Shropshire's copper mines are widely scattered. None was of national significance and *Mineral Statistics* after 1845 record production in only four years: 1866-68, when the maximum output was 98 tons of ore, and 1878 when 325 tons were produced.[19]

Modest quantities of copper ore were found in the Stiperstones mining region. The Pulverbatch census for 1861 records two copper miners living at Lawn Hill (SJ 416036). The workings at Westcott (SJ 402012), where some ruined structures remain, were usually regarded as a copper mine, and were responsible for Shropshire's appearance as a source of copper in *Mineral Statistics* for 1866-68, but they never produced significant quantities.

The small copper mine amongst the squatter cottages on Hayton's Bent Common (SO 517801), Stanton Lacy, on a Craven estate map of the 1770s.

A copper mine on Hayton's Bent Common (SO 517801) in Stanton Lacy parish was established in 1754 by John Lawrence. It appears to have been still working in the 1770s, but Sir Roderick Murchison, noting abandoned adits in the 1830s, remarked that it had never been profitable. Some spoil tips remain.[20]

There are several deposits of copper ores in the sandstones of north Shropshire. The most significant is the Pim Hill Mine (SJ 487214), which was leased to Abraham Darby I and partners in 1710. Its ore doubtless formed part of the charge of the copper smelter which Darby established at Coalbrookdale alongside his iron and brass works, but it is doubtful whether his partners worked the mine for the full 14-year period of the lease. The mine worked again in the 1860s and '70s, but proved unproductive. Three shafts remain about 200m apart, two of them infilled, together with a small open cast working. Malachite (copper carbonate hydroxide) has been recorded in an adjacent quarry. Darby's lease may have included the nearby Yorton Bank Mine (SJ 498238) which was the subject of prospecting in the 19th century.[21]

The Clive or Grinshill Mine (SJ 515142, 513263) was probably the most productive in north Shropshire. There were at least six shafts, one of which (SJ 513238) retains some pumping equipment. In the 1860s the mine provided employment for more than 30 men. 'Mine Cottage' in Clive village was one of the surface buildings. Ore was leeched in 24 stone tanks which were sold in 1869 to the Bryntail Mine near Llanidloes (SN 915869) where eight remain.[22]

Copper ore was also found near Hawkstone and Weston-under-Redcastle, where local gentry agreed to mine it in 1697. There was prospecting in the 1860s at Wixhill Mine (SJ 559287) but only some earthworks which may be the remnants of adits remain visible.[23]

A remnant of the engine house at the 19th-century copper mine at Eardiston (SJ 366246).

The only significant surface monument of copper mining in north Shropshire is the ruin of an engine house at Eardiston (SJ 365246), remnant of a mine that was worked spasmodically for more than 40 years, and supposedly had ten shallow shafts. It was leased in 1827 to David William Jones, a 'limeman' from Crickheath, who quickly abandoned it. From 1836 it was worked by the Eardiston Copper Company under the direction of William Allsopp, who drove a 160m-long drainage adit. In 1839 the company sought 'good steady workmen', offering 'constant employment on tribute, by bargain or by day'. Two years later the workforce consisted of four miners, all lodging with a farm labourer. In 1840 a London company took over the mine and built the engine house, but work ceased in September 1844 and the engine was removed. In 1859 the mine was leased by the Ruabon Spelter Works, who handed it in 1863 to the British Copper Co., a Scottish concern which became insolvent two years later. The mine was never worked again. Its output over four decades was probably less than 500 tons of ore, which was apparently carted to Queen's Head whence it travelled by canal boat to St Helens or Cheadle.[24]

Mining at Llanymynech

Deposits of malachite, galena and calamine (zinc oxide) on Llanymynech Hill have been worked since prehistoric times, and Roman coins have been found in the principal remaining feature of the mine, the 'ogof' or cave on the Welsh portion of the hill. Some ore was being extracted in the early 18th century. Operations in the 19th century were on a modest scale. Only one or two miners were employed before the 1870s, but in 1881 seven lead miners and two copper miners lived at the northern end of the hill. The Crickheath Mine at Pant (SJ 273233) recorded an output of 85 tons of lead ore and 60 tons of zinc ore in 1884, when it provided employment for eight underground and four surface workers. The mine was abandoned in 1886, but one miner was apparently still finding lead ore on the hill in 1891. Spoil tips containing malachite remain on the summit and there are some traces of adits.[25]

Lead ore from Llanymynech Hill was smelted in the 1840s and '50s at Maesbury, although the output from the Hill alone would not have required a sizeable smelter. Three lead furnacemen, all born in Pontesbury were living in the Maesbury area in 1861 but the smelter closed during the following decade. It was located by the canal (SJ 315250) and was called the 'Smelting House' on the tithe map. The site was subsequently occupied by an artificial manure works. The 46m-high chimney, destroyed in 1892, appears to have been part of the smelter rather than the manure factory.[26]

Lead-processing in Shrewsbury

Burrs' works in Shrewsbury was the principal lead-processing plant in the county. Thomas Burr, a London plumber who founded the company, moved to Shrewsbury between 1811 and 1813. The family retained contacts with the lead trade in the capital, leasing in 1853 a works in Commercial Road, Lambeth, managed by John Burr, Thomas' younger son.[27]

The premises of G.W. Dodwell, plumber, at the corner of Wyle Cop and Beeches Lane, Shrewsbury (SJ 494123) which from 1814 until 1854 was the lead works of Burr and Co. While Dodwell, may, as the picture suggests, have used the tall structure at the centre of the complex as a chimney, and it was so regarded by many Salopians, it had been built by the Burrs as a shot tower.

The company's first premises were on the south side of Beeches Lane near its junction with Wyle Cop and St Julian Friars. The property was amalgamated with that on the corner of St Julian Friars when the Century Cinema was constructed in 1914. At the beginning of the 19th century the site was occupied by Wicksteed's starch works, and it was used until 1814 by John Haycock & Co. for the manufacture of soap. Thomas Burr appears first to have set up a workshop to make lead pipes by extrusion, and then to have constructed a shot tower. The Burrs left Beeches Lane in 1854 and the site was subsequently occupied by another plumber, G.W. Dodwell, who probably used the shot tower as a chimney until it was demolished in 1904.[28]

In 1829 Thomas Burr purchased Charles Bage's linen weaving factory in Kingsland, which had been on sale for two years, but the site was probably not developed until the business had

165

been taken over by his sons, Thomas II and William, in 1836. The Burrs purchased the Cann Office estate, west of the Bage factory in 1849, and the property between the factory and Trouncer's brewery in 1852, acquisitions that enabled them to relinquish the Beeches Lane premises.[29]

The 1:500 map of 1882 shows that the core of the Kingsland works was Bage's vaulted weaving shed, 27.43m long and 9.14m wide. Around it were a lead rolling mill, a melting furnace and casting bed, a hydraulic pipe-making machine, two steam engines, furnaces and ovens for the production of red lead, machinery for grinding and dressing red lead, and a mill and smelting furnace for manufacturing white lead. In 1853 a 46m-high shot tower was constructed, and a vehicle ferry installed to convey wagons across the Severn *en route* to the railway depots.

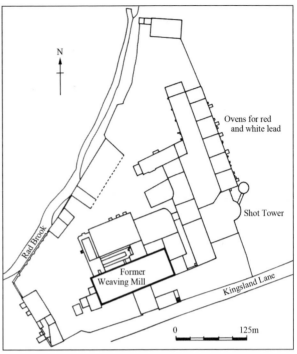

Plan of Burrs' Lead Works, Kingsland, Shrewsbury, re-drawn from the First Edition of the Ordnance Survey 1:500 plan of 1882.

The products were sheet lead, piping, shot and oxides in the form of white and red lead. The workforce in 1861 consisted of 35 men, five boys and a woman. George Burr operated one of the smelters at Pontesford in the 1870s which may have led to the erroneous belief that lead was smelted at Kingsland. Pollution from the works was the subject of many complaints in the 1850s, and as late as 1883.[30]

The lead works closed early in 1894, and was soon demolished, the shot tower collapsing as it was being felled at 11.45am on 3 May 1894.[31] The site became a recreation ground. One building remained, the cottage, No.5 Kingsland Lane, the home in 1890 of William Owen, works foreman, but in 1899 of Samuel Morgan, a gardener. It was standing in 1970 but has since been demolished.

Conclusions

The lead mining region around the Stiperstones is one of the most evocative industrial landscapes in Britain. Its heroic qualities appear the more remarkable in contrast with the modest scale of non-ferrous mining remains elsewhere. Spoil heaps, the ruins of engine houses, the tracks of railways and tramways, the remaining miners' cottages stimulate respect for past achievements at Snailbeach and Roman Gravels, whereas The Bog, denuded of its principal structures, and Tankerville, where evidence remains of how much was expended for little reward, are reminders of the vanity of so many human endeavours.

7 LINEAR LANDSCAPES: THE ARCHAEOLOGY OF TRANSPORT

Transport systems are most rewardingly studied as linear landscapes. A main line railway has more in common with a canal or a turnpike road than with the early railways from which its technology derives. A canal's locks, sluices, bridges and lock-keepers' cottages reflect the company's house styles and engineering practices rather than those of the communities where they happen to be located. Similarly, milestones and tollhouses on turnpike roads, signalling systems and goods sheds on railways, towpath gates on a river navigation, have corporate rather than local characteristics.

Air Transport

It is ironic that Shropshire is one of the best places in Britain for studying the development of aeronautics and the history of air transport. The county has no significant connections with aircraft manufacturing and the only linear landscape features which link it with the air transport industry are the vapour trails of transatlantic airliners heading southwards across the chill dawn skies. It is the museum at Cosford that marks the county out. This began on a small scale in the 1970s and is now part of the Royal Air Force Museum. It houses many military and experimental aircraft, but the collection also illustrates as well as any in the world the development of airliners since the late 1930s. Aircraft which can be seen, not all of them versions for civilian passenger use, include the Avro York, the Douglas C47 (or DC3 Dakota), the Junkers Ju52, the de Havilland Comet 1 and the Bristol Britannia. The restoration workshops at the museum provide insights into the intricacies of aircraft construction and manufacture.

Pipelines

Scarcely more visible than vapour trails are the pipelines that cross Shropshire. The first, from a pumping station on Cosford Brook (SJ 781046) to Tettenhall, was established by Wolverhampton Corporation under parliamentary powers obtained in 1855. Water first flowed through it on 8 October 1858. Between that time and 1914 six further pumping engines were added, two of them supplied by the Lilleshall Company in 1879-82. In 1906 a 1.2km aerial ropeway was constructed to supply the station's boilers with coal from a siding on the Shrewsbury-Wolverhampton railway. The pumping station was converted from steam to electric operation in 1948.[1]

The dams in the Elan Valley designed by James Mansergh created reservoirs from which water was conveyed to Frankley Reservoir near Birmingham by a pipeline 118km long,

The Cosford Brook pumping station (SJ 781046) from which water has been pumped to Wolverhampton since 1858.

The viaduct which carries the pipeline from the Elan Valley reservoirs to Birmingham across the valley of the Corn Brook on the south side of the Clee Hills (SO 606747).

The pumping station and depot on the Elan Valley-Birmingham pipeline at Holywaste (SO 657763) bearing the date 1902 and the arms of the City of Birmingham.

about a third of it passing through Shropshire, which was built between 1896 and 1906. It cuts across Bringewood Chase south of Ludlow, entering Shropshire (SO 495742) before bridging the River Teme (SO 522737) and the Ledwych Brook (SO 537738). The water then flows over a concrete aqueduct at Bennetts End (SO 582744) before entering Studley Tunnel through the limestone between Gorstley Rough and the Novers, and emerging on to another aqueduct. It crosses the Corn Brook (SO 606747) and passes beneath the A4117 Ludlow-Cleobury Mortimer road at Hollywaste (SO 649757) before reaching a pumping station (SO 657763) where four 2ft (0.62m) gauge diesel locomotives were once employed. It crosses the River Rea (SO 675767) north of Cleobury Mortimer and takes an east-north-easterly course through the Wyre Forest to Button Oak (SO 753780) before bridging the Severn (SO 775783) and passing out of the county.[2]

The dam at Lake Vyrnwy, the work of George Deacon, Surveyor and Water Engineer of the City of Liverpool, was the first high masonry dam in Great Britain, and when completed in 1891 impounded the largest artificial reservoir in Europe. The 109km pipeline between the lake and Merseyside enters Shropshire west of Oswestry. The filter beds at Llanforda (SJ 277295) were served by a 2ft (0.6m) gauge railway system worked by diesel-mechanical locomotives until the 1980s. The aqueduct skirts the northern edge of Oswestry, the appropriately named Liverpool Road having been laid out along its course c.1900. It then goes north of and almost parallel to the former Cambrian Railway to Hindford, where it crosses the Ellesmere Canal (SJ 335330) before heading north-east, and passes out of the county west of Brookhill (SJ 412390).[3]

A more recent pipeline runs into the Black Country from Chelmarsh Reservoir (SO 737847), built for the South Staffordshire Water Company in the late 1960s, from which an aqueduct over the River Severn supplies a waterworks on the opposite bank.

Shropshire was also on the route of the pipeline from Ellesmere Port to Fawley (Hampshire) and Shanklin (Isle of Wight) that formed part of the PLUTO (**P**ipe **L**ine **U**nder **T**he **O**cean) network, established in 1944 to supply fuel to the Allied forces in France after the Normandy landings. There was a pumping station near Fordhall Farm (SJ 649330) west of Market Drayton but few visible traces of the pipeline remain.

The Severn Navigation[4]

Shropshire's principal means of long-distance transport in 1660, and the source of much wealth, was the River Severn. Francis Ap Owen of Dowles, who died in 1669, had a trow, a barge and a boat worth £100, and timber to the same value awaiting despatch on the river. Richard Brooke of Madeley, who died in 1670, owned a vessel called the *Jonathan* worth £40. Abel Jones of Shrewsbury, who died in the same year, had a pair of barges worth £42. Edward Jeffries of Bridgnorth, who died in 1673, operated on a lower scale. He owned a barge and a cockell boat, which, with their equipment, were worth only £8, and his movable possessions were valued at only £24.[5] The contrast between the bargemen highlights the two main traffics on the Severn. The wealthier owners were concerned with the carriage to Gloucester and ports downstream, particularly Bristol, of Shropshire's more valuable manufactures – iron, leather, grain, cheese and paper – and with return freights of groceries, tobacco, wine, spirits, Baltic timber and other goods which could not be produced in the county. Many cargoes from Shropshire for the estuary ports were transhipped at Bewdley to the trows which departed fortnightly to meet the spring and neap tides at Gloucester, but the county's wealthier owners had at least some vessels that could survive the dangerous tidal waters below that city. Many bargemen, probably the majority, made their livings by carrying bulk cargoes over short distances, particularly taking coal from the Ironbridge Gorge downstream to Bridgnorth, Bewdley, Worcester, Tewkesbury and Gloucester.

The Severn Navigation had medieval origins but developed when coal from Broseley and Madeley was first mined on a large scale in the 16th century. The Wolverhampton University Port Books project showed that the river was part of a thriving commercial economy by 1700.[6] It made possible the growth of the Shropshire iron industry and in conjunction with the Staffordshire & Worcestershire Canal it carried the produce of Shropshire ironworks to customers in the Black Country and Birmingham. In conjunction with the Shropshire Canal it carried substantial quantities of coal downstream from Coalport, about 50,000 tons a year by c.1802 and 80,000 tons by 1830. The trade in general merchandise was lost to canals and road transport in the early 19th century, and competition from railways caused the navigation to decline after 1840, and particularly after the opening of the Severn Valley Railway in 1862. The last commercial vessel on the Shropshire portion of the river sank after it hit one of the piers of the bridge at Bridgnorth on 25 January 1895.[7]

The Shropshire portion of the Severn was never improved. In 1786 a bill to permit the construction of 16 locks between Diglis (Worcester) and Coalbrookdale, surveyed by William Jessop, the most able canal engineer of the time, was rejected by the House of Commons after pressure from Shropshire bargemen. John Randall observed some 80 years later that 'As a class bargeowners are opposed to innovation', and that the oldest men remembered how when George III was king they shouted themselves hoarse and tossed their caps in honour of victory over attempts to improve the channel. When locks were constructed on the river between Stourport and Gloucester in the 1840s, Shropshire bargeowners were given exemption from tolls, but there was no serious proposal to construct locks further upstream.[8]

The Shropshire Severn remained a river that could be used without payment, and which was free from the kind of bureaucratic controls that generate documentary records. Archaeology is thus of particular importance in gaining understanding of how the navigation operated.

Artefacts contribute but little to that understanding. Some small items survive, such as the anchor (or cedger) displayed in the museum at Ironbridge, but insufficient to justify analysis. No boats used on the Upper Severn remain, so that images provide the most valuable evidence.

George Perry, in describing vessels on the Severn in 1758, distinguished between trows of between 40 and 80 tons, with main, top- and sometimes mizzen-masts, and single-masted barges and frigates of between 20 and 40 tons. Both types were up to 60ft (9.1m) long.[9] He was probably making a distinction between vessels that could safely negotiate the estuary, and those that usually went no further downstream than Gloucester. Analysis of pictorial and documentary evidence shows that Severn bargeowners used a wide range of vessels. Whatever their size, Severn vessels were of similar construction – clinker-built, with D-shaped sterns and masts that could be lowered to pass under bridges. Inventories provide evidence of the equipment carried on board, which included chains, ropes, tarpaulins, hooks, planks, poles, shafts, oars, sails, stays, blocks, windlasses, anchors, beams and scales, pitch, tar, oakum, barrels, chests, shovels and scoops. Some had awnings that could be erected over stern sections to provide accommodation for crews where there was no cabin. The more valuable vessels recorded include the 'great trow at Gloucester' worth £70, the property of Francis Owen of Madeley in 1732, and his 'middle trow' worth £60. A trow belonging to Richard Lacon of Bridgnorth was valued at £67 10s in 1735, while the trow *Loving Brother*, belonging to Thomas Andrews, also of Bridgnorth, was worth £60 in 1723. These vessels, like a half-completed 70-ton trow on the stocks at the Rovings in 1796, could trade in the estuary. Some trows carried 'oars vessels' or 'tow boats' that could be used to get free from sandbanks.[10]

Most vessels trading in Shropshire were smaller and less valuable. Some owners had 'sets' of vessels, like the Shrewsbury man whose fleet in 1812 comprised the *Defiance* of 40 tons, the *Mary* of 35 tons and the *William* of 14 tons. John Rees, also of Shrewsbury, was working until 1835 with the *Cambrian*, a 55-ton barge, the *Hannah*, a 42-ton barge, and a 'capital boat' of seven tons. The 20 boats working from Shrewsbury in 1837 comprised two of 50 tons, one of 45 tons, three of eight tons, and three of six tons. One of the 50-ton barges, the *Eliza*, property of Thomas Bratton, was sketched by William Vandyck Brown while moored at Frankwell Quay.[11] An early 19th-century engraving shows a large vessel moored at Cound Lane End, probably a trow owned by the Dodson family. One of the last depictions of a trow is in a photograph of the Severn Warehouse, Ironbridge, probably taken in the 1880s. An earlier photograph of the boatyard on the other side of the river, probably from the 1860s, provides a rare view of some of the single-masted barges used in the coal trade, some of which also appear in late 19th-century photographs of Bridgnorth held by

Severn barges moored at the premises of Edward Gother, boat builder, at the Bower Yard, Benthall (SJ 667035) in the late 1850s. An unusual picture of the smaller Severn barges used principally for carrying coal.

the Rutter family.[12] The smallest vessels, the 'boats' shown in illustrations of Shrewsbury and Bridgnorth, were probably used to move goods between barges and wharfs. The larger vessels worked with crews of three or sometimes four men. The 1861 census records at Gloucester docks the 50-ton *Endeavour* and the 30-ton *Maria Jane*, both of Ironbridge, each with a crew of three, but four men slept on the *Industry* which was moored at Madeley.

John Wilkinson's celebrated *Trial*, generally regarded as the first iron boat, was launched at Willey Wharf in 1787. In 1857 a newspaper commented that iron barges had been commonplace on the River Severn ever since, although they proved no cheaper than those of conventional construction. The Onions family of ironmasters in 1820 worked four iron barges, one worth £150, while the wrought-iron frigate *Salop* was offered for sale at the Meadow Wharf, Coalbrookdale in 1812. John Randall remembered seeing *Trial* after her working life was ended, half-sunk in the Severn downstream from Coalport Bridge.[13]

The nature of the river meant that much of a bargeman's time was spent waiting. The trade in coal from the Ironbridge Gorge was dependent on 'flushes', sudden increases in the water level. In 1784 it was remarked that when the river level rose, it was commonplace for between 60 and 80 vessels to leave the vicinity of Coalbrookdale carrying as much as 4,000 tons of coal downstream. In consequence remarkable numbers of barges could sometimes be seen in the gorge. In 1836 Charles Hulbert counted 72 from Coalport Bridge. A journey to Gloucester from Ironbridge took about 24 hours, but few vessels were able to accomplish more than 20 voyages a year.[14]

John Randall wrote in the 1850s that Shropshire barges 'go down with the stream and are drawn back by horses'.[15] Bargemen also made use of sails, when and where this was possible. Before the construction of towpaths vessels were dragged upstream by gangs of

Loadcroft Wharf, Coalbrookdale, probably in the late 1880s. There are plateway wagons on the left, and the wharf crane remains in place. The barge is the largest to have been photographed in the Severn Gorge, and has cabins at the stem and stern. Three three-storey warehouses with taking-in doors line the Wharfage.

'bow haulers', who were the subject of moral disapproval from the propertied classes. The small vessels portrayed in some views of the river may have been used by bow haulers to return home after they had dragged up a vessel over the section they were accustomed to work.

The towpath between Bewdley and Coalbrookdale, authorised in 1772, was not completed until 1800. The path from Coalbrookdale to Frankwell Quay, Shrewsbury, received parliamentary assent in May 1809, and was completed, under the direction of William Hazledine, the following November. Hazledine's notebook, with meticulous drawings of the 164 gates by which the path passed through field boundaries, still survives.[16] No towpath was constructed upstream from Frankwell, although some traffic used this stretch of the river until the 1850s. Observation of the circuitous route of the Severn between low sandstone cliffs shows that bowhaulers must have spent some of their time wading through water. The towpath acts designated one side or the other of the river as the right of way, the left bank through Shrewsbury, the right bank from the horse ferry provided by the towpath company at Underdale to Cressage Bridge, the left bank to Coalport and thence on the right bank past the county boundary to Bewdley. Bridges were provided across most of the tributaries at their points of confluence. An iron bridge cast by the Coalbrookdale Company in 1828 crosses the mouth of the Borle Brook (SO 753817), while the Mor Brook (SO 733885) is spanned by a bridge made by Onions of Broseley in 1824. A small stone arch crosses the mouth of the Leighton Brook (SJ 608050). There is no trace of any means of crossing the delta at the mouth of the Cound Brook, although the minutes of the towpath trustees show that they built at least three bridges there. Between Eardington

The bridge built by the towpath trust across the mouth of the Mor Brook near Eardington (SO 733885). It was cast in 1824 by the Broseley foundry of John Onions.

The bridge across the mouth of the Borle Brook downstream from Highley (SO 753817), built by the towpath trust, and cast at Coalbrookdale in 1828.

and Arley evidence can be found of shelves dug to create a level course for the towpath, and erosion reveals that the path was sometimes re-surfaced with waste materials from the Coalport Chinaworks, although initially iron slag and gravel were used. The towpaths were financed by tolls charged on horses – not on boats – and the companies were responsible for clearing fords for the passage of vessels at low water. The Bewdley-Coalbrookdale company relinquished its powers on Lady Day 1885, while those of the Coalbrookdale-Frankwell path were taken over by Shrewsbury Borough Corporation in 1884.[17]

Perry showed that in 1756 there were 313 barges working on the Severn from Bewdley and places upstream, the property of 182 owners. Of these 6% of both owners and barges were to be found in Shrewsbury, 46% of owners and 44% of barges in the Severn Gorge, 30% of owners and 28% of barges in Bridgnorth, and 10% of owners and 15% of barges in Bewdley. There remained 15 owners and 21 barges in smaller settlements, four of each at Pool Quay, three owners and seven barges at Cound, and eight owners and ten barges between Bridgnorth and Bewdley. Evidence from later periods suggests that the relationship between the ports stayed much the same.

At Shrewsbury most warehouses were grouped around the quays at Mardol and Frankwell constructed in 1607 by Rowland Jenks. The area was altered by the construction on a new alignment of the Welsh Bridge in 1796, by the demolition of the buildings on Mardol Quay after the Second World War and by the building of a theatre and local government offices at Frankwell in the early 21st century. There were yards on the two quays specialising in handling timber, and warehouses for hops, cider, spirits, grain and lead. Some cargoes were handled on the upstream side of the English Bridge where Marine Terrace now stands. The Union Wharf near the Castle at the bottom of St Mary's Water Lane was constructed by Thomas Groves from 1823, became the base of the bargeman John Rees, and is evidence of the vitality of the navigation in the early 19th century.[18]

In the Ironbridge Gorge, Stephen Duckworth identified from documentary, cartographic, pictorial and archaeological sources 16 principal wharfs upstream from Coalport Bridge: Meadow, Ludcroft, Wharfage, Bower Yard, Benthall Rails, Ladywood, Barnetts Leasow, Bedlam Furnaces, Coalford, Lloyds Head, Calcutts, Lloyds, Jackfield Rails, Werps, Coalport Chinaworks and the Shropshire Canal terminus, to which can be added Swinney Wharf and Willey Wharf further downstream.[19] Some, like the Coalbrookdale Company's Ludcroft Wharf or the canal terminus and interchange at Coalport, were the results of investment in the late 18th or early 19th centuries. Others, with relatively simple facilities, remained in use with little change from the 16th century until the end of the navigation. Duckworth's meticulous examination of the Calcutts wharf, identifying wooden posts, remnants of wharf walls and towpath levels, showed that plentiful archaeological evidence remains even on a site covered by waste tips and eroded by flooding.

Commercial warehouses were concentrated along The Wharfage, a quay built in the first half of the 18th century that became a through road with the opening of the Iron Bridge. Three remain, with pulleys and taking-in doors making them instantly recognisable as warehouses, together with the Coalbrookdale Company's single-storey transit warehouse, now the Museum of the Gorge, an extraordinary Gothic structure of 1834 designed by Samuel Cookson and regarded as one of those 'convincing and cemented proofs of the March of Improvement'. It must always have been subject to flooding. It was served by plateways running down Coalbrookdale which, from Dale End, also extended in an upstream direction to Meadow Wharf, which in 1816 was handling all the iron despatched by the Lightmoor Company and much of the coal from the Coalbrookdale Company's collieries. The deep water, enabling vessels to moor in summer, was seen as one of the advantages of the wharf.[20]

The interchange at Coalport where the Shropshire Canal reached the riverside repays study in its present condition and has enormous archaeological potential. The north bank of the river is lined by a massive stone wall, topped in places by bricks held together in cast-iron frames. The 20m slope between the canal and the river was crossed by seven diamond-shaped railways, which ran on to drawbridge-like constructions that could be extended above the holds of waiting barges on the river. These devices were probably the 'suspended trams' mentioned by John Randall in his description of Coalport in the late 1850s. They were probably used for loading coal, since pigs or bars of iron were traditionally carried by strong men in the pockets of leather aprons. A five-storey warehouse where small consignments were handled spanned the canal and projected over the river. Huge piles of coal awaiting transit dominated the landscape. It seems astonishing that when the Coalport branch railway opened in 1861, it was anticipated that it would deliver large quantities of freight to be despatched by river barge. The LNWR laid rail connections into the interchange area, but they do not appear to have been extensively used, mine owners and ironmasters preferring to despatch their freight direct to customers by rail. The main topographical features of the interchange were restored in the early 1970s, and the stonework at the end of some of the diamond-shaped railways can still be seen, together with the base of a pillar crane, and a stone bearing the date 1792 from the five-storey warehouse which is incorporated into a modern wall.[21]

In Bridgnorth iron rings to which barges were moored, as depicted on several engravings, remain on the piers of the bridge. The river frontage on Underhill Street is dominated by a mid-19th-century development in the Italianate style, consisting of two three-bay, three-storey blocks, with blind arcading in their front elevations, flanking a two-storey, nine-bay range. Between this building and St Mary's Steps stands the 'Old Malthouse', a two-storey structure, with lucams above the former taking-in doors in the gables. Adjacent to the bridge is the four-storey Ridley's Warehouse, once used for the storage of grain, on the upstream side of which is Riverside, where the level of the roadway was raised in 1887. The hanging nets of fishermen dominated the area in the 1850s. Behind the river frontage are cliffs of soft red sandstone in which are many traces of cave workshops and dwellings, some of which were still occupied in the mid 19th century.[22]

There are few traces of wharfs and warehouses in the smaller riverside settlements. There was a 'common landing place' for timber near the mouth of the River Perry in 1728, and a quay with a warehouse where iron was landed at Pimley in the 1660s. A wharf at Cound Lane End was the base for the Dodson family's fleet of barges. There was a mooring at Cressage from which a barge broke loose and crashed into the temporary bridge at Buildwas in 1791, and a wharf at Sheinton where a man was drowned in 1862. At the Rovings in Barrow parish were a boat-building yard, a wharf where Caughley porcelain was loaded, and a public house traditionally kept by a bargeowner, which closed during the 1860s. Bargate Wharf (SO 753809) in Kinlet, on the border with Arley in Staffordshire, was a point of despatch for timber from the Wyre Forest as was a 'load' used in the 18th century further downstream at Dowles.

During the 18th century barges were constructed in Shrewsbury, on the site now occupied by the Sixth Form College, at the Bower Yard, Benthall, at several sites in Jackfield, at the Rovings and in three yards in Bridgnorth. By 1851 only two barge builders remained, Edward Gother at Benthall and William Oakes at Bridgnorth. The sale of Oakes' yard in 1856 provides an opportunity to identify the principal components of a boat-building establishment. He had oak, ash and elm timbers in the round and in planked form, together with deal planking. Long lengths were leant against each other to form the tent-like structures depicted in several illustrations of the river. Oakes' yard also included a blacksmith's shop, three sawpit sheds and an almost completed 40-ton barge.

The succession of islands in the Severn is one of the river's more curious features. David Pannett showed in the 1970s that all are on the sites of fish weirs, that there are archaeological remains of most of the 28 weirs in the county listed in 1575, and that archaeological and field name evidence identifies the sites of six weirs not on the list. Weirs were fences of stakes encompassing wickerwork fish traps. A weir impeded traffic and was usually by-passed by an artificial channel dug within the parish or manor to which it belonged, thus creating an island, usually called a bylet. Most fish weirs were medieval in origin, and some listed in 1575 probably went out of use soon afterwards. Others remained as significant sources of food. Little Shrawardine weir (SJ 391152) was working in 1661 when the 'Materialls for the Weare or fishing garth' were valued at five shillings in the probate inventory of Edgar Dyos. The weir remained a fishery in the early 19th century. Fitz Weir (SJ 453162) was the subject of a watercolour in 1878, and that at Montford was similarly recorded in 1897. The Preston Boats weir (SJ 510117) was intact in the 1920s. The channels around most weirs have filled with silt, but well-defined islands remain at Holywell (SJ 504134), Pimley (SJ 520142) and Sutton Maddock (SJ 707017), and the stubs of stakes are visible at low water at Montford, Bromley's Forge (SJ 439165) and Preston Boats. A bowling green occupies

Remains of the early 18th-century lock that gave access from the River Severn to the River Tern (SJ 553091).

176

the bylet at Bridgnorth (SO 719929) whose by-pass channel carries only a trickle of water except at times of flood. The barge gutter at Coton Hill (SJ 490134) is similarly silted up. The bylet, called Poplars Island, was the scene of a fête in 1857 after which the bridge of boats linking it to Coton Hill collapsed with the loss of ten lives.[23]

Some of the Severn's tributaries were navigable. The lower reaches of the Vyrnwy were used by barges carrying iron and lead ore in the early 18th century, and in 1824 one Thomas Jones stole a cow's hide from a vessel on the river at Melverley. The Tern also carried barges. A vessel that lay sunk in the river near Attingham Park in 1757 had been used by Joshua Gee, the ironmaster, to convey iron to Upton Forge, and the Coalbrookdale Co. accounts in 1737-38 record the despatch of small quantities of iron to Tern Forge. The best evidence for the navigation is archaeological. In 1969 Dr Michael Lewis excavated the remains of a lock at the mouth of the river (SJ 553091), which had walls of ashlar blocks joined by iron cramps set in lead, and a floor of transverse timbers with brick paving. The lock could have passed a boat 23ft long and 7ft 8in in beam (7m x 2.33m). The lock was probably built c.1710 at the time that Tern Forge was being constructed. About 1797 Humphrey Repton, the landscape gardener, cut away one side and incorporated it into a weir designed to create a lake visible from Attingham Park. The weir collapsed and the lake disappeared in a flood in the 1830s. Several pictures of Ludlow Castle show what appear to be commercial vessels on the River Teme. It would seem sensible to have moved iron from the furnace and forge at Bringewood (Herefordshire) to Ludlow by river, and there is good evidence of navigation on the lower reaches of the Teme, but it is doubtful whether there was ever through navigation from Ludlow to the Severn.[24]

Canals
Shropshire's first canals, some of the earliest in Britain, were an integral part of the economy of the Coalbrookdale Coalfield (see chapter 4, pp.105-08). The first long-distance waterways in the county were products of the 'canal mania' of the 1790s – the Acts of Parliament for the Leominister, Ellesmere and Shrewsbury canals were all passed in 1793. The last two waterways were linked in 1835 when the Birmingham & Liverpool Junction Canal was opened between Autherley and Nantwich, with a branch from Norbury Junction to Wappenshall.

The Shrewsbury Canal
The Shrewsbury Canal linked the tub boat canals of the Coalbrookdale Coalfield with the county town. The company purchased 1.6km of the private Wombridge Canal, which gave it access to the hub of the tub boat system at Donnington Wood. At Trench (SJ 688121) an inclined plane conveyed vessels into a 6.5km stretch along which 11 locks lowered boats to a 19.3km pound extending to the terminus at Shrewsbury, with aqueducts crossing the Tern at Longdon, the Roden at Rodington and the Uffington Brook at Pimley, and a tunnel beneath Haughmond Hill at Berwick. The canal's principal source of water was a reservoir at Trench supplied chiefly from mine workings. The canal opened from Trench to Long Lane in 1793, to Berwick Wharf in 1796 and to Shrewsbury in 1797. Two sections in Shrewsbury were closed respectively in 1922 and 1939, and the whole waterway was closed by the LMSR Act of 1944. Hopes of re-opening in the 1960s were frustrated by the breaking of its line by drainage authorities.[25]

The Trench inclined plane (SJ 689123), which raised boats 22.9m over a distance of 204m, was of the type that had become standard on the tub boat system. Its working life extended for 127 years, and when traffic ceased in 1921 it was the last surviving canal inclined plane in Britain. The stonework of the docks at the head of the incline remained until the 1970s, when a new road obscured all trades of the previous landscape, except for the public house, once the *Shropshire Arms*, now the *Blue Pig*, which features in old photographs of the plane.

The 11 locks were built 6ft 7in (2m) wide for the passage of tub boats. After 1835 locks 10 and 11 were widened to 7ft 4in (2.24m), permitting standard narrow boats to reach Shrewsbury. Boats of 6ft 2in (1.88m) beam, called 'Shroppies' or 'narrer-narrer boats' were constructed to operate to and from Trench. Several years after the canal opened Telford said that the locks were 81ft (24.68m) long, thus capable of admitting trains of four 20ft tub boats, but that they had intermediate gates to enable the economic passage of one or three boats. Tony Clayton in the 1970s discovered traces of grooves, probably the locations of intermediate gates, in the chamber walls of locks 4 and 6, and in-filling in the walls of locks 10 and 11. The locks had

1.	Trench	SJ 683125
2.	Baker's/Castle	SJ 677125
3.	Turnip	SJ 673131
4.	Hadley Park	SJ 671133
5.	Peaty	SJ 670135
6.	Shucks	SJ 669136
7.	Wheat Leasowes	SJ 668137
8.	Britton	SJ 666141
9.	Wappenshall	SJ 663146
10.	Eyton/Drawbridge	SJ 652150
11.	Eyton Lower	SJ 643153

Table 7.1 Locks on the Shrewsbury Canal

vertical lower gates lifted within 'guillotine' frames, with suspended counterbalances. From 1840 cast-iron counterbalances rising and falling in wells at the sides were substituted at locks 1, 2, 3, 5, 7, 8, 9 and 10, thus simplifying the operation of the gates.[26]

The aqueduct that carried the Shrewsbury Canal over the River Roden at Rodington (SJ 589242).

The abutments of the most modest of the three aqueducts on the Shrewsbury Canal, at Pimley, were removed in the 1990s. The aqueduct at Rodington (SJ 589242), demolished *c.*1970, was characteristic of the first generation of canals, a masonry structure of three arches, the crowns of which were a considerable distance below the parapet in order to accommodate the great thickness of puddled clay needed to seal the bottom of the waterway.

The most important surviving monument on the canal is the 57m long, 4.9m high aqueduct over the River Tern at Longdon (SJ 617656). Josiah Clowes, the canal's engineer, died late in 1794, and on 10-12 February 1795 his preparatory works for the aqueduct were damaged by floods. Thomas Telford was appointed to succeed Clowes on 28 February, and was instructed to report on what might be done at Longdon. On 14 March the canal proprietors approved the construction of an iron aqueduct supplied from the Ketley Ironworks by William Reynolds & Co. It was anticipated that the structure would be completed by 14 September 1795, although it was not opened to traffic until 14 March 1796.

The aqueduct consists of a trough whose sections are bolted together through flanges, with a towpath alongside it. Trough and towpath are supported at each end by masonry abutments, and at intermediate points by cruciform cast-iron columns, with diagonal bracing struts of similar section. John Healey pointed out that the hand-made bricks and sandstone used in the eastern abutment resembled the materials used at Rodington, suggesting that it was the work of Clowes, and that it formed part of a planned symmetrical structure consisting of three central arches, flanked on each site by a cutwater and two arches linked to the abutments. The west abutment, which is of sandstone rather than brick, appears to have been built by Telford on foundations provided by Clowes, and appears to be slightly misaligned with the iron structure. Telford used only one of the original pier footings as a base for the columns supporting the trough and placed the other two sets of columns on new foundations. Charles Hadfield demonstrated that Longdon cannot have been a 'trial run' for the construction of the much larger Pontcysyllte Aqueduct, for little progress can have been made at Longdon before the proprietors of the Ellesmere Canal determined to build an iron trough over the River Dee on 14 July 1795.[27]

The aqueduct carrying the Shrewsbury Canal over the River Tern at Longdon (SJ 617656), showing the eastern abutment.

The 887m-long Berwick Tunnel (SJ 535117-SJ 532120) was part of the final section of the waterway opened to traffic in January 1797. From its opening until 1819 it had a 3ft wide cantilevered towpath, beneath which water could circulate, as on the Pontcysyllte Aqueduct. The ends are now sealed.

The Shrewsbury Canal had distinctive accommodation bridges, lifting structures whose decks were raised by chains attached to beams pivoted on upright wooden, square-section columns, sustained by diagonal braces at the bases. The last to survive, at Wappenshall (SJ 661146) and Rodington (SJ 592142), were demolished in the 1970s. Flat, channel-section cast-iron bridges were also used. The largest, Teague's Bridge from Wombridge (SJ 693124), is in the custody of the Ironbridge Gorge Museum, while the smaller bridge that spanned the entrance to the basin at Long Lane (SJ 635155) has been re-used at the Coalport Chinaworks museum. A third remains *in situ* east of Pimley (SJ 523143) at a point where canal water was diverted to supplement the flow to Uffington Mill.

In Shrewsbury an extensive coal wharf was created in the area now bounded by Castle Foregate, New Park Road, Beacalls Lane and Howard Street. Space was taken by coal suppliers including William Hazledine and the Lilleshall Company, but expectations that the canal would reduce the cost of coal in the county town were disappointed. After the canal was linked to the national system the Butter Market was constructed on the southern edge of the wharf, and the waterway was extended up to its doors. When its functions were taken over by Shrewsbury's general market in 1869, the Butter Market was adapted as a railway

The eastern portal of Berwick Tunnel (SJ 535117), 1966.

Minor roads and tracks crossed the Shrewsbury Canal on lifting bridges, all of which have been demolished. This example stood at Rodington (SJ 592142).

warehouse, fulfilling that function for about a century. It was adapted as a night club in the 1980s. In 1840 a boat builder, Edward Evans, occupied a site on the wharf. By 1859 the canal was owned by the London & North Western Railway which constructed a line through a short tunnel under Howard Street, which fanned out into sidings linked by wagon turntables which occupied most of the eastern side of the yard. A travelling crane was constructed alongside the Beacalls Lane boundary, together with a brick goods shed in the north-western corner, to which abutted a small corn mill. By the 1880s the canal was cut back, extending only halfway across the wharf, its route to the former Butter Market being occupied by a railway siding. Canal traffic at the wharf ceased in 1922.[28]

Shrewsbury's gasworks and brickyards in the Castlefields area received coal by canal. Adjacent to Factory Bridge where the canal was crossed by the main road to Market Drayton was a basin where, in 1840, coal from mines at Uffington was unloaded. It was filled in between 1880 and 1900. The principal canal users in this area were the occupiers of the plot that extended back from the frontage now occupied by Nos.106-10 St Michael's Street. Between 1835 and 1838, after the canal was linked to the national system, warehouses were built for three carrying companies, Tilston & Co., Fairhurst & Co. and Crowley Hicklin & Co. The site was subsequently used for milling and malting and was served by a short branch canal. The only users of the section which looped west of the road between Factory Bridge and Comet Bridge were the owners of the Ditherington Flax Mill whose boiler house was on the canal bank. The canal was officially closed south of Comet Bridge in 1939.[29]

The completion of the line from Norbury Junction to Wappenshall in 1835 linked the Shrewsbury Canal with the national network, enabling the Shropshire Union company in the early 20th century to offer carrying services from this warehouse at Longdon (SJ 620154), now demolished, to distant destinations.

The Ellesmere Canal

The Ellesmere Canal took its name from the north Shropshire town where the inaugural meeting of prospective shareholders was held on 31 August 1791. When the promoters obtained their Act of Parliament in 1793 they envisaged a strategic waterway linking the Mersey, the Dee and the Severn. The rivalries and disputes of the years that followed have been elucidated by Charles Hadfield and Edward Wilson. When the company's network was completed, following its merger with the earlier Chester Canal in 1813, it was very different from that originally contemplated. It was constructed under the direction of Thomas Telford, but in accordance with strategic engineering decisions taken by William

Jessop, and in the face of financial constraints. The network comprised a route from the River Mersey to Chester, beginning at the new town of Ellesmere Port, thence along the old Chester Canal to Hurleston near Nantwich, from where the Ellesmere proper ran west to Grindley Brook where it entered Shropshire. It then crossed the mosses to Frankton, where it forked, one line heading south-west to join the Montgomeryshire Canal at Carreghofa, the other north-west, passing through the Oswestry Coalfield and into Wales at Chirk, whence it continued across the Pontcysyllte Aqueduct to Trevor Basin, which served industries around Ruabon and along the Vale of Llangollen. Branches extended into Whitchurch and Ellesmere, while another failed to reach Prees but served a wharf at Edstaston (SJ 517322) and lime kilns at Quina Brook (523330). The intended route to the Severn at Shrewsbury left the Montgomeryshire line below the locks at Frankton but ended in a field south of a wharf at Weston Lullingfields (SJ 419257). The Ellesmere & Chester Canal was linked with the national network in 1835. It was modestly profitable, but, faced with the threat of railway competition, it became a constituent of the Shropshire Union Railway & Canal Co. in 1845, and, with that company, was taken over by the LNWR the following year. Diminishing traffic led to threats of closure as early as the 1870s, and by the 1920s the canal faced competition from road transport as well as railways. The Shropshire section had fallen out of use by 1939. L.T.C. Rolt failed to force a passage through the weeds to Pontcysyllte in 1947, but succeeded in 1949, and in 1952 Edward Wilson and others followed suit. In 1954 it was decided to retain the waterway as a means of supplying reservoirs near Hurleston. It became popular with boaters and for marketing purposes was renamed the Llangollen Canal.[30]

The current main line enters Shropshire north of Grindley Brook locks (SJ 523429) where it is crossed by the road from Whitchurch to Chester. A canalside settlement developed around the bridge, including an elegant lock-keeper's cottage that remains, together with a former cornmill, but limekilns and a boat-building yard have disappeared. A section of the Whitchurch branch has been restored, from its junction with the main line (SJ 527415), where there is a fabricated steel lifting bridge, to the over bridge at Chemistry (SJ 531415). Further along the branch at Sherrymill Hill (SJ 537416) a silkmill and the town gasworks have disappeared, but a cornmill of 1828 remains at the former terminus at New Wharf (SJ 541414).

From Whitchurch the canal pursues a southerly course across the mosses on the borders of Shropshire and Maelor. At Brickwalls (SJ 513377) the canal is crossed by a steel lifting bridge replacing an earlier wooden structure, and the remains of limekilns now stand in a garden. Morris Bridge (SJ 493354) is of the same type. At the junction with the Prees Branch the main line is spanned by a roving bridge. The canal passes into Maelor for a short distance (SJ 481354-SJ 454349) before reaching the remains of the wharf at Hampton Bank (SJ 451344). The circuitous course to Ellesmere, north of Colemere and round the southern edge of Blakemere, reveals some of England's most delightful canal scenery. The canal passes through an 80m tunnel before the junction with the Ellesmere town branch, opposite the elegant Beech House (SJ 401342) of 1806, once the company headquarters. A sundries warehouse remains on the Town Wharf at the end of the branch (SJ 398348), but the adjacent gasworks has disappeared and the creamery which replaced a Victorian foundry was demolished in 1991. The maintenance depot on the main line

Lifting bridges on the Prees branch of the Ellesmere: Canal Starks Bridge (SJ 492347) in the foreground, the Allmans bridge in the distance.

(SJ 400342) is less busy than when Edward Wilson memorably recorded its operations in the late 1940s.[31]

The section of the Prees Branch from the main line to Whixall Marina (SJ 496341) is crossed by the only two remaining wooden lifting bridges on the Ellesmere Canal, Allman's Bridge (SJ 492349) and Starks Bridge (SJ 492347). Beyond the marina a nature reserve extends to Waterloo (SJ 497332), once a busy wharf, where only cottages remain of the settlement, but the site of the limekilns worked by Jebb & Co. in 1828 can still be identified. The remainder of the canal bed is dry. The warehouse overlooking the basin at Edstaston (SJ 517321), once used for sundries traffic, is now part of a residence. In 1816 iron and iron

The warehouse on the wharf at Edstaston (SJ 517322), terminus of the Prees branch of the Ellesmere Canal c.1970.

183

Welsh Frankton (SJ 371318), where the main line of the Ellesmere Canal is joined by the lock flight leading to the lines to Weston Lullingfields and the Montgomeryshire Canal.

castings from the Coalbrookdale Coalfield were despatched from Edstaston, together with locally produced grain, and there was a heavy inward traffic in shop goods for the Coalfield. Two ranks of limekilns remain at the branch terminus at Quina Brook (SJ 523328).

The main line pursues a circuitous course from Ellesmere to Welsh Frankton, where a canalside community grew up along the flight of locks descending from the main line (SJ 371318) to what is now called Weston Arm Junction, where the routes to Carreghofa and Weston Lullingfields (SJ 368311) separate. Boats were often moored for the night at Frankton, where stables provided accommodation for their motive power and the *Old Canal Tavern* refreshment for their crews. A toll collector lived alongside the locks, together with workers at a boat-building yard, with a dry dock alongside the second lock pound that was owned in 1861 by John Evans, who employed six men and two boys. Only two boat builders remained at Frankton in 1901.

The first part of the Ellesmere's line towards Shrewsbury is now a linear nature reserve. A wharf at Horderley (SJ 381311) became the terminus of the branch after the bank of the canal on the Shrewsbury side was breached in 1917. At Weston Lullingfields (SJ 420265) was a bank of four lime kilns, together with a coal wharf, stables, a crane, a weighbridge and a warehouse from which cheese was despatched, but which was a venue for dances in the 1920s and '30s. In the 1960s the various structures were recognisable, an old delivery wagon remained in the yard and the wharf retained much of its atmosphere.

The line towards the Montgomeryshire Canal pursues a south-westerly course from Frankton to Pant. It crossed the River Perry on a low brick aqueduct of three arches (SJ 363298) which was replaced when navigation was restored to this stretch in the 1990s. At Rednal the canal is crossed by the Shrewsbury & Chester Railway. A basin and sidings, the site of which was later used by the artificial manure works of Messrs Richards, provided

The wharf of the Ellesmere Canal at Weston Lullingfields (SJ 419257) photographed c.1966.

exchange facilities for freight in the 1860s. The two-storey canalside building (SJ 351276) opposite the drive to the former Rednal & West Felton station was probably the landing point for those alighting from a short-lived canal passenger service from Newtown connecting with trains which began in 1853. At Queen's Head, where the canal is crossed by the Holyhead Road, a donkey-powered railway, built by 1880 and still working in the 20th century, brought sand to the canal from a quarry to the south. There were limekilns on the north bank and a warehouse remains on the south bank. A three- and four-storey range south of the canal accommodated a steam flourmill.

West of the Holyhead Road are Aston Locks (SJ 332260) and a wharf at Maesbury Marsh alongside the *Navigation Inn* (SJ 314250), which is the current limit of navigation. A crane stands on the wharf but the warehouse where sundries were handled was destroyed by fire in 1968. Canalside industries included a lead smelter and an artificial manure works. Further west is the junction of a branch (SJ 303248) which led to Maesbury Hall Mill.

The canal then enters the Oswestry Coalfield. An early 19th-century railway from pits around Sweeney terminated at Gronwen Wharf (SJ 304246). Its course was traced in the 1940s by Edward Wilson, who found about a hundred stone sleeper blocks and concluded that the rails were *c.*1.37m long.[32] Redwith or Morton Wharf (SJ 301241), where the canal is crossed by the road from Knockin to Llynclys, remains recognisable as a canal installation but there are no traces of its limekilns. At Crickheath Wharf (SJ 292234) the canal was joined by another early 19th-century railway which brought limestone from quarries near Porthywaen. At Pant and Llanymynech other railways brought limestone to kilns and wharfs near the canal (see pp.164-65), which passes into Wales as it goes beneath the bridge carrying the road from Oswestry to Welshpool (SJ 266210).

The current main line of the Ellesmere Canal pursues a north-westerly course from Frankton to Chirk. After passing New Marton locks (SJ 332342, SJ 328347) it reaches

Former warehouses at St Martin's (SJ 314356) on the main line of the Ellesmere Canal

St Martin's Moor (SJ 314356), home of many boatmen in the 19th century where warehouses remain on the east bank. The canal was a vital element in the economy of the Oswestry Coalfield beyond Moreton Hall (SJ 300357). Gledrid Bridge lies near the wharf that was the canalside terminus of the Glyn Valley Tramway in its horse-drawn phase between 1873 and 1888. The bridge marks the beginning of 'Pontcysyllte Aqueduct and Canal', the area designated a UNESCO World Heritage Site in 2011, which extends over the Welsh border, across the great aqueduct itself, and through the Vale of Llangollen to the Horseshoe Falls, the source of the canal's water.[33] At Upper Chirk Bank (SJ 294370) the canal is crossed by the turnpike road from Oswestry on a bridge in which iron ribs sustained timber baulks supporting filling material on which the road was laid. Two similar bridges remain at Trevor Basin.

The aqueduct carrying the Ellesmere Canal over the valley of the River Ceiriog near Chirk (SJ 287372), opened in 1801, and part of the Pontcysyllte Aqueduct and Canal World Heritage Site. Six of the ten arches are in Shropshire.

The first major monument within the World Heritage Site is the 254m long, 25.5m high Chirk Aqueduct (SJ 287372), which carries the canal over the River Ceiriog. The boundary between England and Wales follows an old line of the river, now usually dry, and six of the aqueduct's ten arches are in Shropshire. Charles Hadfield showed that the design was changed many times after William Jessop recommended to the company in July 1795 that an iron trough should be erected. It was probably Thomas Telford who afterwards decided to construct a masonry aqueduct in which, perhaps as late as 1799, it was resolved to insert a cast-iron bottom rather than a thick layer of puddled clay. Iron side plates were added in 1870. The aqueduct opened to traffic late in 1801 and remains the most spectacular way of crossing the frontier between England and Wales.[34]

The Shropshire Union

The Ellesmere Canal was joined to the Shrewsbury Canal by Thomas Telford's 63.5 km Birmingham & Liverpool Junction Canal (B&LJC), from Autherley on the Staffordshire &

Mileposts on the Birmingham & Liverpool Junction Canal reveal its terminal points at Autherley Junction near Wolverhampton and Nantwich, as well as the junction with the 'Newport Arm' at Norbury.

Worcestershire Canal near Wolverhampton to the Ellesmere & Chester Canal at Nantwich. It was authorised, after much political turmoil, in 1826 and opened on 2 February 1835. Its principal source of water is the Knighton Reservoir, the feeder stream from which enters the canal just outside Shropshire (SJ 733274). In 1845, along with the Shropshire, the Shrewsbury, and the Ellesmere & Chester canals, it became part of the Shropshire Union Railway & Canal Company, and its main line is often, in consequence, called the 'Shropshire Union'. The company was leased by the LNWR in 1846, a transaction given parliamentary sanction the following year. The B&LJC carried commercial traffic until the 1970s and is traversed by many touring boats. Its archaeology has been elucidated by Jonathan Morris.[35]

The canal enters Shropshire south-east of Cheswardine (SJ 736274) and continues northwards for about three miles to the Staffordshire border (SJ 694314). At Park Heath Wharf (SJ 731275) the former weighbridge remains. The wharf was used from 1891 by the Whitehouse family for the distribution of coal from Littleton Colliery near Cannock. At Goldstone Wharf (SJ 704294) a warehouse has been adapted as a dwelling, alongside a popular public house. The Cheswardine Road bridge (SJ 700301) frames the entry to Woodseaves Cutting, on the rims of which are piles of spoil from the excavation up to 10m high, which increase the cutting's apparent depth. A small cave high on the western side of the cutting, 350m north of the bridge, appears to have housed a blacksmith's hearth during an early stage of construction. The most celebrated feature of the cutting, thanks to a photograph by Eric de Maré, is a 13.4m high stone-arched accommodation bridge (SJ 697307). De Maré called it the 'Rocket' bridge, but the name is not used locally, and the photographer may have misheard the colloquial name of the cutting, the 'Rockin'.[36]

The canal re-enters Shropshire as it crosses the culverted River Tern (SJ 685343) and remains in the county for about 8km. The basin at Market Drayton (SJ 684346) was in water by 1829 when it was occupied by boats carrying spoil for embankments. It was subsequently used by the principal carrying companies, by William Hazledine who sold coal from Wombridge, and by William Tomkinson who traded in guano, corn and salt. At the north end the mid-19th-century Shropshire Union Carrying Co. warehouse was incorporated in 1914 into a newly-built cornmill which worked until the 1970s. The adjacent *Bleak House* was the home of the canal agent. Victoria Wharf (SJ 678353), where the canal is crossed by the road to Norton-in-Hales, was chiefly used by coal merchants. A cottage at Adderley Wharf (SJ 671391) was once the home of the lime burner who worked the kilns which stood at the side of the winding hole. The five locks at Adderley lower the canal by 9.4m and after passing through them the canal enters Cheshire (SJ 660410).

The 16.9km 'Newport Arm' of the B&LJC, sanctioned in 1827 and opened on 2 February 1835, leaves the main line at Norbury Junction, Staffordshire (SJ 793227) and enters Shropshire south of Forton (SJ 752200) at the foot of the flight of 17 locks which descended from the junction at Norbury.[37] Six further locks completed the descent to the Shrewsbury Canal. The section through Newport is in water, and one canalside warehouse remains, although its onetime neighbour now houses the sawmill at the Blists Hill Museum. After passing through Ticket House Lock (SJ 738194) and Polly's Lock (SJ 733191) the canal heads south-west over the Weald Moors, and crossed Kynnersley Drive on a structure commonly called the Duke's Drive Aqueduct (SJ 686165) which bore the arms of the Dukes of Sutherland. It was demolished during drainage work in the 1960s. To the south was the junction with the 1.3km branch to a wharf at Lubstree (SJ 692152), opened in 1844 and closed in 1922. A warehouse with a canopy over the canal remains at the terminus.

Adderley Locks (SJ 660410)

Wappenshall (SJ 663145), where the Newport Arm of the B&LJC joins the Shrewsbury Canal, was the most significant canal community in Shropshire. The junction occupied land owned by the Dukes of Sutherland, who constructed warehouses which handled shop goods for the whole of the Coalbrookdale Coalfield, where coal and iron produced in the area were despatched, and where limestone for ironmaking was received from Llanymynech

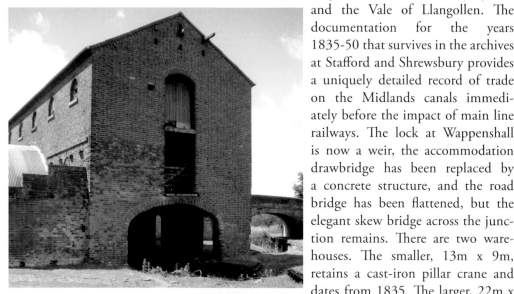

and the Vale of Llangollen. The documentation for the years 1835-50 that survives in the archives at Stafford and Shrewsbury provides a uniquely detailed record of trade on the Midlands canals immediately before the impact of main line railways. The lock at Wappenshall is now a weir, the accommodation drawbridge has been replaced by a concrete structure, and the road bridge has been flattened, but the elegant skew bridge across the junction remains. There are two warehouses. The smaller, 13m x 9m, retains a cast-iron pillar crane and dates from 1835. The larger, 22m x 8m, constructed on arches springing from piles and spanning an arm of

Wappenshall Junction (SJ 663145): the large warehouse of 1838 (top photograph) and smaller warehouse dating from 1835.

A pulley by which goods in narrow boats could be lifted directly to the upper floors of the large warehouse at Wappenshall.

the canal, was begun in 1838. There are remains of a winch in the gable of the south elevation, and a hoist remains on the first floor. Other buildings include the toll clerk's residence, a two-storey, three-bay brick house with a semi-octagonal bow front, the weighbridge house, and a public house, now Bridge House, that was under construction in December 1836. The wharf was purchased in 2007 by Telford & Wrekin Council and is now the headquarters of the Shrewsbury & Newport Canals Trust.[38]

The Leominster Canal

The Leominster Canal, one of the last successful waterways of the Industrial Revolution, was literally marginal to the Shropshire economy, but its archaeological remains are of unusual interest, and most are within the county.[39] The canal, intended to link the Severn at Stourport with Leominster, received parliamentary sanction in 1791 and its construction was directed by Thomas Dadford junior. The section from the Mamble collieries to Woofferton was opened in 1794 and extended to Leominster in 1796, making a total length of 30km along which boats 70ft (3.3m) long and 6ft 10in (2.08m) in beam could be navigated. The canal never reached the Severn, and its only economic function was to carry westwards the produce of Sir Walter Blount's collieries at Mamble. From the wharf at Woofferton it contributed to the coal supply of Ludlow. The canal was sold in 1858 to the Shrewsbury & Hereford Railway, after which it was formally closed and drained, and some of its land was used for the railway between Tenbury and Woofferton.

The most easterly section of the Leominster Canal in Shropshire is in the parish of Neen Sollars which it enters near Southnett Wharf House (SO 673705) and leaves by an aqueduct over the River Rea (SO 651703), a single brick arch. The section between the crossings of the Corn Brook (SO 627686) and the Ledwych Brook (SO 537687) is also in Shropshire, and the canal re-enters the county as it crosses the Teme Aqueduct (SO 537687), a three-arch structure of brick and stone, the central span of which was blown up during a military exercise in the Second World War. The earthworks of the section between the aqueduct and the old railway (SO 533685) are well-preserved, and the site of the wharf at Woofferton (SO 591684) is recognisable. The canal leaves Shropshire south of the wharf (SO 514680).

One of the outer arches of the aqueduct carrying the Leominster Canal over the River Teme (SO 537687). The central arch was destroyed in a military exercise during the Second World War.

Turnpike Roads

Shropshire's roads, particularly the routes into Wales, were notoriously bad in the early 18th century. Some roads had to be raised above flood levels. Celia Fiennes in 1698 noted that the last two or three miles of the approach to Shrewsbury from Whitchurch followed a causeway which can still be recognised in parts of St Michael's Street and Ditherington. John Loveday in 1732 wrote that:

> A causey wide enough for one horse runs from Shrewsbury, with some Interruption, for about 8 miles on the way to Welshpool.

At that time it seems that wheeled vehicles could scarcely progress west of Shrewsbury, but in 1813 an observer remarked that the county's public roads were tolerably good and in a general state of improvement. In Shropshire, as in other counties, transport possibilities were transformed by the activities of turnpike trusts.[40]

The routes towards London were the first to pass into the care of turnpike trusts. In 1725 (12 Geo I, c.9) a trust was constituted for the route from Shrewsbury to Ivetsey Bank near the Staffordshire border, most of which was part of the Roman Watling Street, with a branch from Oakengates to Shifnal that became a component of the principal route to the capital.

Most of Shropshire's main roads and a few minor ones were to come under the control of turnpike trusts during the 18th century.[41] Thirty-eight Acts of Parliament designated new trusts in Shropshire (excluding those in the Halesowen/Oldbury area) of which two were passed before 1750, 24 between 1750 and 1769, four between 1770 and 1799, and eight after 1800. While the period between 1750 and 1769 marked the peak of legislative activity relating to Shropshire's roads, the extent of change brought about by Acts that renewed the powers of trusts (which normally had terms of 21 years) is less easily measured. Some renewal Acts enabled trusts to take over substantial new stretches of road. Paradoxically, some Acts establishing new trusts, such as that for the Atcham-Dorrington road in 1797 (37 Geo III c.172) were for routes of little importance and were probably set up by larger trusts to inhibit the use of lanes avoiding tollgates. Some trusts managed long stretches of road, such as that for the Chester Road established in 1760 (33 Geo II c.51) which extended from Chester through Shropshire to Stonebridge near Coventry, and were broken up into virtually autonomous administrative districts. Some trusts worked closely together. The trustees of the Shrewsbury division of Watling Street, the Welsh Bridge roads and the Coleham Bridge roads sought contractors for collecting tolls in the same advertisement in 1825, for example.

The turnpike road system was wound up in the second half of the 19th century.[42] After amalgamations and separations, some 46 trusts controlled the county's roads in 1850. Some sections of road that had fallen out of use, such as the route from Norton Crossroads through the ford on the Severn at Wroxeter to Acton Burnell, were given up early in the 19th century. The first substantial section of main road to be de-turnpiked was the portion of the Chester Road between Whitchurch and Tern Hill, where tolls ceased to be collected in 1854. Six trusts ceased operation in the 1860s, but most, a total of 35, were disbanded in the following decade, leaving three to follow in the 1880s, with just one, the Wem-Bron-y-Garth Trust, continuing to collect tolls until 1893, when only one other turnpike road remained in Britain.

Shropshire has few ancient signposts. A sandstone pillar outside the *Bell* at Tong (SJ 791081) marking distances to Newport, Chester, Brewood, Lichfield, Shifnal and Salop is probably the only signpost in the county that pre-dates the turnpike era. An obelisk at the crossroads in Craven Arms (SO 433827) gives distances to many towns, amongst them Holyhead, suggesting that it dates from after 1780. A stone at the junction of the London and Wenlock roads in Shrewsbury lists Shifnal, Birmingham and Oxford as staging posts *en route* to London, and gives distances to Bath and Bristol, and is probably also of late 18th-century date.

The most visible remains of turnpike trusts are mileposts and tollhouses, more of which remain in Shropshire than in most counties. The earliest mileposts are in stone. Those on the Bishop's Castle roads are of hard rock with crudely carved inscriptions, while some around Shrewsbury were of soft sandstone which has weathered, rendering inscriptions indecipherable. Those on the Leighton Trust were of roughly-shaped stone with cast-iron plates attached carrying inscriptions. The posts on the road from Wem to Bron-y-Garth road were of neatly-shaped stone, with iron plates attached on which inscriptions were painted. Carved mile-stones were installed along the wholly new Minsterley-Churchstoke turnpike in the mid-1830s. The majority of the surviving mileposts are of cast-iron, are triangular in plan, with the inscriptions on thicker and chamfered sections at the top, and on plinths at the bottom. The Coalbrookdale Company offered several variations of this design in the 1840s.

Nearly 300 houses were used by turnpike trusts in Shropshire for the collection of tolls. Some were adaptations of existing cottages, such as that at Nobold (SJ 474101) on the Shrewsbury-Longden road, but most were purpose-built. The majority have disappeared as a result of road-widening or because the standard of accommodation fell below 20th-century requirements. The tollhouse at Prescot (SJ 426120) on the approach to Baschurch from Shrewsbury, a single-storey two-room building of dressed sandstone blocks, was damaged

The 18th-century obelisk recording distances by road from the Earl of Craven's inn in the parish of Stokesay (SO 433827) which in the 19th century gave its name to the railway town of Craven Arms.

192

*The situation of this otherwise unremarkable cottage at Harpswood (SO 691915) indicates that
it was a tollhouse on the road from Bridgnorth to Ludlow, turnpiked in 1762.
It controls the junction with the branch road to Brown Clee and the crossing of the Mor Brook
in the foreground.*

beyond repair when it was struck by a car in January 1939. Similarities between tollhouses
built by the First and Second Ludlow trusts – semi-octagonal towers, whether of brick
or stone, with triangular-headed windows with pairs of stone lintels – suggest that the
two organisations worked closely together. Several other trusts favoured octagonal or semi-
octagonal towers, such as that built by the Oswestry trust at Porthywaen (SJ 258235).
Some tollhouses are undistinguished in appearance but can be recognised by their situa-
tions near road junctions or river crossings, such as that at Harpswood (SO 691915) which
controls a crossing of the Mor Brook and the junction of the Bridgnorth-Ludlow road
with the route from the Brown Clee to Bridgnorth. Some were idiosyncratic in design, but
without functional features, such as the double-fronted cottage with ogee windows on the
ground floor which controlled the Brockton road at Minsterley (SJ 372051). Others, like
that built at Burcote (SJ 618105) *c.*1805, which 30 years later became redundant when the
Overley Hill diversion on the Holyhead Road was completed (see p.242), are little different
from other contemporary working-class cottages.

The best-preserved turnpike records in Shropshire, those of the two Ludlow trusts,
enable some minor improvements to be recognised.[43] At Henley (SO 533762) on the road
to Bridgnorth, the old line of the road, by-passed by a scheme authorised on 27 November
1828, is clearly visible.

In the 18th century most turnpike trusts either took over existing main roads, such
as Watling Street, or adapted rambling lanes into passable through routes, such as that

A milestone on the Bridgnorth and Cleobury Mortimer turnpike north of Horsford Bridge (SO 699864).

A milestone near Hope (SJ 339010) on the new turnpike road from Minsterley to Churchstoke constructed in the 1830s. It is curious that the trust decided to use stones rather than cast-iron posts at this late date.

A cast-iron milepost erected by the Welsh Bridge Trust on the Shrewsbury-Baschurch road near Leaton (SJ 473180) indicating that it is located in an outlying part of the parish of St Mary.

A cast-iron milepost east of Aston Eyre (SO 656939) on the turnpike road from Morville to Shipton opened in 1843. It is unusual for distances to London to be shown on Shropshire mileposts. The inscription on the right-hand side of the plinth shows the name of the township, Aston Eyre, while the left-hand side is blank.

A cast-iron milepost on the A442 north of Norton (SJ 727005) usually regarded as the road from Telford (or Wellington) to Bridgnorth, but the distance from Shifnal indicates that this was part of a Staffordshire turnpike that extended to Bridgnorth through Newport and Shifnal.

A cast-iron milepost on the Shrewsbury-Bridgnorth road north of Cross Houses (SJ 530081). A foundry moulder has inserted the letter 'N' into the mould the wrong way round.

from Tern Bridge through Leighton to Buildwas Bridge, turnpiked, in anticipation of the construction of the Iron Bridge, in 1778. One of the few wholly new routes was the road from Ludlow to Cleobury Mortimer constructed through the mining landscape on Clee Hill in the 1750s.

After 1800 trusts sought more radical improvements, of which there is plentiful archaeological evidence. In Shrewsbury, the gradient through New Street was eased in 1824, and, some time before, the old route to Baschurch, familiar to many as the access route to the agricultural showground, was abandoned in favour of the present road. A bend was taken out of the route from Coleham Bridge towards Church Stretton when the route through Old Coleham was replaced by the present line along Moreton Crescent, probably in 1815-16. The trustees of the Ellesmere road decided to ease the gradient on Cross Hill by the excavation of a cutting in 1828, following an accident to a coach.[44]

One of the first major schemes was undertaken on the Welshpool road on either side of the Welsh border. West of Halfway House the turnpike road ran past the *Rose and Crown* (SJ 319112) through Lower Winnington towards Buttington, crossing the border at SJ 295102. In 1801 a new line was authorised (41 Geo III c.88) diverging north between mileposts 10 and 11 (SJ 323117), beginning with a straight stretch of 2km running in a north-westerly direction to Plas-y-Court. The road crosses the frontier about 0.5km beyond at Gate Farm. There were gates at Middleton and Trewern, both in Wales, and at the *Rose and Crown* on the old sector which was de-turnpiked on 1 May 1837.

The Kidderminster Trust re-routed the Kidderminster-Bridgnorth road through the parish of Alveley, probably in 1809-10.[45] The Wolverhampton Trust moved their road to Newport some 100m to the east, probably to accommodate an extension of the park at Kilsall Hall. The landscape in the vicinity has been changed by the construction of RAF Cosford and the M54 motorway. The Burlton and Llanymynech Trust constructed the straight road from Ruyton-XI-Towns towards Baschurch in 1837. Greenwood's map of 1826-27 shows the present road from Shrewsbury to Prees Heath, north of the crossroads with the Shawbury-Wem turnpike (SJ 540253) as an 'Intended Road', for which contractors were sought in April 1826. The old line remains, lined with squatter-like cottages. Greenwood also shows the old line of the Shrewsbury-Montgomery road west of the parish boundary of Westbury (SJ 351072) through Aston Pigott and Aston Rogers as far as Littleworth (SJ 332051), which was part of the Bishop's Castle trust. By the 1840s the present route had been constructed and is marked as a 'new road' on the Worthen Tithe Map.[46]

Some schemes were more ambitious. The roads south from Ludford Bridge (SO 512741) towards Richard's Castle and Woofferton, leading to Hereford and Worcester, were re-routed by the Ludlow First Turnpike Trust in the 1830s, and a new tollhouse was built where the roads diverge at Overton (SO 499725). The old line of the Hereford route was preserved as a footpath, but public rights on the former Worcester road were extinguished, and in Ludford a timber-framed inn (SO 513742) was isolated by the diversion.[47]

Three roads were built by newly-constituted turnpike trusts. One, authorised in 1817 (57 Geo III c.12), was responsible for the road from Coalbrookdale to Wellington built as a means of relieving unemployment, although the road was managed as part of the Madeley trust. In 1834 an Act (4 & 5 Wm IV c.11) was obtained for a road from Minsterley to Churchstoke, up the Hope Valley and through the lead mines at Roman Gravels, creating

John Gwynn's bridge at Atcham (SJ 540093) of 1768-76, which remains in its original condition after being by-passed by a concrete bridge in 1929.

a new route from Shrewsbury to Bishop's Castle. The road is a testament to the skills of the last generation of engineers to work for turnpike trusts, with two spacious tollhouses at Plox Green (SJ 367048) and Pultheley (SO 324947). Five years later the last new Turnpike Act affecting Shropshire was passed, authorising a road from Morville to Shipton, creating a low-level route between Bridgnorth and Ludlow avoiding the 1,100ft summit at the *Three Horseshoes* on the turnpike through Burwarton. It opened in 1843.

Many bridges were constructed in Shropshire during the turnpike era, although the larger examples were the responsibility of Quarter Sessions rather than the trusts. The county's bridges were expertly described by the late A.H. Blackwall.[48] The first significant bridge of the 18th century was constructed by the borough of Oswestry across the River Tanat at Llanyblodwell (SJ 241229) in 1710-11, a three-arch structure with a central span of 12m. John Gwynn's bridge at Atcham (SJ 540093), seven arches in Grinshill stone built in 1768-76, remains in unaltered condition, having been by-passed by a concrete bridge in 1929, and is the most important stone bridge in the county. Telford's Montford Bridge (SJ 432153), completed in 1794, a similar structure in red sandstone, has a cantilevered footpath but otherwise is in its original condition, as is the Welsh Bridge in Shrewsbury, built by John Carline and John Tilley in 1796. The English Bridge was much altered in 1927. One of the best of Telford's smaller bridges is Lee Bridge (SJ 558268), now by-passed, a sandstone arch with a span of 11m. Blackwall's research showed that there was considerable investment in bridges in the late 19th century.

Shropshire's iron bridges comprise a unique feature of its Industrial Archaeology. The first of them is discussed in chapter 4. The Coalbrookdale works cast Telford's iron bridge at Buildwas (SJ 645045) in 1795-96. It was replaced in 1905, but an inscribed portion of one of its ribs is displayed alongside the replacement's replacement, completed in 1992. The Cound Arbour bridge (SJ 555053), cast at Coalbrookdale in 1797, may be the oldest iron bridge still open to motor traffic. By *c.*1811 Thomas Telford had developed a standard design for iron bridges, used at Stokesay, Meole Brace, Cound and elsewhere, but the only remaining example in Shropshire is at Cantlop (SJ 517063), now happily by-passed and conserved as part of a picnic site. A rib from Stokesay Bridge (SO 438818), demolished in 1965, is preserved at Coalbrookdale, while ribs from the Cound Bridge of 1818

The bridge at Cound Arbour (SJ 555053) cast by the Coalbrookdale Company in 1797, which may be the oldest iron bridge still open for vehicular traffic.

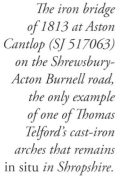

The iron bridge of 1813 at Aston Cantlop (SJ 517063) on the Shrewsbury-Acton Burnell road, the only example of one of Thomas Telford's cast-iron arches that remains in situ *in Shropshire*.

(SJ 558057), demolished in 1967, have been re-used in the centre of Telford. Beneath a modern wooden bridge across the Upper Furnace Pool at Coalbrookdale are parts of an iron bridge erected before 1801. The bridge at Coalport has the most complex history of any iron bridge. It originated as a wooden bridge completed in 1780 whose superstructure was rebuilt on three sets of iron ribs after flood damage in 1795. One half-rib was replaced and two complete ribs added, and an iron superstructure was erected in place of the wooden one in 1818.[49]

The development of stage coach services in Shropshire was memorably described from their own memories by Owen and Blakeway. They noted that in the late 18th century there was 'a vast increase of posting and stage-coaches' in Shrewsbury. Stage coach services can be analysed, since they were advertised. Their fares and timings are known, and estimates can be made of how many horses they employed. Posting – private hire operation – is scarcely documented, yet it accounted for a large part of long-distance passenger traffic. According to Owen and Blakeway, in 1753 a coach from London took four days, with overnight stops, to reach Shrewsbury, reduced to two days in 1764. By the early 1770s coaches were running without overnight stops, and in 1774 one service with a small fast vehicle, the *Modern Machine*, claimed to do the journey in 24 hours, while a larger coach, the *New Fly*, took 36 hours. In 1788 the *Royal Mail* took 22 hours to London and the *Fly* 30 hours. The larger coaches were doing the journey in 27 or 26 hours in the mid-1820s, and by the early 1830s the *Wonder* and the *Nimrod*, both large coaches, were reaching the capital in about 15 hours.[50]

From the late 1770s Shrewsbury became a hub for stage coach services. The principal network was centred on the *Lion*, which had been built by the lawyer John Ashby in 1777. The inn was managed from January 1781 by Robert Lawrence, previously landlord of the *Raven*, who had begun a service to Holyhead in 1779. The road through Shrewsbury superseded that through Chester as the principal route for travellers between London and Dublin. Coaches from Holyhead to London connected at Shrewsbury with services to Bristol and Bath which began in 1779. Direct journeys to and from Liverpool and Manchester, which began in 1807, also connected at Shrewsbury for the south-west. From the 1790s coaches began to run to the coastal resorts of Aberystwyth and Barmouth 'for the bathing season'. Some coaches ran to the Potteries and Macclesfield but no regular pattern of service developed in that direction. On the main routes, to London by various roads, to Bath and Bristol, to Holyhead, to Liverpool and Manchester and to the Welsh resorts, there was competition between the principal Shrewsbury inns. Foremost was the *Lion*, followed by its neighbour the *Raven and Bell*, and by the *Talbot*, built in Market Street in 1775 for the Oteley family of Pitchford Hall, while a few services operated from the *Elephant and Castle* and the *Britannia*.

Shrewsbury's coaching trade was quickly affected by railways. The Liverpool & Manchester Railway, acknowledged as the first main line railway, opened in 1830. By 1834 the *Hawk* coach from Shrewsbury ran to Liverpool, connecting by rail to Warrington and Manchester. In 1837, following the opening of the Grand Junction Railway from Birmingham into Lancashire, services for Liverpool and Manchester ran to Whitmore (Staffs.) where they connected with trains. The following year most of Shrewsbury's London services became feeder coaches, running to the terminus of the London & Birmingham Railway at Curzon Street, Birmingham. Services to the south-west were re-routed to connect with trains at Birmingham from the early 1840s. Shrewsbury's coach operators survived for more than two decades by increasing services which supplemented those offered by the railway companies, but by 1861 only the *Royal Mail* to Aberystwyth remained, and in July of that year the coaching era concluded with the sale of its 30 horses.

Shrewsbury's principal inn was the *Lion*, built by John Ashby 'to promote the general good of this town and county'. Its glory was and is its ballroom, designed as an assembly room for county society. Most of its stabling and coach houses lined the inn yard, but some were on the other side of Belmont Bank at the rear of the yard. The *Talbot* also had extensive stabling off Swan Hill and Cross Hill, while as late as 1903 the *Britannia's* stables were reckoned to accommodate 20 horses.[51]

Outside Shrewsbury the only significant hub for coaching traffic was Ludlow, but in 1811 services amounted only to ten weekly departures from the *Crown* and nine from the *Angel*, fewer than the daily total from Shrewsbury.[52]

The Holyhead Road

The most spectacular road improvement of the Industrial Revolution period was not the achievement of a private turnpike trust but of a public authority.[53] The Act of Union between England and Ireland of 1800 led to complaints by Irish MPs about the routes between London and Dublin. A series of enquiries culminated in the appointment in 1815 of the Holyhead Road Commission (55 Geo III c.151) charged with improving the route from London to Dublin through Coventry, Birmingham, Wolverhampton, Shifnal, Shrewsbury, Oswestry, Llangollen and across Snowdonia to Bangor, over the Menai Straits and across Anglesey to Holyhead. Thomas Telford, county surveyor in Shropshire since 1788, had recommended the route in 1810 and became the Commission's surveyor. An Act of Parliament in 1819 (59 Geo III c.30) vested in the Commission all the powers of the existing turnpike trusts on the route west of Shrewsbury, so that sections of the roads previously managed by Welsh Bridge and Oswestry trusts became the responsibility of the new body.

The work of the Commission in Wales was the subject of a detailed study by Cadw published in 2003, but the survey did not include the section from Shrewsbury to Chirk which was under the same management. The road is lined with elegant mileposts of Telford's design, made in the masons' yard where the stone for the Menai Bridge was worked, and installed in 1828. Most of the Shropshire examples remain *in situ* although much of the Telford's road has been by-passed. Some existing tollhouses continued in use but two new ones were built in Shropshire of similar design to the standard cottage shown in Telford's *Autobiography*. The house at Gallowstree Bank, Oswestry (SJ 296288) was unfortunately demolished in 2015, while that at Shelton (SJ 465122) was re-erected at the Blists Hill Museum in 1973.

From 1815 the Commission's priority was the improvement of the road in Wales, and for some years little work was done in Shropshire. West of Wellington improvements were delayed because Telford hoped to build an entirely new road direct to Chirk, avoiding the county town. The proposal was eventually dropped and schemes in the vicinity of Shrewsbury were implemented. The cutting up to The Mount (SJ 484130) was completed in 1829 and most of the road from Frankwell to Shelton was re-aligned. A direct approach to the English Bridge cutting through the precincts of the abbey was completed to Telford's

The Gallowstree Bank tollhouse on the Holyhead Road at Oswestry (SJ 296288), which until its demolition in 2015 was the only tollhouse designed by Thomas Telford that remained in Shropshire.

design in 1837. More drastic schemes to create boulevards taking traffic directly through the centre of Shrewsbury were abandoned.[54] The re-aligning of the road over Montford Bank west of Shrewsbury was one of the last major projects on the Holyhead Road, and was completed in 1838, four years after Telford's death.

East of Shrewsbury the Commission worked with turnpike trusts, and during the 1820s the road through Shifnal was re-aligned, a by-pass was built avoiding Priorslee village and the centre of Oakengates, and a high embankment carried the road across the Ketley Brook (SJ 669110). The last substantial project on this part of the road was the re-alignment of the road around Overley Hill west of Wellington, completed in 1835.

The stages for the principal Holyhead coaches were the *Jermingham Arms* at Shifnal, to which horses hauled coaches from Wolverhampton, the *Falcon* at Haygate, Wellington (actually in Wrockwardine parish), the *Lion* and the *Raven & Bell* in Shrewsbury, and the *Wynnstay Arms* in Oswestry, from where the next stage concluded at Llangollen.

Twentieth-century road transport

When turnpike trusts relinquished their powers in the 1860s and '70s their duties relating to roads passed to Highway Districts, set up by Quarter Sessions, while Quarter Sessions itself took responsibility for bridges, the number in the care of the county increasing from 169 to 269 between 1878 and 1886. From 1888 main roads were the responsibility of the county council, which first purchased a steam roller in 1890.[55]

Within 15 years the new authority faced problems of managing change. By 1903 some 125 motor cars had been registered. According to complaints, many took to the roads in spring, driven by *cads* and *foreigners*, blowing their horns and covering cyclists in white dust.[56] From 1911 the 'white roads of Shropshire' were blackened as tarred surfaces were laid down. Garages were established, some developing from coach-making businesses, and F.A. Legge's garage in Abbey Foregate, Shrewsbury, was supposedly Britain's first roadside filling station, opened early in 1914.

After the First World War Shropshire increasingly attracted motoring tourists and char-abanc parties. As many as 30 coaches might arrive in the Carding Mill Valley on a summer Sunday, and in the mid-1930s the roads flanking the Mere at Ellesmere were heavily congested. The County Surveyor, W.H. Butler, introduced an enlightened programme of road improvements. The county's first by-pass, at Gobowen (SJ 30633–SJ 303336), avoiding notoriously dangerous bends, was opened in 1926. A by-pass for Lower Corve Street in Ludlow, including a new concrete bridge, opened in 1931, and the St George's by-pass taking Watling Street traffic away from the shopping centre in Oakengates, was built in 1931-32 under an unemployment relief scheme. Construction of the first Shrewsbury by-pass, most of which followed existing lanes east and south of the town, began in 1931 and it opened in 1933. The Church Stretton by-pass was not quite complete when war broke out in 1939.[57]

Many buildings in Shrewsbury were adapted to cater for motoring. Benbow House on Coton Hill was converted to a garage by the coachbuilder Mark Davies in 1911. The cruck house at No.18 Abbey Foregate became Strefford's (later Cureton's) garage in the mid-1920s. The *George Hotel* in Market Street by the mid-1930s had a garage, fitted with a turntable, which could accommodate 20 cars.

Motor buses appeared in Shropshire from the second decade of the 20th century. Early in 1913 the landlord of the *Unicorn* in Shrewsbury began to run a service from the town centre to Bayston Hill, using a double-decked vehicle which alarmed the town council. The service soon ceased but in 1915 the London-based Allen Omnibus Co. began to operate in the town. On 1 April 1916 the Birmingham & Midland Motor Omnibus Co. (the 'Midland Red') purchased the operation and established a garage at Ditherington in 1920. The company dominated bus services around Wellington, Bridgnorth and Ludlow as well as in the county town, although private concerns continued to work some services through the period of nationalisation after the Second World War and into the era of deregulation from the 1980s. Services in the northern part of the Coalbrookdale Coalfield were shared between the Midland Red and the Shropshire Omnibus Association, a group of small private operators one of whom worked Shropshire-built buses into the late 1960s.[58]

Motoring created new landscapes. Prees Heath (SJ 556381), where the A49 from South Wales to Lancashire intersects with the A41 from London to Merseyside, is an archetypal early-20th-century roadside settlement. The *Raven* is an imposing mock-timbered wayside

The Midway Truckstop at Prees Heath (SJ 555380)

inn. Next to it, along what appears to be the original line of the road, stand the rustically-inspired Breckland Café and the cheerfully modernist Midway Truckstop. Ye Olde Raven Garage of the 1930s became a car auction showroom. On the opposite side of the main road was the *Cherry Tree Inn*, eccentrically timber-framed, and another garage, and the landscape is completed by a scatter of semi-detached houses and bungalows. Prees Heath awaits detailed analysis.

The county's most imposing roadhouse was the *Nautical William* at Fenn Green, Alveley (SO 771833), opened in 1937 and designed 'to give the impression of a liner's superstructure' for Derick Burcher, a 'live wire in the motor industry', an agent for Riley cars and a competitor in the hill climb trials at Shelsey Walsh. In the 1990s the building was post-modernised and adapted as a nursing home.[59]

Mainline Railways

Shropshire's role as one of the birthplaces of English railway technology is described in chapter 4. Mainline railways, of which it is generally accepted that the Liverpool & Manchester Railway, opened in 1830, was the first, came relatively late to the county. The intricate railway politics of the 1840s have been described by previous writers. Two local companies, the Shrewsbury & Birmingham and the Shrewsbury & Chester, opened in 1848, and the Shrewsbury & Chester, opened to Wolverhampton the following year, became involved in conflict in the late 1840s and early 1850s with the London & North Western Railway which had taken over the Shropshire Union Railway & Canal Co. in

1846. A newspaper observed in 1853 that 'the struggle between the rival Great Western and North Western companies for the possession of the Shrewsbury & Birmingham line has now assumed an almost national importance'. Ultimately the Shrewsbury companies made an alliance with the Great Western Railway, whose broad gauge line reached Wolverhampton in 1854.[60]

The LNWR and the GWR eventually established a *modus vivendi* in December 1854, and on 1 January 1855 their destructive competition ceased. From 1863 Shrewsbury became the centre of a network managed by a Joint Committee that operated until the last Joint Superintendent retired in 1932. The line from Chester through Shrewsbury to Wolverhampton became part of the Great Western's route from Paddington to Merseyside which by 1870 was entirely standard gauge. From Shrewsbury to Wellington the line was shared with the LNWR, as were the routes to Hereford and Welshpool. The management of Shrewsbury station was similarly a joint responsibility. The LNWR had its own route to Crewe, while the GWR approached Crewe from Wellington via Market Drayton. By the 1870s a network of branch lines crossed the county. North Shropshire was served by the Oswestry, Ellesmere & Whitchurch and Oswestry & Newtown sections of the Cambrian Railways, and Oswestry became the headquarters of the company and the location of its engineering works. The North Staffordshire Railway ran to Market Drayton from Stoke-on-Trent via Silverdale. The Potteries, Shrewsbury & North Wales Railway, an ambitious concern in the 1870s which hoped to reach a ferry port for Ireland on the Lleyn Peninsula, became a by-way from Shrewsbury to Llanymynech and Criggion. It closed in 1880 to re-open as the Shropshire & Montgomeryshire Light Railway in 1909. It was operated by the War Department between 1941 and 1960, after which the oil sidings near the abbey remained in use until the late 1980s. The Shrewsbury Railway Heritage Trust is restoring the former Abbey Station. The Bishop's Castle Railway, a gloriously anarchic private concern, opened in 1866 and operated until 1935. The Cleobury Mortimer & Ditton Priors Light Railway, opened in 1908, did much to stimulate the economy of the Clee Hills region.

Shrewsbury Station (SJ 493129), jointly operated by the GWR and the LNWR, and designed by Thomas Penson. The lower storey was added during large-scale alterations in 1899-1903.

For many years the GWR and LNWR competed for London traffic but after the shortening of the Great Western Route by the opening of the 'Bicester cut-off' in 1910, that company gained an advantage. Nevertheless, into the 1930s the 10.35 from Euston to Shrewsbury of the LMSR, successor to the LNWR, was a large train, carrying through portions for Swansea and Aberystwyth. Some of the most important services passing through Shropshire were those on which the two major companies co-operated, linking Lancashire and Scotland with the west of England through the Severn Tunnel, which began in 1888 and continued until 1969.

Shropshire's main lines still bear traces of their origins. Richard Morriss analysed the county's passenger stations and identified 157, of which less than 20 remain open. Some archaeological evidence remains of the first decades of Shrewsbury's railway history, when each of the companies whose trains ran into the town was nominally independent and had its own locomotive shed, carriage sidings and freight depot.[61] Shrewsbury Station, extending over the bridge spanning the Severn, was shared by the two companies. The building, in Tudor Revival style, was designed, like other stations on the Shrewsbury & Chester Railway, by Thomas Penson. The complex was radically altered between 1899 and 1903 when the present ground floor was added beneath Penson's original building. The bridge over the Severn was widened with fabricated steel girders carried on cast-iron columns. The track layout was extended to the north, and the junction with the line to Crewe re-aligned, necessitating the widening of the bridge across Castle Foregate and alteration of the line of Howard Street. The enlargement of the station made possible the abandonment of ticket platforms which had been erected in 1886 on the line from Wellington by the Underdale Road bridge, and on the Hereford line at the end of the Abbey Foregate triangle. Part of the station's all-over roof remained until 1964.

Shrewsbury Station (SJ 493129), jointly operated by the GWR and the LNWR, and designed by Shrewsbury Station in the early 1960s before the removal of the overall roof. 'Castle' class 4-6-0 No. 7026 Tenby Castle awaits departure with a train for Wolverhampton.

The original locomotive depot of the Shrewsbury & Chester Railway (SJ 492132)
north of Shrewsbury Station, now adapted as apartments.

The Shrewsbury & Chester Railway established a freight depot off Castle Foregate, which from 1858 was bounded by the LNWR's route from Crewe. From 1862 it was shared by the West Midland Railway which worked the Severn Valley line and in 1863 was taken over by the Great Western. The volume of traffic subsequently became too great for the facilities and the GWR built another depot north of the Ellesmere Road bridge. The LNWR's freight depot was the 'New Yard', separated from the GWR by the Bagley Brook, for which the road access was also from Castle Foregate. The LNWR, which incorporated the Shropshire Union Railway & Canal Co., also used the canal basin as a freight depot, gaining access to it by a siding under Howard Street authorised in 1859.

The Shrewsbury & Birmingham locomotive depot lay south of its tracks near to the Underdale Road Bridge, with the Shropshire Union depot on the other side of the line. By 1864 both had become coal yards and were worked jointly. The reservoir which provided water for Shropshire Union locomotives remained well into the 20th century. The Shrewsbury & Chester company built a depot on the south side of their line behind the *London Apprentice* public house, which served its original function for about two decades. It

The engine sheds at Coleham, Shrewsbury (SJ 499119) with 'Castle' class 4-6-0 No. 5097 Sarum Castle, for many years a Shrewsbury engine.

The 'Shelf' sidings alongside the Shrewsbury & Hereford Railway (SJ 497116) south of Shrewsbury which accommodated numerous redundant steam locomotives in 1967-69.

was put to other railway purposes for a century, became part of a garage and is now adapted as housing. The joint locomotive sheds at Coleham, well remembered in Shrewsbury, originated in 1856, were much enlarged in the 1880s, but have now disappeared except for the former railwaymen's club.

The Shrewsbury & Hereford company carriage sheds on the eastern side of its tracks outside the station were enclosed within the Abbey Foregate triangle when the direct connection between the Hereford and Wellington lines was completed in 1867. The Shropshire Union kept its carriages north of its line between the Underdale Road and Monkmoor Road bridges, and the Severn Valley Railway alongside its tracks south of Sutton Bridge Junction. The 'shelf' sidings alongside the line to Hereford probably originated as the Shrewsbury & Hereford company's marshalling yard. They were celebrated in the late 1960s as a dump for the last generation of steam locomotives, redundant in Lancashire and Cheshire and *en route* to scrap yards in South Wales.

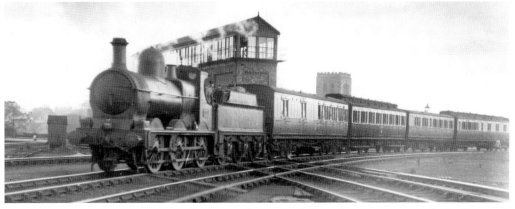

An image of the 1930s epitomises the 'joint' character of Shrewsbury Station. In the background is the LNWR Severn Bridge Junction signal box (SJ 496126) that still remains. A GWR 'Dean Goods' 0-6-0 locomotive brings in a train, probably from the Welshpool direction since it includes ex-Cambrian Railways coaches.

The Shrewsbury & Hereford railway signal box, freight depot and passenger station buildings on Shropshire's southern border at Woofferton (SO 513682). In the background is the distinctive outline of Titterstone Clee.

Nine signal boxes once controlled trains through Shrewsbury. Two, the LNWR buildings at Severn Bridge Junction and Crewe Bank, are listed, the latter as the largest manually-operated signal box remaining in Britain. Along the Shrewsbury & Hereford line early signal boxes, with low-pitched slate roofs, remain at Dorrington (SJ 489033), Church Stretton (SO 456936), Bromfield (SO 496775) and Woofferton (SO 515685).

Through passenger services between Shropshire and Paddington were withdrawn in 1967 and replaced by a single daily return service between Shrewsbury and Euston via the newly electrified West Coast Main Line. Services by this route were increased in the 1980s, but were withdrawn by Virgin Trains in 1998 after privatisation of the railways. From April 2008 the Wrexham, Shropshire & Marylebone company (WSMR) operated five return trains daily to London under an Open Access agreement. The journey time from Shrewsbury was longer than the schedules for steam-worked services in the 1950s, and the operation proved unviable. It was withdrawn in January 2011. Models of the rolling stock and the WSMR's Class 67 locomotives will be a reminder of the company for generations to come.

Shropshire's outstanding railway bridges include the Belvidere Bridge (SJ 520125),

The former Cambrian Railways station at Ellesmere (SJ 396350), opened in 1863 and closed in 1964.

The ex-GWR goods warehouse at Hodnet (SJ 621278) on the line from Wellington to Market Drayton and Crewe.

The ex-LNWR signal box at Whitchurch (SJ 550415)

The goods shed of the North Staffordshire Railway station at Pipe Gate (SJ 737408).

an iron arch by the Coalbrookdale Company by which the Wellington line from Shrewsbury crosses the Severn, and the Albert Edward Bridge (SJ 660037) of 1862 by which the line from Wellington and Madeley Junction crossed the Severn to Buildwas Junction, another iron arch cast at Coalbrookdale. The viaduct across the Ceiriog at Chirk (SJ 287371) was originally a masonry structure of ten arches, with spans of timber construction at either end, but the wooden arches were replaced by stone ones in 1858. The longest tunnel, at Oakengates on the Shrewsbury & Birmingham line, extends for 430m. There are short tunnels at Ludlow and Bridgnorth.

Craven Arms is a railway junction town.[62] Before 1850 it consisted of little more than the wayside inn built for the Earls of Craven and taking their name. The opening of the Shrewsbury & Hereford line in 1852, and of lines to Knighton, Bishop's Castle and Much Wenlock, stimulated growth. A locomotive depot, carriage sidings and a small marshalling yard were built, and freight facilities included cattle docks, a crane for loading timber, sidings for the town gasworks, an oil depot, the yard of a farmers' co-operative and a woodworking concern. At Gobowen, junction for the Shrewsbury & Chester's Oswestry branch, a similar range of facilities grew up around Thomas Penson's elegant Italianate passenger station.

Little remains of the routes of the Cambrian Railways in Shropshire apart from the track between Oswestry and Blodwell Junction which may become part of a heritage railway

Hollinswood Sidings (SJ 704092), used by the GWR as a local marshalling yard, and as the junction with the mineral railway of the Lilleshall Company. In August 1965 an ex-LMSR class 8F locomotive is about to deliver a class 3F 0-6-0T tank engine to join other engines awaiting scrapping.

extending over ex-GWR tracks to Gobowen. The company's outstanding monuments are the passenger station buildings at Oswestry (SJ 295298) and Ellesmere (SJ 396351), together with the locomotive and carriage works at Oswestry. A former goods shed at Pipe Gate station on the line from Silverdale to Market Drayton is one of the few surviving structures in Shropshire built by the North Staffordshire Railway.

The Severn Valley Railway from Hartlebury through Bewdley, Bridgnorth and the Ironbridge Gorge to Shrewsbury opened in 1862, too late to invigorate the economy of the region which 70 years previously had been amongst the most dynamic in Britain. Its history was undistinguished, rather more than a by-way but never a main line, until, after its formal closure, it was developed from 1966 into one of Britain's premier heritage railways. In some respects it has moved away from its own history. A Bridgnorth a substantial depot houses more steam locomotives than would ever have operated on the line in the past. Some trains are hauled by locomotives that never normally worked there. Nevertheless, the railway's achievements are substantial. The craft of repairing steam locomotives is cherished at Bridgnorth, and the Engine House accommodating currently unused rolling stock at Highley sets high standards in conservation as well as providing splendid views over the Severn Valley. Furthermore, at Highley Station (SO 749830) the landscape of an early 20th-century railway has been sensitively re-created, and when a train of Great Western stock hauled by a small Great Western locomotive calls, there is a powerful evocation of the past.

8   PERSPECTIVES

This book is based on the premise that Industrial Archaeology, the study of recent centuries through physical evidence of all kinds, adds significantly to our understanding of our past. Some justification is appropriate for the omission of three areas of studies which are not explored here, nor, by convention, in most other works on Industrial Archaeology.

The Italianate farmstead at Trewern near Oswestry (SJ 293328)

Omissions

It is philosophically indefensible to exclude agriculture from archaeological studies of recent centuries. Its omission can be partly justified on pragmatic grounds such as limited space, the author's lack of expertise, or the lack of coherent secondary works. A more cogent reason might be that agricultural buildings evolve over long periods, and that barns, dairies, ploughs and wagons of recent centuries are better seen in an extended context than within a closely defined chronological setting. Nevertheless, the model farm buildings constructed between 1760 and 1860, such as those on the Lilleshall estate of the Dukes of Sutherland,[1] or the extraordinary Italianate farmstead at Trewern (SJ 293328) near Oswestry, have much in common with contemporary industrial buildings in their sources of power, their transmission systems and in the iron machines they housed.

Similarly, there can be no philosophical grounds for omitting the study of Shropshire's polite architecture. Any industrial archaeologist must take account of the activities of Thomas Farnolls Pritchard, re-invigorator of old country houses and designer of the Iron Bridge. Charles Bage, surveyor and wine merchant, designed three textile mills of international consequence. Thomas Telford designed churches and villas before applying his sense of proportion to bridges and tollhouses. Samuel Cookson of the Coalbrookdale ironworks toyed with the Gothic style in a riverside warehouse at Ironbridge and in a school at Dawley. Thomas Penson, architect of Chester, provided the Shrewsbury & Chester Railway with its varied stations. The most prolific designer of industrial buildings was A.B. Deakin, whose works in Shrewsbury included the wool warehouse on the Welsh Bridge, the Perseverance Ironworks and the maltings in Mardol. Arthur Edward Oswell, who worked on churches and schools, designed branches for Lloyds Bank, the Alliance Insurance office in Shrewsbury, and the Sentinel Waggon Works. Frank Shayler was responsible for the offices and printing works of the *Shrewsbury Chronicle* as well as suburban houses in Shrewsbury in the Arts and Crafts style, together with No.31 Shelton Road, which in 1934 marked the appearance of German-style Modernism in the county. There are essential common concerns between the industrial archaeologist and the historian of architecture.[2]

Military structures are also significant in the history of the industrial past. The medieval walls of Ludlow sustain an electricity sub-station while Belfast hangars, airfield control towers, Nissen huts and a sergeants' mess are amongst the 20th-century wartime buildings put to industrial use in Shropshire. Industrial archaeologists share concerns with military historians investigating the original purposes and uses of such buildings.

Definitions

Analysis of contrasting landscapes in Shropshire puts the 'industrial revolution' in its context. If any part of England experienced 'revolution' in the 18th century it was the Coalbrookdale Coalfield. The consequences of innovations made there in ironworking, in mechanical and structural engineering, in the organisation of production and in the application of science to manufactures and mining, were momentous, and shaped events across Great Britain and, ultimately, in other countries. Yet these changes were paralleled in lesser coalfields, which also adopted steam engines and plateways, used turnpike roads and became involved in ironmaking. The insignificance of such enterprises throws into focus the magnitude of the changes which occurred in and around the Ironbridge Gorge. The small scale of 'vernacular' textile manufactures similarly emphasises the significance of Shrewsbury's colossal textile mills. The 'industrial revolution' is also reflected in ambitious projects whose prospects seem, with hindsight, always to have been forlorn, such as the cottonmill at Stottesdon, the Leominster Canal and James George's ironworks at Knowbury.

Study of Shropshire reveals something of the evolution of the 'factory', the complex where varied processes are applied to manufacture products which may be capital items such as steam engines supplied to coal mines, material for secondary processes such as thread supplied to tailors or shoemakers, or consumer goods such as frying pans, teapots or cheese. The Coalbrookdale Ironworks, producing pots and pans for customers in the borderland and overseas in the mid 18th century, was perhaps the county's first 'factory' in this sense, but while it made castings for steam engines it did not evolve into an 'engineering works' making complete machines until the 1790s, at the same time that the Hazledine brothers were setting up 'factories' in Shrewsbury and Bridgnorth. The Caughley porcelain works of the 1770s was clearly a 'factory' in every sense of the word, to the extent of having a public clock to impose time discipline, and it began a line of development that can be traced through the larger china factory at Coalport of the 1790s and the well-organised brick and roofing tile works of the 1850s and '60s to Charles Lynam's vast decorative tile factories at Jackfield of the 1870s and '80s. The textile mill of 1790 in Coleham and the Ditherington flaxmill of 1796-97 represented something new in Shropshire but they had precedents elsewhere. Engineering factories developed in most towns in the mid 19th century, and in a national context establishments like the locomotive and carriage works of the Cambrian Railway at Oswestry and the Perseverance Ironworks in Shrewsbury were not innovatory. By the time of the First World War the Sentinel works, making complex steam wagons, could be moved wholesale from Glasgow to the edge of Shrewsbury and go quickly into production. In the last quarter of the 20th century, large factories were established in Shropshire making electronic devices, plastics and yogurt, using technologies imported from Germany, Korea or Japan.

Archaeological study also highlights the tradition of adaptive re-use of buildings and structures which began long before the process became a fashionable concept in the 1970s. Iron forges were adapted to grind grain or make paper in the early 19th century, when the silkmill at Whitchurch became a cheese warehouse, and Charles Bage's weaving mill at Kingsland was the nucleus of a lead-processing plant. Around 1900 William Jones adapted a flaxmill and a steam cornmill as malt houses. A cornmill at Hanwood was converted into a bleach works which in turn became a barytes mill. A sawmill at Minsterley passed through a spell as a military forage depot before being adapted as a creamery. In the 1930s hangars and concrete sheds built during the First World War for the Royal Flying Corps came to serve as factories and workshops, and by the late 1960s many military buildings of the Second World War had been similarly adapted. In the 1940s and '50s premises in the Ironbridge Gorge left derelict by ironworking and ceramics concerns became nurseries for new manufactures.[3]

Retrospectives

Some of the seeds of the discipline of Industrial Archaeology germinated in Shropshire, although there were other green shoots in Manchester, the Bristol area and in Ulster. On 20 February 1953 the *Shrewsbury Chronicle* used the heading 'Industrial Archaeology' above a report that Michael Rix, deputy warden of the Shropshire Adult College, Attingham Park, 'an expert on the archaeology of industry', had called for more to be done to save such monuments as the Longdon Aqueduct and the Ditherington Maltings. Two years later, in 1955, Rix published an article in *The Amateur Historian* in which the term 'Industrial Archaeology' first appeared in print in a national context. Earlier still, in 1951, the Wrekin Trades Council discussed a lecture that members heard at Attingham on 'the world significance of Coalbrookdale', and affirmed that Shropshire's part in the rise of modern industry should be better known.[4] Some elements of a concern for the industrial heritage can be observed in Shropshire before the Second World War. The Iron Bridge was scheduled an

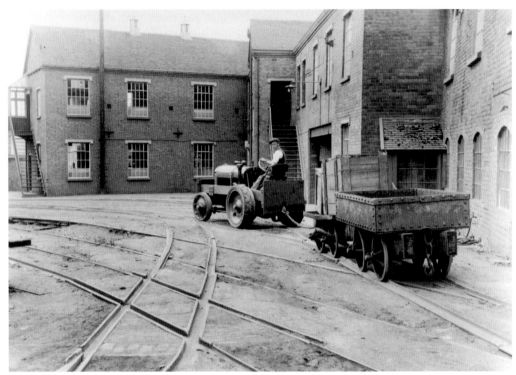

The Coalbrookdale Coalfield as seen by L.T.C. Rolt in the 1940s:
a tractor hauling wagons on the plateway system at Horsehay (SJ 672071).

Hampton Bank (SJ 451344) on the Ellesmere Canal, where L.T.C. Rolt spent the summer
of 1947 before the future of the canal was secured in 1954.

Ancient Monument in 1934. In 1938 Dr D.H. Robinson delivered to a field society a paper on the county's canals which had a sound archaeological foundation, and, given the lack of secondary literature, a remarkable degree of accurate historical detail. When thanking him, the antiquarian W.J. Slack affirmed that Shropshire had a proud industrial history whose monuments merited study and protection.[5] Canal cruising was established on a commercial basis on the Shropshire Union and Ellesmere canals during the 1930s.[6] The Darby family of Coalbrookdale were among the subjects of a study of Quaker industrialists published by Paul Emden in 1939, 14 years before Arthur Raistrick's *Dynasty of Ironfounders* influenced Allied Ironfounders Ltd to establish a museum at Coalbrookdale.[7] During the Second World War L.T.C. Rolt visited Ironbridge as a government inspector, and was impressed by the ruins of the Bedlam furnaces, the use of horse-drawn plateways at Horsehay in the fabrication of landing craft, a coal pit wound by a horse gin, and, above all, by 'the great black semi-circle of Darby's iron bridge springing over the Severn'.[8]

It can be argued that the growth of the industrial conservation movement arose from particular features of English society in the years after the Second World War.[9] The 'successes' of the movement in Shropshire are well chronicled. In 1954 the future of the main line of the Ellesmere Canal was assured, and its popularity as a cruising waterway made possible the beginning of the restoration of the Montgomeryshire arm of the canal. A meeting in Kidderminster on 6 July 1966 established the Severn Valley Railway and the first train ran along the restored line into Bridgnorth on 25 March 1967. The project subsequently evolved into one of the best heritage railways.[10] Shropshire has also featured in the main line running of preserved locomotives. The routes through Shrewsbury from Chester and Crewe to Hereford and Newport have been amongst the most popular for such excursions.

The Severn Valley Railway at its best. A train of GWR stock enters Highley behind a GWR 'Large Prairie' locomotive, March 2013.

The beginnings of conservation at Coalbrookdale.
The Old Furnace (SJ 667048) before it was uncovered in 1959.

The rolling mill at the G.R. Morton Ironworks at the Blists Hill museum, which takes its name from the Ironbridge Gorge Museum Trust's first Honorary Curator.

Since 1980 the remains of the Snailbeach lead mine and the canal wharf at Llanymynech have been evaluated and presented to the public. The Ditherington flaxmill ceased to be used for malting in 1987 and has been regarded as 'heritage at risk', but its status as a Grade I listed building has ensured its survival. Its future uses have yet to be determined although some small buildings have already, in 2016, been adapted to welcome visitors.[11]

There are many smaller-scale indications that industrial heritage has been appreciated in Shropshire. Individual initiatives have saved some of the county's best watermills. Local authorities have paid attention to industrial monuments in the designation of country parks, in the Town Park and the Granville Country Park in Telford, the Old Shrewsbury Canal Park, the Severn Valley Country Park at Highley and Alveley and at Llanymynech, even if some structures have subsequently been neglected.[12] The Shrewsbury & Newport Canal Trust, formed in 2000, has transformed the wharf at Wappenshall and has ambitions to bring back navigation on the Shrewsbury Canal and the Newport Arm. English Heritage have listed such structures as the signal boxes in Shrewsbury. Private collectors of porcelain, decorative tiles and Sentinel steam wagons contribute to the base on which our understanding of the industrial past is founded.

The Ironbridge Gorge Museum is, in a global context, the most significant industrial conservation project in Shropshire. In 1959 Allied Ironfounders Ltd uncovered the Old Furnace at Coalbrookdale and established a small museum nearby. Although open only during the summer and for only four hours a day, the museum attracted many visitors and its success was one justification for the establishment of the Ironbridge Gorge Museum Trust in 1967. The Trust was founded at the initiative of Telford Development Corporation as the result of pressure from local and national organisations to accord protection to the industrial monuments of the Gorge. During the 1970s and '80s most of its prime objectives were achieved, and it set standards by which the conservation and interpretation of industrial monuments came to be judged in an international context. The museum, like similar institutions established in the 1950s and '60s throughout Europe, faces challenges in combining popular appear with the retention of its scholarly foundations.[13]

There is a symbiotic relationship between effective conservation policies and the growth of historical scholarship. Monuments will only be conserved and interpreted if they are understood, and the justification for conserving buildings must be based on arguments derived from evidence, and not on the mindless assertion of questionable superlatives. It can be argued that the 'successes' in industrial conservation in Shropshire have depended on sound historical understanding of why buildings and structures are important, and on eloquent advocacy of that importance. Once the future of a monument is ensured, it can remain the object of study, and its significance can continually be reassessed as thinking progresses.

Industrial archaeological scholarship in Shropshire as elsewhere is less healthy than when the first edition of this study appeared in 1996. Archive, library and archaeological services, as elsewhere, have been fiercely truncated. Neither local authorities nor universities now organise evening classes, monthly research groups or weekend schools on historical topics. Postgraduate courses in Industrial Archaeology are no longer taught at Ironbridge although supervision of higher degrees is provided by the University of Birmingham on the Edgbaston campus at the Centre for West Midlands History and the Ironbridge International Institute for Cultural Heritage. It is fortunate that voluntary societies in Shropshire continue to be concerned with the county's history.

Archaeological study persistently raises new questions about the industrial past at the same time that it stimulates respect for past achievements. Understanding of Ditherington flaxmill has increased because it has been possible continually to re-examine the structure and because it has been reinterpreted in a succession of contexts, not just as a landmark in the history of structures, but as a building designed to house particular technologies and adapted to accommodate others, as a workplace, and as the focus of a suburb. Its recent reinterpretation would have been scarcely imaginable in 1960 when it was simply 'the world's first iron-framed building'.[14] Our understanding of our industrial heritage, as of any aspect of our past, increases from qualitative, not just quantitative gains, from better directed research and creative thinking rather than merely from the accumulation of more data. It is hoped that this book will provide a foundation for future studies in Shropshire, and that it poses questions which will stimulate understanding of the industrial past in its widest contexts.

Appendix 1   Water-power sites in Shropshire

Most of Shropshire is drained by the River Severn and its tributaries. The list works **up** the Severn, taking each tributary in turn, then listing the mills on each side in **downstream** order. Streams flowing into the principal tributaries are likewise listed in downstream order. The River Teme, which flows into the Severn downstream from Shropshire, is treated first, together with its tributaries.

The list includes only sites which are known to have worked since 1660 and those considered likely to have done so. Mills of which there is only place name or archaeological evidence, or which were out of use by 1660, are not included.

There are no mills on the Shropshire portions of watercourse shown in brackets.

Names of streams in inverted commas have been bestowed for the sake of brevity and convenience. They have no historical authenticity.

Rivers and Streams are listed in the following order:

TEME
Cwmhouse Brook
Crochen Brook
'Stowe Brooke'
Clun
  Redlake
  'Treverward Brook'
Kemp
  'Hurst Brook'
  Unk
Onny
  West Onny
  East Onny
    Darnford Brok
  Quinny Brok
    Byne Brook
      Heath Brook
  'Stokesay Brook'
Corve
  Easthope Brook
  'Abdon Brook'
  'Diddlebury Brook'
  Siefton Brook
  Clee Brook

Ledwych Brook
  (Dogditch Brook)
    Benson Brook
  Colly Brook
Corn Brook
Rea
  Winterburn Brook
  Cleobury Brook
  Farlow Brook
  Burrell Brook
  Hopton Brook

SEVERN
Dowles Brook
Borle Brook
  Crunells Brook
Bowhills Brook
Dudmaston Brook
Potseething Brook
Cantern Brook
Worfe
  'Atwell Park Brook'
  Neachley Brook
    Kilsall Brook
    Albrighton Brook

Wesley Brook
  Nedge Brook
  Badger Brook
  Stratford Brook
    Brantley Brook
    'Gatacre Brook'
Linley Brook
Dean Brook
'Swinney Brook'
Wash Brook
'Calcutts Brook'
Benthall Brook
Calde Brook
  Horsehay Brook
  Lyde Brook
Farley Brook
Sheinton Brook
  'Kenley Brook'
Leighton Brook
Cressage Brook
Cound Brook
  Combley Brook
  Betchcott Brook
  Lynall Brook
  Bullhill Brook

Tern
  Coal Brook
  Bailey Brook
  Rosehill Brook
Meese
  Lynn Brook
  'Woodcote Stream'
  Wagg's Brook
  Ellerton Brook
  Plat Brook
Strine
  Lilleshall Brook
  Humber Brook
  Ketley Brook
    Hadley Brook
Roden
  Lyneal Brook
  Sleap Brook
  Sulton Brook
Uffington Brook
Rea Brook
  Lowerfield Brook
  Worthen Brook
  Brockton Brook
  Aston Brook

217

		(DEE)	(WEAVER)
Yockleton Brook	(Vyrnwy)		Duckow
'Winnington Brook'	(Tanat)	(Ceiriog)	
Minsterley Brook	Cynlaith	Morlas Brook	
Habberley Brook	Morda	Shll Brook	
Perry	'Sweeney Brook'	Emral Brook	
Meadow Brook	'Aston Stream'		
Weir Brook	Pwll Trewern		
'Kinnerley Stream'	Camlad		
	Pellmell Brook		
	Caebitra		
	Aylesford Brook		

ABBREVIATIONS

BGM:	Boring Mill
BKM:	Bark Mill
BLM:	Blade Mill
BNM:	Bone Mill
BRM:	Barytes Mill
CEM:	Cement Mill
CDM:	Cider Mill
CGM:	Ceramics Grinding Mill
CPW:	Calico Print Works
CTM:	Cotton Mill
CRM:	Corn Mill*
ELG:	Electric Generator
HCM:	Horse Cloth Mill
FLM:	Fulling Mill
IBF:	Iron Blast Furnace
IFD:	Iron Foundry
IFG:	Iron Forge (may include IRM and/or ISM)
IRM:	Iron Rolling Mill
ISM:	Iron Slitting Mill
LNM:	Linen Mill
LTM:	Leather Mill (may include BKM)
OLM:	Oil Mill
PFB:	Power for barn machinery
PTM:	Paint Mill (may include BRM)
PPM:	Paper Mill
SKM:	Silk Mill
SWM:	Saw Mill
WLM:	Woollen Mill (may include FLM)
WPM:	Water Pump

*No distinction is made between types of corn mill, flour mills, grist mills, provender mills, kibbling mills &c.

** The second column in each table shows the ancient parish in which the mill is situated.

TEME

The source of the Teme is 6 km. south of Newtown, from where the river flows south east, beyond Felindre forming the border between Shropshire and Wales. It is joined by the River Clun near Leintwardine, before veering north round Bringewood Chase. It is joined by the Onny at Bromfield, then flows round Ludlow where it is joined by the Corve, and then in a generally easterly direction, west of Burford forming the boundary between Shropshire and Worcestershire, eventually flowing out of the county at Monks Bridge. Its confluence with the Severn is at Powick, downstream from Worcester.

Vron or Doly Carn	Bettws-y-Crwyn	SO 167818	CRM
Coed-y-Hendre	Llanfair Waterdine	SO 212785	CRM
Silurian Mills	Knighton	SO 287725	WLM
Stowe	Stowe	SO 310729	CRM
Bromfield	Bromfield	SO 482767	CRM
Bromfield Saw Mill	Bromfield	SO 491768	SWM
Castle Mill	Ludlow	SO 507745	CRM IFD
Mill Street Mill	Ludlow	SO 511742	CRM SKM
Broad Street Mill	Ludlow	SO 512742	CRM WLM
Old Street (Hockey's) Mill	Ludlow	SO 514742	CRM
Ludford Mill	Ludford	SO 514742	CRM
Ludford (Temeside) Mill	Ludlow	SO 519743	CRM PPM
Barretts Mill	Richard's Castle	SO 523692	CRM
Ashford Carbonel	Ashford Carbonel	SO 511711	CRM ELG SWM WPM

Cwymhouse Brook

A tributary of the Teme which rises on the southern slope of the Black Mountain and flows south to join the Teme north west of Beguildy at SO 190802.

Moat Farm Mill	Bettws-y-Crwyn	SO 188806	CRM

Crochen Brook

A tributary of the Teme originating from two sources in the western part of Llanfair Waterdine which join at Cymbrain (SO 231779). The stream flows into the Teme at SO 232768.

Melyn-y-Grog	Llanfair Waterdine	SO 233769	CRM

'Stowe Brook'

A small stream which rises on Stowe Hill and flows south east to join the Teme at SO 331732.

Weston Farm Mill	Stowe	SO 329734	CRM

Clun

A tributary of the Teme which rises near the Anchor on the Welsh border, flows east to Clun, where it is joined by the Unk, and at Aston-on-Clun turns south through Clungunford to join the Teme at Leintwardine.

Newcastle Mill	Clun	SO 248823	CRM
Hurst Mill	Clun	SO 318811	CRM FLM
Clunton Mill	Clunton	SO 334812	CRM
Purslow Farm Mill	Clunbury	SO 358807	CRM PFB
Beckjay Mill	Clungunford	SO 396779	CRM

Redlake

A tributary of the Clun which flows from several sources in the hills in the south of Clun parish, first in a south-easterly direction to Bucknell, and then east-north-east to join the River Clun at SO 394738.

Quern Mill	Clun	SO 324760	CRM
Bucknell Upper (Walk) Mill	Bucknell	SO 344743	CRM
Bucknell Lower Mill	Bucknell	SO 346741	CRM

'Treverward Brook'.

A small stream joining the River Redlake from the east.

Treverward Farm	Clun	SO 282782	CRM

Kemp

A tributary of the Clun which springs from several sources in the hills south of Bishop's Castle, provides water for the ornamental pools at Walcot, and then flows south to join the River Clun at Aston-on-Clun.

Brockton Mill	Lydbury North	SO 325859	CRM
Oaker (Aston) Mill	Hopesay	SO 384816	CRM ELG

'Hurst Brook'

A stream which flows north to join the River Clun immediately upstream of Clun Castle.

Hurst Saw Mill	Clun	SO 317806	SWM

Unk

A substantial stream which flows from the hills west of Mainstone to join the River Clun at Clun.

Mainstone Mill	Mainstone	SO 179879	CRM
Birches Mill	Clun	SO 286845	CRM
Bicton Farm Mill	Clun	SO 289827	PFB
Clun Mill	Clun	SO 304813	CRM

Onny

A tributary of the Teme, with two branches joining at Eaton (SO 377896). Both branches rise at the south end of the Stiperstones range, the West Onny below Shelve Hill and the East Onny west of Ratlinghope Hill. Beyond the confluence at Eaton the river flows in a south-easterly direction past Horderley, Stokesay and Onibury to join the Teme at Bromfield (SO 484766).

Plowden (Cock's, Cox) Mill	Lydbury North	SO 384872	CRM
Halford Mill	Halford	SO 436833	CRM
Stokesay Mill	Stokesay	SO 437815	CRM
Wootton Mill	Onibury	SO 459783	CRM

West Onny

Lydham Mill	Lydham	SO 334911	CRM

East Onny

Upper Mill	Wentnor	SO 381940	CRM WLM
Whitcot Mill	Norbury	SO 378918	CRM

Darnford Brook
A brook which rises east of Ratlinghope Hill round which it flows to join the East Onny at Bridges (SO 393964).

Ratlinghope Mill	Ratlinghope	SO 403970	CRM

Quinny Brook
A tributary of the Onny which flows south from the Stretton Gap, where it is known as the Marsh Brook, to join the Byne Brook at Strefford (SO 449858). It joins the Onny north of Craven Arms (SO 435843).

Queenbatch Mill	Church Stretton	SO 449903	CRM
Marsh Mill	Wistanstow	SO 448880	CRM
Berry Mill	Wistanstow	SO 438845	CRM

Byne Brook/Eaton Brook/Lakehouse Brook
A stream which rises south-west of Cardington and flows south-west through Rushbury and Eaton-under-Heywood, where it is known at the Eaton Brook. In its lower reaches it is known as the Byne Brook, before it joins the Quinny Brook at Strefford (SO 449858).

Newhall Mill	Eaton	SO 489890	CRM
Affcot Mill	Wistanstow	SO 450858	CRM

Heath Brook
A tributary of the Byne Brook which rises west of Cardington on the southern slopes of Wilstone Hill, flows east through Cardington, then south to join the Byne Brook near Rushbury (SO 517909).

Cardington Mill	Cardington	SO 511949	CRM
Cardington Lower (Gretton) Mill	Cardington/Rushbury	SO 513945	CRM

'Stokesay Brook'
A stream extending less than 2km. in an easterly direction, joining the Onny near Stokesay Castle.

Stokesay Castle Mill	Stokesay	SO 435817	PFB

Corve
A tributary of the River Teme which rises in Spoonhill Wood, south of Much Wenlock, and flows south-east to join the Teme at Ludlow.

Broadstone Mill	Munslow	SO 547901	CRM
Hungerford Mill	Munslow	SO 537893	CRM LTM
Stanton Lacy Mill	Stanton Lacy	SO 493790	CRM
Corve Mill	Ludlow	SO 511753	BKM

Easthope Brook
A tributary of Corve originating with springs at the northern end of Wenlock Edge which flows south-east to join the Corve south of Brockton (SO 588932).

Easthope (Greenpool) Mill	Easthope	SO 568946	CRM

'Abdon Brook'
A stream which flows from the Five Springs between Abdon Burf and Clee Burf, through Cockshutford, north-west to Tugford and south-west to join the Corve south of Munslow (SO 526863).

Abdon Furnace	Abdon	SO 567867	IBF
Tugford Mill	Tugford	SO 558870	CRM
Broncroft Mill	Diddlebury	SO 547867	CRM

'Diddlebury Brook'

A stream that has several sources south of Middlehope. It flows south through Diddlebury to join the Corve south of the village (SO 504838).

Turnhalls (Fernhall) Mill	Diddlebury	SO 498867	CRM
Bache Mill	Munslow	SO 501861	CRM

Siefton Brook

A stream that rises near Westhope and flows north to join the Corve at Culmington (SO 484819).

Siefton Mill	Culmington	SO 483833	CRM

Clee Brook/Pye Brook

A tributary of the Corve which originates on the southern slopes of Nordy Bank and flows west, then south-west, to join the Corve near Culmington (SO 498817). Known as the Pye Brook on its lower reaches.

Clee St Margaret Mill	Clee St Margaret	SO 561844	CRM
Bouldon Mill	Holgate	SO 547850	CRM IBF PPM

The mill at Bouldon in the Corvedale (SO 547850) where the water system also powered a blast furnace and a paper mill.

Ledwyche Brook

A tributary of the Teme which rises near Scrimage in the parish of Cold Weston, flows south-east towards Stoke St Milburgh, then south and south-west. It is joined by the Dogditch Brook at Henley (SO 528766), then takes a south-westerly direction to join the Teme at Burford (SO 581671).

Stoke St Milburgh Mill	Stoke St Milburgh	SO 568821	CRM
Henley Mill	Bitterley	SO 541763	CRM
Caynham Mill	Caynham	SO 544729	CRM
Burford (Ledwyche) Mill	Burford	SO 575684	CRM

Dogditch Brook/Bensons Brook

A tributary of the Ledwyche Brook which rises north of Titterstone Clee near Wheathill and flows south-west to be joined west of Bitterley (SO 551777) by Bensons Brook, and joins the Ledwyche Brook at Henley (SO 528766). No mills have been identified on the Dogditch Brook. Bensons Brook rises on the south slopes of Titterstone Clee and flows west through Bitterley to join the Dogditch Brook.

Bitterley Mil	Bitterley	SO 559773	CRM

Colly Brook/Stoke Brook

A tributary of the Ledwyche Brook which flows south from Hope Bagot and joins the Ledwych Brook west of Greete (SO 564704).

Rockhill Mill	Burford	SO 517722	CRM

Corn Brook

A tributary of the Teme which rises on the south slopes of Titterstone Clee and flows south to join the Teme at Monks Bridge (SO 617683).

Cornbrook Furnace	Coreley	SO 604683	IBF
Boraston Mill	Burford	SO 618702	CRM
Coreley (Bossell) Mill	Coreley	SO 615731	CRM
Tilsop Furnace	Burford	SO 616725	IBF
Whatmore (Wetmore) Mill	Burford	SO 615715	CRM

Rea

A tributary of the Teme which rises north of Ditton Priors and flows south-east through Neenton to be joined by the Cleobury Brook (SO 654848) after which it takes a southerly course through Stottesdon to Cleobury Mortimer, and is joined by the Hopton Brook (SO 657707) before crossing the Worcestershire border and joining the Teme near Newnham Bridge (SO 636686).

Middleton Mill	Ditton Priors	SO 628894	CRM	
Duddlewick Mill	Stottesdon	SO 654832	CRM	
Hardwick Forge	Stottesdon	SO 660818	IFG	
Prescott Mill	Stottesdon	SO 662810	CRM	IFG
Stottesdon Factory	Stottesdon	SO 662804	CTM	IFG
Detton Mill	Stottesdon	SO 663792	CRM	
Walfords Mill	Neen Savage	SO 675767	CRM	PPM
Lloyds Mill	Neen Savage	SO 677763	PPM	
Cleobury Corn Mill	Cleobury Mortimer	SO 679757	CRM	
Cleobury Upper Forge	Cleobury Mortimer	SO 687757	IFG	
Cleobury Lower Forge	Cleobury Mortimer	SO 688747	IFG	
Tetstill Mill	Neen Sollars	SO 661715	CRM	

Winterburn Brook

A tributary of the Rea which originates on Neenton Heath and joins the River Rea south-east of Neenton (SO 564854).

Faintree Pump	Chetton	SO 656890	WPM
Lower Faintree Mill	Chetton	SO 658885	CRM

Cleobury Brook

A tributary of the River Rea which rises between Cleobury North and Neenton and flows south-east to join the Rea (SO 654848).

Cleobury North Mill	Cleobury North	SO 626872	CRM	
Charlcotte Paper Mill	Aston Botterell	SO 637862	CRM	PPM
Charcotte Furnace	Aston Botterell	SO 637861	CRM	IBF
Wrickton Mill	Stottesdon	SO 642858	CRM	
Straffords Mill	Stottesdon	SO 646853	FLM	

Farlow Brook

A tributary of the River Rea. The Farlow Brook and its tributaries the Match Brook, Ingardine Brook and Wheathill Brook rise east of Wheathill and flow east to join the Rea at Prescott (SO 662810).

Silvington Mill	Silvington	SO 621799	CRM
Farlow Mill	Farlow	SO 638813	CRM

Burrel Brook, or Pudding Brook

A stream which rises west of Cleobury Mortimer, and flows roughly parallel to and south of the main street of the town before joining the River Rea (SO 679759).

Pinkham Mill	Cleobury Mortimer	SO 678758	CRM
Lower Mill	Cleobury Mortimer	SO 678759	CDM CRM

Hopton Brook, or Mill Brook

A stream which rises on the east side of Titterstone Clee, flows south through Hopton Wafers, and joins the Rea south of Neen Sollars (SO 657707). It is known as the Mill Brook on its lower reaches.

Upper Mill	Hopton Wafers	SO 638769	PPM
Middle Mill	Hopton Wafers	SO 639766	PPM
Lower Mill	Hopton Wafers	SO 638762	BLM PPM
Ditton Mill	Cleobury Mortimer	SO 641736	CRM
Langley Mill	Neen Sollars	SO 653730	PPM
Sturts (Bradley) Mill	Neen Sollars	SO 654712	CRM PPM

SEVERN

The Severn rises on Plym Llimon, passes through Llanidloes, Newtown and Welshpool, receiving the waters of the Camlad and Pwlll Trewern, both of which flow partly through Shropshire, before entering the county at its confluence with the Vyrnwy south of Melverley (SJ 327158). The river forms the frontier with Wales for about 2km. and flows east towards Shrewsbury and then south towards Ironbridge and Bridgnorth. It is joined by the Perry at Bromley's Forge (SJ 440166), the Rea near Coleham Bridge (SJ 496124), the Tern at Atcham (SJ 553092), the Cound Brook at Cound (SJ 565063) and the Worfe at Pendlestone (SJ 724944). Downstream from Bridgnorth the Severn is joined by the Mor Brook at Eardington (SO 733885) and the Borle Brook near Highley (SO 753817) before passing across the county boundary about a mile downstream (SO 753809).Part of the west bank further downstream in Dowles parish was in Shropshire until 1895.

Isle	Bicton	SJ 456158	CRM WLM
Berwick	Shrewsbury	SJ 470148	WPM
Waterworks, English Bridge	Shrewsbury	SJ 496123	WPM
Calcutts Mill	Broseley	SJ 686030	CRM
Waterworks	Bridgnorth	SO 718929	WPM

Dowles Brook

A stream which originates east of Cleobury Mortimer and east of Furnace Mill forms the boundary between Shropshire and Worcestershire as far as its confluence with the Severn at Dowles (SO 779763) where the ancient boundaries have been changed.

Furnace Mill	Cleobury Mortimer	SO 719765	CRM

Baveny Brook

A stream flowing south from several sources around Baveney Wood to join the Dowles Brook (SO 709765).

'Baveney Furnace'	Cleobury Mortimer	SO 711764	IBF

Borle Brook

A tributary of the Severn which rises near Upton Cresset and flows south-east to join the Severn downstream from Highley (SO 753817).

The Down Mill	Chetton	SO 681898	CRM
Eudon Mill	Chetton	SO 689897	CRM
Glazeley Mill	Glazeley	SO 706886	CRM
Borle Mill	Highley	SO 793827	CRM
Lockwood (Logwood) Mill	Highley	SO 740820	CRM

Crunnells/Horseford Brook

A stream which rises near Middleton Scriven, and flows parallel to the Horseford Brook which it joins at Horseford Mill, and then flows east to join the Borle Brook at Huntsbottom (SO 715863), the section below Horseford Mill is known as Crunnells Brook.

Horseford Mill	Deuxhill	SO 700864	CRM

Bowhills Brook/Paper Mill Brook

A tributary of the Severn which originates from several streams in the south-eastern part of Alveley parish and flows north-west to join the Severn at Hampton Loade (SO 746864).

Bowells (Allum Bridge) Mill	Alveley	SO 771853	CRM
Coton Mill	Alveley	SO 765856	PPM
Gortens Mill	Alveley	SO 763858	CRM
Crows Mill	Alveley	SO 755860	CRM LTM PPM
Hampton Loade Forge	Quatt	SO 748864	IFG

Daddle Brook/Lybatch Brook

A stream which rises south of Alveley and flows north to join the Bowhills Brook (SO 757858).

Checkars Mill	Alveley	SO 676843	CRM

Hempton Brook/Chelmarsh Brook

A tributary of the Severn whose main source rises north of Chelmarsh and flows south-east to join the Severn (SO 745876). The stream was dammed in the 1960s to create the Chelmarsh reservoir.

Hempton Mill	Chelmarsh	SO 742874	CRM

Mor Brook

A tributary of the Severn which originates in a series of streams rising on the slopes of Wenlock Edge south of Much Wenlock, chief amongst them the Walton Brook or Beggarhill Brook. The Mor Brook flows south-east and joins the Severn at Eardington (SO 733885).

Acton Round Mill	Acton Round	SO 641955	CRM
Callaughton Mill	Much Wenlock	SO 621975	CRM
Aldenham Mill	Morville	SO 651956	CRM
Lye Mill	Morville	SO 676932	CRM
Hubbals Mill	Morville	SO 691915	IFG
Harpsford Mill	Morville	SO 692916	CRM
Eardington Mill	Quatford	SO 717898	CRM LNM
Eardington Upper Forge	Quatford	SO 726897	IFG
Eardington Lower Forge	Quatford	SO 734895	IFG

Beaconhill Brook
A stream which rises in the hills west and south of Monkhopton and flows north and north-east to join the Mor Brook east of Acton Round (SO 642957).

Monkhopton Mill	Monkhopton	SO 627934	CRM

'Aldenham Brook'
A stream rising south of Shirlet that flows through Aldenham Park to join the Mor Brook at Morville (SO 670937).

Hurst	Morville	SO 672958	IFG

Dudmaston Brook
A tributary of the Severn which rises south-east of Quatt and flows in a south-westerly direction through several ornamental pools in the grounds of Dudmaston to join the Severn (SO 736888).

Dudmaston Mill (1)	Quatt	SO 737896	BNM
Dudmaston Mill (2)	Quatt	SO 736896	CRM

'Potseething Brook'
A tributary of the Severn, less than a mile long, with sufficient flow of water to sustain one mill.

Daniels Mill	Quatford	SO 718917	CRM

Canters Brook
A stream that originates near Astley Abbots and flows in a south-easterly direction to join the Severn (SO 725950).

Cantern Mill	Astley Abbots	SO 716940	CRM

Worfe
A tributary of the Severn which rises near Woodhouse (SJ 712119), north of Watling Street, between the Telford conurbation and Sherrifhales. It turns south at Burlington Pool, the section past Ruckley Grange being known as the Ruckley Brook, and the length further south as the Cosford Brook, and is then joined by the Neachley Brook (SJ 782053), and after forming the south-eastern boundary of the park at Hatton Grange, is joined at Ryton (SJ 759028) by the Wesley Brook. Its confluence with the Severn is at Pendlestone (SO 724951).

Crackley Bank Mill	Sheriffhales	SJ 766112	CRM		
Burlington House Mill	Sheriffhales	SJ 774113	CRM		
Lizard Mill	Tong	SJ 786098	CRM		
Lizard Forge	Tong	SJ 788088	IFG		
Tong Forge	Tong	SJ 783083	IFG		
Ryton Mill	Ryton	SJ 759028	CRM	PPM	SLM
Higford Mill	Stockton	SJ 745006	CRM		
Badger Hall	Badger	SJ 757990	WPM		
Stableford Hall	Worfield	SJ 762988	WPM		
Worfield Mill	Worfield	SJ 758958	CRM		
Davenport House	Worfield	SJ 753951	WPM		
Burcote Mill	Worfield	SJ 746954	CRM	LNM	WLM
Rindleford Mill	Worfield	SJ 738955	CRM	FLM	OLM
Pendlestone Mill	Worfield	SJ 724944	CRM	IFG	WLM

'Atwell Park Brook'

A stream which rises south of Lilleshall Park and joins the Worfe north of Crackley Bank (SJ 756113).

| Atwell Park Farm | Sheriffhales | SJ 756127 | CRM PFB WPM |

Neachley Brook

A tributary of the Worfe which begins as the Pickmere Brook, originating near Picmoor Wood on the Staffordshire border just north of Watling Street. It forms the county boundary south of Watling Street to the north end of Norton Mere before joining the Worfe (SJ 782053). The brook powers Weston Mill in Staffordshire.

| Tong Castle Mill | Tong | SJ 790067 | CRM |

Kilsall Brook/Morning Brook

A tributary of the Neachley Brook which originates with several streams rising east of Boscobel. It flows east to join the Neachley Brook below Tong Castle (SJ 791067)

| Shackerley Mill | Donington | SJ 808063 | CRM |

Albrighton Brook/Humphreston Brook

The source of the brook is on the Staffordshire/Shropshire border west of Chillington Park from where it flows east to join the Neachley Brook at Cosford (SJ 781047).

Humphryston Mill	Albrighton	SJ 814047	CRM
Clock Mill	Albrighton	SJ 807044	CRM
Cosford Mill	Albrighton	SJ 789041	CRM
Cosford Grange Mill	Albrighton	SJ 786046	CRM

Wesley Brook/Sal Brook

A tributary of the Worfe which rises near Priorslee in a lake that was once a reservoir for the Lilleshall Company's ironworks, first created by damming a stream, then by subsidence. It was landscaped by Telford Development Corporation in 1977-78. The lake now consists of The Flash (SJ 720204) and The Reservoir (SJ 712102). The railway embankment separating the two parts was once the Lilleshall Company's mineral line to Woodhouse Colliery. The brook flows south-east through Shifnal to join the Worfe at Ryton (SJ 759028).

Haughton Mill	Shifnal	SJ 742087	CRM SWM
Shifnal Manor Mill	Shifnal	SJ 741067	CRM IBF
Patcher's	Shifnal	SJ 741056	PPM
(Paltey's,			
Hem Paper Mill,			
Shifnal Paper Mill)			
Evelith Mill	Shifnal	SJ 743051	CRM
Kemberton Mill	Kemberton	SJ 744045	CRM IBF PPM
Hinnington Mill	Shifnal	SJ 752036	CRM WPM
Grindle Forge	Ryton	SJ 753034	IFG PPM

Nedge Brook/Granny's Brook

A tributary of the Wesley Brook which rises near Malins Lee and flows east to join the Wesley Brook at the foot of Lodge Hill (SJ 741062).

| Hem Mill | Shifnal | SJ 724059 | CRM |

Badger Brook
A tributary of the Worfe which rises north-east of Beckbury and flows south then west through Badger to join the Worfe near Stableford (SJ 762988).

| Badger Heath Mill | Badger | SJ 783996 | CRM |
| Badger Mill | Badger | SJ 767994 | CRM |

Stratford Brook
A tributary of the Worfe which originates in streams rising on the county boundary east of Albrighton, and flows through Patshull Pool, powering Pasford Mill in Staffordshire, then through Chesterton, and, after its confluence with the Brantley Brook at Hilton (SJ 773955) joins the Worfe south of Worfield (SJ 758948).

| Chesterton Mill | Worfiled | SJ 792978 | CRM FLM PPM |

Brantley/Claverley/Hilton/Churl/Cut Throat Brook
A tributary of the Stratford Brook which rises near Six Ashes, flows north-east skirting Bobbington and forming a short stretch of the county boundary, then north through Claverley, where it is known as the Claverley Brook, then the Hilton Brook, then the Churl, joining the Stratford Brook at Hilton (SJ 773955).

Ashford Bank (Robbins) Mill	Claverley	SJ 802933	CRM BNM
Powkhall Mill	Claverley	SJ 791933	CRM
Sutton Mill	Claverley	SJ 789945	CRM PPM
Hopstone Mill	Claverley	SJ 786946	CRM

'Gatacre Brook'
A stream which rises in Gatacre Park and joins the Brantley Brook south-east of Claverley (SJ 803922).

| Sytch House Farm | Claverley | SJ 782905 | CRM |
| Lower Beobridge Mill | Claverley | SJ 784911 | CRM |

Linley Brook
A tributary of the Severn which rises east of the high ground at Shirlett and flows south through the pools of Willey Park then by a circuitous but generally easterly course to join the Severn near Wrens Nest (SJ 705983).

Old Willey Furnace	Willey	SO 672979	IBF
Smithies Mill	Willey	SO 674977	CGM CRM SWM
Nordley (Littlefords) Mill	Astley Abbots	SO 687981	CRM
Frog Mill	Astley Abbots	SO 698976	CRM
Wrens Nest Forge (Upper)	Astley Abbots	SO 701981	IFG
Wrens Nest Forge (Lower)	Astley Abbots	SO 706983	IFG

Dean Brook
A tributary of the Severn which rises south of Broseley and flows east through woodland to join the Severn near Hifnal (SO 705988).

| New Willey Furnace | Willey | SJ 673007 | IBF |
| Dean Mill | Willey | SJ 683000 | CRM |

Swinney Brook

A short stream in the parish of Sutton Maddock that flows south into the Severn (SJ 706017).

Swinney Mill	Sutton Maddock	SJ 706017	CGM CRM OLM

Wash Brook/Hay Brook

A stream which rises south of Dawley and flows through Lee Dingle in Madeley parish to join the Severn upstream from Coalport (SJ 693027).

Madeley Court Mill	Madeley	SJ 695052	CRM
Clock Mill	Madeley	SJ 700041	CRM CEM
Washbrook Mill	Madeley	SJ 699039	CRM

Calcutts Brook

A tributary of the Severn which rises east of Broseley and flows north to join the Severn at The Calcutts (SJ 687030).

Calcutts Upper Mill	Broseley	SJ 684027	CRM
Calcutts Lower Mill	Broseley	SJ 685028	CRM
Calcutts Ironworks	Broseley	SJ 686030	BGM IBF IFG

Benthall Brook

A tributary of the Severn which rises west of Broseley and flows north to join the Severn immediately downstream of the Iron Bridge (SJ 673034).

Benthall Ironworks	Benthall	SJ 672030	BGM IBF
Benthall Mill	Benthall	SJ 672032	CRM

Calde Brook

A natural stream whose course is now almost entirely artificial as a result of its adaptation to provide power for the ironworks in Coalbrookdale. It now originates in the Upper Furnace Pool, Coalbrookdale, which is supplied with water by the Lyde Brook and Horsehay Brook, and extends about a mile south to join the Severn at Dale End (SJ 665036).

Coalbrookdale Mill	Madeley	SJ 669049	CRM
Upper Furnace	Madeley	SJ 667048	IBF
Lower Furnace	Madeley	SJ 667045	IBF
Upper Forge	Madeley	SJ 669042	CRM IFG
Middle Forge	Madeley	SJ 668041	BGM IFG
Lower Forge	Madeley	SJ 667040	IFG

Horsehay Brook

A tributary of the Calde Brook which rises in the western part of Dawley parish, flows south to Lightmoor and then west to join the Lyde Brook at the head of Coalbrookdale, in the period covered by this survey, on the east side of the Upper Furnace Pool.

Horsehay Ironworks	Dawley	SJ 673071	CRM IBF
Lightmoor Ironworks	Dawley	SJ 682053	CRM IBF
Park Lane Forge	Madeley	SJ 681048	IFG

Lyde Brooke

A tributary of the Calde Brook which rises west of Little Wenlock and takes a south-westerly course to join the Horsehay Brook at the head of Coalbrookdale, in the period covered by this survey, on the western side of the Upper Furnace Pool (SJ 667049).

Little Wenlock Mill	Little Wenlock	SJ 663057	CRM

Farley Brook

A tributary of the Severn which rises south of Much Wenlock and flows in a north-north-easterly direction to join the Severn near Buildwas Abbey (SJ 642045).

Downs Mill	Much Wenlock	SJ 630007	CRM
Farley Upper Mill	Much Wenlock	SJ 631007	CRM
Farley Lower Mill	Much Wenlock	SJ 633022	CRM
Buildwas Mill	Buildwas	SJ 641039	CRM

Sheinton/Harley Brook

A stream which rises at the foot of Wenlock Edge between Longville and Plaish and flows north-east through Hughley, where it is known as the Hughley Brook, and then to Harley where it takes a more northerly course to its confluence with the Severn (SJ 607049).

Plaish Mill	Cardington	SO 535964	CRM
Holy (Preen) Mill	Cardington	SO 550955	CRM
Hughley Mill	Hughley	SO 564979	CRM
Harley Forge	Harley	SJ 588001	IFG
Harley Mill	Harley	SJ 600011	CRM
Wigwig Mill	Much Wenlock	SJ 608018	CRM
Sheinwood Mill	Sheinton	SJ 615026	CRM
Sheinton Forge	Sheinton	SJ 607041	IFG

'Kenley Brook'

A stream which rises south of Kenley and flows east to join the Harley Brook (SO 570984).

Kenley Furnace	Kenley	SJ 564985	IBF

Leighton Brook

A stream originating on the south slopes of the Wrekin which flows south-west through Leighton to its confluence with the Severn (SJ 608050).

Dingle Mill	Leighton	SJ 617062	CRM
Upper Mill	Leighton	SJ 612058	CRM
Leighton Furnace	Leighton	SJ 610055	CRM IBF

Cressage Brook

A tributary of the Severn which originates in several streams rising south and west of the village and flows north to its confluence with the Severn (SJ 593043).

Cressage Mill	Cressage	SJ 592040	CRM

Cound Brook

A tributary of the Severn which rises at the north end of the Stretton Gap and flows north through Leebotwood where it is joined by the Walkmills Brook (SO 477987). Its northerly course continues through Longnor to Condover from where it follows a circuitous but generally easterly route to the delta where it joins the Severn (SJ 565063).

Carding Mill	Church Stretton	SO 445945	WLM
Dudgeley (Dagers) Mill	Church Stretton	SO 466960	CRM
Leebotwood Mill	Leebotwood	SO 475986	CRM
Longnor Mill	Longnor	SJ 488006	CRM SWM
Longnor Forge	Longnor	SJ 485013	IFG PPM
Dorrington Forge	Dorrington	SJ 484021	IFG
Condover Mill	Condover	SJ 479046	CRM
Upper Mill	Condover	SJ 493057	CRM
Widnall Mill	Condover	SJ 502060	LTM
Cantlop Mill	Berrington	SJ 523062	CRM
Pitchford (Eaton Mascott) Forge	Pitchford	SJ 534054	CRM IFG
Upper Cound Mill	Cound	SJ 553050	PPM
Lower Cound Mill	Cound	SJ 555055	CRM

Betchcott Brook/Walk Mills Brook

A tributary of the Cound Brook which originates as a series of streams on the north slope of the Long Mynd and flows west from Smethcott to join the Cound Brook at Leebotwood (SO 477987).

Upper Mills	Smethcott	SO 448992	FLM
Woolstaston Mill	Woolstaston	SO 457994	CRM ELG
Fulling Mill	Woolstaston	SO 462993	FLM
Fulling Mill	Leebotwood	SO 466993	FLM

Lynall Brook

A stream which rises near Ruckley and flows north through Acton Burnell to join the Cound Brook (SJ 545052).

Acton Burnell Mill	Acton Burnell	SJ 530020	CRM

Bullhill Brook

A stream which rises near Langley and flows north to join the Cound Brook (SJ 555053).

Langley Mill	Langley	SJ 545005	CRM
Grange Mill	Cound	SJ 551003	CRM

Tern

A tributary of the Severn which originates from springs between Woore and Madeley (Staffordshire), enters Shropshire near Willoughbridge Farm, flows south-west through Market Drayton and turns south after its confluence with the Bailey Brook north-east of Hodnet (SJ 629315). It is joined by the Strine at Crudgington (SJ 639176), by the Meese at Bolas (SJ 639208) and by the Roden at Walcot (SJ 593124), and reaches the Severn at Atcham (SJ 553091).

Bearstone Mill	Mucklestone	SJ 725390	CRM
Norton Forge	Norton-in-Hales	SJ 704379	IFG
Betton (Oakley) Mill	Market Drayton	SJ 698366	CRM
Tunstall Hall	Market Drayton	SJ 692352	WMP
Tunstall Mill	Market Drayton	SJ 691352	CRM
Hinsley Mill	Market Drayton	SJ 686345	CRM
Turley (Tern) Mill	Market Drayton	SJ 679337	CRM PPM
Tanyard Mill	Market Drayton	SJ 677338	BKM
Walk (Drayton, Victoria) Mill	Market Drayton	SJ 671334	CRM PPM
Buntingsdale Mill	Market Drayton	SJ 657331	CRM

Bearstone Mill, the first mill on the River Tern in Shropshire, upstream from Market Drayton (SJ 725390).

New Mill	Market Drayton	SJ 636316	CRM
Wollerton Mill	Hodnet	SJ 626298	CRM
Peplow Mill	Hodnet	SJ 643243	CRM
Eaton Mill	Stoke-upon-Tern	SJ 649231	CRM
Longdon Mill	Longdon-on-Tern	SJ 617153	CRM
Allscott Mill	Wrockwardine	SJ 613133	CRM FLM LTM
Walcot Mill	Wellington	SJ 594124	CRM FLM
Tern Works	Atcham	SJ 551098	CRM IFG

Coal Brook

A stream which rises in the Bishops Wood area and flows north-west to join the Tern at Market Drayton (SJ 683340). For about 2 km. north of Chipnall it forms the boundary between Shropshire and Staffordshire.

Chipnall Mill	Cheswardine	SJ 736324	CRM
Shakeford Mill	Hinstock	SJ 677284	CRM
Drayton Old Mill	Market Drayton	SJ 656331	CRM PPM

Bailey Brook

A stream which originates in the low-lying land south of Moreton Say and flows south to join the Tern south of Tern Hill (SJ 627314).

| Sandford Mill | Prees | SJ 581341 | CRM OLM |

Rosehill Brook

A tributary of the Tern which rises south of Market Drayton and flows south-west to join the Tern at Stoke-on-Tern (SJ 637280).

| Rosehill Mill | Market Drayton | SJ 657306 | CRM |

Meese

The River Meese originates with several streams which flow into Aqualate Mere from which the main stream flows north-west towards Standford Bridge. It takes a circuitous but generally south-westerly course to Tibberton, then heads west before joining the Tern at Bolas (SJ 639208).

Chetwynd Mill	Chetwynd	SJ 735215	CRM	WPM
New Caynton Mill	Edgmond	SJ 694230	CRM	IFG
Old Caynton Mill	Edgmond	SJ 692214	CRM	OLM
Tibberton Mill	Edgmond	SJ 681204	PPM	SLM
Cherrington Mill	Edgmond	SJ 670207	CRM	
Great Bolas Mill	Great Bolas	SJ 648208	CRM	PPM

Lynn Brook/Moreton Brook/Back Brook/Mill Brook

A tributary of the Meese which originates on the Staffordshire border near Great Chatwell from where it flows north. It is called the Lynn Brook, then the Moreton Brook, then the Back Brook and then the Mill Brook before it flows into Aqualate Mere (SJ 776200).

Chadwell Mill	Sheriffhales	SJ 786145	CRM	PFB
Lynn (Lindon) Mill	Sheriffhales	SJ 787155	CRM	

'Woodcote Stream'

A tributary of the Lynn Brook which rises south of Woodcote Hall and flows north, eventually through underground channels and apparently finds its way into the Lynn Brook.

Woodcote Mill	Sheriffhales	SJ 767154	SWM

Wagg's Brook

A tributary of the Meese which rises west of Bishop's Wood and forms the boundary between Shropshire and Staffordshire for 8km. as far south as Ellerton before flowing into the Meese (SJ 716236).

Doley Mill	Cheswardine	SJ 739295	CRM	
Ellerton Mill	Cheswardine	SJ 714260	CRM	PPM
Sambrook Mill	Cheswardine	SJ 713248	CRM	IFG

Goldstone/Ellerton/Showell Brook

A tributary of the Meese which rises east of Cheswardine and flows south towards Sambrook and its confluence with the Meese near Deepdale Farm (SJ 713327).

Westcott Mill	Cheswardine	SJ 709290	CRM
Hinstock Mill	Hinstock	SJ 693262	CRM
Showell Mill	Edgmond	SJ 718242	CRM

Plat Brook

A tributary of the Tern which originates on the eastern side of Sandford Heath and takes a circuitous but generally easterly course to join the Tern near Bolas (SJ 638207).

Wood Mill	Stanton-upon-Hine-Heath	SJ 262230	CRM

Strine

A tributary of the Tern which rises south-east of Newport and flows past the northern side of the town, then in a generally south-westerly direction and through several channels across the Weald Moors where it is joined by the Lilleshall, Humbers and Hurley brooks, and passing through numerous artificial channels joins the Tern at Crudgington (SJ 269176). Drainage authorities since the 17th century have created other outlets to the Tern.

Longford Mill	Longford	SJ 717181	CRM

Lilleshall Brook

A tributary of the Strine which rises in the woods east of Lilleshall Abbey, flows north-west past the southern edge of Lilleshall village, and is joined by a tributary flowing from the south at Honnington Grange. The brook continues in a north-westerly direction to its confluence with the Strine (SJ 685165).

Abbey Mill	Lilleshall	SJ 734144	CRM
'Middle Mill'	Lilleshall	SJ 733146	CRM
Towns End Mill	Lilleshall	SJ 727149	CRM
Honnington Grange	Lilleshall	SJ 723149	CRM IBF

Humber Brook

A stream which has its origins on the northern fringe of Donnington and flows north-west past the Humbers to join the Strine Brook (SJ 685164).

| Lubstree Forge | Lilleshall | SJ 693153 | IFG |

Wombridge Brook/Trench Brook

A stream which flows in a north-westerly direction across Wombridge parish and ultimately joins the Crow Brook which subsequently flows into the Strine (SJ 668156).

| Wombridge Mill | Wombridge | SJ 692115 | CRM IBF |

Hadley Brook

A stream which flows north through the township of Hadley to join the Crow Brook which subsequently flows into the Strine (SJ 668156).

| Hadley Mill | Wellington | SJ 676135 | CRM |

Ketley/Hurley Brook

A tributary of the Strine which rises near Lawley and flows north falling steeply until it is crossed by the Holyhead Road at the settlement of Ketley Brook. Its subsequent course is less steep and from Leegomery Mill it is known as the Hurley Brook. From Wappenshall to its confluence with the Strine most of its present course is in the former bed of the Shrewsbury Canal.

Newdale Ironworks	Wellington	SJ 672097	IBF
Ketley Ironworks	Wellington	SJ 688061	IBF
Leegomery Mill	Wellington	SJ 667128	CRM
Eyton Mill	Eyton-upon-the-Weald-Moors	SJ 653151	CRM

Roden

A tributary of the River Tern which rises east of Ellesmere, flows south towards Wem after which it follows a circuitous course through Leebrockhurst, Stanton-upon-Hine-Heath and Shawbury, before turning south and joining the Tern at Walcot (SJ 593124).

Wytheford Forge	Shawbury	SJ 569188	IFG
Ercall Mill	High Ercall	SJ 585164	CRM
Harcourt Mill	Stanton-upon-Hine-Heath	SJ 559246	CRM
Stanton Mill	Stanton-upon-Hine-Heath	SJ 566241	CRM
Moreton Mill	Shawbury	SJ 574226	CRM KFG SWM
Wem Mill	Wem	SJ 512285	CRM

Lyneal Brook
A stream which flows south of Colemere to join the Roden north of Loppington (SJ 462315).

Lyneal Mill	Ellesmere	SJ 453325	CRM

Sleap Brook
A tributary of the River Roden which originates on either side of the A528 between Cockshut and Myddle and flows east to join the Roden south of Wem (SJ 505281).

Burlton Mill	Loppington	SJ 459272	CRM

Soulton Brook
A tributary of the River Roden which originates south of Whitchurch with several streams flowing in a southerly direction east of Prees, then across the Dog Moor eventually coming together to join the Roden downstream from Wem.

Prees Mill	Prees	SJ 551337	CRM

Uffington Brook
A tributary of the Severn which rises between Astley and Battlefield and flows south through Sundorne, where it was dammed to create ornamental lakes, and reaches the Severn near Pimley (SJ 525141). A mill stream was diverted to flow towards Uffington and joins the Severn further downstream (SJ 527139).

Pimley Mill	Uffington	SJ 523144	CRM
Uffington	Uffington	SJ 527138	CRM IRM

Rea Brook
A tributary of the River Severn which originates in Marton Pool (SJ 295026) and pursues a north-easterly course towards Shrewsbury where it now joins the Severn upstream from the English Bridge (SJ 496124). The confluence was more complex in the past.

New Mill	Pontesbury	SJ 407075	CRM
Cruckmeole Mill	Pontesbury	SJ 429094	CRM
Cruckton Mill	Pontesbury	SJ 431095	CRM
Hanwood Upper Mill	Hanwood	SJ 441093	BRM CRM FLM
Hanwood Mill	Hanwood	SJ 449100	CRM
Redhill (Hanley) Mill	Meole Brace	SJ 468095	CRM
Pulley Mill	Meole Brace	SJ 484102	CRM
Meole Brace Mill	Meole Brace	SJ 487106	CRM
Sutton Old Mill	Sutton	SJ 497108	CRM
Sutton New Mill	Sutton	SJ 504107	BRM CRM IFG
Burnt Mill	Shrewsbury	SJ 503113	CRM
Monks' (Prince's) Mill	Shrewsbury	SJ 502121	CRM
Abbey Mill	Shrewsbury	SJ 497124	CRM
Coleham Factory	Shrewsbury	SJ 496123	WLM

Lowerfield Brook
A tributary of the Rea Brook which runs east of Trylistan and flows in a south-easterly direction into Marton Pool (SJ 295029).

Marton Mill	Chirbury	SJ 285033	CRM

Worthen/Brockton Brook

A tributary of the Rea Brook which originates as the Rowley Brook and the Tantree Brook which drain the eastern side of the Long Mountain. The stream joins the Rea Brook south-east of Worthen (SJ 344043).

Walton Mill	Worthen	SJ 298055	CRM
Brockton Mill	Worthen	SJ 318046	CRM
Worthen Mill	Worthen	SJ 327045	CRM

Aston Brook

A stream which rises south of Caus Castle and joins the Rea Brook due east of Worthen (SJ 347048).

Aston Rogers Mill	Worthen	SJ 343064	CRM

Yockleton Brook

A stream which drains the eastern slopes of the Long Mountain north of Caus Castle and joins the Rea Brook west of Hanwood (SJ 433097).

Vennington Mill	Westbury	SJ 338095	CRM
Upper Mill	Yockleton	SJ 396013	CRM
Lower Mill	Yockleton	SJ 404103	CRM

'Winnington Brook'

A stream which rises in the Winnington area and flows south-east to join the Yockleton Brook east of Westbury (SJ 375095).

Hayford Mill	Alberbury	SJ 359107	CRM

Minsterley Brook

A tributary of the Rea Brook which flows north through the Hope Valley where it is joined by several streams from the east. Its confluence with the Rea is at Malehurst (SJ 384064).

Hope Mill	Worthen	SJ 353019	CRM
The Waterwheel	Westbury	SJ 365024	BRM CRM
Hogstow Mill	Westbury	SJ 366032	CRM FLM
Minsterley Mill	Westbury	SJ 374045	BRM CRM FLM

Habberley/Pontesbury Brook

A tributary of the Rea Brook which rises east of the Stiperstones and flows north to join the Rea north of Pontesford (SJ 407075).

Habberley Mill	Pontesbury	SJ 403036	CRM
Skin Mill	Pontesbury	SJ 415051	CRM LTM
Pontesford Upper Mill	Pontesbury	SJ 412065	CRM
Pontesford Lower Mill	Pontesbury	SJ 408065	CRM SWM
Hinton Mill	Pontesbury	SJ 406075	CRM

Perry

A tributary of the River Severn which originates in the hills south of Selattyn and flows in an easterly direction north of Gobowen, then turns south past Halston, and continues in a generally southern direction across the Baggy Moors through Ruyton-XI-Towns, turning east towards Baschurch then south-east to join the Severn near Bromley's Forge (SJ 440166).

Park Mill	Selattyn	SJ 294325	CRM
Fernhill Forge	Whittington	SJ 318333	IFG

Rednall Mill	West Felton	SJ 373294	CRM
Ruyton Mill	Ruyton-XI-Towns	SJ 391225	CRM
Platt Mill	Baschurch	SJ 403224	CRM
New Mills	Ruyton-XI-Towns	SJ 405213	CRM
Milford Mill	Baschurch	SJ 419211	CRM
Bent Mill	Baschurch	SJ 422203	CRM FLM
Adcote Mill	Baschurch	SJ 422196	CRM
Yeaton Upper Mill	Baschurch	SJ 433193	CRM
Yeaton Lower Mill	Baschurch	SJ 435193	CRM
Fitz Mill	Fitz	SJ 443181	CRM
Mytton Mill	Fitz	SJ 441176	CRM
Bromley's Forge	Montford	SJ 441166	IFG

Meadow Brook

A stream which rises north of Oswestry and flows east to join the River Perry north of Whittington (SJ 329325).

Oak (Derwen, Fernhill) Mill Whittington	SJ 312327	CRM

Weir Brook

A tributary of the River Perry which rises south of West Felton and flows east to join the Perry east of Wykey (SJ 396250).

Sandford Mill	West Felton	SJ 338236	CRM
Heath Mills	West Felton	SJ 323244	CRM

'Kinnerley Stream'

A tributary of the River Severn which rises south of West Felton and joins the Severn east of Melverley (SJ 345170).

Kinnerley Mill	Kinnerley	SJ 348200	CRM

Vyrnwy

A tributary of the River Severn which enters Shropshire downstream from Llanymynech Bridge, interweaves with the county boundary for a mile or so, probably reflecting a former course in this flat country. It continues in a south-easterly direction, forming the county boundary as far as *Cymmerau*, its confluence with the Severn south of Melverley (SJ 337158). It is joined by the Morda, on which there are many mills, at Mill House, Pentheylin (SJ 304194), and by the Tanat (SJ 244206), on whose tributary the Cynllaith there is a single mill. Otherwise there are no mills on the Vyrnwy and its tributaries in Shropshire.

Tanat

The River Tanat enters Shropshire at its confluence with the Cynllaith in Llanyblodwell (SJ 215238). For 0.5km. it forms the county boundary through the village of Llanyblodwell, re-entering Wales for 0.5km. before its confluence with the Vyrnwy west of Llanymynech (SJ 244206).

Cynllaith

A tributary of the River Tanat which rises in the hills west of Offa's Dyke in the parish of Llansilin, forms the boundary between Shropshire and Wales north of Pont Pentregwyn (SJ 217284), then flows south for 5 km. through Llangedwyn before re-entering Shropshire for 0.5 km. and joining the Tanat.

Penybont Mill	Llanyblodwell	SJ 215238	CRM

Morda Brook

A tributary of the Vyrnwy which rises in the hills west of Offa's Dyke in the parish of Llansilin, and enters Shropshire at Llawnt (SJ 249308) whence it flows south to Llanforda Mill (SJ 255283) and then east past Morda and Maesbury, turning south towards Llanmynech and its confluence with the Vyrnwy near Pentreheylin Hall (SJ 304194).

Llanforda Mill	Oswestry	SJ 255283	CRM
Penyllan Mill	Oswestry	SJ 278281	CRM
Morda Upper Mill	Oswestry	SJ 287280	CRM WLM
Morda Corn Mill	Oswestry	SJ 287281	CRM
Morda Lower Mill	Oswestry	SJ 289281	CPW PPM WLM
Weston Upper Mill	Oswestry	SJ 293277	CRM CTM
Weston Lower Mill	Oswestry	SJ 297275	CRM WLM
Ball Mill	Oswestry	SJ 304265	CRM
Maesbury Mill	Oswestry	SJ 304259	CRM PTM
Maesbury Hall Mill	Oswestry	SJ 303250	CRM
Llantidmon (Redwith) Mill	Llanymynech	SJ 290210	CRM
Pentreeylin Mill	Kinnerley	SJ 304194	CRM

Weston Lower Mill on the Morda Brook (SJ 297275)

Morda Mill (SJ 287280) near Oswestry

'Sweeney Brook'

A tributary of the Morda, originating in streams rising on Sweeney Mountain which, once united, flow east to join the Morda south of Maesbury (SJ 305247).

Sweeney Mill	Oswestry	SJ 285253	CRM

'Aston Stream'

A stream which rises south of Aston and joins the Morda north of Osbaston (SJ 316237).

Aston Mill	Oswestry	SJ 321269	CRM
Park Mill	Oswestry	SJ 320250	CRM

Pwll Trewern

A tributary of the Severn which rises on the north slopes of Heldre Hill at the north-eastern end of the Long Mountain, where it forms the boundary between Shropshire and Wales, and then flows west through Montgomeryshire to join the Severn east of Pool Quay (SJ 266118).

Dingle Mill	Alberbury	SJ 294108	CRM
Old Dingle Mill	Alberbury	SJ 296104	CRM
Hall Mill	Alberbury	SJ 317107	CRM

Camlad

A tributary of the River Severn which rises on Corndon Marsh near Hyssington, flows south to the Roveries Bridge, when west to Churchstoke, forming for 4km. the southern border of a salient of Shropshire. From Churchstoke it turns north, through Shropshire, passing through the Marrington Gorge east of Chirbury. It is joined by the Aylesford Brook, flowing west out of Marton Brook near Stockton (SJ 266008), and then follows a circuitous but basically westward course in which for two sections, each of c.1km, it forms Shropshire's boundary with Wales. It joins the Severn near Forden (SO 209005).

Bromley's Mill	More	SO 333917	CRM
Marrington Mill	Chirbury	SO 272975	CRM
Walk Mill, Marrington	Chirbury	SO 272979	FLM
Walk Mill, Heightley	Chirbury	SO 276998	FLM
Heightley Mill	Chirbury	SO 273988	CRM
Stockton Mill	Chirbury	SJ 265007	CRM

Pellmell Brook

A stream which originates in several springs west of Lydham and joins the River Camlad near Snead (SO 320918).

White (Wheat) Mills	Lydham	SO 320918	CRM

Caebitra

A stream which rises south of Montgomery and flows north-east to join the River Camlad at Churchstoke (S) 270940). Between Melin-y-wern (SO 234966) and its confluence with the Lack Brook near Churchstoke (SO 167940) it forms the border between Shropshire and Wales.

Brompton Mill	Churchstoke	SO 251931	CRM
Mellington Mill	Chirbury	SO 259908	CRM

Aylesford Brook

A stream which flows in a south-westerly direction out of Marton Pool to join the Camlad near Stockton (SJ 266008). A tributary rises north of Middleton and flows north, then west to join the brook north of Wotherton (SJ 284017).

Rorrington Mill	Chirbury	SJ 266007	CRM

Ceiriog

A tributary of the River Dee which enters Shropshire at Pen-y-bryn (SJ 264375) whence it and the Dee which it joins north east of Chirk (SJ 318395) form the county's western and northern boundary for 12km. to the Dee's confluence with the Shell Brook (SJ 350413). In modern times all mills on the Ceiriog and Dee have been on the Denbighshire bank, but those sections where the boundary and the river do not coincide probably indicate the existence of ancient mill sites.

Morlas Brook

A tributary of the River Ceiriog which rises 1.5km. west of Offa's Dyke and enters Shropshire at Craignant (SJ 253349). It is the only tributary of the Ceiriog with mills in Shropshire.

Old Paper Mill	St Martin's	SJ 273344	PPM
Wern Mill	St Martin's	SJ 275345	CRM PPM
New Mills	St Martin's	SJ 277345	CRM
Weston Rhyn Paper Mill	St Martin's	SJ 282347	PPM
Weston Mill	St Martin's	SJ 28450	CRM
Erescob Mill	St Martin's	SJ 308362	CRM
Glynmorlas Mill	St Martin's	SJ 313377	CRM SWM

Shell Brook

A tributary of the River Dee which rises at Trench, 2km. north of Ellesmere, and in its lower reaches forms the boundary between Shropshire and Wales.

Pant Mill	Ellesmere	SJ 354400	CRM

Emral Brook

A tributary of the River Dee whose sources rise north of Ellesmere and join on the country boundary (SJ 425390) and then flow north to Worthenbury before joining the Dee (SJ 423494).

Brook Mill	Ellesmere	SJ 418389	CRM
Wood Mill	Ellesmere	SJ 417381	CRM

'Whitchurch Stream'

A stream which rises south of Whitchurch and flows through the town to its confluence with the Red Brook on the county boundary, then heads north-west to join the Worthenbury Brook which in due course joins the River Dee.

Whitchurch Mill	Whitchurch	SJ 541414	CRM
Chemistry Mill	Whitchurch	SJ 528415	CRM

Duckow

A tributary of the River Weaver whose main stream rises on the eastern edge of the park at Cloverley Hall, Calverhall. It flows south and east then turns north, passes Shavington Park before forming Shropshire's boundary with Cheshire for 3km. before it passes out of the county 2km. south of Audlem. It then flows north to its confluence with the Weaver near Nantwich.

Moreton Mill	Moreton Say	SJ 631354	CRM

Appendix 2   Turnpike Road Data

This list details as far as is possible in the present state of knowledge, the principal turnpike roads in Shropshire and their tollhouses. Some questions about the county's turnpikes awaiting resolution, particularly those concerning the merging and separation of trusts. Some of turnpike trusts listed had roads in more than one county, but only Shropshire sections and the tollhouses on them are listed here. The list shows each road system at its maximum extent. The responsibilities of some trusts were reduced as others were established – the section of the Shrewsbury-Oswestry road beyond the tenth milestone, part of the Welsh Bridge Trust from 1756, passed to the Oswestry Trust in 1763, and to the Holyhead Road Commission in 1819. Not all the tollhouses listed were necessarily in operation at any one time. Tollhouses administered by the Holyhead Road Commission are listed under the turnpike trusts that had been responsible for those sections of road before the Commission gained powers over them in 1819. Dates of de-turnpiking are taken from SA QA/4 (SA 560/739). Grid references of tollhouses of which there is no cartographic evidence (marked *) are approximations only.

1. Shrewsbury-Crackley Bank & Shifnal

Original Act of Parliament: 12 Geo I, c 9; 1725

Extent:
Shrewsbury-Crackley Bank
Oakengates-Shifnal
Crudgington-the *Swan*, Watling Street
Cotwall-Shawbirch-Hadley-Oakengates
The *Horseshoes*, Uckington-Wroxeter-Longnor Green.
Atcham Bridge-Cross Houses

Dates of de-turnpiking: 1866 (Wellington district); 1875 (Shifnal district); 1877 (Shrewsbury district).

Tollhouses:

Acton Burnell/Frodesley	SJ 521020
Bratton Field	SJ 633141
Burcot (1)	SJ 616105
Burcot (2)	SJ 618106
Cock, Wellington	SJ 659110
Cronkhill Lane	SJ 537087
Emstrey Hill	SJ 520107
Hadley	SJ 675120
Leegomery	SJ 662135
Long Lane	SJ 635157
Long Waste/Longdon	SJ 614157
Priorslee	SJ 720092
Red Hill/Limekiln Bank	SJ 731108
Shawbirch	SJ 648132
Tern Bridge	SJ 550093
Watling Street	SJ 663111
Wroxeter	SJ 565088*

The tollhouse at Burcot (SJ 616105)
on the Shrewsbury-London road. It was
by-passed in the 1830s by the Overley Hill
diversion on the Holyhead Road.

The 'Umbrella House' at Burcot (SJ 618106),
a tollhouse built in the 1830s for the Overley Hill
diversion, and rendering redundant
the earlier tollhouse.

2. Wolverhampton Roads

Original Act of Parliament: 21 Geo II, c 25; 1748

Extent:
Shifnal – county boundary on the road to
    Wolverhampton.
Hales Heath – Tong, Albrighton – county boundary
    on road to Wolverhampton

Date of de-turnpiking: 1 November 1880

Tollhouse:

Shifnal	SJ 749073

3. Ludlow First Turnpike

Original Act of Parliament: 24 Geo II, c 29; 1751.

Extent:
Ludlow-Woofferton-Monksbridge on the road to
    Worcester
Ludlow-*Maidenhead* at Oreton, on the road to
    Hereford

Date of de-turnpiking: 1 January 1873

Tollhouses:

Ashford	SO 515704
Burford	SO 586685
Ledwich Bridge	SO 575684
Little Hereford Bridge	SO 546682
Ludford	SO 513741
Ludford Park	SO 508734
Monksbridge	SO 613687
Overton	SO 509725

The tollhouse at Overton (SO 499725)
built by the Ludlow First Turnpike Trust
in the 1830s where new routes to Worcester
and Hereford diverged south of Ludlow.

4. Shrewsbury-Wrexham

Original Act of Parliament: 25 Geo II, c 22; 1752

Extent:
Shrewsbury-Ellesmere-Wrexham
Ellesmere-West Felton-Moreton Bridge-Oswestry
Harmer Hill-Wem-Cotton Wood
Shawbury-Wem-Sandford

Date of de-turnpiking: 1 November 1871 (Wem division); 31 December 1872 (Overton division)

Tollhouses:

Blackwaters	SJ 393327
Coton	SJ 530340
Coton Hill, Shrewsbury	SJ 492134
Creamore	SJ 516298
Edstaston	SJ 522323
Hardwick	SJ 380339
Harlescott	SJ 497165
Palms Hill	SJ 520276
Rednal	SJ 365281
Soulton/Round Hill	SJ 523292
Stockett	SJ 425315
Stone & Cross	SJ 526340
Tilley	SJ 522283
Whip Lane	SJ 321233

5. Shrewsbury-Much Wenlock-Bridgnorth

Original Act of Parliament: 25 Geo II c 49; 1752.

Extent:
Shrewsbury-Much Wenlock-Bridgnorth
Bridgnorth-Smithy Brook
Much Wenlock-Church Stretton
Bridgnorth-Black Brook
Atcham-Condover-Dorrington
Wall-Blackwood Lime Kilns.

Date of de-turnpiking: 31 March 1875

Tollhouses:

Boreton	SJ 502065
Chilton	SJ 530091
Cressage	SJ 587042
Harley	SJ 600010
Hazler	SO 468933
King Street	SJ 518075
Morville	SO 671939
North Gate, Bridgnorth	SO 715938
Rushbury	SO 513916
Weeping Cross	SJ 513104
Wenlock	SO 624994
Wenlock Bank	SO 613995
West Gate, Bridgnorth	SO 709932
Westwood	SO 595983
Wheel Green	SO 763952*

6. Bewdley Roads

Original Act of Parliament: 26 Geo II c 3; 1753.

Extent:
Bewdley-Kinlet

Date of de-turnpiking: 1 November 1878

Tollhouses:

Burton Bridge	SO 735791
Dowles	SO 735791

7. Ludlow Second Turnpike

Original Act of Parliament: 29 Geo II c 59; 1756

Extent:

Ludlow-Henley-Clee Hill-Cleobury Mortimer
Ludlow-Sheet-Ledwych Bridge (Caynham)
Ludlow-Steventon-*Serpent Inn* (Ashford Carbonel)
Ludlow-Elton-Court House (Wigmore)
Ludlow-Leintwardine-Pervine Brook (near Knighton)
Ludlow-Lowse Gate on the road from Bromfield
    Wood to Mocktree
Ludlow-Bromfield-Wistanstow-Church Stretton
Ludlow-Munslow-Beambridge on the road to Much
    Wenlock
Craven Arms-Bouldon
Ludlow-Fishmore-Hayton-Bouldon
Ludlow-Middleton- the *Three Horseshoes* on the road
    to Bridgnorth
Pedlars' Rest (Culmington)-Craven Arms
Whitcliffe-Wigmore
Ashford Bowdler-Ledwych-the turnpike road on Clee
    Hill

Tollhouses:

Angel (Bitterley)	SO 573759*
Caynham	SO 564767
Cleobury Mortimer	SO 668757
Corve Gate, Ludlow	SO 508753
Fishmore Brook	SO 514764
Hopton	SO 640760
Little Stretton	SO 443919
Lower Galdeford	
(Temeside), Ludlow	SO 517742
Ludford (on Wigmore road)	SO 504743
Maryknowl	SO 482737*
New Bridge	SO 506743*
Old Street, Ludlow	SO 513742*
Peaton Strand	SO 536847*
Pedlars' Rest	SO 486844
Sandpits	SO 515753
Stoke Bridge	SO 438818*
Sutton	SO 516830*
Whettleton	SO 460827*

Date of de-turnpiking: 1 January 1873

The stone tollhouse erected by the Second Ludlow Turnpike Trust at Temeside, Lower Gaolford (SO 517742). Elements of the octagonal plan, and the chevron-headed windows were used by the trust on other tollhouses. This tollhouse controlled the road to Steventon, in order to deter long-distance travellers from using it rather than because of potential revenue.

8. Roads leading into Much Wenlock

Original Act of Parliament: 29 Geo II c 60; 1756

Extent:
Much Wenlock-Buildwas Bridge
Much Wenlock-Broseley-Nordley Common
Much Wenlock-Beambridge
Much Wenlock-Barrow-Willey-Nordley Common
Much Wenlock-Gleedon Hill-Cressage

Date of de-turnpiking: 1 November 1870

Tollhouses:

Beambridge	SO 532882
Bourton	SO 619996
Buildwas	SJ 639038
Linley	SO 683992
Marsh	SO 646997
Much Wenlock	SO 628997
Posenhall	SJ 657016
Sheinton	SJ 618037
Willey	SJ 674006

9. Roads from Coleham Bridge, Shrewsbury, to Longden and Church Stretton

Original Act of Parliament: 29 Geo II c 61; 1756

Extent:
Coleham Bridge-Church Stretton
5th milestone near Longden to Castle Pulverbatch
3rd milestone to the village of Condover

Date of de-turnpiking: 1 November 1877

Tollhouses:

Condover Turn	SJ 486085
Meole Brace	SJ 491110
Nobold	SJ 474101
Nobold, Stanley Lane	SJ 480107
Sutton Lane End	SJ 491107

10. Roads from Shrewsbury to Preston Brockhurst, Shawbury and Shreyhill

Original Act of Parliament: 29 Geo II c 64; 1756

Extent:
Shrewsbury-Preston Brockhurst-Prees Heath
Shrewsbury-Shawbury
Shrewsbury-Shreyhill-Newport
Waters Upton-Hinstock Heath
Crudgington-Hodnet
Harlescott-Uffington-Atcham
Edstaston-Lacon-Cotton-Prees-Prees Lower Heath

Date of de-turnpiking: 1 January 1873

Tollhouses:

Berwick	SJ 543107
Castle Foregate	SJ 494132
Chetwynd Lane End	SJ 738198
Cotwall	SJ 602174
Crudgington	SJ 631181
Darliston	SJ 579325
Harlescott	SJ 512156
Holloway	SJ 555283
Old Heath	SJ 504145
Prees	SJ 555321
Prees Lower Heath	SJ 576328
Quina Brook	SJ 523329
Roden	SJ 571165

11. Welshpool, Oswestry and Llangollen roads

Original Acts of Parliament: 29 Geo II c 68, 1756 &
3 Geo II c 43; 1763

Extent:
Oswestry-10th milepost from Shrewsbury
Gobowen-Queen's Head
Oswestry-Welshpool
Llanrhaidr-Knockin
Oswestry-Llanfyllin
Oswestry-Pontcysyllte
Oswestry-Wrexham
Mileoak-collieries near Oswestry
Oswestry-Rhydycroesau-Llansilin
Llynynmaen Coalwork-Pentrechannel & Treflach
    Limeworks
Aston-Llynclys
New Inn-Glyn Ceiriog-Llansaintffraid

Dates of de-turnpiking: 1 May 1879 (3rd district);
    12 May 1882 (4th district); 1 May 1885 (1st and
    2nd districts)

Tollhouses:

Bryn-y-groes	SJ 248230*
Church Street, Oswestry	SJ 288292
Coed-y-go	SJ 279277
Craignant	SJ 254350
Croes Wylan	SJ 287287
Fernhill	SJ 308257
Gallowstree Bank	SJ 296288
Glyn	SJ 239218
Lawnt	SJ 249308
Llanforda	SJ 283290
Llynclys & Pwllycrwrw	SJ 282241
Llwyn, Oswestry	SJ 297302
Llwynymaen	SJ 272283*
Lodge	SJ 283354
Maesbury	SJ 308257
Mile End	SJ 333299
Mile Oak	SJ 301277
Penyllan	SJ 267281*
Porthywaen	SJ 258234
Queen's Head	SJ 340267
Redwith	SJ 302241
Rhydycroesau	SJ 241307
Selattyn	SJ 267339*
Wern-issa	SJ 233238*
Weston Chain	SJ 296276*
Whittington Chain	SJ 327409*
Willow Street, Oswestry	SJ 287299
Woodhill	SJ 273268
Woolston	SJ 320242*

12. Roads leading into Tenbury

Original Act of Parliament: 30 Geo II c 38; 1757

Extent:
Burford-Knowle Gate-Clee Hill

Date of de-turnpiking: 1 November 1870

Tollhouses:

Heath/Titrail	SO 593747
Hope Bank	SO 592690
Knowle Gate	SO 598734

13. Roads leading from the Welsh Gate and Coton Hill in Shrewsbury

Original Act of Parliament: 31 Geo II c 67; 1758

Extent:
Welsh Bridge-Yockleton-Westbury
Welsh Bridge-Hanwood-Pontesbury-Minsterley
Welsh Bridge-Wattlesborough Heath-Welshpool
Welsh Bridge-Montford Bridge-Nesscliff-Oswestry
Winnington-Middleton-Trewern-Buttington Hall
Coton Hill-Baschurch

Date of de-turnpiking: 1 November 1877

Tollhouses:

Copthorne	SJ 468123
Coton Hill	SJ 489134
Minsterley	SJ 374050
Hanwood	SJ 470113
Kingsland Lane	SJ 478132*
Middleton	SJ 310127
Montford Bridge	SJ 431153
Mount	SJ 484130
New Street	SJ 485127*
Poulton	SJ 387059
Prescot	SJ 426210
Shelton	SJ 465132
Rose & Crown	SJ 319111
Wolf's Head	SJ 371208

14. Roads leading into Kidderminster

Original Act of Parliament: 33 Geo II c 50; 1760

Extent:
Kidderminster-Bridgnorth

Date of de-turnpiking: 1 November 1873

Tollhouses:

Quatt	SO 755881

15. Chester-Stonebridge

Original Act of Parliament: 33 Geo II c 51; 1760

Extent:
Cheshire border-Whitchurch-Prees Heath-Sandford-
  Bletchley-Newport-Welsh Harp at Stonnall (Staffs)
Whitchurch-Ightfield-Cloverley-Bletchley

Dates of de-turnpiking: 31 July 1854 (Whitchurch-
  Tern Hill); 1 November 1867 (Newport-Tern
  Hill); 30 June 1870 (Newport – Stonnall);
  1 November 1877 (Chester-Whitchurch)

Tollhouses:

Bletchley	SJ 624334
Dodington	SJ 538419*
Grindley Brook	SJ 522431
Hinstock (Four Alls)	SJ 695254
Newport	SJ 744196*
Sandford	SJ 580340*
Sedgeford	SJ 551442
Tern Hill	SJ 522431

16. Roads from Bridgnorth and Cleobury Mortimer

Original Act of Parliament: 2 Geo III c 79; 1762.

Extent:
Cleobury Mortimer-Cross Houses-Bridgnorth
Cross Houses-Morville
Cross Houses-Cleobury North-Ditton Priors-Brown
   Clee
Glazeley-Oldbury-Bridgnorth
Cleobury Mortimer-Abberley Hill
Cleobury Mortimer-Milson-Tenbury
Cleobury Mortimer-Bewdley

Dates of de-turnpiking: 1 November 1878 (Cleobury
   Mortimer District); 1 November 1879 (Cleobury
   North and Ditton Priors District)

Tollhouses:

The Barns	SO 622717
Baveney Wood	SO 698787
Billingsley	SO 706853
Branstrey	SO 658747
Cleobury North	SO 627874
Ditton Priors	SO 609892
Halfway House	SO 707909
Harpswood	SO 691915
Lightwood	SO 643908
Oldbury	SO 716924
Overwood	SO 681799
Poulters	SO 696755
Six Ashes	SO 683773
Towns End	SO 687760*
Wall Town	SO 692783*
Weston	SO 694758
Yew Tree	SO 721820

17. Stafford-Sandon

Original Act of Parliament: 3 Geo III c 59; 1763

Extent:
Newport-Eccleshall
Woodcote-Shifnal-Sutton Maddock-Bridgnorth
Newport-Donnington-Watling Street
Harp-Brockton-Edgmnd-Chetwynd End
Eccleshall-Ireland's Cross
Hilton-Honnington

Tollhouses:

Hem	SJ 727056
Kemberton	SJ 722051
Lilleshall	SJ 731164
Worfe Bridge	SO 732958

Dates of de-turnpiking: 1 November
   1867 (most of system); 1 November
   1877 (Bridgnorth-Shifnal)

18. Madeley Turnpike Roads

Original Act of Parliament: 4 Geo III c 84; 1764

Extent:
Buck's Head, Watling Street-New Inns and Beckbury
Birches Brook-the handpost in Kemberton

Date of de-turnpiking: 1 November 1867

Tollhouses:

Cucko Oak	SJ 704048
Hills Lane	SJ 700044
Lawley	SJ 672089
Meadow Wharf	SJ 660039
Rudge Heath	SJ 788961

19. Whitchurch-Nantwich & Newcastle-under-Lyme

Original Act of Parliament: 7 Geo III c 92; 1767

Extent:
Whitchurch-Burleydam-Audlem-Woore-Madeley
(Staffs)-Madeley Heath
Hinstock-Drayton-Adderley-Nantwich

Date of de-turnpiking: 1 July 1875

Tollhouses:

Adderley	SJ 662397
Gravenhunger	SJ 737423
Hinstock	SJ 693264
Spoonley	SJ 666356
Sydnall	SJ 688306

20. Marchwiel-Bangor-Dodington (Whitchurch)

Original Act of Parliament: 7 Geo III c 104; 1767

Extent:
Marchwiel-Bangor-on-Dee-Hanmer-Dodington
Redbrook-Welshhampton

Date of de-turnpiking: 29 September 1875

Tollhouse:

Redbrook	SJ 515412

21. Roads leading into Bishop's Castle

Original Act of Parliament: 8 Geo III c 51; 1768

Extent:
Bishop's Castle & Montgomery-Westbury
Brockton-Minsterley
Bishop's Castle-Ludlow & Clun
Bishop's Castle-Pentre-Montgomery
Bishop's Castle-Churchstoke-Montgomery
Bishop's Castle-Clun & Knighton
Clun-Newton Green (Craven Arms)
Bishop's Castle-Pulverbatch (& Shrewsbury)
Bishop's Castle-Churchstoke & Welshpool
Snead-Lydham

Dates of de-turnpiking: 1 November 1876
(Montgomery and 2nd district); 1 May 1878
(Bishop's Castle & 1st district)

Tollhouses:

Acton	SO 322850
Aston	SJ 352075
Basford	SO 394854
Bishop's Castle, Church	SO 323884*
Bishop's Moat	SO 289895
Bridges/Overs Brook	SO 393965
Clun	SO 303808
Clun Churchyard	SO 300805
Crow Gate/Stank Lane	SO 331877
Edgton	SO 385855
Eyton	SO 371875
Foul Lane End	SO 330891
Hall Orchard/Little Field	SO 326883
Heblands	SO 323902
Horderley	SO 409868
Kempton	SO 361830
Kerry Lane	SO 320886
Knighton	SO 292723
Lagden Lane	SO 327869
Long Lane	SO 420838
Milebrook	SO 312729
Minsterley	SJ 372051
Park Lane	SO 423826
Pulverbatch	SJ 424023
Ridgeway	SO 395864
Twitchen	SO 367793
Westbury	SJ 355090
Wintle Pool/Welsh Street	SO 321892
Wittingslow	SO 426888

The tollhouse built by the Bishop's Castle Trust on the road to Brockton at Minsterley (SJ 372051)

22. Shawbury-Newcastle-under-Lyme &c

Original Act of Parliament: 9 Geo III c 55; 1769

Extent:
Shawbury-Market Drayton-Newcastle-under-Lyme
Shawbury-High Ercall

Dates of de-turnpiking: 10 August 1866
(Shawbury district); 6 November 1872 (Market
Drayton-Newcastle-under-Lyme).

Tollhouses:

Audley's Cross	SJ 722356
Edgbolton	SJ 752220
Hodnet	SJ 614281
Shawbury	SJ 563213*
Tern Hill	SJ 634323
Walton	SJ 590183
Wollerton	SJ 620297*

23. Welshpool roads

Original Act of Parliament: 9 Geo II c 56; 1769

Extent:
Montgomery-Marton
Bishop's Castle-Forden
Four Crosses-Pavement Gate

Date of de-turnpiking: 1 November 1876

Tollhouses:

Alberbury	SJ 363141
Aston	SJ 352075
Aylesford	SJ 274013
Chirbury	SO 263982
Chirbury	SO 262983
Llanymynech	SJ 266211

24. Wem - Bronygarth

Original Act of Parliament: 11 Geo III c 95; 1771

Extent:
Wem-Ellesmere-St Martin's-Bron-y-garth

Date of de-turnpiking: 1893

Tollhouses:

Bronygarth	SJ 267370
Bryng-willa	SJ 303362
Eachley	SJ 452343
Horton	SJ 484302
Loppington	SJ 470293*
Newton	SJ 420342
Northwood	SJ 463333
Palmontmawr	SJ 290359
St Martin's	SJ 317362
Trimpley	SJ 396348
Wolverley	SJ 475310

25. Burlton, Knockin & Llanymynech

Original Act of Parliament: 12 Geo III c 96; 1772

Extent:
Burlton-Knockin-Llanymynech
Knockin-the Llanraidr Road
Plas Carrick Lane–Coid Iffa
Wolf's Head-Knockin Lane

Date of de-turnpiking: 1 November 1877

Tollhouses:

Knockin	SJ 334223
Knockin	SJ 329223
Llwyntidmon	SJ 286207
Marton	SJ 443239
Plas Garreg	SJ 275213
Platt Bridge	SJ 404223

26. Tern Bridge-Leighton-Birches Brook

Original Act of Parliament: 18 Geo III c 88; 1778

Extent:
Tern Bridge-Leighton-Buildwas Bridge-Birches Brook

Date of de-turnpiking: 1 November 1875

Tollhouses:
Briar Hill	SJ 582071
Leighton	SJ 61006

27. Roads leading into Dudley

Original Act of Parliament: 30 Geo III c 102; 1790

Extent: Dudley-New Inns

Date of de-turnpiking: 1 November 1876

Tollhouses:
none in Shropshire

28. Stourbridge-Worfield & Bridgnorth

Original Act of Parliament: 56 Geo III c 16; 1816

Extent:
Stourbridge-Bridgnorth

Date of de-turnpiking: 1 May 1877

Tollhouse:
Barsley/Old Lodge	SO 761915

29. Coalbrookdale-Wellington

Original Act of Parliament: 57 Geo III c 12; 1817

Extent:
Coalbrookdale-Lawley-Wellington
Lawley-Balls Hill (Dawley)

Date of de-turnpiking: 1 November 1875

Tollhouses:
Arleston	SJ 664102
Coalbrookdale	SJ 668049
Lawley	SJ 674082

A rare photograph of a tollhouse when it was still operational, in this case at Coalbrookdale on the new road to Wellington built in 1816-17. The boards listing tolls and the name of the collector are evident, as it the wicket gate that allowed pedestrians to pass through without payment. The photograph was taken before the construction of the railway through Coalbrookdale in 1862.

30. Tarporley-Whitchurch

Original Act of Parliament: 10 Geo IV c 77; 1829

Tollhouses:
none in Shropshire

Extent:
Tarporley-Whitchurch

Date of de-turnpiking: 1 November 1876

31. Minsterley-Churchstoke

Original Act of Parliament: 4 & 5 Wm IV c 11; 1834

Tollhouses:

Plox Green	SJ 367048
Pultheley	SO 324947

Extent: Minsterley-Churchstoke

Date of de-turnpiking: 1 November 1879

The spacious toll collector's cottage at Plox Green (SJ 367048) on the new road from Minsterley to Churchstoke built in the 1830s.

32. Shipton-Morville

Original Act of Parliament: 2 Vic c 30; 1839

Tollhouses:

Marlbrook	SO 574941*
Weston	SO 597928

Extent:
Morvill-Shipton
Weston-Brockton-Easthope Cross

Date of de-turnpiking: 1 November 1872

APPENDIX 3   ORGANISATIONS CONCERNED WITH INDUSTRIAL ARCHAEOLOGY

Cambrian Railways Society: www.cambrianrailways.com
County of Salop Steam Engine Society Ltd: www.shrewsburysteamrally.co.uk
Daniel's Mill Trust, Eardington: www.danielsmill.co.uk
Ironbridge Gorge Museum Trust: www.ironbridge.org.uk
Llanymynech Heritage Partnership: www.llanymynech.org.uk
Royal Air Force Museum, Cosford: www.rafmuseum.org.uk
Sentinel Drivers Club: www.sentinelwaggons.co.uk
Severn Valley Railway: www.svr.co.uk
Shrewsbury & Newport Canal Trust: www.snct.co.uk
Shrewsbury Railway Heritage Trust: www.shrewsburyrht.org.uk
Shropshire Archaeological and Historical Society: www.shropshirearchaeology.co.uk
Shropshire Archives: www.shropshire.gov.uk/archives
Shropshire Caving & Mining Club: www.shropshirecmc.org.uk
Shropshire Council Museum Service: www.discovershopshire.org or www.shopshire.gov.uk/museums
Shropshire Mines Trust: www.shropshiremines.org.uk
Shropshire Union Canal Society: www.shropshireunion.org.uk
Tiles and Architectural Ceramics Society: www.tilesoc.org.uk
Whitchurch Heritage Centre: www.whitchurch-heritage.co.uk
Wrekin Local Studies Forum: www.wlsf.org.uk

BIBLIOGRAPHY

For abbreviations see p.*viii.*

Books

Adams, D.R., & Hazeley, J., *Survey of the Church Aston and Lilleshalll Mining Area* (1970). Church Aston: Shropshire Mining Club.

Aikin, A., *Journal of a Tour through North Wales* (1797). London: Johnson.

Albert, W., *The Turnpike Road System in England 1663-1840* (1972). Cambridge: Cambridge University Press.

Alfrey, J. & Clark, K., *The Landscape of Industry: patterns of change in the Ironbridge Gorge* (1993). London: Routledge.

Anderson, R.C., *A History of Midland Red* (1984). Newton Abbot: David & Charles.

Angerstein, R.R., *R.R. Angerstein's Illustrated Travel Diary 1753-1755: Industry in England and Wales from a Swedish perspective* (trans. T. & P. Berg, 2001). London: Science Museum.

Anon., *The History of Isaac Jenkins* (n.d.). Wellington: Houlston.

Ashman, G., ed., *The Ironbridge Hornpipe: a Shropshire Tune Collection from John Moore's Manuscripts* (1991). Ashington: Crescent.

Bagshaw, S., *History, Gazetteer and Directory of Shropshire* (1851). Sheffield: Bagshaw.

Bailey, W., *Bailey's Western and Midland Directory* (1783). Birmingham: Pearson & Rollason.

Baker, N., *Shrewsbury Abbey: Studies in the archaeology and history of an urban abbey* (2002). Shrewsbury: Shropshire Archaeological & Historical Society.

Bannister, G.F., *Great Western Steam off the Beaton Track* (1975). Truro: Bradford Barton.

Barnard, A., *The Noted Breweries of Great Britain and Ireland* (1889). London: Causton.

Barnes, J., *Thomas Barnes of Farnworth and the Quinta: a Chronicle of a Life* (Oswestry: Quinta Press, 2012).

Barnwell, P.S., Palmer, M., & Airs, M., eds., *The vernacular workshop from craft to industry, 1400-1900* (2004). York: CBA.

Baxter, B., *Stone Blocks and Iron Rails* (1966). Newton Abbot: David & Charles.

Beale, C., *The Ironbridge Spirit: a history of the Ironbridge Gorge Museum Trust* (2014). Telford: Ironbridge Gorge Museum Trust.

Beck, K.M., *The Great Western North of Wolverhampton* (1991). London: Ian Allan.

Beddoes, K., & Smith, W.H., *The Tenbury and Bewdley Railway* (1995). Didcot: Wild Swan.

Bick, D.E., *The Old Metal Mines of Mid-Wales: West Montgomeryshire* (1977). Newent: The Pound House.

Birch, A., *The Economic History of the British Iron and Steel Industry 1784-1879* (1967). London: Cass.

Bishton, J., *Salop: Report to the Board of Agriculture* (London: Board of Agriculture: 1794).

Blackwall, A., *Historic Bridges of Shropshire* (1985). Shrewsbury: Shropshire Libraries.

Booth, D.T.W., *Watermills on the River Rea in South Shropshire* (3rd edn., 2011). Birmingham: Midlands Wind and Watermills Group.

Bridges, A.J., *Industrial Locomotives of Cheshire, Shropshire and Herefordshire* (1977). London: Industrial Locomotive Society.

Brook, F., *The Industrial Archaeology of the British Isles: 1. The West Midlands* (1977). London: Batsford.

Brook, F., & Allbutt, M., *The Shropshire Lead Mines* (1973). Leek: Moorland.

Brooks, R. J., *Shropshire Airfields in the Second World War* (2008). Newbury: Countryside Books.

Brown, I.J., *The Coalbrookdale Coalfield: Catalogue of Mines* (1968). Shrewsbury: Salop County Library.

Brown, I.J., *The Mines of Shropshire* (1976). Ashbourne: Moorland.

Brown, I.J., *A History of Limestone Mining in Shropshire* (1977). Newport: Shropshire Mining Club.

Brown, I.J., *Images of England: The East Shropshire Coalfields* (1999). Stroud: Tempus.

Brown, I.J., *West Shropshire Mining Fields* (2001). Stroud: Tempus.

Brown, I.J., *A List of Fatal Accidents in Shropshire Mines 1850-1979* (2005). Telford: Shropshire Caving & Mining Club.

Brown, I.J., & Trinder, B., *The Coalport Tar Tunnel* (1971). Telford: Ironbridge Gorge Museum Trust.

Brown, J., & Grimmett, N., *Rickards of Ludlow: Ironmongers for 140 years* (2008). Ludlow Historical Research Group.

Brown, Y., *Ruyton-XI-Towns: Unusual Name: Unusual History* (1988). Studley: Brewin.

Burt, R., Waite, P., & Burnley, R., *The Mines of Shropshire & Montgomeryshire with Cheshire & Staffordshire: Metalliferous and Associated Minerals 1845-1913* (1990). University of Exeter Press.

Carlon, C.J., *The Gallantry Bank Copper Mine, Bickerton, Cheshire, with a review of mining in the Triassic rocks of the Cheshire-Shropshire Basin* (1981). Sheffield: Northern Mines Research Society.

Carlon, C.J., *The Eardiston Copper Mines, Shropshire* (1981). Kendal: Peak District Mines Historical Society.

Carpenter, R, *The Criggion Branch of the Shropshire & Montgomeryshire Light Railway* (1990). Didcot: Wild Swan.

Carr, A.M., *Shrewsbury: a Pictorial History* (1994). Chichester: Phillimore.

Cathrall., W., *The History of Oswestry* (1855). Oswestry: George Lewis. (Reprint, c. 1974, Shrewsbury: Salop County Council).

Chapman, S.D., *The Early Factory Masters: The Transition to the Factory System in the Midlands Textile Industry* (1967). Newton Abbot: David & Charles.

Chrimes, M., ed., *The Civil Engineering of Canals and Railways before 1850* (1997). Aldershot: Ashgate.

Christiansen, R., *A Regional History of the Railways of Great Britain: VII: The West Midlands* (1973). Newton Abbot: David & Charles.

Christiansen, R., & Miller, R.W., *The Cambrian Railways* (1967). Newton Abbot: David & Charles.

Christiansen, R., & Miller, R.W., *The North Staffordshire Railway* (1971). Newton Abbot: David & Charles.

Clarke, N.J., *Railways of East Shropshire Through Time* (2015). Stroud: Amberley Publishing.

Clarke, N.J, *Waterways of East Shropshire through Time* (2015). Stroud: Amberley Publishing.

Clarke, N.J., ed., *The Industrial Heritage of the Parishes around The Wrekin: Parts I and II* (2008). Telford: Wrekin Local Studies Forum.

Clarke, N.J, *Crossing the River: Fords and Ferries on the Shropshire Severn* (2015). London: Railway & Canal Historical Society.

Clemens, M., *The Last Years of Steam in Shropshire and the Severn Valley* (2014). Oxford: Fonthill.

Clow, A., & N., *The Chemical Revolution* (1952). London: Batchworth.

Coleman, D.C., *The British Paper Industry 1495-1860: A Study in Industrial Growth* (1958). Oxford: Clarendon Press.

Cooke, E., *Who killed Prees Heath?* (1991). Shrewsbury: Shropshire Wildlife Trust.

Cossons, N., *The BP Book of Industrial Archaeology* (3rd edn., 1993). Newton Abbot: David & Charles.

Cossons, N., ed., *Perspectives on Industrial Archaeology* (2000). London: Science Museum.

Cossons, N., & Trinder, B., *The Iron Bridge: Symbol of the Industrial Revolution* (2nd edn., 2002). Chichester: Phillimore.

Cragg, R., *Civil Engineering Heritage: West Midlands* (2010). Stroud: Phillimore.

Cryer, G., *Shropshire Railways.* (2014). Ramsbury: Crowood Press.

Davies, A.S., *The Charcoal Iron Industry of Powysland* (1939). Welshpool: Powysland Club.

Davies, D.L., *The Glyn Valley Tramway* (1962). Lingfield: Oakwood Press.

Dawson, F., *John Wilkinson: King of the Ironmasters* (2011). Stroud: The History Press.

de Maré, E., *Bridges of Britain* (revised edn., 1975). London: Batsford.

Denton, J.H., *Canals and Railways: a list of plans and related documents deposited at the Shirehall, Shrewsbury* (1969). Shrewsbury: Salop County Council.

de Soissons, M., *Telford: the making of Shropshire's New Town* (1991). Shrewsbury: Swan Hill.

Donaldson-Hudson, R., *An Historical Survey of the Parish of Cheswardine* (1939). Shrewsbury: Wilding.

Douet, J., ed., *Industrial Heritage Re-tooled: the TICCIH guide to Industrial Heritage Conservation* (2012). Lancaster: Carnegie.

Duggan, T.C., *The History of Whitchurch, Shropshire* (1935). Whitchurch: Whitchurch Herald.

Dutens, J.H., *Mémoires sur les Travaux Publiques de l'Angleterre* [Studies of public works in England] (1819). Paris: L'Imprimerie Royale.

Earnshaw, D., et al., *Whitchurch Remembered* (1980). Shrewsbury: Shropshire Libraries.

Eckel, E.C., *Cements and Plasters* (1928). London: John Wiley.

Edwards, I., *Davies Brothers, Gatesmiths: Eighteenth Century Wrought Ironworks in Wales* (1977). Cardiff: Welsh Arts Council.

Emden, P.H., *Quakers in Commerce: a record of business achievement* (1939). London: Sampson Lowe.

Falconer, K., *Guide to England's Industrial Heritage* (1980). London: Batsford.

Fiennes, C., *The Journeys of Celia Fiennes* (ed. C. Morris, 1947). London: Cresset.

Forrest, H.E., *The Old Houses of Wenlock* (1914). Shrewsbury: Wilding.

Forrest, H.E., *The Old Houses of Shrewsbury: their history and associations* (5th edn., 1935). Shrewsbury: Wilding.

Foulkes, F.W., *Hooked on Cheese* (1985). Shrewsbury: Shropshire Libraries.

Foxall, H.D.G., *A Gazetteer of Streets, Roads and Place Names in Shropshire* (1967). Shrewsbury: Salop County Council.

Foxall, H.D.G., *Shropshire Field Names* (1980). Shrewsbury: Shropshire Archaeological Society.

Gale, W.K.V., & Nicholls, C.R., *The Lilleshall Company Limited: a history 1764-1964* (1979). Ashbourne: Moorland.

Gasquoine, C.P., *The Story of the Cambrian: a Biography of a Railway* (1922). Oswestry: Caxton Press.

George, J., *Daniel's Mill: its history, millers and restoration* (no date). Bridgnorth: privately published.

Giles, C., & Williams, M., eds., *Ditherington Mill and the Industrial Revolution* (2015). Swindon: English Heritage.

Giles, C., & Goodall, I., *Yorkshire Textile Mills 1770-1930* (1992). London: HMSO.

Gough, R., *The History of Myddle* (ed. D. Hey, 1981). Harmondsworth: Penguin.

Green, C., *Severn Traders: The West Country Trows and Trowmen* (1999). Witney: Black Dwarf.

Gregory, T., *The Shropshire Gazetteer* (1824). Wem: Gregory.

Griffith, E., *The Bishop's Castle Railway, Shropshire, 1865-1935* (1969). Farnham: privately published.

Griffiths, R., & Smith, P., *The Directory of British Engine Sheds, vol.1* (1999). Shepperton: Oxford Publishing Co.

Griffiths, S., *Griffiths' Guide to the Iron Trade of Great Britain* (1873; new edn. with introduction by W.K.V. Gale, 1967). Newton Abbot: David & Charles.

Griffin, A.R., *Coalmining* (1969). London: Longmans.

Gwyn, D., *Gwynedd: Inheriting a Revolution* (2006). Chichester: Phillimore.

Hadfield, C., *The Canals of South Wales and the Border* (1960). Cardiff: University of Wales Press.

Hadfield, C., *The Canals of the West Midlands* (1966). Newton Abbot: David & Charles.

Hadfield, C., *The Canal Age* (1968). Newton Abbot: David & Charles.

Hadfield, C., *World Canals* (1986). Newton Abbot: David & Charles.

Hadfield, C., *Thomas Telford's Temptation* (1993). Cleobury Mortimer: Baldwin.

Hamilton, J., *Turner's Britain* (2003). London: Merrell.

Harris, J.R., *The British Iron Industry 1700-1850* (1988). Basingstoke: Macmillan Education.

Harris, J.R., *Industrial Espionage and Technology Transfer: Britain and France in the Eighteenth Century* (1998). Aldershot: Ashgate.

Hatcher, J., *The History of the British Coal Industry, I. Before 1700: Towards the Age of Coal.* (1993). Oxford: Clarendon Press.

Hatchett, C., *The Hatchett Diary* (ed. A Raistrick, 1967). Truro: Bradford Barton.

Hayman, R., Horton, W., & White, S., *Archaeology and Conservation in Ironbridge* (1999). York: CBA.

Herbert, A.T., & Huggins, K., *The Decorative Tile in Architecture and Interiors* (1995). London: Phaidon.

Hey, D.G., *An English Rural Community: Myddle under the Tudors and Stuarts* (1974). Leicester University Press.

Hobbs, J.L. *Shrewsbury Street Names* (1954). Shrewsbury: Wilding.

Holland, J., *The History and Description of Fossil Fuel, the Collieries and the Coal Trade of Great Britain* (1835, reprint 1968). London: Cass.

Hollox, G., *John Doughty & Son: The Story of a Jackfield Brick and Roofing Tile Manufacturer* (2014). Broseley: privately published.

Hughes, W.J., & Thomas, J.L., *'The Sentinel': A History of Alley & MacLellan and the Sentinel Waggon Works, I, 1875-1930* (1975). Newton Abbot: David & Charles.

Hulbert, C., *History and Description of the County of Salop* (1837). Hadnall: Hulbert.

Hulbert, C., *Memoirs of Seventy Years of an Eventful Life* (1852). Shrewsbury: Hulbert.

Hussey, D.P., *et al.*, *The Gloucester Coastal Port Books 1575-1765: a Summary* (1995). University of Wolverhampton.

Hyde, C.K., *Technological change and the British Iron Industry, 1700-1800* (1977). Princeton University Press.

Ince, L., *The Knight Family and the British Iron Industry 1695-1902* (1991). Solihull: Ferric Publications.

Industry Hall, *Report of the School called Industry Hall in the Parish of Prees, Shropshire* (1804).

Ionides, J., *Thomas Farnolls Pritchard of Shrewsbury: Architect and Inventor of Cast Iron Bridges* (1999). Ludlow: Dog Rose.

Jenkins, A.E., *Titterstone Clee Hills: Everyday Life, Industrial History and Dialect* (1988). Orleton: privately published.

Jenkinson, A., *Shropshire's Wild Places: a Guide to the County's Protected Wildlife Sites* (1992). Church Stretton: Scenesetters.

Jones, K.B., *The Wenlock Branch: Wellington to Craven Arms* (1998). Usk: Oakwood.

Jones, K.B., *Pitmen, Poachers and Preachers* (2009). Ludlow: Dog Rose.

Labouchere, R., *Abiah Darby 1716-1793 of Coalbrookdale: Wife of Abraham Darby II* (1988). York: Sessions.

Lazarus, B., *Country Reflections around Cheswardine* (1988). Cheswardine: privately published.

Lee, L.J., *A Full List and Partial Abstract of the Quarter Sessions Rolls, 1696-1800* (no date). Shrewsbury: Salop County Council.

Lee, L.J., and Venables, R.G., *A Full List and Partial Abstract of the Quarter Sessions Rolls 1801-20* (no date). Shrewsbury: Salop County Council.

Leonard, J., Preshous, D., et al., *The Gale of Life: Two Thousand Years in South-West Shropshire* (2000). Little Logaston: Logaston.

Lerry, G.G., *Henry Robertson: Pioneer of Railways into Wales* (1949). Oswestry: Woodall.

Lewis, M.J.T., *Early Wooden Railways* (1970). London: Routledge & Kegan Paul.

Lewis, M.J.T., ed., *Early Railway 2: Papers from the Second International Early Railway Conference* (2003). London: Newcomen Society.

Lewis, W.J., *Lead Mining in Wales* (1967). Cardiff: University of Wales Press.

Livesey Ltd., *Handbook to the Shropshire & Montgomeryshire Railway* (no date, reprint 1977). Shrewsbury: Salop County Council.

Lloyd, D., *Broad Street: its houses and residents through eight centuries: Ludlow Research Paper No.3* (1979). Birmingham: Studio Press.

Lloyd, D., Howell, P., & Richards, M., *The Feathers: Ludlow Research Paper No. 5* (1986). Ludlow Historical Research Group.

Lloyd, D., *Archives Photograph Series: Ludlow* (1995). Stroud: Chalford.

Lloyd, D., *et al.*, *Victorian Ludlow* (2004). Bucknell: Scenesetters.

Loch, J., *An Account of the Improvements on the Estate of the Marquess of Stafford in the Counties of Stafford & Salop* (1820). London: Hurst, Rees, Orme & Brown.

Lyons, E., *A Historical Survey of Great Western Engine Sheds* (1972). Oxford: Oxford Publishing Co.

MacDermot, E.T., *History of the Great Western Railway* (3 vols., 1927, 1931, revised edn., ed. C.R. Clinker, 1964). London: Ian Allan.

MacDonald, W., *An Illustrated Guide to Shrewsbury* (1897). London & Edinburgh: MacDonald.

McMillan, B.L., *History of a water supply to Wolverhampton 1847-1947* (1947). Wolverhampton Corporation.

Markham, S., *John Loveday of Caversham 1711-1789: the Life and Times of an Eighteenth Century Onlooker* (1984). Wilton: Russell.

Marshall, J., *The Severn Valley Railway* (1989). Nairn: David St John Thomas.

Mendenhall, T.C., *The Shrewsbury Drapers and the Welsh wool trade in the sixteenth and seventeenth centuries* (1953). Oxford University Press.

Mercer, E., *English Architecture to 1900: The Shropshire Experience* (2003). Little Logaston: Logaston.

Merchant, H., *Wem: History and Guide* (1907). Wem: Prince.

Merry, E., *A History of Minsterley* (1976). Minsterley: privately published.

Middleton, V, & Smith, K, *Branch Line to Shrewsbury: the Shropshire & Montgomeryshire Railway.* (1991). Midhurst: Middleton.

Middleton, V, & Smith, K, *Branch Lines around Cleobury Mortimer.* (2007). Midhurst: Middleton.

Middleton, V, & Smith, K, *Kidderminster to Shrewsbury.* (2007). Midhurst: Middleton.

Middleton, V, & Smith, K, *Ludlow to Hereford.* (2007). Midhurst: Middleton.

Middleton, V, & Smith, K, *Shrewsbury to Ludlow.* (2008). Midhurst: Middleton.

Middleton, V, & Smith, K, *Shrewsbury to Newtown.* (2008). Midhurst: Middleton.

Middleton, V, & Smith, K, *Craven Arms to Wellington.* (2008). Midhurst: Middleton.

Middleton, V, & Smith, K, *Branch Lines around Oswestry.* (2009). Midhurst: Middleton.

Middleton, V, & Smith, K, *Wolverhampton to Shrewsbury.* (2009). Midhurst: Middleton.

Middleton, V, & Smith, K, *Ludlow to Hereford.* (2010). Midhurst: Middleton.

Middleton, V, & Smith, K, *Oswestry to Whitchurch.* (2010). Midhurst: Middleton.

Middleton, V, & Smith, K, *Shrewsbury to Chester.* (2010). Midhurst: Middleton.

Middleton, V, & Smith, K, *Shrewsbury to Crewe.* (2013). Midhurst: Middleton.

Middleton, V, & Smith, K, *Branch Lines around Market Drayton.* (2014). Midhurst: Middleton.

Middleton, V, & Smith, K, *Stafford to Wellington.* (2014). Midhurst: Middleton.

Milner, J., & Williams, B., *The Rails to Glyn Ceiriog: the History of the Glyn Valley Tramway 1857-1903.* (2011). Chester: Rail Romances.

Moran, M., *Vernacular Buildings of Shropshire (2003).* Little Logaston: Logaston.

Morgan, J.S., *The Colonel Stephens Railways: a Pictorial History* (1978). Newton Abbot: David & Charles.

Morgan, R.C., *The Life of Richard Weaver: the Converted Collier* (1861). London: Morgan & Chase (rep. 2014, Charleston SC: Nabu).

Morris, B., & Morris, D., *Market Drayton and Norton-in-Hales* (1989). Loggerheads: Brampton.

Morris, C., *On Tour with Thomas Telford* (2004). Longhope: Tanner's Yard.

Morris, J., *The Shropshire Union Canal: a towpath guide ... from Autherley to Nantwich* (1991). Shrewsbury: Management Update.

Morriss, R., *Rail Centres: Shrewsbury* (1986). London: Ian Allan.

Morriss, R., *Railways of Shropshire: a brief history* (1983). Shrewsbury: Shropshire Libraries.

Mullins, S.P., *Much Wenlock: a town trail* (1991). Shrewsbury: Shropshire Leisure Services.

Murchison, R., *The Silurian System* (1839). London: John Murray.

Murchison, R., *Siluria* (5th edn., 1872). London: John Murray.

Muter, W.G., *The Buildings of an Industrial Community: Coalbrookdale and Ironbridge* (1979). Chichester: Phillimore.

Mutton, N., *An Engineer at work in the West Midlands: the Diary of John Urpeth Rastrick for 1820* (1969). Wolverhampton College of Technology.

Nankivell, J.W., *Chapters from the History of Ellesmere* (1983). Birmingham: Lazanica Press.

Neal, T., *Shropshire Airfields* (2005). Telford: Langrish Caiger.

Nef, J.U., *The Rise of the British Coal Industry* (1932). London: Routledge.

Newman, J., & Pevsner, N., *The Buildings of England: Shropshire* (2006). London & New Haven: Yale University Press.

Nightingale, J., *The Beauties of England and Wales, or Original Delineations of Each County, vol. 13, part 1, Shropshire* (1813). London: Harris.

Oppitz, L., *Lost railways of Shropshire* (2004). Newbury: Countryside Books.

Organ, J., *Craven Arms to Llandeilo* (2008). Midford: Middleton.

Owen, H., & Blakeway, J.B., *A History of Shrewsbury* (1825). London: Harding Lepard.

Palmer, V., *Chirk and the Glyn Valley Tramway: a Portrait in Old Picture Postcards* (1988). Market Drayton: S.B. Publications.

Pannett, D., & Trinder, B., *Old Maps of Shrewsbury* (1972). Shrewsbury: Field Studies Council

Pattison, A., *On Severn Shore: the story of the Drill Hall, Coleham, Shrewsbury* (2004). Shrewsbury: privately published.

Partridge, C.A., *Handbook to Ludlow* (1878). Ludlow: Partridge.

Pawson, E., *Transport and Economy: the Turnpike Roads of Eighteenth-Century Britain* (1977). London: Academic Press.

Pearce, A., *Mining in Shropshire* (1995). Shrewsbury: Shropshire Books.

Pearson, L., *Tile Gazetteer: A Guide to British Tile and Architectural Ceramic Installations* (2005). Shepton Beauchamp: Richard Dennis.

Penfold, A., ed., *Thomas Telford: Engineer* (1980). London: Thomas Telford.

Pennant, T., *Tours in Wales* (1883). London: Hughes.

Pidgeon, H., *Memorials of Shrewsbury* (1837). Shrewsbury: Eddowes.

Pocock, R.W., & Whitehead, T.H., *British Regional Geology: the Welsh Borderland* (2nd edn., 1948). London: HMSO.

Pococke, R., *Travels through England of the Revd Richard Pococke* (ed. J. Cartwright, 1889). London: Camden Society.

Post Office, *The Post Office Directory of Shropshire* (1856). London: Kelly.

Powell, J., *Ironbridge Gorge through Time* (2009). Stroud: Amberley.

Powell, J. & Vanns, M., *The Archives Photographs Series: South Telford* (1995), Chalford: Chalford Publishing.

Powell, J. & Vanns, M., *The Archives Photographs Series: North Telford* (1995), Chalford: Chalford Publishing.

Preshous, J., *Bishop's Castle Well-remembered* (1990). Bishop's Castle: privately published.

Price, M., *The Cleobury Mortimer and Ditton Priors Light Railway* (1964). Lingfield: Oakwood Press.

Pybus, M., *Under the Buttercross: Market Drayton: a town of Good Food* (1986). Market Drayton Civic Society.

Quartermain, J., Trinder, B., & Turner, R., *Thomas Telford's Holyhead Road: the A5 in North Wales* (2003). York: CBA.

Rackham, O., *The History of the Countryside* (London: Dent, 1986).

Raistrick, A., *Quakers in Science and Industry* (1950; rep. 1993). York: Sessions.

Raistrick, A., *Dynasty of Ironfounders* (1953). London: Longmans.

Randall, J., *The Severn Valley* (1862). London: Virtue.

Randall, J., *The Clay Industries including the Fictile and Ceramic Arts on the Banks of the Severn* (1877). Madeley: Salopian and West Midland Office.

Randall, J., *Broseley and its Surroundings* (1879). Madeley: Randall.

Randall, J., *History of Madeley* (1880). Madeley: Wrekin Echo.

Ranger, W., *Report to the General Board of Health on a preliminary report into ... Bridgnorth* (1853). London: Eyre & Spottiswoode.

Ranger, W., *Report to the General Board of Heatlh on a preliminary report into ... Shrewsbury* (1854). London: Eyre & Spottiswoode.

Rayska, U., *Victorian and Edwardian Shropshire from old photographs* (1977). London: Batsford.

Rayska, U., & Carr, A.M., *Telford Past and Present* (1978). Shrewsbury: Shropshire Libraries.

Rees, W., *Industry before the Industrial Revolution* (1968). Cardiff: University of Wales Press.

Review Publishing, *Industry of Shropshire: Business Review* (1891). Birmingham: Review Publishing Co.

Richards, E., *The Leviathan of Wealth: the Sutherland Fortune in the Industrial Revolution* (1973). London: Routledge & Kegan Paul.

Riden, P., *A Gazetteer of Charcoal-fired Blast Furnaces in Great Britain in use since 1660* (1987). Cardiff: privately published.

Riley, G., *The Water Mills of the Borough of Newcastle* (1991). The Borough of Newcastle-under-Lyme.

Rimmer, W.G., *Marshall's of Leeds, 1788-1886* (1960). Cambridge University Press.

Robinson, D.H., *The Wandering Worfe* (1980). Albrighton: Waine Research Publications.

Robinson, D.H., *The Sleepy Meese* (1988). Albrighton: Waine Research Publications.

Robinson, Son & Pike, *Shrewsbury Illustrated* (1894). Brighton & London: Robinson, Son & Pike.

Rolt, L.T.C., *Narrow Boat* (1944). London: Eyre Methuen.

Rolt, L.T.C., *Thomas Telford* (1958). London: Longman.

Rolt, L.T.C., *Landscape with Canals* (1977). London: Allen Lane.

Rowley, N. & S.V., *Market Drayton: a Study in Social History* (1966). Market Drayton: privately published.

Rowley, R.T., *The Shropshire Landscape* (1972). London: Hodder & Stoughton.

Rutter, M., & Dent, H., *Bridgnorth: a Pictorial History* (1998). Chichester: Phillimore.

Sayers, R.S., *Lloyds Bank in the History of English Banking* (1957). Oxford: Clarendon Press.

Scard, M.A., *The Building Stones of Shropshire* (1990). Shrewsbury: Swan Hill.

Scarfe, N., ed., *Industrial Espionage: the La Rochefoucauld Brothers' Tour of England in 1785* (1995). Woodbridge: Boydell.

Scott, W.J., *The Great Great Western, 1889-1902* (1972). Newton Abbot: David & Charles.

Seaby, W.A., & Smith, A.C., *Windmills in Shropshire, Hereford and Worcester: a contemporary survey* (1984). Stevenage Museum Publications.

Sentinel Wagon Works Ltd., *Sentinel Patent Locomotives* (1931). Shrewsbury: Sentinel Wagon Works.

Shaw, M., *The Lead, Copper & Barytes Mines of Shropshire* (2009). Little Logaston: Logaston.

Shorter, A.H., *Water Paper Mills in England* (1966). London: Society for the Preservation of Ancient Buildings.

Shrewsbury Chronicle and Shropshire Libraries, *The Changing Face of Shrewsbury* (1981). Shrewsbury: Shrewsbury Chronicle and Shropshire Libraries.

Shropshire Federation of Women's Institutes (SFWI), *Shropshire Within Living Memory* (1992). Newbury: Countryside Books.

Shropshire Railway Society, *Shropshire Railways Revisited* (1982). Shrewsbury: Shropshire Libraries.

Shropshire Records & Research Unit, *Shrewsbury Then and Now* (1991). Shrewsbury: Shropshire Books.

Simpson, S., *The Agreeable Historian or the Compleat English Traveller* (1746). London: R. Walker.

Skempton, A.W., ed., *Civil Engineers and Engineering in Britain, 1600-1830* (1996). Aldershot: Variorum.

Smith, D.J., *The Severn Valley Railway* (1967). Bracknell: Town & Country Press.

Smith, S.B., *A View from the Iron Bridge* (1979). London: Thames & Hudson.

Smith, W.J., & Beddoes, K., *The Cleobury Mortimer & Ditton Priors Light Railway* (1980). Oxford: Oxford Publishing Company.

Stembridge, P.K., *The Goldney Family: a Bristol Merchant Dynasty* (1998). Bristol: Bristol Record Society.

Stopes, H., *Malt and Malting* (1885). London: Unwin.

Stratton, M., *The Terracotta Revival: Building Innovation and the Image of the Industrial City in Britain and North America* (1993). London: Gollancz.

Stratton, M., *Ironbridge and the Electric Revolution* (1994). London: John Murray.

Stratton, M., & Trinder, B., *The English Heritage Book of Industrial England* (1997). London: Batsford.

Stratton, M., & Trinder, B., *Twentieth-Century Industrial Archaeology* (2000). London: Spon.

Sutherland, R.J.M., ed., *Structural Iron, 1750-1850* (1997). Aldershot: Ashgate, 1997.

Tann, J., *The Development of the Factory* (1970). London: Cornmarket.

Tann, J., ed., *The Selected Papers of Boulton & Watt: Volume 1: The Engine Partnership 1775-1825* (1981). London: Diploma Press.

Tew, D., *Canal Inclines and Lifts* (1984). Gloucester: Alan Sutton.

Thomas, A.R., & Thomas, J.L, *'The Sentinel': A history of Alley & MacLennen and The Sentinel Wagon Works*, vol. II 1930-1980 (1987). Worcester: Woodpecker Publications.

Thomas, E., *Coalbrookdale and the Darbys* (1999). York: Sessions.

Toghill, P., *Geology in Shropshire* (1990). Shrewsbury: Swan Hill Press.

Toghill, P., *Onny Valley, Shropshire Geology Teaching Trail* (1992). London: Geologists' Association.

Toghill, P., & Chell, K., *Shropshire Geology: Stratigraphic and Tectonic History* (1984). Taunton: Field Studies Council.

Tonks, E.S., *The Shropshire & Montgomeryshire Railway* (1972). London: Industrial Railway Society.

Tonks, E.S., *The Snailbeach District Railway* (1974). Birmingham: Industrial Railway Society.

Townson, R., *Tracts and Observations in Natural History and Physiology: A Sketch of the Mineralogy of Shropshire* (1799). London: J. White.

Trinder, B., *A Description of Coalbrookdale in 1801* (1970). Telford: Ironbridge Gorge Museum Trust.

Trinder, B., *The Industrial Revolution in Shropshire* (1973, 3rd edn. 2000). Chichester: Phillimore.

Trinder, B., *The Darbys of Coalbrookdale* (1974, 2nd edn. 1992). Chichester: Phillimore.

Trinder, B., ed., *The Most Extraordinary District in the World: Ironbridge and Coalbrookdale* (1977, 3rd edn., 2005). Chichester: Phillimore.

Trinder, B., *The Making of the Industrial Landscape* (1982, 3rd edn. 1997). London: Orion.

Trinder, B., ed., *Victorian Shrewsbury: Studies in the History of a County Town* (1984). Shrewsbury: Shropshire Libraries.

Trinder, B., ed., *The Blackwell Encyclopedia of Industrial Archaeology* (1992). Oxford: Blackwell.

Trinder, B., *A History of Shropshire* (1983, 2nd edn., 1997). Chichester: Phillimore.

Trinder, B., *The Market Town Lodging House in Victorian England* (2001). Friends of the Centre for Local History, University of Leicester.

Trinder, B., *English Market Towns and their Suburbs in recent centuries* (2005). University of Cambridge Institute of Continuing Education.

Trinder, B., *Barges & Bargemen: A Social History of the Upper Severn Navigation 1660-1900* (2005). Chichester: Phillimore.

Trinder, B., *Beyond the Bridges: the Suburbs of Shrewsbury 1760-1960* (2006). Chichester: Phillimore.

Trinder, B., *Britain's Industrial Revolution: the making of a manufacturing people* (2013). Lancaster: Carnegie.

Trinder, B., & Cox, J.,eds, *Yeomen & Colliers: the probate inventories of Dawley, Lilleshall, Wellington and Wrockwardine* (1980). Chichester: Phillimore.

Trinder, B., & Cox, N., eds., *Miners and Mariners of the Severn Gorge: the probate inventories of Benthall, Broseley, Little Wenlock and Madeley* (2000). Chichester: Phillimore.

Tucker, G., *Some Watermills of South-West Shropshire* (1991). Birmingham: Midland Wind & Water Mills Group.

Turner, K., & Turner, S., *The Shropshire & Montgomeryshire Light Railway* (1982). Newton Abbot: David & Charles.

Victoria History of Shropshire, Volume 8, the Hundreds of Condover and Ford (1968). Oxford University Press.

Victoria History of Shropshire, Volume 3, County Government (1979). Oxford University Press.

Victoria History of Shropshire, Volume 11, Telford (1985). Oxford University Press.

Victoria History of Shropshire, Volume 10, Wenlock, Upper Corve Dale and the Stretton Hills (1998). Oxford University Press.

Victoria History of Shropshire, Volume 6, part 1, Shrewsbury: General History and Topography (2014). Woodbridge: Boydell & Brewer.

Wakelin, P., ed., *Pontcysyllte Aqueduct and Canal: Nomination as a World Heritage Site* (2008). Wrexham: Wrexham Borough Council.

Wakelin, P., *Pontcysyllte Aqueduct and Canal: World Heritage Site* (2015). Milton Keynes: Canals & Rivers Trust.

Walker, C., *The Steam Railway: Shrewsbury* (1971). Oxford: Oxford Illustrators Ltd.

Wanklyn, M., ed., *The Diary of George Gitton of Bridgnorth for 1866* (1998). University of Keele Centre for Local History.

Ward, A.W., *The Bridges of Shrewsbury* (1935). Shrewsbury: Wilding.

Ward, C., *Cotters and Squatters: Housing's Hidden History* (2002). Nottingham: Five Leaves.

Ward, T.O., *The Medical Topography of Shrewsbury* (1841). Worcester: Deighton.

Warner, A., *Newport, Shropshire: Past and Present* (1983). Newport: privately published.

Watkin, I., *Oswestry, with an account of its old houses, shops &c.* (1920). Oswestry: Owen.

Watkins, G., *The Stationary Steam Engine* (1968). Newton Abbot: David & Charles.

Watkins-Pitchford, W., *The Port of Bridgnorth* (1935). Bridgnorth: R.S. Fallows.

Watson, M., & Musson, C., *Shropshire from the Air: Man and the Landscape* (1993). Shrewsbury: Shropshire Books.

Watson, M., & Musson, C., *Shropshire from the Air: An English County at Work* (1993). Shrewsbury: Shropshire Books.

Watson, N., *A family business: Morris & Co. 1869-1994* (1995). Shrewsbury: Morris & Co.

Webb, B., *A Ludlow Album: a collection of old photographs* (1981). Shrewsbury: Shropshire Libraries.

Whitehead, T.H., Robinson, T., Pocock, R.W., & Dixon, E.E.L., *Memoirs of the Geological Survey of England and Wales: the country between Wolverhampton and Oakengates* (1928). London: HMSO.

Wightman, J., *Annals of the Rescued* (1860). London: James Nisbet.

Wilding & Son, *Shropshire: a Beautiful English County* (1935). Shrewsbury: Wilding.

Williams, G., *The Wenlock Limestone Industry: an historical note* (1990). Telford: Williams.

Williams, G., *Much Wenlock's Limestone Quarries* (revised edn., 2014). Much Wenlock: Ellingham Press.

Wilson, E., *The Ellesmere and Llangollen Canal: an historical background* (1975). Chichester: Phillimore.

Woodward, I., *The Story of Wem and its Neighbourhood* (1951). Shrewsbury: Wilding.

Wrekin Local Studies Forum, *Proceedings of the Thomas Telford Day School 2007* (2007). Telford: Wrekin Local Studies Forum

Wrekin Local Studies Forum, *Proceedings of the John Randall Day School 2010* (2011). Telford: Wrekin Local Studies Forum.

Wrekin Local Studies Forum, *Proceedings of the Ken Jones Local History Day 2013* (2013). Telford: Wrekin Local Studies Forum

Wren, W.J., *The Tannat Valley – the Railways and Industrial Archaeology* (1968). Newton Abbot: David & Charles.

Wright, T., *The History and Antiquities of the town of Ludlow* (1826). Ludlow: Proctor & Jones.

Yate, B., *By Great Western to Crewe. The Story of the Wellington to Nantwich and Crewe Line.* Usk: Oakwood.

Yate, B., *The Railways and Locomotives of the Lilleshall Company* (2008). Clophill: Irwell.

Yate, B., *The Shropshire Union Railway. Stafford to Shrewsbury including the Coalport Branch* (2003). Usk: Oakwood.

Young, A., *Tours in England and Wales* (1932). London: LSE Reprints.

Articles and contributions to Symposia

Allbutt, M., & Brook, F., 'The South Shropshire Lead Mines', *Journal of Industrial Archaeology*, vol.10 (1973).

Baker, N.J., 'The Talbot Chambers Site, Market Street, Shrewsbury', *TSAS*, vol. 66 (1989).

Baldwin, M., 'Ironworking in Cleobury Mortimer, Part 1', *Cleobury Chronicles*, vol. 3 (1994).

Belford, P., 'Forging Ahead in Coalbrookdale: Historical Archaeology at the Upper Forge', *IAR*, vol. 25 (2003).

Belford, P., & Ross, R.A, 'Industry and Domesticity: exploring historical archaeology in the Ironbridge Gorge', *Post-Medieval Archaeology*, vol. 38 (2004).

Bergeron, L., ed., Papers from the Pontcysyllte International Conference: *Patrimoine de l'industrie*, vol. 17 (2007).

Binnie, G.M., 'Masonry and Concrete Dams 1880-1941', *IAR*, vol. 10 (1987).

Blake Roberts, D., & Blake Roberts, G., 'The results of recent excavations at Coalport, Shropshire', *English Ceramic Circle Transactions*, vol. 2 (1981).

Boucher, C.T.G., 'Broadstone Mill', *TNS*, vol. 36 (1963-64).

Allbut, M., & Brook, F., 'The South Shropshire Lead Mines', *Journal of Industrial Archaeology*, vol. 10 (1973).

Brown, I.J., 'Notes on the Mines of the Madeley Court Company', *SNL* No. 38 (1970).

Brown, I.J., 'Underground in the Ironbridge Gorge', *IAR* vol. 3 (1979).

Burke, J.P., 'Railway Crossroads of the North-West: Shrewsbury', *Modern Railways*, vol. 17 (1963).

Burne, E.L., 'On Mills, by Thomas Telford', *TNS*, vol. 17 (1936-37).

Carpenter, R., 'Bishop's Castle Station', *British Railway Journal*, No. 38 (1991).

Champion, W.A., 'John Ashby and the history and environs of the Lion Inn, Shrewsbury', *TSAS*, vol. 75, (2000).

Chaplin, R., 'The alteration of the route of Watling Street between Atcham Bridge and Norton', *SNL*, No. 14 (1961).

Chaplin, R., 'A Forgotten Industrial Valley', *SNL*, No.36 (1969).

Charlesworth, M., 'The "penny bridge" celebrates its 100th birthday', *Shropshire Magazine*, July 1992.

Clarke, N.J., 'The Aqueduct: an east Shropshire industrial settlement', *SNL*, Nos.39/40 (1970-71).

Clarke, N.J., 'The Eytons and the Shrewsbury Canal: three generations of involvement', *JRCHS*, No. 211 (2011).

Clarke, N.J., 'The Railway Interests of a Shropshire Landed Gentleman', *JRCHS*, No. 215 (2012).

Collingwood, R., 'The Early Paper Mills of Shropshire: an update', *TSAS*, vol. 80 (2005).

Cossons, N., 'Ironbridge: the First Ten Years', *IAR*, vol.3 (1979).

Cox, N., 'Imagination and Innovation of an Industrial Pioneer: the first Abraham Darby', *IAR*, vol.12 (1990).

Cromarty, R., 'The water supply in Shrewsbury 1550-1835', *TSAS*, vol 75 (2000).

Crossley, D., 'The survival of early blast furnaces: a world survey', *Journal of the Historical Metallurgy Society*, vol. 18 (1984).

Davidson, I., 'George Deacon (1843-1909) and the Vyrnwy Works', *TNS*, vol. 59 (1987-88).

Day, W., 'The Shropshire Portion of the Chester-Cardiff road in 1675', *TSAS*, vol. 60 (1975-76).

de Haan, D., 'The Iron Bridge – New Research in the Ironbridge Gorge', *IAR*, vol. 26 (2004).

Denton, J.H., & Lewis, M.J.T., 'The River Tern Navigation', *JRCHS*, vol. 23 (1977).

Dickinson, H.W., & Lee, A., 'The Rastricks: Civil Engineers', *TNS*, vol. 4 (1923-24).

Edmundson, R.S., 'Coalport China Works, Shropshire: a comparative study of the premises', *IAR*, vol. 3 (1979).

Edmundson, R.S., 'Bradley & Co., Coalport Pottery, 1796-1800', *Transactions of the Northern Ceramic Society*, vol. 4 (1981).

Edwards, I., 'The early ironworks of north-west Shropshire', *TSAS*, vol. 56 (1957-60).

Evans, R.C., 'A Year in the Life of Thomas Telford', *WMS*, vol. 4 (1970-71).

Falconer, K.A., 'Fireproof Mills – the widening perspectives', *IAR*, vol. 16 (1993).

Goodman, K.W.G., 'Tilsop Furnace', *WMS*, vol. 13 (1980).

Green, H., 'New Factory, Severn Street, Castlefields', *Bulletin of the Association for Industrial Archaeology*, No.25 (1976).

Green, H., 'The Linen Industry of Shropshire', *IAR*, vol. 5 (1981).

Hancox, T.C., 'Two East Shropshire Paper Mills', *SNL*, No. 37 (1969).

Hancox, T.C., 'Ludford Paper Mill', *Transaction of the Woolhope Naturalists' and Field Club*, vol.41 (1973).

Hayman, R., 'The Cranage brothers and eighteenth-century forge technology', *Historical Metallurgy*, vol. 38 (2004).

Hayman, R., 'Charcoal Ironmaking in Nineteenth-century Shropshire', *EcHR*, vol 61 (2008).

Herbert, A.T., 'Jackfield Decorative Tiles in Use', *IAR*, vol. 3 (1979).

Hibbs, J., 'The Shropshire Omnibus Association: a note on a producers' co-operative'. *Transport History*, vol. 2 (1969).

Houghton, A.W.J., 'The Caughley Porcelain Works near Broseley, Salop', *Industrial Archaeology*, vol. 5 (1968).

Hulme, E.W., 'The Statistical History of the Iron Trade, 1717-50', *TNS*, vol. 9 (1928-29).

Hughes, M., 'Telford, Parnell and the Great Irish Road', *Journal of Transport History*, vol. 6 (1964).

Hyde, C.K., 'The Iron Industry of the West Midlands in 1754: Observations from the Travel Account of Charles Wood', *WMS*, vol. 6 (1973).

Ince, L., 'The introduction of coke iron at the Stour forges of the Knight family', *Journal of the Historical Metallurgical Society*, vol. 24 (1991).

Jenkins, R., 'The Industries of Herefordshire', *TNS*, vol. 17 (1936-37).

Johnson, B.L.C., 'The Foley Partnerships', *EcHR*, 2nd series, vol. 4 (1952).

Jones, I C., 'Electricity Supply in Shropshire before Nationalisation', *IAR*, vol. 18 (1996).

Jones, K., Hunt, M., Malam, J., & Trinder, B., 'Holywell Lane: A Squatter Community in the Shropshire Coalfield', *IAR*, vol. 6 (1982).

Kanefsky, J., & Robey, J., 'Steam Engines in 18th-century Britain: A Quantitative Assessment', *Technology & Culture*, vol. 21 (1980).

Kay, G., 'Charles Lynam – an Architect of Tile Factories', *Journal of the Tiles and Architectural Ceramics Society*, vol. 4 (1992).

King, P.W., 'Sir Clement Clarke and the Adoption of Coal in Metallurgy', *TNS*, vol.73 (2001).

King, P.W., 'The choice of fuels in the eighteenth-century iron industry: The Coalbrookdale Accounts re-considered', *EcHR*, vol. 64 (2011).

Lawson, J., 'Sir Basil Brooke and Bromley's Forge', *SNL*, No. 44 (1973).

Lloyd, L.C., 'Paper-Making in Shropshire', *TSAS*, vol. 44 (1937-38).

Lloyd, L.C., 'Paper-Making in Shropshire: Supplementary Notes', *TSAS*, vol. 53 (1949-50).

Malam, J., 'White Salt-glazed Stoneware Manufacture at Jackfield', *West Midlands Archaeology*, vol. 24 (1981).

Malley, M., 'Martin Billing & the Ownership of Tibberton Paper Mill', *British Association of Paper Historians Quarterly*, No. 84 (Oct. 2012).

Marsh, P., 'Shrewsbury Markets in the Nineteenth Century', Trinder, B., ed., *Victorian Shrewsbury* (1984).

Morriss, R., 'A Gazetteer of Passenger Railway Stations in Shropshire', *TSAS*, vol. 64 (1983-84).

Mutton, N., 'The Forges at Eardington and Hampton Loade', *TSAS*, vol. 58 (1965-68).

Mutton, N., 'Charlcott Furnace 1733-79', *Bulletin of the Historical Metallurgy Group*, vol. 6 (1966).

Mutton, N., 'Eardington Forges and Canal Tunnel', *Industrial Archaeology*, vol. 7 (1970).

Mutton, N., 'Investigations of the Sites of Charcoal Blast Furnaces at Shifnal and Kemberton', *SNL*, No.43 (1972).

Nair, G., & Poyner, D., 'The Coming of Coal: Industrial Development in a South Shropshire Parish', *Midland History*, vol. 18 (1993).

Nankivell, C.R.T., 'Three dwellings in the Dark Lane Rows', *SNL*, No.41 (1971).

Nichol, J.D., 'Social and Political Stability in 18th-century Provincial Life: a study of the career of John Ashby (1722-1779) of Shrewsbury', *TSAS*, vol. 59 (1969-70).

Pannett, D., 'A note on Bromley's Forge', *SNL*, No. 36 (1969).

Pannett, D., 'Fish Weirs of the River Severn', *SNL*, No.42 (1971).

Pannett, D., 'The River Severn – some historical observations', *Shropshire Conservation Trust Bulletin*, No.29 (1973).

Pannett, D., 'Fish Weirs on the River Severn in Shropshire', *SNL*, No. 44 (1975).

Pannett, D., 'The River Severn at Wroxeter', *TSAS*, vol. 66 (1980).

Pannett, D., 'Fish Weirs of the River Severn', Aston, M., ed., *Medieval Fish, Fisheries and Fishlords in England* (1988). Oxford: British Archaeological Reports.

Pape, T., 'The Early Glass Industry in North Staffordshire', *Transactions of the North Staffordshire Field Club*, vol. 67 (1933).

Pape, T., 'An Elizabethan Glass Furnace', *The Connoisseur*, vol. 92 (1933).

Powell, J., 'Early Steam in Ironbridge', *Ironbridge Quarterly*, 1990:2.

Poyner, D., & Evans, R., 'The Wyre Forest Coalfield', *Cleobury Chronicles*, vol. 3 (1994).

Preston, R.A., 'The *Eliza*: a 19th-century Trow at Shrewsbury', *TSAS*, vol. 68 (1993).

Prestwich, J., 'On the Geology of the Coalfield of Coalbrookdale', *Transactions of the Geological Society*, vol. 5 (1840).

Rhodes, J., 'Lead Smelting in the Severn Gorge', *SNL*, No. 41 (1971).

Riden, P., 'Eighteenth-Century Blast Furnaces: a New Checklist', *Journal of the Historical Metallurgy Society*, vol. 12 (1978).

Rimmer, W.G., 'Castle Foregate Flax Mill, 1797-1886', *TSAS*, vol. 56 (1957-60).

Rix, M., 'Industrial Archaeology', *The Amateur Historian*, vol. 2 (1955),

Roberts, S., 'Hinksay Rows', *SNL*, No.44 (1973).

Robinson, D.H., 'An account of the Shropshire Canals', *Transactions of the Caradoc & Severn Valley Field Club*, vol. 11 (1939-42).

Scard, M.A., 'The Development and Changing Organisation of Shropshire's Quarrying Industry, 1750-1900', *IAR*, vol. 11 (1989).

Scott, H., 'Colliers' Wages in Shropshire 1830-50', *TSAS*, vol. 53 (1949-50).

Shearing, E.A., 'The Shropshire Union Canal and the Peatswood Estate at Tyrley', *JRCHS*, vol. 29 (1987).

Shorter, A.H., 'The Excise Numbers of Paper Mills in Shropshire', *TSAS*, vol. 53 (1949-50).

Silvester, R.J., 'John Probert of Copthorne: A Georgian Land Agent', *TSAS*, vol 84 (2009).

Skempton, A.W., 'Telford and the Design for a new London Bridge', in Penfold, A., ed., *Thomas Telford: Engineer* (1980). London: Thomas Telford.

Smith, S.B, 'The Construction of the Blists Hill Ironworks', *IAR*, vol. 3 (1979).

Smith, E.C., 'Joshua Field's Diary of a tour through the provinces, 1821, Part 2', *TNS*, vol. 13 (1932-33).

Smith, R.S., 'England's first rails: a re-consideration', *Renaissance & Modern Studies*, vol.4 (1960). [Reproduced in Chrimes, M., ed., *The Civil Engineering of Canals and Railways before 1850* (1997). Aldershot: Ashgate].

Smith, W.H., 'Craven Arms & Stokesay Station', *British Railway Journal*, No. 32 (1990).

Strachan, S., 'Henry Powell Dunnill: a Victorian Tilemaster', *Journal of the Tiles and Architectural Ceramics Society*, vol. 3 (1990).

Tolley, R.S., 'The Changing Industrial Geography of Eastern Shropshire', *WMS*, vol. 5 (1972).

Tonkin, J.W., 'Hinksay Row, Dawley', *SNL*, No. 33 (1967).

Tonkin, S.M., 'Trevithick, Rastrick and the Hazledine Foundry, Bridgnorth', *TNS*, vol. 26 (1947-49).

Trinder, B., 'The Wooden Bridge at Cressage', *SNL*, No.35 (1968).

Trinder, B., 'The First Iron Bridges', IAR, vol. 3 (1979). [Reproduced in Sutherland, R.J.M, *Structural Iron, 1750-1850* (Aldershot: Ashgate, 1997. (1997), 247-56].

Trinder, B., 'Coalport Bridge: A Study in Historical Interpretation', *IAR*, vol. 3 (1979).

Trinder, B., 'The Holyhead Road: an engineering project in its social context', in Penfold, A., *Thomas Telford* (1980).

Trinder, B., 'The Severn Navigation at Dowles', *TSAS*, vol. 64 (1983-84).

Trinder, B., 'The Development of the Integrated Ironworks in the Eighteenth Century', *Institute of Metals Handbook* (1988-89).

Trinder, B., 'Ditherington Flax Mill – a Re-evaluation', *Textile History*, vol. 23 (1992).

Trinder, B., 'The Textile Industry in Shrewsbury in the late Eighteenth Century', Clark, P. and Corfield, P., *Industry and Urbanisation in Eighteenth-Century England* (1994). Centre for Urban History University of Leicester.

Trinder, B., 'The Shropshire Coalfield', Clark, P. and Corfield, P., *Industry and Urbanisation in Eighteenth-Century England* (1994). Centre for Urban History University of Leicester.

Trinder, B., 'Recent Research on Early Shropshire Railways', Lewis, M.J.T., *Early Railways 2: Papers from the Second International Early Railways Conference* (London: The Newcomen Society, 2003).

Trinder, B., '18th- and 19th-century Market Town Industry: an analytical model', *IAR*, vol. 24 (2002).

Trinder, B., 'The Heritage of the Iron Industry in the Coalbrookdale Coalfield, Shropshire, England 1959-2005', in Kiem, K., ed., *Konversionen: Zum Umgang mit Bauten der Eisenindustrie in Europa* [Conversion: Dealing with the buildings of the iron industry in Europe] (2007). Aachen, Shaker Verlag.

Trinder, B., 'William Reynolds: Polymath – A Biographical Strand through the Industrial Revolution', *IAR*, vol. 30 (2008).

Trinder, B., 'Food in Probate Inventories 1660-1750', *TLH*, vol. 38 (2009).

Trinder, B., 'John Fletcher's Parishioners: Reflections on Industrial Revolution and Evangelical Revival in the Ironbridge Gorge', Hammond, G., & Forsaith, P.S., *Religion, Gender and Industry* (2011). Eugene, Oregon: Wipf & Stock.

Trinder, B., 'Country carriers revisited', *TLH*, vol. 42 (2012).

Trinder, B., 'Was there a Shropshire Enlightenment?', *WMH*, vol. 1 (2013).

Trinder, B., 'Ironbridge and beyond: Reflections on 30 years of Change', Albrecht, H., & Hansell, F., *Industrial and Mining Landscapes within World Heritage Context* (2014). Freiberg: Sächsisches Industriemuseum/TU Bergakademie Freiberg.

Tucker, D.G., 'Electricity Generating Stations for Public Supply in the West Midlands, 1888-1977', *WMS*, vol. 10 (1977).

Upton, C., 'From Paper to Pipes: Public Health, Clean Water and the Elan Valley Scheme, 1892-1905', *WMH*, vol. 2 (2014).

Wanklyn, M., 'John Weld of Willey (1585-1665): An enterprising landowner of the early 17th century' *WMS*, vol. 3 (1969).

Wanklyn, M., 'John Weld of Willey: Estate Management 1631-1660', *WMS*, vol. 4 (1970-71).

Wanklyn, M., 'Iron and Steelworks in Coalbrookdale in 1645', *SNL*, No.44 (1973).

Wanklyn, M., 'Industrial Development in the Ironbridge Gorge before Abraham Darby', *WMS*, vol. 15 (1982).

Wanklyn, M., 'The Severn Navigation in the seventeenth century: the long-distance trade of Shrewsbury boats', *Midland History*, vol. 13 (1988).

Wanklyn, M., 'Urban Revival in Early Modern England; Bridgnorth and the River Trade, 1660-1800', *Midland History*, vol. 18 (1993).

Ward, W.W., 'Richard Groom of Wellington', *Methodist Magazine*, vol. 62 (1893).

Watson, M., 'Broadford Works Aberdeen', *Textile History*, vol. 23 (1992).

White, R., 'A Recent Archaeological Survey at Charlcotte and Titterstone Clee, Shropshire', *TSAS*, vol. 79 (2004).

Williams, A.B., 'The Rural Industries of Llanymynech', *Montgomeryshire Collections*, vol. 47 (1941).

Williams, W.H., 'The Canal Inclined planes of East Shropshire', *Journal of Industrial Archaeology*, vol. 2 (1963).

Parliamentary Papers

Report of the Assistant Commissioner ... for Hand Loom Weavers (1840), XXXIV.

First Report from the Select Committee on Private Business, the Severn Navigation (1841), IX.

Reports from Commissioners, Railways, Gauges, Oxford, Worcester & Wolverhampton and Oxford & Rugby Railway Bills (1845), XI.

Report of the Select Committee on Railway Bills (1846), XIII.

Report to the Admiralty upon the Improvements of the River Severn (1847-48), XXXI.

Report of the Commissioners appointed to enquire into the application of iron to railway structures (1849). XXIX.

Report of the Inspector of Mines for 1874 (1875), XVI.

Theses and Academic Assignments

Andreae, C., *A Historical and Structural History of Sheinwood Mill, Shropshire* (1990-91) Ironbridge Institute assignment.

Butterfield, R., *The Records of the Canal Wharf at Wappenshall* (1989-90). Ironbridge Institute assignment.

Duckworth, S., *The Severn Navigation and River Wharf sites in the Ironbridge Gorge with particular reference to the site at The Calcutts* (1987-88). Ironbridge Institute dissertation.

Eaves, M., & Hall, S., *Water Power System and Blast Furnace at Leighton, Shropshire* (1993-94). Ironbridge Institute assignment.

Edwards, H., *The Commercial Centres of Madeley and Dawley 1790-1940* (1988-89). Ironbridge Institute dissertation.

Ensum, J., *Highley – Settlement/Community* (1993). Wolverhampton University dissertation.

Fenwick, P., *The Smithies Sawmill* (1989-90). Ironbridge Institute assignment.

Goff, A.D., *A Study of the Former Coach-building Workshops, No.1 Church Street, Bishop's Castle* (1992-93). Ironbridge Institute assignment.

Goodman, K.W.G., *Hammerman's Hill: the Land, People and Industry of the Titterstone Clee Area of Shropshire from the 16th to the 19th centuries* (1978). University of Keele, PhD thesis.

Guthrie, J., & Pudney, C., *Wappenshall Junction, Shropshire: a Survey of the Canal Developments and the Industrial Buildings* (1988-89). Ironbridge Institute assignment.

Hayman, R., *The Shropshire Wrought-Iron Industry c. 1600-1900: A Study of Technological Change* (2003). University of Birmingham, PhD thesis.

Healey, J., *Longdon-upon-Tern Aqueduct: a building survey and study of the masonry abutments.* (1988-89). Ironbridge Institute dissertation.

Hewitt, P.B., *The Mining, Quarrying and allied industries of the Cleehill Regions from the 1800s to 1930* (1991). CNAA (Wolverhampton Polytechnic) M.Phil. thesis.

Higgins, D.A., *The Interpretation and Regional Study of Clay Tobacco Pipes: a Case Study of the Broseley District* (1987). University of Liverpool, PhD thesis.

Holmes, D., *The Working of the Silurian Wenlock Limestone in South-East Shropshire* (1986-87). Ironbridge Institute dissertation.

Johnson, B.L.C., *The Charcoal Iron Trade in the Midlands 1690—1720* (1950). University of Birmingham, MA thesis.

Jones, I.C., *A Survey of Longwood Brickworks, Shropshire* (1991-92). Ironbridge Institute assignment.

Jones, I.C., *The Industrial Archaeology of Coleham, Riverside* (1992-93). Ironbridge Institute assignment.

Kent, J., *The Barrow Farm Maltings, Barrow* (1991-92). Ironbridge Institute assignment.

McDonald, M.R., *The wash-house: an archaeological and functional evaluation with special reference to the "brew-us" of the Ironbridge/Coalbrookdale area* (1987-88). Ironbridge Institute dissertation.

Morris, Jonathan, *The Birmingham and Liverpool Junction Canal* (1984-85). Ironbridge Institute dissertation.

Morris, Julie, *The Brick and Pipeworks, Woodhouse Fields, Bourton, Much Wenlock, Shropshire* (1990-91). Ironbridge Institute assignment.

Norris, G., *A Survey of the Heavy Erecting Shop, Coalbrookdale* (1989-90). Ironbridge Institute assignment.

Pattison, A., *William Hazledine: Shropshire Ironmaster & Millwright: a reconstruction of his life and his contributions to the development of engineering 1786-1840* (2011). University of Birmingham, MPhil. thesis.

Rogers, E., *Water Power on the Ketley Brook, Shropshire: an archaeological perspective* (1992-93). Ironbridge Institute dissertation.

Rowley, R.T., *The History of the South Shropshire Landscape 1086-1800* (1967) University of Oxford B.Litt. thesis.

Smith, N., *An investigation into the commercial life, trades and craft industries of 19th-century Much Wenlock and an evaluation of their physical remains* (1988-89). Ironbridge Institute dissertation.

Temple, J.C., *Industrial Archaeology of Aviation in Shropshire* (1983-84). Ironbridge Institute dissertation.

Terry, R., *Industrial History and Archaeology of the Linley Brook* (1988-89). Ironbridge Institute dissertation.

Wakelin, P., *Historical Applications of British Fire Insurance Records.* Ironbridge Institute dissertation, 1984.

Watts, S., *All's Grist to the mill: a survey of Rindleford Mill in the parish of Worfield* (1988-89). Ironbridge Institute dissertation.

Whall, J., *An Interpretive Scheme Providing Proposals for Presenting the Water Mills at Ludlow to the Public* (1990-91) Ironbridge Institute assignment.

Research Papers and Consultancy Reports

Beale, R., *The Old Wind: a Preliminary Report* (1988). Telford: Ironbridge Gorge Museum Archaeology Unit.

Clark, K., & Alfrey, J., *Coalbrookdale: First Interim Report of the Nuffield Survey* (1986). Telford: Ironbridge Institute.

Clark, K., & Alfrey, J., *Coalport and Blists Hill: Second Interim Report of the Nuffield Survey* (1986). Telford: Ironbridge Institute.

Clark, K., & Alfrey, J., *Benthall and Broseley Wood: Third Interim Report of the Nuffield Survey* (1987). Telford: Ironbridge Institute.

Clark, K., & Alfrey, J., *Jackfield and Broseley: Fourth Interim Report of the Nuffield Survey* (1987). Telford: Ironbridge Institute.

Edwards, H., *et al.*, *Madeley Wood Powder House: a building survey* (1987). Telford: Ironbridge Gorge Museum Archaeology Unit.

Elsworth, J., & White, K., *Granville Country Park: further archaeological investigations* (1988). Telford: Ironbridge Institute.

Higgins, D., *Lightmoor Blast Furnaces* (1988). Telford: Ironbridge Gorge Museum Archaeology Unit.

Higgins, D., Morriss, R., & Trueman, M., *The Broseley Pipeworks: an archaeological and historical evaluation* (1988). Telford: Ironbridge Institute.

Ironbridge Gorge Museum Archaeology Unit, *The Upper Forge Coalbrookdale: Severn Gorge Repairs Project Report 13* (1996). Ironbridge Gorge Museum for English Heritage.

Isaac, S., *Granville Colliery Horse Gin* (1987). Telford: Ironbridge Gorge Museum Archaeology Unit.

Jones, A., *Finds Typologies: Pottery 1: The Coarse Earthenwares* (1988). Telford: Ironbridge Gorge Museum Archaeology Unit.

Jones, A., Higgins, D., & Trueman, M., *11 Benthall Lane* (1987). Telford: Ironbridge Gorge Museum Archaeology Unit.

Macleod, M., Stratton, M., & Trinder, B., *Llanymynech Hill: an Archaeological and Historical Evaluation (1987)*. Telford: Ironbridge Institute.

Macleod, M., Trinder, B., & Worthington, M., *The Ditherington Flax Mills, Shrewsbury: a survey and historical evaluation* (1988) Telford: Ironbridge Institute.

Marriott, J., Reid, M., Barratt, G. & White, R., *A Conservation Plan for the Historic Mining Landscape of the Clee Hills, South Shropshire* (2 vols., 2008). University of Birmingham for English Heritage.

Meeson, R.A., & Meeson, J., *Sandford Mill, Prees, Shropshire: an archaeological record of the standing structure* (1998).

Stratton, M., *Interpreting the Industrial Past* (1987). Telford: Ironbridge Institute.

Terry, R., *The Swan Malthouse, Ironbridge* (1988). Telford: Ironbridge Gorge Museum Archaeology Unit.

Trinder, B., *Fifty Years in Ellesmere: a report on an adult education class held in the autumn term 1986*. Typescripts in Shropshire Archives and Ironbridge Gorge Museum.

Trueman, M., *Archaeology in Ironbridge 1985-86* (1986). Telford: Ironbridge Gorge Museum Archaeology Unit.

Trueman, M., *28 Waterloo Street, Ironbridge* (1987). Telford: Ironbridge Gorge Museum Archaeology Unit.

Trueman, M., Macleod, M., & Jones, A., *The Upper Works, Coalbrookdale: a Rescue Excavation* (1988). Telford: Ironbridge Gorge Museum Archaeology Unit.

Trueman, M., & Ryan, J., *33 Hodge Bower, Ironbridge* (1987). Telford: Ironbridge Gorge Museum Archaeology Unit.

Trueman, M., Ryan, J., & Edwards, H., *Benthall Mill: a building survey* (1987). Telford: Ironbridge Gorge Museum Archaeology Unit.

Whittingslow, M., & Smith, P., *Lightmoor Brickworks* (1988). Telford: Ironbridge Gorge Museum Archaeology Unit.

Winkworth, A., *et al.*, *Willey Round House: a building survey* (1987). Telford: Ironbridge Gorge Museum Archaeology Unit.

Wrexham County Borough Council and RCAHMW, *Pontcysyllte Aqueduct & Canal: Nomination as a World Heritage Site* (2011).

Newspapers

Aris's Birmingham Gazette; Berrow's Worcester Journal; Bridgnorth Journal; Eddowes Salopian Journal; Ironbridge Weekly Journal; Ludlow & Wenlock Express; Shrewsbury Chronicle; Shropshire Star; Wellington Journal; Wenlock Express.

Printed Maps

Barnes, H., *A New Map of the Kington-Leominster-Stourport Canal* (1977). Tenbury Wells: G.R.Kendrick.

Baugh, R., *Map of Shropshire* (1808, reprinted 1983). Shrewsbury: Shropshire Archaeological Society.

Dean, R.J., *Map of the Kington, Leominster and Stourport Canal* (1968). Caterham: Railway & Canal Historical Society.

Greenwood Pringle & Co., *A Map of the County of Salop from an actual Survey made in the years 1826 & 1827* (1828, reprinted 2009). Shrewsbury: Shropshire Archaeological Society.

Toghill, P., & Chell, K., *A Geological Map of Shropshire* (1984). Taunton: Field Studies Council.

REFERENCES

Chapter 2

1. *Report of the School called Industry Hall in the Parish of Prees, Shropshire* (1804); Bishton, J., *Report to the Board of Agriculture* (1794).
2. Gough, R., *The History of Myddle* (ed. Hey, D., 1981), 108, 126-27; Hey, D., *An English Rural Community* (1974), 153-67.
3. *VCH* vol.8, 76, 103, 121, 137, 144, 166; Booth, D.T.W., *Watermills on the River Rea* (1990); Tucker, G., *Some Watermills of South-west Shropshire* (1991).
4. Booth, *op.cit.*, 7-8, 12, 17; Boucher, C.T.G., 'Broadstone Mill', *TNS*, vol.36 (1963-64), 159-63.
5. George, J., *Daniel's Mill* (n.d.).
6. Booth, *op.cit.*, 7-8.
7. Watts, S., *All's Grist to the Mill: a Survey of Rindleford Mill* (Ironbridge Institute dissertation, 1986-87).
8. Robinson, D.H., *The Sleepy Meese* (1980), 22-25.
9. Tucker, *op.cit.*, 38.
10. Goodman, K.W.T., 'Tilsop Furnace', *WMS*, vol. 13 (1980), 40-46.
11. Mutton, N., 'Charlcotte Furnace', TSAS, vol. 58 (1965-68), 84-88; Mutton, N., Charlcotte Furnace 1733-79', *Bulletin of the Historical Metallurgy Group*, vol. 6 (1966), 18-49; White, R., 'A Recent Archaeological Survey at Charlcotte and Titterstone Clee, Shropshire', *TSAS*, vol. 79 (2004).
12. Eaves, M., & Hall, S., *Water Power System and Blast Furnace at Leighton* (Ironbridge Institute assignment, 1993-94); Angerstein, R.R., *R.R. Angerstein's Illustrated Travel Diary* (2001), 330. The drawing of Leighton in the original diary in the archives of the Jernkontoret in Stockholm is not reproduced in that edition.
13. I am indebted to James Lawson for much of the information in this table.
14. *SC* 11 Jan. 1793, 18 April 1794, 2 Aug. 1811.
15. *SC* 18 April 1794, 2 Aug. 1811.
16. Cox, N., 'Imagination and Innovation of an Industrial Pioneer', *IAR*, vol. 12 (1990), 130-34
17. Mutton, N., 'Eardington Forges and Canal Tunnel, *Industrial Archaeology*, vol. 7 (1970), 53-59; Mutton, N., 'The Forges at Eardington and Hampton Loade', *TSAS*, vol. 58 (1965-68),

235-43; Trinder, B., *Barges & Bargemen* (2006), 127-28.
18. SA 625/1.
19. Pape, T., 'The Early Glass Industry in North Staffordshire', *Transactions of the North Staffordshire Field Club*, vol. 67 (1933), 116-20.
20. Lloyd, L.C., 'Paper Making in Shropshire', *TSAS*, vol. 44 (1937-38), 121-87; Lloyd, L.C., 'Paper Making in Shropshire: Supplementary Notes' *TSAS*, vol. 53 (1949-50), 152-63.
21. *SC* 6 Sep. 1816.
22. HRO, inventories of Richard Fosbrook of Alverley (1730); William Fosbrook of Claverley (1731).
23. *SC* 26 Jan. 1788, 25 Feb. 1825.
24. Lloyd, L.C., 'Paper Making in Shropshire', *TSAS*, vol.44 (1937-38), 179-81; Robinson, *op.cit.*, 92.
25. Booth, *op.cit.*, 25.
26. Robinson, *op.cit.*, 90-91; *ESJ* 3 Dec. 1829.
27. Robinson, D.H., *The Wandering Worfe* (1980), 116-18.
28. Trinder, B., *The Industrial Revolution in Shropshire* (2000), 91.
29. LJRO, inventory of Thomas Sandford of Prees, 1726; Meeson, R.A., & Meeson, J., *Sandford Mill, Prees, Shropshire: an archaeological record of the standing structure* (1998).
30. Seaby, W.A., & Smith, A.C., *Windmills in Shropshire, Hereford and Worcester* (1984), 5-6, 9-12, 18-20; the Pearson picture was formerly in the Old House, Dogpole, Shrewsbury.
31. *VCH*, vol. 8, 210; Toghill, P., *Geology in Shropshire* (1990), 92.
32. Scard, M.A., 'The Development and Changing Organisation of Shropshire's Quarrying Industry 1750-1900', *IAR* vol. 11 (1988), 173; see also Scard, M.A., *The Building Stones of Shropshire* (1990).
33. Scard, M.A., 'The Development and Changing Organisation of Shropshire's Quarrying Industry 1750-1900', *IAR* vol. 11 (1988), 173-83.
34. *VCH*, vol.8, 281.
35. *ex inf.* the late Dr Donald Harris.
36. Whitehead, T.H., Robertson, T., Pocock, R.W. & Dixon, E.E., *Memoirs of the Geological Survey of England and Wales: the Country between Wolverhampton and Oakengates* (1928); Robinson, D.H., *The Wandering Worfe* (1980), 29; SFWI,

Shropshire Within Living Memory (1992), 187-88; Wilson, E., *The Ellesmere & Llangollen Canal* (1975), 96-97.

37. Prees Parish Records, *ex inf.* Meriel Blower; *Historic Buildings in Telford, No.18, Apley Castle.*

38. Morris, J., *The Brick and Pipeworks, Woodhouse Fields, Bourton, Much Wenlock* (Ironbridge Institute assignment, 1990-91).

39. Smith, W., & Beddoes, K., *The Cleobury Mortimer & Ditton Priors Light Railway* (1980), 39, 53; Gwyn, D., *Gwynedd: Inheriting a Revolution* (2006), 193-94.

40. Williams, G., *The Wenlock Limestone Industry: an historical note* (1990); Williams, G., *Much Wenlock's Limestone Quarries* (revised edn., 2014): Holmes, D., *The Working of the Silurian Limestone in South-East Shropshire* (Ironbridge Institute dissertation, 1986-87); Jones, K.B., *The Wenlock Branch* (1998), 97-109.

41. Trinder, B., 'The Wooden Bridge at Cressage', *SNL* No.35 (1968), 1-6.

42. Brown, I.J., *A History of Limestone Mining in Shropshire* (1977), 20, 23.

43. *VCH*, vol. 8, 210.

44. MacLeod, M., Stratton, M., & Trinder, B., *Llanymynech Hill: An Archaeological and Historical Evaluation* (research paper, 1987); Aikin, A., *Journal of a Tour through North Wales* (1797), 5-7; Pennant, T., *Tours in North Wales* (1883), vol. 3, 168, 204.

45. *ESJ* 6 Jan. 1841.

46. Kent, J., *The Barrow Farm Maltings, Barrow* (Ironbridge Institute assignment, 1991-92).

47. Rowley, R.T., *The History of the South Shropshire Landscape 1086-1800* (1967), 219-20.

48. Nightingale, J., *The Beauties of England and Wales, vol. 13, pt. 1, Shropshire* (1813), 36.

49. I am grateful to Dr Peter Hobson, formerly of the University of Wolverhampton for his guidance on the history of Wyre Forest.

50. *ESJ* 15 April 1868.

51. *Ironbridge Weekly Journal* 22 Feb. 1871.

52. *VCH*, vol. 11, 316.

53. Wilson, *op.cit.*, 97-98; *SC* 29 Jan. 1892.

54. Ellis, R., *The Industries of the Dudmaston Estate* (Ironbridge Institute dissertation, 1984-85).

55. LJRO, inventories of Richard Furber (1660), William Tankard (1695).

56. University of Wolverhampton, Port Books Database.

57. Trinder, B., 'The Archaeology of the British Food Industry 1660-1960: a preliminary survey', *IAR*, vol. 15 (1993), 129-30.

58. Kelly & Co., *Directory of Shropshire* (1879), 479.

59. Trinder, *op.cit.*, 134.

60. Trinder, *op.cit.*, 133-34.

61. *RM* vol 84 (1939), 372; vol 85 (1939), 302.

62. *Ex inf.* Mr J. Wilde of Oswestry. I am grateful to Mrs Jessie Hanson for this information.

63. *VCH*, vol. 11, 232.

64. *SC* 20 Feb., 26 Mar., 7/21 May, 20 Aug., 29 Oct., 19 Nov., 1920, 25 Mar. 1921, 14 April 1922; Cooke, E., *Who killed Prees Heath?* (1991).

65. *Ex inf.* Mr R.M.J. Freeman of Pimley Manor, Shrewsbury.

Chapter 3

1. Eliot, G., *The Mill on the Floss* (Nelson edn., n.d.), 129.

2. Trinder, B., '18th- and 19th-century Market Town Industry: an analytical model', *IAR*, vol. 24 (2002).

3. Marsh, P., 'Shrewsbury Markets in the Nineteenth Century', Trinder, B., ed., *Victorian Shrewsbury* (1984), 19-23; *SC* 30 April, 28 May, 6 Aug., 17 Sep. 1819; 25 Jan. 1822.

4. *ESJ* 9, 16, 23 Jan., 7, 21 Feb. 1861.

5. Marsh, *op.cit.*, 24-28.

6. *Ibid*, 23-24.

7. *ESJ* 25 April 1888.

8. Earnshaw, D., *et al.*, *Whitchurch Remembered* (1980), 14.

9. *Ibid*, 19.

10. Seaby, W.A., & Smith, A.C., *Windmills in Shropshire, Hereford and Worcester* (1984), 5-6; *SC* 11 Sep. 1846.

11. *SC* 26 Mar. 1858; *ESJ* 14 Nov. 1877.

12. Woodward, I., *The Story of Wem* (1951), 61.

13. Trinder, B., & Cox, J., *Yeomen & Colliers in Telford* (1980), 69, 111-12; LJRO, inventory of William Podmore, 1744.

14. Nankivell, J.W., *Chapters from the History of Ellesmere* (1983), 27-28.

15. Watkin, I., *Oswestry* (1920), 150-52.

16. *ESJ* 9 May 1888.

17. *ESJ* 27 Feb. 1856

18. *VCH*, vol. 6 (1), 252; MacDonald, W., *An Illustrated Guide to Shrewsbury* (1897), 36-37; *SC* 4 May 1923; Giles, C., & Williams, M., *Ditherington Flax Mill and the Industrial Revolution* (2015), 120-28.

19. *SC* 18 Jan., 1820; 15 Sept. 1830; 22 Dec. 1905; Hulbert, C., *Memoirs of Seventy Years* (1852), 263; *ESJ* 4 March 1868.

20. *ESJ* 1 July 1868; Review Publishing, *Industry of Shropshire* (1891), 26.

21. *ESJ* 2 Jan. 1828; MacDonald, *op.cit.*, 38-39; Hulbert, *op.cit.*, 263; Jones, I.C., *The Industrial Archaeology of Coleham Riverside* (Ironbridge Institute assignment, 1992-93).

22. *Ex inf.* Dr David Jenkins.

23. *SC* 26 Aug. 1932 (for detailed description of the tannery), 21 Sep. 1956.

24. Smith, N., *An investigation into the commercial life … of Much Wenlock* (1988-89), 26.

25. Jones, *op.cit.*; Hulbert, C., *Memoirs of Seventy Years* (1852), 263; Hulbert, C., *History & Description of the County of Salop* (1837), 308.

26. *SC* 4 Feb. 1831.

27. Wright, T., *History and Antiquities of … Ludlow* (1826), 198-200; BPP 1840, XXIV, *Report of the Assistant Commissioner for Hand Loom Weavers*, 543.

28. Wilding & Son, *Shropshire* (1935), 73-74; MacDonald, *op.cit.*, 47.

29. *VCH*, vol.11, 230.

30. Trinder, B., *Britain's Industrial Revolution* (2013), 539-40.

31. *Ludlow & Church Stretton Chronicle* 14 Jan. 1911; Review Publishing, *op.cit.*, 25; *ESJ* 24 Feb. 1864; *SC* 11 April 1890; 27 April 1894.

32. *SC* 3 March 1854; 4 Jan. 1867; 26 Jan., 18 March 1892.

33. *VCH* vol. 11, 230; the late Mr T.W. Pollard kindly arranged for me to see the Tan Bank works.

34. Goff, A.A., *A Study of the former Coachmaking Workshops, No. 1 Church Street, Bishop's Castle* (Ironbridge Institute assignment, 1992-93).

35. Trinder, B., *Britain's Industrial Revolution* (2013), 92-93.

36. I am grateful to Professor Jennifer Tann, formerly of the University of Birmingham, and to Ron Fitzgerald for observations on the Soho Foundry and the Round Foundry.

37. Tonkin, S.M., 'Trevithick, Rastrick and the Hazledine Foundry, Bridgnorth', *TNS* vol.26 (1947-49), 171-84; Dickinson, H.W., & Lee, A., 'The Rastricks: Civil Engineers', *TNS*, vol. (1923-24), 48-63; *SC* 9 Nov. 1810; 18 Feb. 1812; 16 April 1830; BPP 1849 XXXX, *Report of the Commissioners appointed to enquire into the application of iron to railway structures*, 287, 387.

38. Cossons, N., & Trinder, B., *The Iron Bridge: Symbol of the Industrial Revolution* (2nd edn., 2002), 86-87, 123

39. Smith, E.C., 'Joshua Field's Diary of a tour through the Provinces, 1821, part 2', *TNS*, vol. 13 (1932-33), 18-19; SA, Phillips MSS, vol.5,

267; Jones, I.C., *op.cit.*, MacDonald, *op.cit.*, 44; *SC* 30 Oct. 1840; *ESJ* 6 Sep. 1876, 10 April 1878, 15 Jan. 1879.

40. Trinder, B., *Beyond the Bridges* (2006), 85-86; Pattison, A., *William Hazledine* (University of Birmingham thesis, 2011), *passim*.

41. *VCH*, vol. 6 (1), 256; Pattison, *op.cit.*, 54, 103; *SC* 5 Oct. 1827.

42. Trinder, *Beyond the Bridges*, 134; *ESJ* 2 May 1838; 28 April 1847; 12 May 1865; 22 Jan. 1879; *SC* 26 Oct. 1832; 24 April 1840.

43. *Shropshire Conservative* 18 June 1842; *ESJ* 1 May 1878; *VCH*, vol. 6 (1), 256-57; Trinder, *Beyond the Bridges*, 146-47.

44. MacDonald, *op.cit.*, 40-41; Review Publishing Co., *op.cit.* 12-13; *ESJ* 8 Jan. 1868; 3 June 1868; 5 Aug. 1868; 3 March 1869; 29 Dec. 1876; 25 Feb. 1885; *SC* 17 Nov. 1893; 13 July 1917; *Wellington Journal* 13 May 1905; 25 Nov. 1905. The winnower at Long Beach was observed by Henri Quinn.

45. I am grateful to Dr. David Jenkins for information about foundries at Market Drayton.

46. *Ludlow Advertiser* 14 July 1888, 15 Oct. 1892; inscriptions on Hodges family grave, St Giles, Ludford.

47. Earnshaw, *op.cit.*, 62; *SC* 15 Mar. 1907.

48. *Friends of the Ironbridge Gorge Museum Newsletter*, No. 30 (1978).

49. Jones, K.B., *The Wenlock Branch* (1998), 37; *SC* 25 April, 7 Nov. 1856, 8 Jan. 1893.

50. Christiansen, R., & Miller, R.W., *The Cambrian Railways* (1967), vol. 1, 138; vol. 2, 20, 110, 156-58; Watkins, *op.cit.* 333.

51. SA Deposited Plan, No 371, 30 Nov 1857; *VCH*, vol. 6 (1), 248; Trinder, *Beyond the Bridges*, 49-50; *SC* 4 Dec. 1863; *ESJ* 30 Oct. 1878.

52. Trinder, *Beyond the Bridges*, 50; *SC* 28 Nov. 1890.

53. Hughes, W.J., & Thomas, J.L., *The Sentinel*, vol.1 (1975); vol. 2 (1987), *passim*; *Steaming*, No.33 (1990).

54. Baldwin, M., Elliott, W., & Davis, J., *Cleobury Chronicles*, vol. 1 (1991), 40-47.

55. MacDonald, *op.cit.*, 42; *ESJ* 30 Jan. 1867; 3 March, 21 July 1880; 18 Jan. 1882; 12 Jan., 9 July 1887; *SC* 15 Dec. 1893; 13 March 1894; 19 June 1903; 26 Jan. 1940.

56. Trinder, *Beyond the Bridges*, 29-33.

57. *SC* 24 Oct 1975; Trinder, *Beyond the Bridges*, 150.

58. *ESJ* 14 May 1879; 31 Dec. 1884. I am grateful to Mrs. Stella Straughen for information on Kingsland.

59. Trinder, *Beyond the Bridges* (2006), 108-112.

60. *ESJ* 13 Oct. 1880, 18 May 1881; *SC* 1 May 1925, 7 April 1933; Trinder, *Beyond the Bridges*, 138-40.
61. *SC* 16 Dec. 1831; 6 Dec. 1865.
62. MacDonald, *op.cit.*, 47.
63. Wilding & Co., *Shropshire* (1914), 121; Trinder, *Beyond the Bridges*, 31.
64. *Daily News* 2 Nov. 1912.
65. Trinder, *Beyond the Bridges* (2006), 127-28.
66. Lee, M.J., 'Cherry Orchard: the Growth of a Victorian Suburb', in Trinder, B., ed., *Victorian Shrewsbury* (1984), 115-26; Trinder, *Beyond the Bridges*, 57, 122.
67. *ESJ* 6 Nov. 1865; 18 April 1866; Trinder, *Beyond the Bridges*, 91-93.
68. Lee, *op.cit.*, 119; Trinder, *Beyond the Bridges*, 59-61.
69. *SC* 31 Oct. 1851; *ESJ* 23 Feb., 2 March, 16 Aug. 1853; 9 May, 6 June 1866; 16 Jan. 1867; Trinder, *Beyond the Bridges*, 37-38.
70. Lee, *op.cit.*, 119-22; Trinder, *Beyond the Bridges*, 61-62.
71. Trinder, *Beyond the Bridges*, 96.
72. *ESJ* 26 Jan. 1853.
73. Hughes & Thomas, *op.cit.*, vol. 2, 120-28; Trinder, *Beyond the Bridges*, 164-65.
74. Trinder, *Beyond the Bridges*, 164-65; Wilding & Co., *Shropshire* (1935), 76-78; *SC* 15 Jan. 1926; Chatwood Security Co., leaflet, copy in Ironbridge Gorge Museum Library.
75. Trinder, *Beyond the Bridges*, 38-44.
76. *ex.inf.* the late Mr G.R. Fletcher; *SC* 13 April 1934; Trinder, *Beyond the Bridges*, 36, 165-66.
77. Temple, J.T., *Industrial Archaeology of Aviation in Shropshire* (1984); Trinder, *Beyond the Bridges*, 62-3.
78. Hardy, T., *The Life and Death of the Mayor of Casterbridge* (1886, Pan edn., 1978), 260-61.
79. I am grateful to Dr David Jenkins for information about Little Drayton.
80. Partridge, C.A., *Handbook to Ludlow* (1878), 129.
81. *VCH*, vol. 6 (1), 239-40; 281-82; Trinder, *Beyond the Bridges*, 19.
82. The engines were recorded on a 45 rpm record, *The Music of Machinery: Shrewsbury Pumping Station*, Big Ben Records, MOM1; Trinder, *Beyond the Bridges,* 20, 85.
83. Giles, C., & Williams, M., eds., *Ditherington Flax Mill and the Industrial Revolution* (2015), 105-11.
84. Trinder, *Beyond the Bridges,* 20; *VCH*, vol. 6 (1), 282.
85. Stratton, M., *Ironbridge and the Electric Revolution* (1994), 49-56.
86. Tucker, D.G., 'Electricity Generating Stations for Public Supply in the West Midlands, 1888-1977', *WMS*, vol. 10 (1977), 8-28.
87. *Shropshire Magazine*, Oct. 1976; *Ironbridge Quarterly*, 1993, No.4.
88. SC 1 June 1923, 27 Jan. 1938. *Ex inf* Mrs Jen Davies.
89. *Ludlow Advertiser* 8 Aug. 1947.
90. Stratton, M., & Trinder, B., *Twentieth Century Industrial Archaeology* (2000), 111.

Chapter 4

1. Toghill, P., *Geology in Shropshire* (1990), 130-31.
2. Ward, T.O., *The Medical Topography of Shrewsbury* (1841), 63.
3. Murchison, Sir R., *The Silurian System* (1839), 92-94; *Shropshire Conservative* 24 April 1841.
4. *VCH*, vol. 8, 279-80; *SC* 8 May 1812, 29 Jan. 1831; SFWI, *Shropshire within Living Memory* (1992), 52; *ESJ* 15 April 1868.
5. *VCH*, vol. 8, 322.
6. Brook, F., & Allbutt, M., *The Shropshire Lead Mines* (1973), 65-66.
7. *ESJ* 22 March 1843; *Shropshire Magazine* January 1970, 28-29.
8. *VCH*, vol. 8, 83; *SC* 27 Mar. 1846; for Lower Long Wood see chapter 2, 23-24, 26.
9. Murchison, *op.cit.*, 83; *VCH*, vol. 8, 211; *ESJ* 3 June 1835.
10. *VCH*, vol.8, 103; *SC* 26 Jan. 1810; 25 Dec. 1874.
11. *VCH*, vol.8, 280; Brown, I.J., *The Mines of Shropshire* (1976), 80-81.
12. *VCH*, vol.8, 257, 279-80; Morgan, R.C., *The Life of Richard Weaver* (1861).
13. Poyner, D., & Evans, R., 'The Wyre Forest Coalfield', *Cleobury Chronicles*, vol. 3 (1994), 7-17.
14. Nair, G., & Poyner, D., 'The Coming of Coal: Industrial Development in a South Shropshire parish', *MH*, vol. 18 (1993), 87-103; *SC* 17 May 1878.
15. Nair & Poyner, *op.cit.*; *SC* 16 April 1804, 23 Dec. 1813, 4 Jan., 1 March 1815, 8 Aug., 15 Aug. 1817.
16. Smith, W., & Beddoes, K., *The Cleobury Mortimer & Ditton Priors Light Railway* (1980), 23, 80; *SC* 27 May 1881.
17. Poyner & Evans, *op.cit.*, 11-16; Brown, *op.cit.* 68-77.
18. SSWI, *op.cit,* 29, 45.
19. *SC* 19 Sep. 1919.
20. Toghill, *op.cit.*, 129-30.
21. Thomas, R.D., *Industries of the Morda Valley* (1939), 12-18.
22. *Ibid*, 18-19.
23. *Ibid*, 11.
24. Stratton, M.J., *The Terracotta Revival* (1993), 51.

25. Barnes, J., *Thomas Barnes of Farnworth and the Quinta* (2012); Newman, J., & Pevsner, N., *The Buildings of England: Shropshire* (2006), 683-85.

26. Bridges, A.J., *Industrial Locomotives of Cheshire, Shropshire and Herefordshire* (1977), 78-79; Brown, *op.cit.*, 82; *SC* 23 July 1915.

27. *ESJ* 8 July 1857.

28. Toghill, *op.cit.*, 132-34; Marriott, J., Reid, M., Barratt, G. & White, R., *A Conservation Plan for the Historic Mining Landscape of the Clee Hills, South Shropshire* (2 vols., 2008). University of Birmingham for English Heritage, provides a comprehensive multi-period interpretation.

29. Smith & Beddoes, *op.cit.*, 73-84.

30. Murchison, *op.cit.*, 122.

31. *Ibid*, 123.

32. Goodman, K.W.G., *Hammerman's Hill* (University of Keele thesis, 1978).

33. Anon, *The History of Isaac Jenkins* (n.d.), 12.

34. Hewitt, P.B. *The Mining, Quarrying and allied industries of Clee Hill* (Wolverhampton Polytechnic thesis, 1991).

35. HRO, inventory of Richard Plummer of Ludlow, 1692.

36. Hewitt, *op.cit.*, 26-58; *SC* 18 June 1778, 30 Dec. 1780.

37. Commonplace Book relating to Thomas Botfield, *penes* A.M.W. Smith of Ivy Hatch, Kent.

38. *ESJ* 11 June 1845, 20 April 1853; *SC* 18 April 1851.

39. *ESJ* 18 May 1887.

40. Hewitt, *op.cit.*, 75, 83, 108, 173-74.

41. *Ibid*, 187.

42. *ESJ* 16 Oct. 1861.

43. Hewitt, *op.cit.*, 15, 187, 169; Jenkins, A.E. *Titterstone Clee Hills* (1988), 29-32; *ESJ* 12 Jan. 1876.

44. SA, GWR, *Regulations for the Clee Hill Branch* (1933).

45. *ESJ* 11 May, 13 July 1881; *SC* 15 July 1881.

46. Jenkins, *op.cit.*, 35.

47. Hewitt, *op.cit.*, 169.

48. Toghill, *op.cit.*, 125-29.

49. Wanklyn, M., 'Industrial Development in the Ironbridge Gorge before Abraham Darby, *WMS*, vol. 15 (1982), 3-7; Trinder, B., *The Industrial Revolution in Shropshire* (3rd edn., 2000), 1-19.

50. Alfrey, J., & Clark, K., *The Landscape of Industry* (1993), 115, 149-50; Trinder, *op.cit.*, 138-40.

51. Alfrey & Clark, *op.cit.*, 180.

52. *Ibid.*, 184-85; Trinder, *op.cit.*,140-41.

53. Trinder, *op.cit.*, 141-43; Jones, K., Hunt, M.W., Malam, J., & Trinder, B., 'Holywell Lane', *IAR*, vol. 6 (1982), 163-85.

54. Trinder, *op.cit.*, 154; *ESJ* 4 Jan. 1860.

55. Alfrey & Clark, *op.cit.*, 136-39; Cossons, N., & Trinder, B., *The Iron Bridge* (2002), 39-46.

56. Edwards, H., *The Commercial Centres of Madeley and Dawley* 1790-1940 (Ironbridge Institute dissertation, 1988-89).

57. Trinder, B., 'Recent Research on Early Shropshire Railways', Lewis, M.J.T., *Early Railways 2:* (2003), 10-24.

58. Smith, R.S., 'England's first rails: a re-consideration', *Renaissance & Modern Studies*, vol.4 (1960), 119-34; Alfrey & Clark, *op.cit.*, 70-74; Lewis, M., *Early Wooden Railways* (1970), 95-102.

59. Jones, N.W., 'A Wooden Wagon Way at Bedlam Furnace', *PMA*, vol.21 (1987), 259-66.

60. Trinder, B., ed., *The Most Extraordinary District* (2005), 39-40.

61. Trinder, *Industrial Revolution in Shropshire* (2000), 61-62.

62. *Ibid*, 71-75; Alfrey & Clark, *op.cit.*, 70-74; Lewis, *op.cit.*, 157-79, 193-94; Trinder, B., 'Recent Research on Early Shropshire Railways', Lewis, M.J.T., *Early Railways 2:* (2003), 10-24.

63. Trinder, *Industrial Revolution in Shropshire* (2000), 107; *IQ*, 1990 (3), 4-5.

64. *SNL* No. 39 (1970), 6-7.

65. Gale, W.K.V., & Nicholls,C.R., *The Lilleshall Company* (1979), 76.

66. Bridges, *op.cit.*, 83-84.

67. Trinder, *Industrial Revolution in Shropshire* (2000), 63-64.

68. *Ibid*, 64-70.

69. Williams, W.H., 'The Canal Inclined Planes of East Shropshire', *Journal of Industrial Archaeology*, vol.2, 37-56; Tonkinson, R. Ll., *Inclined Planes on the Shropshire Canals* (Birmingham School of Architecture thesis, 1964).

70. Alfrey & Clark, *op.cit.*, 74; Beal, R., *The Old Wind: a Preliminary Report* (research paper, 1988); Trinder, *Industrial Revolution in Shropshire* (2000), 67-70.

71. *ESJ* 26 June, 17 July 1861.

72. Wanklyn, *op.cit.*, 3-7.

73. Alfrey & Clark, *op.cit.* 40-46.

74. Brown, I.J., 'Underground in the Ironbridge Gorge', *IAR*, vol. 3 (1979), 158-69.

75. Trinder, *Industrial Revolution in Shropshire* (2000), 45-54; *VCH*, vol. 11, 46.

76. Leese, J.S., 'Old English Power Plants', *Power* (New York), vol. 36 (1912), quoted in Trinder, *The Most Extraordinary District* (2005), 133-34.

77. Isaac, S., *Granville Colliery Horse Gin* (research paper, 1988).

78. Holmes, D., *The Working of the Silurian Wenlock Limestone in South-East Shropshire* (Ironbridge Institute dissertation 1986-87); Williams, G., *The Wenlock Limestone Industry: an historical note* (1990); Alfrey & Clark, *op.cit.*, 34-37; Williams, G., *Much Wenlock's Limestone Quarries* (revised edn., 2014).

79. Alfrey & Clark, *op.cit.*, 34-37; Smith, S.B., *A View from the Iron Bridge* (1979), 40-42, 50-51; Brown, I.J., *The Mines of Shropshire* (1976), 50; Brown, I.J., 'Underground in the Ironbridge Gorge', *IAR*, vol. 3 (1979), 60-62.

80. Trinder, *Industrial Revolution in Shropshire* (2000), 44.

81. Trinder, B.S., *Barges & Bargemen* (2005), 132.

82. Adams, D., & Hazeley, J., *Survey of the Church Aston-Lilleshall Mining Area* (1970).

83. Trinder, *Industrial Revolution in Shropshire* (2000), 43; Brown, I.J., *The Mines of Shropshire* (1976), 13-17.

84. Alfrey & Clark, *op.cit.*, 172-73.

85. *Ibid*, 49-55, 101-04.

86. Gale & Nicholls, *op.cit.*, 40-41.

87. Jones, A., *Finds Typologies: Pottery I: the coarse earthenwares* (research paper, 1988).

88. Alfrey & Clark, *op.cit.*, 95-98.

89. Jones, A., Higgins, D. & Trueman, M., *11 Benthall Lane* (research paper, 1987); Higgins, D.A., *The Interpretation and Regional Study of Clay Tobacco Pipes: a Case Study of the Broseley District* (University of Liverpool, PhD thesis, 1987).

90. Higgins, D., Morriss, R., & Trueman, M., *The Broseley Pipeworks: an archaeological and historical evaluation* (research paper, 1988).

91. Trinder, *Industrial Revolution in Shropshire* (2000), 87; Alfrey & Clark, *op.cit.*, 98-99; Houghton, A.W.J., 'The Caughley Porcelain Works', *Journal of Industrial Archaeology*, vol. 5 (1968), 184-92.

92. Trinder, *Industrial Revolution in Shropshire* (2000), 87-90; Edmundson, R., 'Coalport China Works', *IAR*, vol. 3 (1979), 122-45; Edmundson, R., 'Bradley and Coalport Pottery 1796-1800', *Transactions of the Northern Ceramic Society*, vol. 4 (1981), 127-55; Blake Roberts, D., & Blake Roberts, G., 'The results of recent excavations in Coalport', *English Ceramic Circle Transactions*, vol. 2 (1981), 71-81.

93. Alfrey & Clark, *op.cit.*, 106-08; Herbert, A.T., 'Jackfield Decorative Tiles in Use', *IAR*, vol. 3 (1979), 146-52; Strachan, S., 'Henry Powell Dunnill', *Journal of the Tiles & Architectural Ceramics Society*, vol. 3 (1981), 71-81; Herbert, A.T., & Huggins, K., *The Decorative Tile* (1995),

51-57; Pearson, L., *Tile Gazetteer: A Guide to British Tile and Architectural Ceramic Installations* (2005).

94. Cox, N., 'Imagination and Innovation … the first Abraham Darby', *IAR*, vol. 12 (1990), 130-31.

95. Trinder, *Industrial Revolution in Shropshire* (2000), 16-17, 91; Simpson, S., *The Agreeable Historian* (1746), 839-40, quoted in Trinder, *The Most Extraordinary District* (2005), 19-20.

96. Trinder, *Industrial Revolution in Shropshire* (2000), 16, 91-92.

97. *Ibid*, 94.

98. *Ibid*, 16.

99. *Ibid*, 90, 105-06; Brown, I.J., & Trinder, B., *The Coalport Tar Tunnel* (1971).

100. Trinder, *Industrial Revolution in Shropshire* (2000), 92-94; *SC* 3 Dec. 1830; Gale & Nicholls, *op.cit.*, 52, 61-62, 65, 82, 90; Trinder, *The Most Extraordinary District* (2005), 133.

101. Trinder, *Industrial Revolution in Shropshire* (2000), 53; *VCH*, vol. 11, 328; *SC* 11 Feb. 1831.

102. Stratton, M.J., *Ironbridge and the Electric Revolution* (1994).

103. The sources on pit girls are reproduced in a teaching pack, *Shropshire Pit Girls*, published by the Ironbridge Gorge Museum in 1986.

104. Alfrey & Clark, *op.cit.*, 61-70.

105. King, P.W., 'Sir Clement Clarke and the Adoption of Coal in Metallurgy', *TNS*, vol.73 (2001).

106. Cox, N., 'Imagination and Innovation … the first Abraham Darby', *IAR*, vol. 12 (1990); Trinder, *Industrial Revolution in Shropshire* (2000), 21-26. For Tern Forge see chapter 2, pp.15-17.

107. Ince, L., The Knight Family and the British Iron Industry (1991), 33-45; Cox, op.cit. 131-32; Trinder, *Industrial Revolution in Shropshire* (2000), 26-32; King, P.W., 'The choice of fuels in the eighteenth-century iron industry: The Coalbrookdale Accounts re-considered', *EcHR*, vol. 64 (2011), 132-56.

108. *SC* 11 Nov., 9 Dec. 1904.

109. *SC* 7 June, 4 Oct. 1872, 14 Nov. 1873; Smith, S.B., 'The Construction of the Blists Hill Ironworks', *IAR*, vol 3 (1979), 170-78; Trinder, *Industrial Revolution in Shropshire* (2000), 90.

110. Hayman, R., 'The Cranage brothers and eighteenth-century forge technology', *Historical Metallurgy*, vol. 38 (2004); Ironbridge Gorge Museum Archaeology Unit, *The Upper Forge Coalbrookdale* (research paper, 1996).

111. Trinder, *Industrial Revolution in Shropshire* (2000), 77; *VCH*, vol. 10, 352; Terry, R., *History*

and *Archaeology of the Linley Valley* (Ironbridge Institute assignment, 1988-89).

112. Alfrey & Clark, *op.cit.*, 89-91; *SC* 3 Jan. 1806.

113. Belford, P., 'Forging Ahead in Coalbrookdale: Historical Archaeology at the Upper Forge', *IAR*, vol. 25 (2003), 59-62; Wanklyn, M., 'Iron and Steelworks in Coalbrookdale in 1645', *SNL* No. 44 (1973), 3-6.

114. *VCH*, vol. 11, 260-61; 29 April 1870, 4 Jan. 1878.

115. *VCH*, vol. 11, 164.

116. Trinder, *Industrial Revolution in Shropshire* (2000), 80-82.

117. Norris, G., *A Survey of the Heavy Erecting Shop, Coalbrookdale* (Ironbridge Institute dissertation, 1980-90).

118. *ESJ* 17 Jan. 1866; I am grateful to Myfanwy Eaves and David Reynolds of the New Zealand Historic Places Trust for confirming that the statue remains *in situ*.

119. Cossons, N., & Trinder, B., *The Iron Bridge* (2nd edn.,2002), 9-56.

Chapter 5

1. Young, A., *Tours in England and Wales* (1934), 162.

2. BPP, 1840, XXIII, *Report … Hand Loom Weavers*, 352.

3. Trinder, B., & Cox, J., eds., *Yeomen & Colliers* (1980), 61-64; Trinder, B., & Cox, N., eds., *Miners and Mariners* (2000), 73-75.

4. Green, H., 'The Linen Industry of Shropshire', *IAR*, vol. 5 (1981), 115; Nightingale, J. *The Beauties of England and Wales, vol. 13, pt. 1 Shropshire* (1813), 35.

5. Williams, A.B., 'The Rural Industries of Llanymynech', *Montgomeryshire Collections*, vol. 47 (1974), 67-74.

6. Booth, D.T.W., *Watermills on the River Rea* (1990), 9; *VCH*, vol. 8, 156, 175; vol. 11 316; Trinder, B., & Cox, J., *Yeomen & Colliers* (1980), 64.

7. *SC* 25 Nov. 1814.

8. Lloyd, D., *Broad Street* (1979), 57; BPP, 1840, XXXIV, *Report … Hand Loom Weavers*, 543.

9. Thomas, R.D., *Industries of the Morda Valley* (1978), 29.

10. Bagshaw, S., *History, Gazetteer and Directory of Shropshire* (1851), 529. I am grateful to Ann Pritchett for information about Carding Mill.

11. Tucker, G., *Some Watermills of South-west Shropshire* (1991), 11-12.

12. LJRO, inventories from the Peculiar of Bridgnorth.

13. Mendenhall, T.C., *The Shrewsbury Drapers* (1953); *VCH*, vol. 6 (1), 140-42, 203-04.

14. Pennant, T., *Tours in Wales* (1883), vol. 3, 224; Owen, H., & Blakeway, J.B., *The History of Shrewsbury* (1826), 551; *ESJ* 3 Dec. 1794; *VCH*, vol. 6 (1), 204, 252.

15. Trinder, B., & Cox, J., *Yeomen & Colliers* (1980), 47-61; LJRO, inventories from Shrewsbury.

16. *ESJ* 3 Dec. 1794.

17. Aikin, A., *Journal of a Tour through North Wales* (1797), 77; *ESJ* 18 Feb., 3 Mar., 23 June, 28 July 1824.

18. *ESJ* 18 June 1800; *SC* 15 June 1830; Nightingale, *op.cit.*, 164.

19. SC 9 Oct. 1795; Hulbert, C., *Memoirs of Seventy Years* (1852), 194-95, 222-23; Hulbert, C., *History and Description of the County of Salop* (1837), 307-08.

20. Hulbert, C., *Memoirs of Seventy Years* (1852), 194-95, 222-23; Hulbert, C., *History and Description of the County of Salop* (1837), 307-08.

21. Jones, I.C., *The Industrial Archaeology of Coleham Riverside* (Ironbridge Institute assignment 1991-92); SA holds a copy of the photograph; Trinder, B., *Beyond the Bridges* (2006), 82-84; *VCH*, vol. 6 (1), 253.

22. Thomas, *op.cit.*, 25-28.

23. Higgins, D., Morriss, R., & Trueman, M., *The Broseley Pipeworks* (research paper, 1988), 11.

24. *SC* 24 Aug. 1804, 8 July 1808, 17 Jan. 1902.

25. The authoritative work on the Ditherington Flax Mill is now Giles, C., & Williams, M., eds., *Ditherington Flax Mill and the Industrial Revolution* (2015). Its historiography can be traced through the following: Bannister, T., 'The First Iron-framed Buildings', *Architectural Review*, no. 107 (1950), 231-46; Rimmer, W.G., *Marshalls of Leeds* (1960); Skempton, A.W., & Johnson, H.R., 'The First Iron Frames', *Architectural Review*, no.131 (1962), 175-86; Tann, J., *The Development of the Factory* (1970), 135-37; Macleod, M., Trinder, B., & Worthington, M., *The Ditherington Flax Mills, Shrewsbury: a survey and historical evaluation* (Ironbridge Institute research paper 1988); Trinder, B., 'Ditherington Flax Mill – a re-evaluation', *Textile History*, vol. 23, 189-224; Trinder, B., *Beyond the Bridges* (2006), 151-55; *VCH*, vol. 6 (1), 254-56.

26. Skempton, A.W., 'Telford and the Design for a new London Bridge', Penfold, A., ed., *Thomas Telford: Engineer* (1980), 71, 74-76.

27. Giles & Williams, *op.cit.*, 103-04.

28. *SC* 1 Sep. 1797.

29. Giles & Williams, *op.cit.*, 49-55.

30. Giles & Williams, *op.cit.*, 73-90.

31. Giles, C., & Goodall, I., *Yorkshire Textile Mills 1770-1930* (1992); Watson, M., 'Broadford Works Aberdeen', *Textile History*, vol. 23 (1992), 225-42; Falconer, K.A., 'Fireproof Mills – the Widening Perspectives', *IAR*, vol. 16 (1993), 11-26.

32. Giles & Williams, *op.cit.*, 93-103.

33. SA, Salop Fire Office Registers, 4791/1/4, 81, policy no. 2061; 4791/1/5, 404, policy no. 3819; 4791/1/9, 381, policy no. 10833; J.B. Lawson, 'Thomas Telford in Shrewsbury', Penfold, A., *op.cit.* 17-18; Hobbs, J.L. *Shrewsbury Street Names* (1954), 106; Wakelin, P., *Historical Applications of British Fire Insurance Records* (Ironbridge Institute dissertation, 1984); Giles & Williams, *op.cit.*, 112-16.

34. SA (formerly Shrewsbury Borough Library Collection), D13322.

35. Macleod, Trinder & Worthington, *op.cit.*, 14; *SC* 17, 24 Dec. 1897.

36. Tann, *op.cit.*, 42-43; Hulbert, C., *History and Description of the County of Salop* (1837), 312; ESJ 9 Aug. 1837, 14 March 1838.

37. Green, H., 'The Linen Industry of Shropshire', *IAR*, vol. 5 (1981), 114-21; Trinder, *Beyond the Bridges*, 155-57; *SC* 3 Nov. 1843.

38. Green, *op.cit.*, 114-21; Hulbert, C., *Memoirs of Seventy Years* (1852), 195, 234, 255.

39. Hulbert, C., *History and Description of the County of Salop* (1837), 308; SA, Pidgeon MS 3056, 15, 55; *SC* 5 Oct. 1827; Trinder, *Beyond the Bridges*, 87.

40. Wright, T., *History & Antiquities of Ludlow* (1826), 81-82; *SC* 26 July 1777, 15 March 1786.

41. Bagshaw, S., *History, Gazetteer & Directory of Shropshire* (1851), 342; *SC* 14 Oct. 1831.

42. BPP, 1840, XXXIV, *Report ... Hand Loom Weavers*, 541; *SC* 13 July 1798, 5 May 1815, 22 Nov. 1844.

43. *ESJ* 17 April, 17 July 1811.

44. Rowley, N. & S., *Market Drayton: a study in social history* (1966), 55-56. I am grateful to Dr. David Jenkins for advice on industry in Market Drayton.

Chapter 6

1. Toghill, P., *Geology in Shropshire* (1990), 65-67.

2. Trinder, B., *Industrial Revolution in Shropshire* (2000), 16-17.

3. Brook, F., & Allbut, M., *The Shropshire Lead Mines* (1973), 23-26; Burt, R., Waite, P., & Burnley, R., *The Mines of Shropshire & Montgomeryshire* (1990), 40.

4. Brook & Allbut, *op.cit.*, 64-73.

5. Burt, Waite & Burnley, *op.cit.*, xi-xv.

6. SA, Watton Colln., vol. 2, 332.

7. Burton, Waite & Burnley, *op.cit.*, xxv-xxix.

8. Burt, Waite & Burnley, *op.cit.*, 27-32; *VCH*, vol. 8, 322.

9. Brook & Allbut, *op.cit.*, 65-66.

10. Tonks, E.S., *The Snailbeach Railway* (1974), 11.

11. *Ibid*, 23-24, 33, 36, 42.

12. Burt, Waite & Burnley, *op.cit.*, 20-22; Brook & Allbut, *op.cit.*, 32-43.

13. Burt, Waite & Burnley, *op.cit.*, 14, 34; *SC* 22 Aug. 1902.

14. Brook & Allbut, *op.cit.*, 44-50.

15. *SC* 15 Jan. 1830.

16. *VCH*, vol. 8, 155, 179-80; *SC* 18 Nov. 1832; *ESJ* 1 Feb. 1843; *Shropshire Magazine*, April 1959, 21-22; Allbut, M., & Brook, F., 'The South Shropshire Lead Mines', *Journal of Industrial Archaeology*, vol. 10 (1973), 50-54; *SC* 1 Aug. 1845. For smelters in the Ironbridge Gorge see chapter 4, pp.117-18.

17. Brown, I.J., *The Mines of Shropshire* (1976), 102; *VCH*, vol. 8, 137; Reminiscences of Mr J. Wylde of Oswestry, copy in Ironbridge Gorge Museum.

18. Brown, *op.cit.*, 105; *VCH*, vol. 8, 124, 181.

19. Burton, Waite & Burnley, *op.cit.*, xxvi.

20. Murchison, R., *The Silurian System* (1839), 188; Rowley, R.T., *The History of the South Shropshire Landscape* (University of Oxford thesis, 1967), 186.

21. Carlon, C.J., *The Gallantry Bank Copper Mines* (1981), 10-13; Cox, N., 'Imagination and Innovation ... the first Abraham Darby', *IAR*, vol. 12 (1990), 130-31.

22. Carlon, *op.cit.*, 13-14; Burt, Waite & Burnley, *op.cit.*, 7.

23. SA 322/62. I am grateful to Professor Peter Edwards for this reference.

24. Carlon, *op.cit.*, 8-9; Carlon, C.J., *The Eardiston Copper Mine* (1981); Burt, Waite & Burnley, *op.cit.*, 18; *ESJ* 28 Aug. 1839.

25. Macleod, M., Stratton, M., & Trinder, B., *Llanymynech Hill* (research paper, 1987), 17-18; Burt, Waite & Burnley, *op.cit.*, 8.

26. *ESJ* 15 Nov. 1854; *SC* 9 Oct. 1863.

27. SA (formerly Shrewsbury Borough Library) MS 6387.

28. SA QR/390/196, January 1844; Ward, T.O., *Medical Topography of Shrewsbury* (1841), 65; *ESJ* 12 June 1878; *SC* 19 June 1914.

29. SA (formerly Shrewsbury Borough Library), MS 18673; Trinder, B., *Beyond the Bridges* (2006), 87.

30. Ranger, W., *Report to the General Board of Health on ... Shrewsbury* (1854), 68-71; *ESJ* 18 May 1853; *SC* 31 March 1883.

31. *SC* 27 April, 4 May, 25 May 1894.

Chapter 7

1. Robinson, D.H., *The Wandering Worfe* (1980), 73-74; MacMillan, B.I., *History of a water supply to Wolverhampton 1847-1947* (1947), 33, 38-39, 45, 53.

2. Bridges, A.M., *Industrial Locomotives of Cheshire, Shropshire & Herefordshire* (1977), 75.

3. Davidson, I., 'George Deacon and the Vyrnwy Works', *TNS*, vol. 59 (1987-88), 81-96.

4. The Upper Severn Navigation is described in detail in Trinder, B., *Barges & Bargemen* (2005).

5. LJRO, probate inventories from the Diocese of Lichfield and the Peculiar of Bridgnorth.

6. University of Wolverhampton, Gloucester Port Books database.

7. Trinder, B., *Industrial Revolution in Shropshire* (2000), 54-59; Trinder, *Barges & Bargemen* (2005), 136-37; *SC* 1 Feb. 1895; *Wellington Journal* 23 March 1895; Powell, J. & Vanns, M.A., *South Telford* (1995), 113.

8. SA, Watton Colln., vol. 10, 280; Trinder, *Barges & Bargemen*, 98, 115-18.

9. *Gentlemen's Magazine*, vol. 28 (1758), 277; reproduced in Trinder, *Barges & Bargemen* (2005), 143-44.

10. Trinder, *Barges & Bargemen* (2005), 22-37; Smith, S.B., *A View from the Iron Bridge* (1979), *passim*.

11. *SC* 25 Sep. 1812; Hulbert, C., *History & Antiquities of … Salop* (1837), 5-6; Preston, R.A., 'The *Eliza*: a Nineteenth century Trow at Shrewsbury', *TSAS*, vol. 68 (1993), 116-17.

12. Harral, T., *Picturesque Views of the Severn* (1824), 206; Trinder, *Barges & Bargemen* (2005), 22-35, 134.

13. Trinder, *Barges & Bargemen* (2005), 98-99; *SC* 27 Nov. 1857.

14. Hulbert, C., *op.cit*, 343-48; reproduced in Trinder, *Barges & Bargemen* (2005), 144-45; *SC* 4 Dec. 1784.

15. Quoted in Trinder, *Most Extraordinary District* (2005), 113-16.

16. SA 7112.

17. Trinder, *Barges & Bargemen* (2005), 64, 136; *SC* 25 Oct. 1805.

18. Trinder, *Barges & Bargemen* (2005), 42-45.

19. Duckworth, S., *The Severn Navigation and River Wharf sites in the Ironbridge Gorge* (1987-88). Ironbridge Institute dissertation.

20. Trinder, *Barges & Bargemen* (2005), 52-58.

21. *Ibid*, 56-57; Trinder, *Most Extraordinary District* (2005), 113-16.

22. Trinder, *Barges & Bargemen* (2005), 48-51.

23. Pannett, D.M., 'Fish Weirs of the River Severn', *Folk Life*, vol. 26 (1987-88), 54-61; *SC* 10 July 1857; Trinder, *Barges & Bargemen* (2005), 16-18.

24. Trinder, *Barges & Bargemen* (2005), 15-16; Denton, J.H., & Lewis, M.J.T., 'The River Tern Navigation', *JRCHS*, vol. 23 (1977), 56-63.

25. Hadfield, C., *Canals of the West Midlands* (1966), 159-65.

26. Clayton, A.R.K., 'The Shrewsbury and Newport canals', Penfold, A., ed., *Thomas Telford* (1980), 23-40.

27. Hadfield, C., *Thomas Telford's Temptation* (1993), 81-87; Healey, J., *Longdon-upon-Tern Aqueduct* (Ironbridge Institute dissertation, 1989-90).

28. Trinder, *Beyond the Bridges* (2006), 142-44.

29. *Ibid*, 149-50.

30. Hadfield, C., *Canals of the West Midlands* (1966), 166-96, 231-51; Wilson, E., *The Ellesmere & Llangollen Canal* (1975), *passim*.

31. Wilson, *op.cit.*, 49-57.

32. *Ibid*, 71-73.

33. Wrexham County Borough Council and RCAHMW, *Pontcysyllte Aqueduct & Canal: Nomination as a World Heritage Site* (2011); Wakelin, P., *Pontcysyllte Aqueduct and Canal: World Heritage Site* (2015).

34. Hadfield, *Thomas Telford's Temptation* (1993),33-34, 39-40, 94-99.

35. Morris, J., *The Shropshire Union Canal* (1991).

36. *Ibid*, 63; Hadfield, *Canals of the West Midlands* (1966), 192.

37. Hadfield, *Canals of the West Midlands* (1966), 231-35.

38. Butterfield, R., *The Records of the Canal Wharf at Wappenshall* (1989-90); Guthrie, J., & Pudney, C., *Wappenshall Junction, Shropshire* (1989-90), both Ironbridge Institute dissertations; Trinder, B., *Industrial Revolution in Shropshire* (2000), 128-30.

39. Hadfield, C., *The Canals of South Wales and the Border* (1960), 191-98; Barnes, A., *A New Map of the Kington-Leominster-Stourport Canal* (1977); Dean, R.J., *Map of the Kington, Leominster and Stourport Canal* (1968).

40. Markham, S., *John Loveday of Caversham* (1984), 121; Fiennes, C., *The Journeys of Celia Fiennes* (1947), 226; Nightingale, J., *The Beauties of England & Wales, vol. 13, pt.,1, Shropshire* (1813), 38.

41. For the background to the turnpike road system and chronological lists of Acts, see Albert, W., *The Turnpike Road System in England 1663-1841* (1972), Pawson, E., *Transport & Economy: the Turnpike Roads of Eighteenth-century England* (1977).

42. SA 560/739. See Appendix Two.

43. SA 356/23/307-09; SA 356/23/312-13.
44. *SC* 7 April 1824; *ESJ* 30 Nov. 1815, 4 June 1818, 2 July, 17 Sep. 1828; Trinder, *Beyond the Bridges* (2006), 79-81, 120, 137.
45. *SC* 20 Sep., 15 Dec. 1809
46. Brown, Y., *Ruyton-XI-Towns* (1988), 63-66; *SC* 7 April 1826.
47. Trinder, B., *The Making of the Industrial Landscape* (1996), 136-38.
48. Blackwall, A.H., *Historic Bridges of Shropshire* (1985).
49. Blackwall, *op.cit.*, 16-22, 47-53; Cossons, N., & Trinder, B., *The Iron Bridge* (2002), 31-51, 76-78, 83; Trinder, B., 'Coalport Bridge: A Study in Historical Interpretation', *IAR*, vol. 3 (1979), 153-57.
50. Owen, H., & Blakeway, J.B., *History of Shrewsbury* (1826), 516-19; Evason, C., 'Downhill Journey: Stage Coaching in Shrewsbury 1833-61', Trinder, B., ed., *Victorian Shrewsbury* (1984), 78-95.
51. *ESJ* 12 Aug. 1857; *Pugh's Hereford Journal* 7 Oct. 1779; SA Watton Colln., vol 8, 102; Ironbridge Gorge Museum, *Sale Catalogue, Britannia Hotel*, Shrewsbury (1903); Champion, W.A., 'John Ashby and ... the *Lion Inn*, Shrewsbury', *TSAS*, vol. 75, (2000), 49-55.
52. Lloyd, D., *Broad Street* (1979), 31-32; Lloyd, D., Howell, P., & Richards, M., *The Feathers* (1986).
53. Quartermain, J., Trinder, B., & Turner, R., *Thomas Telford's Holyhead Road: the A5 in North Wales* (2003). Trinder, B., 'The Holyhead Road: an engineering project in its social context', in Penfold, A., *Thomas Telford* (1980), 41-61; Hughes, M., 'Telford, Parnell and the Great Irish Road', *Journal of Transport History*, vol. 6 (1964), 199-209.
54. Trinder, *Beyond the Bridges* (2006), 48-49, 128-29.
55. *VCH*, vol. 3, 173, 193.
56. *Wellington Journal* 30 May 1903.
57. *SC* 16 April 1926, 14 Feb. 7 March 1930; 6 Feb., 13 March 1931, 26 May 1933; *VCH* vol. 3, 193-95; *Trinder, Beyond the Bridges* (2006), 19.
58. *Trinder, Beyond the Bridges* (2006), 23; Hibbs, J., 'The Shropshire Omnibus Association: a note on a producers' co-operative'. *Transport History*, vol. 2 (1969).
59. *SC* 19 March 1937.
60. MacDermott, E.T., *A History of the Great Western Railway* (2nd edn., 1964), vol. 1, 177-204; Christiansen, R., *A Regional History of the Railways of Great Britain, vol. 7, The West Midlands* (1973), 80-92, 154-61; *SC* 23 Sep. 1853; 5 Jan. 1855.
61. Morriss, R., *Rail Centres: Shrewsbury* (1986); Morris, R., *Railways of Shropshire* (1963); Morriss, R., 'A Gazetteer of Passenger Railway Stations in Shropshire', *TSAS*, vol. 64 (1983-84), 89-106; Burke, J.P., 'Railway Cross-roads of the North-west: Shrewsbury', *Modern Railways*, vol. 17 (1963), 47-56; *VCH*, vol 6 (1), 246-48.
62. Smith, W.H., 'Craven Arms & Stokesay Station', *British Railway Journal* No. 32 (1990), 90-107.

Chapter 8

1. Loch, J., *An Account of the Improvements on the Estate of the Marquess of Stafford in the Counties of Stafford & Salop* (1820).
2. Mercer, E., *English Architecture to 1900: The Shropshire Experience* (2003); Newman, J., & Pevsner, N., *The Buildings of England: Shropshire* (2006).
3. Tolley, R.S., 'The Changing Industrial Geography of Eastern Shropshire', *WMS*, vol. 5 (1972), 1-10.
4. Rix, M., 'Industrial Archaeology', *The Amateur Historian*, vol. 2 (1955), 225-29; *SC* 19 Jan. 1951, 20 Feb 1953.
5. Robinson, D.H., 'An account of the Shropshire Canals', *Transactions of the Caradoc & Severn Valley Field Club*, vol. 11 (1939-42), 44-52.
6. Trinder, B., *Fifty Years in Ellesmere* (1986); *SC* 22 Apl. 1934.
7. Emden, P.H., *Quakers in Commerce* (1939); Raistrick, A., *Dynasty of Ironfounders* (1953).
8. Rolt, L.T.C., *Landscape with Canals* (1977), 54-56.
9. Trinder, B., 'Industrial Archaeology in the twentieth-century context', Cossons, N., *Perspectives on Industrial Archaeology* (2000), 39-56.
10. Marshall, J., *The Severn Valley Railway* (1989), 168-69.
11. Giles, C., & Williams, M., eds., *Ditherington Flax Mill and the Industrial Revolution* (2015).
12. Trinder, B., 'The Heritage of the Iron Industry in the Coalbrookdale Coalfield ... 1959-2005', Kiem, K., ed., *Konversionen: Zum Umgang mit Bauten der Eisenindustrie in Europa* (2007), 43-56.
13. Cossons, N., 'Ironbridge – The First Ten Years', *IAR*, vol. 3 (1979), 179-86; Beale, C., *The Ironbridge Spirit* (2014).
14. Giles, C., & Williams, M., *Ditherington Flax Mill and the Industrial Revolution* (2015).

Index of Names
including companies & organisations

INDEX OF PLACES

Places named in this index are in Shropshire unless otherwise indicated. The ancient parishes of entries which are not themselves ancient parishes are indicated: e.g. *Adeney, Edgmond*; and cross-references are provided to all entries which relate to particular ancient parishes: e.g. *Alberbury*, see also *Bulthey, Bragginton, Criggion, Little Shrawardine, Loton Park, Rowton, Wattlesborough*. No attempt has been made to distinguish between ancient parishes within the towns of Bridgnorth and Shrewsbury.

INDEX OF SUBJECTS

This index follows the system of classification devised by Robert Vogel of the Smithsonian Institution, Washington DC used in *The Blackwell Encyclopedia of Industrial Archaeology*, ed. Barrie Trinder (Oxford: Blackwell, 1992), pp.861-72.

1. TRANSPORT

Air transport
aircraft museum 167

Inland navigation

Types:
canal 37, 74, 81,105-08,111, 148, 177-90
river navigation 5, 75-76,100, 110, 134, 169-77

Structures, installations, practices:
accommodation bridge 180, 182-83, 188
aqueduct 107, 177-79, 184, 186-88, 190
boat-building yard 171, 175-76, 184
bow hauling 172-73
canal tunnel 106, 180
fish weir 176-77
inclined plane 106-08, 177-78
locks 10, 170, 177-78, 182, 184-85, 188
towpath 172-74
tunnel-and-shaft system 105-06, 108
warehouses/wharfs 171-75, 180-90

Vessels:
Barge/trow 169-72,174, 176
iron boat 172
tub boat 105-08, 177-78

Rail transport

Types of railway:
Birkinshaw rails 102, 104
double way 101
heritage railway 207-08, 213
iron railway 101
Jubilee rails 104, 111

light railway 202
'main line' railway 104-05, 135, 198, 201-08
mineral railway 26, 74-76, 78, 79, 81, 85, 90-92, 104-05, 159, 169, 185-86, 208
narrow gauge railway 158
plateway 26-29, 101-04,134, 175, 212
wooden railway 100-01

Railway installations & structures:
carriage shed 205
crossing shelter 105
inclined plane 27, 79, 88, 91-92, 103-04, 108, 134
locomotive depot/shed 91-92, 105, 204-05, 207-08
railway bridge 103-04, 203, 206-07
railway freight depot 105, 204, 207-08
railway station 202-03, 206-08
railway tunnel 207
signal box 205-07, 215

Railway motive power:
diesel locomotive 60, 169
Sentinel 60-61
steam locomotive 58, 104-05

Railway vehicles:
railcar 58-59
railway carriage 58-59
railway wagon 58-59

Road transport

Types of road:
bypass 200
highway district 200
turnpike 89, 111, 191-96, 199-200

Road vehicles:
motor bus/coach 60-61, 200-01
motor car 200
motor lorry 61
post coach 197
stage coach 197-98
steam wagon 59-61

Road transport installations & structures:
bridges 196-97, 200
garage 200-01, 205
inn 198, 200-01
milepost 192, 194, 199
signpost 192
tollgate & tollhouse 191-93, 195-96, 199, 241-52

Aerial ropeway

79, 92, 162

2. CIVIL ENGINEERING

Bridges:
concrete bridge 196
iron bridge/aqueduct 179, 196-97, 206-07
stone bridge 196

Iron-framed 'fireproof' construction:
142-51

Sewage disposal
pumping station 70

Water supply:
aqueduct 168-69
dam 167, 169
pipeline 167-69
pumping station 70, 167-69